Global Mission

# GLOBAL MISSION

## A STORY TO TELL

An Interpretation
of Southern Baptist Foreign Missions

# WINSTON CRAWLEY

615
**BROADMAN PRESS**
Nashville, Tennessee

Dewey Decimal Classification: 266.023
Subject Headings: MISSIONS, FOREIGN // FOREIGN MISSION BOARD
Library of Congress Catalog Card Number: 85-3752

Printed in the United States of America

Unless otherwise noted, all Scripture quotations are taken from the King James Version of the Bible.

All Scripture quotations marked RSV are taken from the Revised Standard Version of the Bible, copyrighted 1946, 1952, © 1971, 1973.

All Scripture quotations marked GNB are taken from the *Good News Bible*, the Bible in Today's English Version. Old Testament: Copyright © American Bible Society 1976; New Testament: Copyright © American Bible Society 1966, 1971, 1976. Used by permission.

**Library of Congress Cataloging in Publication Data**

Crawley, Winston, 1920-
  Global mission.

  Bibliography: p. 388
  Includes index.
  1. Southern Baptist Convention.   Foreign Mission
Board.   2. Southern Baptist Convention—Missions.
I. Title
BV2520.A5S683   1985     266'.6132     85-3752
ISBN 0-8054-6340-2

*To all my mentors and colleagues
in the telling of Christ's story
to the nations*

# Foreword

Doing missions has been more characteristic of Southern Baptists than writing about missions. This imbalance is now receiving more attention by competent Southern Baptist writers. This book is a significant contribution to that endeavor.

The author has a clear comprehension of the whole as well as awareness of detail. He is able to explain the complexity of Southern Baptist missions in understandable terms.

There are several distinguishing marks of the Southern Baptist mission program. The nature of a Convention with multiple concerns makes it different from a society with a single thrust. The financial support system is distinctive. The purpose, methodology, and philosophy have characteristics which deserve understanding.

The pivotal emphasis on career missionaries and the complementary role of volunteers is a rather uncommon combination in missions today. This needs understanding by Southern Baptists.

All these elements blend into a "mission" which relates both to stateside constituents and local Convention leadership. Doing so properly is a never-ending challenge. How can nationalism; remnants of a colonialistic mind-set; and the urgency of an indigenous approach be creatively fused into a productive whole? What is the direction of missions in the future?

These factors and many others cause this book to be important reading for anyone with a serious interest in current foreign missions. It should be required reading for all Southern Baptists. Doubtless it will be in great demand among those whom God has "called out" as they fill a variety of leadership roles in the life of a missions-minded people called Southern Baptists.

R. KEITH PARKS, President
Foreign Mission Board, SBC

# Contents

# Introduction

Southern Baptists have a story to tell. In relation to our global mission, this is true in at least three ways.

We have a story to tell to the world. It is "the old, old story of Jesus and his love." How we tell that story to the part of the world that lies outside our national borders is the subject of this book.

We have a story to tell to other Christians, many of whom have wondered about the rapid growth of our foreign missions work and the principles on which our work is based.

We have a story to tell to ourselves. Even within our own Southern Baptist fellowship, many are uninformed about our foreign missions work. Much of what church members have heard has been piecemeal or anecdotal. Broader concepts and more basic principles may not be generally understood. Even serious students of our foreign missions undertaking and persons directly involved as missionaries have found no ready source of comprehensive information about Southern Baptist foreign missions principles and strategy.

"Why doesn't the Foreign Mission Board give us a comprehensive written strategy guide?" New missionaries have asked this question fairly frequently during their orientation for missionary service. Since the Foreign Mission Board is 140 years old, one might well expect that such a document would have been prepared long ago. The question is reasonable and deserves a careful answer.

Why has no book of this sort been produced earlier? I suppose the primary reason is that earlier generations did not expect formal written statements to the extent that this one does. Planning was much more informal in earlier years. Persons made ad hoc strategy decisions in specific circumstances, without any awareness of the concept of strategy. For over a century, the Foreign Mission Board took no official notice of such terms as *missions philosophy* and *missions strategy*.

In 1974, at the request of the Southern Baptist Convention's Historical Commission, Jesse C. Fletcher (then director of the Mission Support Division of the Foreign Mission Board) reviewed minutes of the Foreign Mission Board from 1845 to report on the development of "Foreign Mission Board strategy." He found that it was 1965 when the Board first "officially spoke to the word *strategy*." He pointed out that the earlier absence of the word did not mean a lack of strategic planning. In fact, his article traced a number of strategy principles in Southern Baptist foreign missions, even from the very early years.[1]

Our times place much more emphasis on formal comprehensive planning documents. A program statement for the Foreign Mission Board was adopted by the Southern Baptist Convention in June 1966.[2] In June 1976 the Convention approved a detailed plan for new foreign missions outreach through the remainder of the century under the title "Foreign Missions Looks Toward AD 2000."[3] In 1978 the Foreign Mission Board developed and adopted a foreign missions philosophy statement. Already in 1970 the Board's administrative staff had prepared an outline of "Strategy for the 70's" for use in foreign missions administration. A new strategy statement was developed in early 1982 for current staff use. (See Appendixes 1-3.)

Planning process, like strategy, has evolved in recent years from very informal to well-defined formal approaches. A comprehensive and integrated planning process for the Foreign Mission Board was developed in 1981 and 1982.

All of these developments indicate a difference in style and expectations today. Informal approaches were taken for granted in earlier generations. (Lottie Moon never heard of a formal job description.) Today we expect everything to be spelled out carefully.

The time problem is another major reason that no comprehensive review of Southern Baptist foreign missions principles and strategy was prepared earlier. Persons in the best position to prepare the document would be those with administrative responsibilities in Southern Baptist foreign missions. They know the realities of the work, the principles being followed, and the ways in which strategy is developed and implemented—but the demands of administrative responsibility are so pressing that time is not available for the writing of a book. Part of the purpose of setting up an Office of Planning when the Foreign Mission Board's administrative staff was reorganized in 1980 was to have a staff member free from administrative pressures and available to help develop formal interpretations of foreign missions principles. From the time of reorganization, Foreign Mission Board President R. Keith Parks has encouraged the writing of this book to tell what Southern Baptists are doing in foreign missions, and why, and how.

There are still several possible problems in a formal interpretation of this sort. One is the serious practical problem of scope and limitations. Foreign missions principles touch on a wide range of topics (theology, comparative religions, world history and current events, anthropology, ecclesiology, economics and development—to name only a few). In a book reasonably limited in size and dealing with such a complex subject, many important issues can receive only brief or incidental treatment. It may be hard both for the author and for the reader to be content with what seems inadequate attention to vital matters.

A further complication is that no one person can speak authoritatively about Southern Baptist foreign missions. An official document would require agreement by Foreign Mission Board members and administrative staff. Group process to develop such consensus would be quite time-consuming. (The brief philosophy statement adopted by the Foreign Mission Board took many hours of work by a special committee of Board members and staff. Such a process would be utterly impossible for a full-length book.) This problem has hindered the development of formal statements which might be taken as representing the position of the Foreign Mission Board.

A further problem is that missionaries might be inclined to ascribe too much weight to any formal written statement. One of my surprises, when I became an area director, was that an offhand comment I might make could be understood by some missionaries as a firm expression of Foreign Mission Board policy. There seems to be an element in human nature that likes to have a set of rules. Missions strategy needs to be dynamic—and there is danger that a formal statement may be taken as final and may short-circuit the dynamism of strategy planning.

In spite of the problems, there have been at least some partial accounts of Foreign Mission Board principles and strategy. For example, there were the article by Jesse Fletcher mentioned earlier and the more recent philosophy and strategy statements developed by the Foreign Mission Board and its staff. A missions study book, *By All Means,* written by six Foreign Mission Board administrators and published in 1959, gave "an account of the various missionary 'means' or methods used by Southern Baptists in lands beyond their own."[4] In 1974 strategy for foreign missions was the theme of the foreign missions series for study in Southern Baptist churches. The adult book, *How in This World* by Leland Webb, then managing editor and now editor of the Foreign Mission Board's periodical *The Commission,* has been the best published summary of Southern Baptist approaches in foreign missions.[5]

There have been other helpful unpublished materials and materials of limited availability.[6] Much information presented in this book will be based on in-house documents of the Foreign Mission Board. But none of these brief treatments, published or unpublished, meets the need for a comprehensive telling of the story of Southern Baptist foreign missions.

There is no shortage of books on missions. Many books have been written from the perspective of nondenominational or parachurch missions organization. Others reflect the perspective of mainline denominations or councils of churches. Some represent one or another current concern or school of thought related to foreign missions. Southern Baptist missions philosophy and strategy are not identical with any of these, though holding many points in common with some or all of them. Fairly frequently someone will comment that it is strange to have so many books on missions and so little representing the Southern Baptist approach. Since we have a story to tell, it surely should now be told.

A primary audience for the telling is students in Southern Baptist seminaries so that they may have available, as either a text or a reference, information about the global mission of our own churches. There are many other secondary audiences—students in Baptist colleges, Southern Baptist missionaries and potential missionaries, pastors and other church leaders, colleagues serving with other Southern Baptist agencies or institutions, church and school libraries, and also (one may hope) those in other Christian denominations who are interested in the spread of the gospel throughout the world. Also, of course, Mr. or Ms. Interested Southern Baptist will be welcomed as a reader.

What kind of book is this to be? Please note the subtitle: An Interpretation of Southern Baptist Foreign Missions. This means that *understanding* is the main intention—understanding what we are doing in Southern Baptist foreign missions, and why, and how. This is not a history of Southern Baptist foreign missions. That book already exists, now revised and updated as *Advance to Bold Mission Thrust, 1845-1980.*[7] This is not a summary of current work. That exists also, in "Partners in Missions, 1985," an annual free distribution item produced by the Foreign Mission Board and in the Board's official annual report released each April.

The emphasis of this book is on explaining the principles and the strategy processes and guidelines that are typical of Southern Baptist foreign missions, in comparison with and sometimes in contrast with the principles and strategy of other Christian missions organizations.

In other words, the content of the book is *missiology*—the current term for the study of missions principles and methods. But there is no attempt to make this a comprehensive textbook in missiology. (A Bibliography for broader study of the subject is included at the back of the book.) Furthermore, since many concerns of importance in missiology are pursued at length in other books, there is no attempt to repeat what can be found readily elsewhere. Instead, the points at which Southern Baptist principles relate to or differ from the approaches of others will be given special emphasis.

Please note carefully that the subtitle defines this book as "an" interpretation—not "the" interpretation. It represents a personal perspective, not final, not authoritative, not binding on the Foreign Mission Board or on my colleagues of the Foreign Mission Board staff. This is, of course, an insider's view, based on nearly 40 years experience in Southern Baptist foreign missions, including 30 years on the administrative staff of the board in assignments directly involved with missions philosophy and strategy. Therefore, perhaps the interpretation can have a kind of "semi-official" validity.

Please note also that there is an implied time frame. This is an interpretation of Southern Baptist foreign missions as of 1984-85. Strategy is dynamic. New circumstances will add further insights and other elements to Southern Baptist foreign missions.

Please note further that at a number of points the interpretation will be idealized. That is, I shall be describing what we and our missionaries have intended to do, realizing that human weaknesses and inadequacies have caused us to fall short of our intention. A principle can still be a guiding principle, even if its fulfillment is less than perfect.

Southern Baptist foreign missions principles and strategy are like a flowing stream. Many of the principles can be identified as far back as Southern Baptist beginnings in 1845. Tributaries (concepts and personal influences) have come into the stream from time to time. A cross section of the stream at any time shows the mixture of elements that compose the stream, plus some sediment of personal frailties and shortcomings being carried along. I have been part of the flow for three decades, contributing some influence to it, but primarily being merged into and carried along by the ongoing flow of Southern Baptist missions.

My missiological concepts have been shaped by personal experience and observation, by reading and conferences, and by the mentors and colleagues to whom this book is dedicated, including Dr. Parks and my co-workers on the Foreign Mission Board staff, along with missionaries around the world. Especially I acknowledge the influence of W. O. Carver, under whose teaching I began my formal study of missions; H. Cornell Goerner, who guided my graduate studies in missiology (or "the theory and practice of missions" as the subject was then called); and Baker J. Cauthen, the missions administrator to whom I was directly responsible for 7 years as a missionary and my first 25 years on the Foreign Mission Board staff.

(I appreciate suggestions about this manuscript from the following Foreign Mission Board staff colleagues: R. Keith Parks, William R. O'Brien, Charles W. Bryan, A. Clark Scanlon, Harlan E. Spurgeon, and Johnni Johnson Scofield. Of course, no one of them is to be held accountable for any shortcomings in the finished product. I appreciate also the valuable supportive assistance of Eris Anderson, H. Victor Davis, Terry Hanks, Pam Jones, and others on the Foreign Mission Board staff.)

Certainly I do not claim that anything written in these pages is the final word on the subject. My orientation has been more to the practical aspects of missions than to the academic. I hope only that the reader will feel helped to an understanding of the basic concerns and basic directions of Southern Baptist foreign missions and will feel also a stimulus both to further study and to greater and more effective personal involvement in the global mission of telling the story of Jesus.

The Foreign Mission Board recognizes the role of men and women in missions, ministry, and as leaders in churches. Throughout this volume, as a matter of style, I use he and other masculine pronouns in a generic sense.

### Notes

1. Jesse C. Fletcher, "Foreign Mission Board Strategy," *Baptist History and Heritage,* vol. 9, no. 4 (1974): 221.

2. Southern Baptist Convention, *Annual,* 1966, pp. 60-67.

3. SBC, *Annual,* 1976, pp. 111-113; and Frank K. Means, "Foreign Missions Looks Toward AD 2000," *The Commission,* vol. 39, no. 6 (June 1976).

4. Genevieve Greer, "Preface," in *By All Means,* Baker J. Cauthen and others (Nashville: Convention Press, 1959), p. v.

5. Leland Webb, *How in This World* (Nashville: Convention Press, 1974).

6. In helping develop the official program statement for foreign missions, adopted by the Southern Baptist Convention in 1966, the Foreign Mission Board staff produced an unpublished booklet, "Foreign Missions: A Southern Baptist Perspective." Also, a number of reports by Winston Crawley to the Foreign Mission Board as director of the Overseas Division (1968-80) and more recently as vice-president for planning have been compiled into a background resource collection for use with new missionaries in missionary orientation.

7. Baker J. Cauthen and Frank K. Means, *Advance to Bold Mission Thrust* (Richmond: Foreign Mission Board, SBC, 1981).

# Part I
# Situation

# 1
# Look What Has Happened!

When Jimmy Carter made his successful run for the American presidency, news media and the American people began to take special notice of Southern Baptists. Many began inquiring or interpreting what it means to be "born again." Even President Carter's home church in Plains, Georgia, was swamped by press and visitors. Southern Baptists were in the national spotlight.

A few interpreters of the American Christian scene have thought of Southern Baptists as a sort of stepchild (or perhaps problem child) among the American denominations. But outside the South, until fairly recently, most Americans have paid little attention to Southern Baptists and have known very little about them. Impressions often have been confused or stereotyped.

To Southern Baptists who have grown up in areas where Baptists have been the predominant Christian group, it has been something of a shock to go to other parts of the United States and seldom see a Baptist church of any kind—or to go abroad and learn that many Christian leaders in other lands are not even aware of the existence of a Southern Baptist denomination.

That situation has been changing, as Southern Baptist mission work has expanded to all 50 states and to more than 100 foreign countries. Southern Baptists now have by far the largest foreign missions operation of any denominational mission board. In total number of missionaries, only Wycliffe Bible Translators, a nondenominational mission drawing personnel from many countries, is larger.[1] In total financial resources for foreign missions, only World Vision, also nondenominational, with financial backing from many countries, is comparable.[2] In circles knowledgeable about foreign missions, Southern Baptists are noted as a remarkable phenomenon. Persons learning for the first time about Southern Baptist missions generally are surprised by what they learn. They see Southern Baptist mission work, both in the United States and overseas, and are inclined to say, "Look what has happened!"

There are many reasons why Southern Baptists and our mission work have not been widely known earlier. For much of our history, we were a small regional body. Only fairly recently Southern Baptists have become unusually large and strong—by now the largest non-Catholic denomination in the United States. Most of the expansion of Southern Baptists throughout the nation has taken place since World War II.

Since World War II has come the great expansion of Southern Baptist missions overseas also. We now have about six times as many missionaries in five times as many countries as we had in 1945.

Prior to World War II, Southern Baptists were not as heavily involved in national life. Most of our churches were rural and small-town churches. Most members were ordinary people. There was a leaning toward provincialism, and a strong strain of pietism kept many Southern Baptists withdrawn from public activities that were considered worldly. To be sure, these are generalizations to which there were many specific exceptions—but I believe persons who experienced Southern Baptist life in those days will find the generalizations a fair likeness of Southern Baptists then.

Furthermore, Southern Baptists have avoided involvement in most interdenominational organizations. The Southern Baptist Convention is not related to the National Council of Churches or to the World Council of Churches. Thus the Foreign Mission Board is not a part of the missions sections of those councils. Neither is the Convention related to the National Association of Evangelicals or the World Evangelical Fellowship, and the Foreign Mission Board is not affiliated with the Evangelical Foreign Missions Association. Our absence from these interdenominational groups has meant that we are not as well known to their leaders as we would be otherwise.

What has been true on the national and world scene has also generally been true locally: Southern Baptists have not been much involved in ongoing interdenominational organizations and programs.

All of this has given many persons the impression that we are loners—not too friendly or sociable, feeling no need for relationships with other Christians.

In the past 40 years, since World War II, the entire picture has been changing. We are more numerous. We are more widely spread. We are stronger economically and culturally. We are more involved in public affairs. We relate more to other Christians. We are becoming better known.

Perhaps we have become less fearful of being contaminated by contacts with the world and with other Christians, and more aware that we have a story to tell to others—that something distinctive has happened, something worth notice. At times no doubt we are tempted to feel proud of Southern Baptist growth and Southern Baptist strength. This is a continuing danger (sermons at our Conventions have been liberally sprinkled with references to our "great denomination"). Perhaps though, with full awareness of the danger of pride, we can try to look at what has happened as something that God has been doing among us and with us. It is a work of grace, and it is a stewardship (like that referred to by Paul in Eph. 3:2).

Baptists in general and Southern Baptists in particular have had remarkable growth. Baptists now constitute the largest free church denomination (not an official state church anywhere) in the world, with well over 30 million members and a total community including relatives and inquirers that may come to about 50 million.[3]

Southern Baptists, who numbered about 350,000 in a little over 4,000 churches in 1845, now number more than 14 million in 36,000 churches. Though the numbers are inflated by millions of nonresident and inactive members, the growth still is remarkable. It creates a base of considerable strength for world outreach.

Southern Baptists have been not only a growing denomination

but also a spreading denomination. Up to World War II there were state conventions in 19 states and the District of Columbia (plus a convention in Hawaii, which was still a territory rather than a state). By 1984 there were 37 state and regional conventions encompassing all 50 states.[4] Before too many years pass, every county in the United States may have a Southern Baptist church.

Southern Baptists have become a multiethnic denomination. Home Mission Board leaders estimate that on any Sunday morning Southern Baptists worship in more than 80 different languages. C. Peter Wagner of Fuller Theological Seminary's School of Church Growth has been quoted as saying, "Compared to what Southern Baptists are doing with ethnic groups in the United States, other churches are not even a close second." Oscar Romo of the Home Mission Board staff refers to Southern Baptists as "the most integrated denomination in the United States."[5] Currently Korean churches are the most rapidly growing segment of Southern Baptists.

Most Southern Baptists are not aware that there were many black churches and members in the Convention in its earlier years—before the black churches formed their own conventions about a century ago. Many Southern Baptists and other American Christians do not know that there are again today significant numbers of black Southern Baptists. The total is estimated at about 300,000. Perhaps 250,000 of them are in about 800 predominantly black Southern Baptist churches. The others are in predominantly nonblack churches.[6]

Southern Baptists are also a multicultural denomination. Forms of worship and styles of preaching vary greatly from place to place and from church to church. Common Southern Baptist worship patterns in earlier days may be well represented by a story told of James Byrnes, former Secretary of State, who had come from a small town in South Carolina. The British ambassador asked him about his church affiliation and he replied that it was Southern Baptist. The ambassador, not familiar with Southern Baptists, did have a general impression which he expressed: "I believe that is low church, isn't it?" To which Mr. Byrnes knowingly replied, "Sir, you have no idea how low."

Of course there are still many Southern Baptist churches with extremely informal worship, but there are also some that tend toward "high church," with formal choir processionals, robed ministers, and divided chancel. In large cities of America today, a Baptist can choose between churches that have varying "personalities" to reflect the cultural patterns of their members. Cultural differences are at the root of many of the tensions in Southern Baptist life today, but cultural variety also constitutes one of the major elements of Southern Baptist strength.

Vitality in Southern Baptist churches is evident in a number of ways. One of the most striking is the continuing increase in seminary enrollments. Enrollments have increased 103 percent in the past ten years, to a current total of 26,999.[7] This has been true in a period when a number of other denominations are short of candidates for the ministry. The larger Southern Baptist seminaries have much larger student bodies than any seminaries of other denominations, and even the smallest is still much larger than most of the theological seminaries in the United States. The potential of so many students preparing for Christian ministry is staggering.

Another evidence of Southern Baptist vitality is the extent to which our churches supply personnel for Christian agencies outside our own denomination. Many of the missionaries of independent nondenominational missions agencies come from Southern Baptist churches. Some Southern Baptist teachers and ministers have moved on to places of leadership with other Christian groups.

Continuing Southern Baptist growth in missions giving has amazed persons of other denominations. In some cases missions giving in other denominations has leveled off or declined. The Cooperative Program and the special offerings for home and foreign missions have continued to thrive. Per-member giving for foreign missions, adjusted for inflation, has increased 10 percent in the last 16 years.

Probably the most amazing part of the Southern Baptist phenomenon in these recent decades has been the expansion of the global missions program.[8] Southern Baptist foreign missionaries increased from 625 at the end of 1947 to 1,901 at the end of 1964, and then have nearly doubled in the past two decades to a total of 3,432. This rapid growth has taken place while most other denominational mission boards have grown little if any. The number of missionaries from denominations affiliated with the National Council of Churches has been declining steadily. Even missions agencies related to the conservative Evangelical Foreign Missions Association and Interdenominational Foreign Mission Association have grown only moderately.[9] In addition, while many other missions agencies have shifted largely to short-term personnel, nearly 90 percent of the Southern Baptist forces are career missionaries.

While growing rapidly in number of missionaries, Southern Baptist foreign missions has been spreading rapidly also. The number of countries served increased from 19 at the end of 1947 to 57 at the end of 1964 and then grew by another 84 percent in the next 20 years to a current total of 105. This was taking place at the same time that some mission boards were retrenching, and some missions spokesmen were lamenting that "doors were closing" to American missionaries all around the world.

While reaching out to many additional countries with a much larger missions force, Southern Baptists have also greatly expanded the variety of their missions ministries. Prior to 1950, missionary forces consisted almost entirely of preachers and women evangelists, teachers, doctors, and nurses. Since then many specialized ministries have been added, such as agriculture, relief and development, social work, student ministries, music, religious education, broadcasting—in fact, a total of about 80 categories of missionary ministry.

A notable part of the Southern Baptist phenonemon more recently has been Bold Mission Thrust—the stated plan of the denomination for accelerated missions in the homeland and around the world during the final quarter of this century. (Bold Mission Thrust will be described more fully in a later chapter.)

In summary, look what has happened! God has been at work in our generation to grow an unusual people. He has been overcoming some of their prejudices and provincialism. He has brought them to cultural and ethnic diversity. In spite of their many faults, He has kept stirring up spiritual vitality within them. In spite of their tensions, He has sought to keep them united in their missionary purpose.

What does this Southern Baptist phenomenon mean in the

purpose of God? Apparently God has been preparing an instrument which He can use in world evangelization. That is how we interpret what has happened. God in His wisdom and in His providence has chosen to use human tools in the accomplishing of His kingdom purposes. We Southern Baptists want to be usable tools.

### Notes

1. "Is Wycliffe Biggest?" *Mission Frontiers* (January-February 1984): 6. The Wycliffe missionaries with a United States base actually serving outside the United States in 1984 numbered just over 2,200 (according to a Wycliffe staff response to a telephone inquiry).

2. Ibid.

3. "Baptist World Alliance Membership Statistics," SBC, *Annual,* 1983, 228-31; and "Organized Christianity: Churches and Global Memberships in 7 Ecclesiastical Blocs and 156 Traditions, AD 1970-1985" (Global Table 27), *World Christian Encyclopedia,* ed. David B. Barrett (London: Oxford University Press, 1982), pp. 792-93.

4. "Minnesota-Wisconsin Becomes 37th Convention," story released by Baptist Press, November 15, 1983.

5. Sid Smith, "A New Day in the Southern Baptist Convention," *Ethnicity,* vol. 2, no. 2 (Winter 1984): 1.

6. Ibid.

7. "Seminaries—1983–1984" (Table), *The Quarterly Review,* vol. 44, no. 4 (July, August, September 1984): 59; and "Seminaries, Academies, Bible Schools—1973–1974" (Table), *The Quarterly Review,* vol. 34, no. 4 (July, August, September 1974): 60. The total enrollment is for all programs including continuing education and the Seminary External Education Division of Southern Baptist Seminaries.

8. This has been true in home missions as well as foreign. The Home Mission Board sponsors about 3,800 missionaries in various categories of full or partial support.

9. Robert T. Coote, "The Uneven Growth of Conservative Evangelical Missions," *International Bulletin of Missionary Research,* vol. 6, no. 3 (July 1982): 118-23.

# 2
# Who Are We?

"Southern Baptists: A Missions People." This current communications theme of the Foreign Mission Board expresses the essence of who we are.

What would Southern Baptists be without missions? What if there had been no William Carey, no Adoniram Judson, no Luther Rice? What if Baptist churches in the United States more than a century ago had not really cared about new frontiers among Western pioneers or in lands afar? These are pointless questions, for it is practically impossible to think about our Baptist heritage without thinking of missionary vision and enthusiasm.

Distinctively, Baptists have been a missionary people. Johann Gerhard Oncken, the famous German Baptist leader who generated the spread of Baptists through central and eastern Europe, expressed it well with his catch phrase, "every Baptist a missionary."

Zeal for the sharing of the gospel has made us what we are. Without it, we would have remained small, weak, and limited to only a few places in the United States and in the rest of the world. Without missionary passion we would likely have turned cold or narrow and rigid.

The very existence of Southern Baptists as a denomination came from missionary concern. The Southern Baptist Convention was established as a channel for mission efforts. The main actions of the organizing Convention in 1845 were the setting up of home and foreign mission boards.

From 1845 to the present, when we analyze ourselves, we think of evangelistic and missionary zeal as the dominant trait of the people called Southern Baptists.

## Shaped by Our History

Baptists have not always been missionary. For a century and a quarter after the beginning of the Baptist movement by John Smyth in 1609 there was little sign of any unusual missionary zeal on the part of Baptists. In that regard, Baptists were like all the main Protestant denominations that had resulted from the Reformation.

Even apart from holding views and pursuing concerns similar to those of other Christians around them, Baptists had two further reasons for slowness in developing missionary zeal. They were a small group, often misunderstood and opposed, and therefore inevitably devoted major energies to becoming firmly established, identifying themselves, and defending their views. Furthermore, many and perhaps most Baptists in those early generations were strongly Calvinistic, so emphasizing the sovereignty of God and the doctrine of election as to make human missionary effort seem inappropriate or even impertinent.

In America, the first Baptist church began in 1639. By about 1734, after a century, as reported by Albert McClellan, "there were only forty-seven known Baptist churches in America, of which all but seven were in the North." McClellan states the obvious conclusion that Baptists generally were not growing, and comments that "this was in times when other groups were rapidly developing."[1] Up to that time, Baptists clearly were not strongly evangelistic and missionary.

In contrast with the earlier picture, McClellan asserts that in America "by 1800 missions had become the dominant thrust of the Baptists."[2] With other Baptist historians, he attributes the change to four developments: the organizing of a general Baptist body, the Philadelphia Association; the influence of the Great Awakening; the experiences of expansion to the Western frontiers; and the effect in America of the new missions undertaking initiated in England by William Carey.

William Carey, widely recognized as "the father of modern missions," is an important part of our spiritual ancestry. Baptists have thrived as we have repeated Carey's pilgrimage from hyper-Calvinism to missionary zeal. Portions of his experience still place their mark upon us, distinguishing us from other groups (even some Baptist groups) that have been antimissionary or nonmissionary.

Carey's early attempt to raise the question of the missionary obligation of Christians was reportedly met by the well-known rebuff, "Young man, sit down: when God pleases to convert the heathen, He will do it without your aid or mine."[3] Carey's response was the publishing of a treatise entitled *An Enquiry into the Obligations of Christians to Use Means for the Conversion of the Heathens*. His famous sermon theme has modified our Calvinism by teaching us not only to "expect great things from God" (in good Calvinist fashion), but also to "attempt great things for God."

Carey and his colleagues in 1792 formed the Particular Baptist Society for Propagating the Gospel Among the Heathen. Such organizing specifically for cooperation in missions became the rallying point that would ultimately pull together Baptists of many scattered backgrounds—Particular and General, Regular and Separate. Cooperation in missions has continued to be the main unifying factor among Baptists, who by nature and by belief are easily subject to fragmenting tendencies.

What Carey began in England and through the English Baptist mission to India became effective among Baptists in America through Adoniram Judson and Luther Rice, who also are of major importance in our spiritual ancestry. When the Judsons and Rice moved to Baptist convictions on the way to India and were baptized there, the Judsons thereby became the first foreign missionaries of American Baptists. Rice, returning to America to develop support for them, did far more: He became the architect of the Baptist denomination in the United States—a denomination built around the framework of support for missions. The result was "the General Missionary Convention of the Baptist Denomination in the United States of America for Foreign Missions," organized in 1814 and popularly known as the Triennial Convention.[4]

Southern Baptist foreign missions began through the Triennial Convention. Lott Carey, a black from Richmond, Virginia, was sent to Liberia, and others were sent later. In 1835 J. Lewis Shuck and his 17-year-old bride, Henrietta Hall, became the first China missionaries from the Baptist churches of the South. Later, when the Southern Baptist Convention was organized, Shuck and Issachar Roberts, who were already in China under the Triennial Convention, became two of our new denomination's early missionaries.

Slavery was the issue that caused the formation of the Southern Baptist Convention, but missions was the purpose for which the Convention was created. Immersion in sectional culture, which has characterized Southern Baptists for much of our denominational history, produced the tensions over slavery that led to a break with the Triennial Convention. The Southern Baptist Convention was organized at Augusta, Georgia, in 1845. Its constitution, borrowing language from the Triennial Convention, stated the convention's purpose as "carrying into effect the benevolent intentions of our constituents, by organizing a plan for eliciting, combining, and directing the energies of the whole denomination in one sacred effort, for the propagation of the Gospel."[5] The central purpose of the denomination's "sacred effort" was reflected in the major actions of the constituting convention: the establishing of mission boards for home and foreign missions.

The nature of the new Convention was especially significant. Earlier organization of the several denominations for missions followed the society pattern. According to that pattern, each Christian purpose would have a special sponsoring society, made up of those interested in that particular purpose. (That pattern is still widely followed today by nondenominational mission boards and by parachurch agencies.) The new pattern adopted by Southern Baptists in 1845 was that of a convention, through which all participating churches would share in every appropriate cooperative Christian effort. The various specific purposes are assigned to boards and agencies created by and responsible to the Convention.

Gradually through succeeding decades, the scattered Baptists of the South, while retaining a high degree of diversity, did blend into an effective unity for cooperation in missions. Southern Baptist historian Walter Shurden has identified four streams of tradition which merged into who we are as Southern Baptists. He describes a Charleston tradition characterized by order, a Sandy Creek tradition characterized by ardor, a Georgia tradition representing sectionalism, and a Tennessee tradition representing successionism.[6]

The Sandy Creek tradition is especially relevant for the missionary zeal that is in the spiritual genes of Southern Baptists. Shubal Stearns established the Sandy Creek Church in North Carolina in 1755. By 1758 there were three churches with 900 members, and they organized the Sandy Creek Association. Within 17 years, according to a history of the Baptist denomination that was published in 1813, the Sandy Creek Church had become "mother, grandmother, and great-grandmother to 42 churches, from which sprang 125 ministers."[7] Albert McClellan noted that "in some ways Shubal Stearns with his fiery evangelism, his unlimited vision, and his genius of organization was the spiritual forerunner of Southern Baptists."[8]

The nature of Southern Baptists as "a missions people" was reflected in the beginning of a department of missions at The Southern Baptist Theological Seminary in 1900 under Professor William Owen Carver—the first such department in any American theological seminary. The influence of that department and of Carver's teaching and writing spread to other Southern Baptist seminaries as they came into being and also widely through Southern Baptist life.

Concern for missions has motivated the major advances of more recent Southern Baptist history. A surge of missions interest after World War I called the Seventy-Five Million Campaign into being, and that led to the formation of the Cooperative Program in 1925. After the setback of the Depression and its years of Southern Baptist debt, a new surge of missions outreach following World War II led to the adoption of a program of foreign missions advance in 1948, under the leadership of Foreign Mission Board Executive Secretary M. Theron Rankin. This was followed by the Baptist Jubilee Advance culminating in 1964 and by the adoption of Bold Mission Thrust plans for the remainder of the century in 1976, under the leadership of the Board's executive director, Baker James Cauthen. (The Home Mission Board has been involved in parallel advances.) The experiences of these decades have molded today's Southern Baptists.

The first few years after World War I raised high hopes in Southern Baptist missions. The democracies had won the war, and the young League of Nations gave encouragement that peace lay ahead. Our nation was entering a decade of prosperity. The Student Volunteer Movement had called out among Southern Baptists (as from every denomination) a growing number of young people offering themselves for missionary service in line with the movement's theme, "The Evangelization of the World in this Generation."

Southern Baptists responded to the enthusiasm of the times by appointing far more missionaries than in earlier years. During the first five years after the war, large groups of new missionaries were sent to reinforce work in established fields; and six new fields were entered.

Before many years passed, however, high hopes began to melt into disappointment and discouragement. The Depression which began in 1929 plunged the Foreign Mission Board and other denominational agencies into serious debt. Missionaries could not be returned to their fields, and new missionaries could not be appointed. Before the end of the Depression, war in Asia and Europe brought difficulty and tragedy to many mission areas.

Most disappointing of all was the fact that several years before the Depression began, while Southern Baptists were still prosperous and total gifts through the churches were still increasing, gifts for missions began to decline. Pledges made during the Seventy-Five Million Campaign were not fulfilled. Churches became increasingly caught up in their own local needs. The vision of Southern Baptists for evangelizing the world seemed to be fading. Perhaps our passing through the deep waters of Depression and the fires of war helped us find renewed dedication to world missions.

In 1945 the Southern Baptist Convention and the Southern Baptist Foreign Mission Board were 100 years old. The ending of a second great world war opened a new opportunity for missions. M. Theron Rankin, executive secretary of the Foreign Mission Board, had a vision of a remarkable advance by Southern Baptists. In 1948 in response to his challenge, the Convention adopted a program of world missions advance, calling for expanding work to many new lands and nearly tripling the number of missionaries.

Though many Southern Baptists felt initially that the missions advance proposed by Rankin and his colleagues was visionary, a great new tide of concern for world missions was rising in Southern Baptist life. The expansion projected in the advance program materialized and merged into the Baptist Jubilee Advance which culminated in 1964. Southern Baptists joined with other Baptists of America in celebrating at that time 150 years of missions outreach since the forming of the Triennial Convention.

Beginning with the challenge presented to the Southern Baptist Convention in Memphis in 1948 and culminating in Jubilee celebrations at Atlantic City in 1964, Southern Baptist foreign missions grew from a staff of 625 missionaries serving in 19 countries to more than 1,800 missionaries assigned to 54 countries. By the end of 1975, just prior to the adoption of Bold Mission Thrust, there had been much further growth, to a total of 2,667 missionaries in 82 countries.[9]

By 1985 we are more than a third of the way through the Bold Mission Thrust period that spans the final quarter of the century. Continuing missions advance (0000 missionaries in 000 countries at the end of 1984) identifies us as still "a missions people." And we are still being shaped by our ongoing history.

## Character

In light of Southern Baptist origin and history, what are the major qualities that affect our missions principles and strategy? Those missionary principles have been distilled from 140 years of denominational experience.[10] They are reflected in documents developed by the Foreign Mission Board in recent years

and are expressed in missions strategy that is being implemented across the world. Both the principles and the resulting
strategy are rooted in some fundamental characteristics of who
we are as Southern Baptists.

### Biblical Convictions

Missionary concern is rooted in what persons believe. Behind
beliefs are personal experiences with Jesus and the continuing
presence of the Holy Spirit. Experience interpreted in the light of
Scripture produces deep and compelling beliefs.

This is not primarily a matter of doctrines, such as may be
written in creeds or statements of faith. What matters is not the
statements to which we may give assent, but rather those beliefs
held so deeply that they determine who we are and how we live.
*Convictions* is doubtless a better word here than *beliefs:* Biblical
convictions are the soil in which missions grows.

As Southern Baptists, we envision ourselves as under the
lordship of Christ. No true missionary motivation can exist apart
from vital personal experience and relationship with Jesus.

We envision ourselves also as "people of the Book." We look to
the Bible, as interpreted to us by the Holy Spirit, as our rule of
faith and practice.

Convictions about Jesus as Savior and Lord, the helpless
condition of sinful man, the universal loving purpose of God,
and the responsibility of Christians and of the church sustained
missionary vision and outreach in New Testament days. Similarly, clear and deeply held biblical faith results in missionary
outreach today. The evangelistic and missionary zeal that characterizes Southern Baptists is rooted in our commitment to basic
biblical convictions. One danger today is that such convictions
may become diluted to the point of having no compelling force
in our lives. The decline in missionary outreach in some Christian groups seems to be related to doubt or uncertainty about
biblical views of Jesus, the nature of man, the purpose of God,
and the responsibility of the church. If our convictions weaken,
our missionary zeal will diminish.

This is not essentially a question of stated beliefs. We can keep
repeating the same strong Baptist themes and claiming the same

doctrinal positions, but lose the conviction, compassion, and concern that would move us to missionary outreach.

In principle, we Southern Baptists "believe the Bible." In principle, we acknowledge the lordship of Christ. But, unfortunately, many in our churches are aware only of having accepted Jesus as Savior, without having yet consciously made Him Lord of Life. In actual practice, our use of the Bible can easily center in those portions that comfort us (and perhaps criticize others), rather than in those portions that challenge us.

This ambivalence in our biblical convictions is reflected both in the phenomenal missionary outreach of Southern Baptists reported in chapter 1 and in those weaknesses and failures of our missionary efforts that may be seen on closer examination.

### Evangelism

Part of the charge brought against Baptists in American colonial days was that they could not "meet a man upon the road but they must ram a text of scripture down his throat."[11] That image of aggressive evangelism is part of the impression many persons still have of Southern Baptists. We generally would not state it or act it out so forcefully, but we would generally agree that evangelism is a major element in our concept of ourselves.

*Evangelism* may be the best of all the "good words" as perceived by Southern Baptists. We like to think of ourselves as evangelistic, and we hope this will be the impression that others will have of us. We like to preach about evangelism and to use the word in our Convention themes and slogans. We are more likely to attend evangelism conferences than other kinds of Christian gatherings. Evangelism is obviously one of our very good words.

The major attention given by Southern Baptists to evangelism is both appropriate and important. This is a central part of who we are. More basically, it is central to the God-given mission of the church. However, we sometimes seem to belabor the point, or to "protest too much," as if seeking by much talk about evangelism to make up for an actual decline in evangelistic fervor.

In other ways too the fact that evangelism is such a good word can lead to problems in our missions outreach. Sometimes narrow or superficial concepts of evangelism can hinder effective sharing of the gospel in another culture, or lead to misreading and misreporting what is happening. But these are manageable problems—and the strong concern for evangelism that the problems reflect is very valuable.

### Missions

Concern for missions obviously is another central element in how we see ourselves as Southern Baptists. This is shown by the recurring emphasis on missions advance reviewed previously. It is evident in the rapid growth of our foreign missions outreach described in chapter 1.

*Missions*, like evangelism, is one of the very good words in the Southern Baptist vocabulary. That is entirely fitting, since we are convinced that missions is thoroughly biblical, that missionary outreach with the gospel to the ends of the world is the will of God. This emphasis on missions as a good word helps us to keep holding the missionary challenge in view.

But missions as a good word can have disadvantages too. In wanting to appear very missionary, we are sometimes tempted to label as missions many things in our church life (and our church budgets) that are primarily ministering to ourselves, our families, our immediate neighbors, our own kind of people. By doing so, we kid ourselves into thinking that we are more missionary than we really are, and the meaning of missions becomes watered down until it has little force. A stirring missionary concept like Bold Mission Thrust can be made meaningless by the use of the term in reference to denominational business as usual—as though taking a new budget which hardly advances enough to match inflation and calling it a Bold Mission Thrust budget would make it bold!

Emphasis on missions is axiomatic for Southern Baptists. But it is only a small step from "axiomatic" to "taken for granted" and only another small step from there to "neglected." At times it seems that we feel we have fulfilled our missionary calling when we have recognized missions appropriately in our Convention themes and programs, have spoken resoundingly about the urgency of missions—and then can go home and continue doing what comes naturally: meeting urgent needs of our own churches and church families, and treating missions as an "extra" to be handled from the leftovers of our resources.

Southern Baptists have exceeded most major American denominations in continuing growth both in number of missionaries and in giving for foreign missions. However, we need to keep this quite remarkable growth in perspective. Several independent, nondenominational missions societies have been growing even more rapidly (groups such as Wycliffe Bible Translators, Campus Crusade, Youth with a Mission). Some of the smaller denominations, such as Assemblies of God, have missionary forces that are growing at a much more rapid percentage rate. In ratio of missionaries to church members, we fall far short of Baptists in many other lands (Australia, New Zealand, Sweden, and Canada, for example).

The same is true of our giving for foreign missions. An analysis of per-member giving for foreign missions by 40 American denominations shows Southern Baptists ranking 31st.[12] A major problem is that Southern Baptists have an inflated church membership, by comparison with most smaller denominations. We report about one fourth of our membership as nonresident.[13] Many other members are entirely inactive. It would help if churches reported membership figures based on those who give at least minimal evidence that Christian faith and church membership mean something to them.

Even making allowance for our inflated membership and for the probability that average per-capita income of Southern Baptists is lower than in some other denominations, we still are not doing anything spectacular in per-member giving for foreign missions.

Regretfully, we are not doing as well in missions giving as we did in earlier years. Southern Baptist giving for all missions causes in 1983 amounted to slightly over 15 percent of total gifts through our churches. The percentage was better in the depths of the Depression 50 years ago. It had been even better in 1925, when the Cooperative Program was established. It was better still during the Seventy-Five Million Campaign, in the early 1920s, when the proportion reached 40 percent one year.[14]

If per-member giving for missions in this era of Bold Mission Thrust, in proportion to the probable per-capita income of Southern Baptists, is to reach the level of missions giving during the Seventy-Five Million Campaign, it will have to increase to a level two and one-half times higher than the current level.

All of this seems to say that concern for global missions is indeed an important part of who we are as Southern Baptists, but that we are probably not as strongly missionary or as different from other Christians in this respect as we have sometimes imagined ourselves to be.

### New Testament Polity

We think of Southern Baptist churches as modern expressions of the New Testament church. Our concepts of regenerate church membership, congregational church government, the priesthood of all believers, the symbolism of the ordinances, and other elements of church life are grounded in New Testament principles.

Baptist polity has important effects on our ways of doing missions. Many of the differences between Southern Baptist foreign missions and the work of other missions agencies (as to viewpoints, objectives, approaches, and methods) grow out of Baptist polity. We seek to harmonize our ways of working with our understanding of the nature of the church.

There is, however, one major complication not usually recognized by persons who have never lived and worked in a cultural setting other than their own. Our understandings of the church include elements that come from our own culture. It is not always easy to distinguish between the biblical principle and the cultural expression. Therefore, special effort must be made in overseas missions to let New Testament principles of church life be expressed in ways appropriate to the local culture.

### Independence

I am somewhat amused when I see a sign saying "Independent Baptist Church." Every Southern Baptist church I know stoutly maintains its independence. This is an indelible part of who we are. We accept it as a fundamental premise that a New

Testament church should be subject to no authority except that of Christ, its Head. Therefore, we resist firmly (some would say stubbornly) any attempt to place demands or restrictions upon us.

It is not surprising that Southern Baptists have had a reputation in many places of being dogmatically sectarian or isolationist. And it is no doubt true that there have been many times when we have leaned too far backward in seeking to preserve our independence, avoiding relationships that would have been helpful. Only rarely have Southern Baptists followed the extreme "separation" doctrine that becomes almost paranoid, but fairly often we may have isolated ourselves from others to the point of remaining provincial.

Now, increasingly, Southern Baptists are learning better how to relate beneficially without giving up independence.

### Cooperation

For Southern Baptists, independence and cooperation are like two sides of the same coin. The very existence of a Southern Baptist Convention is an expression of cooperation. The fact that our organization for missions is of the convention type rather than the society type shows cooperation as a central element in who we are. Our central system for financing missions is very appropriately called the Cooperative Program.

Southern Baptist missions is cooperative missions. This quality distinguishes Southern Baptist missions from independent missions. Ability to function as part of a team is essential for the Southern Baptist missionary. In Southern Baptist missions, the element of teamwork mingles with and remains in tension with individual freedom.[15]

### Diversity

Southern Baptists today are a "mixed bag." Our denomination encompasses a wide range of differences.

In the beginning, in 1845, Southern Baptists were remarkably homogeneous—geographically, racially, culturally, and economically. There were differences, of course, but there were many more similarities. The denomination occupied only one section of the country. Its church members were of white Anglo-Saxon lineage. They lived predominately on farms and in small towns. Relatively few were wealthy or highly educated. There was much agreement in points of view and similarity in forms of church life.

Now there are Southern Baptists in all the states of the Union. Church members include persons of many ethnic backgrounds. Urbanization has produced a wide gap between the circumstances and the attendant cultural traits of different groups of Southern Baptists. The poor and those with less education are still represented, but now so are prosperous persons, highly educated, and some leaders in society. Both sectional differences and differing degrees of sophistication have led to a wide range of viewpoints and greatly differing forms of church life.

A large and growing proportion of Southern Baptists is made up of persons who have come from other denominational backgrounds and who have not fully assimilated the central principles that have made Southern Baptists who we are.

Our diversity is both a blessing and a problem. It is a main source of the tensions that trouble Southern Baptist life. Those tensions have less to do with the substance of our Christian faith than with varieties of emphasis and differing ways of expressing ourselves.

On the other hand, and far more significantly, our diversity makes possible multifaceted ministry. It demonstrates the triumph of Christian love over human differences. It reflects the ideal nature of the church as made up of all kinds of people. And it points toward the even greater diversity of the church (and the Baptist family) throughout the world.

### Change

Southern Baptists are probably changing more than most other American denominations. Certainly the change from a sectional to a national and multiethnic denomination in 40 years is highly unusual.

We are continuing to change. Social ministries are becoming more widely appreciated. The place of women in our churches is being debated. We are being affected by changes in the surrounding culture, such as trauma affecting the American family. Affluence, for good or bad (or both), affects our values—and our possibilities.

All of these changes, like the other Southern Baptist characteristics that have been mentioned and like still others that might be mentioned, influence the way in which we move across the world in foreign missions.

## Summary

Every aspect of Southern Baptist foreign missions, beginning with the concept of missions and extending all the way to the details of mission methods, is colored by who we are. This is true of both the form and the content of our mission efforts, as will be detailed in further chapters of this book.

Out of our history we have brought the great strengths of our biblical convictions and our democratic polity, but we have brought also some dangers—the possibility that we may be naïve, or narrow, or even colonial in our missionary approaches.

More recently we have run the risk of absorbing and reflecting in our mission efforts some current elements of American culture: the spreading relativism that considers all religions the same; the new isolationism and focus on homeland problems that arose in the 1960s; the superficiality of quick projects that may ignore cross-cultural realities; and the generalizing of mission until urgency and thrust are lost.

Who are we? We are a people whom God has molded into an instrument He wants to use marvelously in world evangelization.

### Notes

1. Albert McClellan, *Meet Southern Baptists* (Nashville: Broadman Press, 1978), p. 15.
2. Ibid., p. 23.
3. F. Deanville Walker, *William Carey: Missionary Pioneer and Statesman* (Chicago: Moody Press, 1925), p. 54 (and note).
4. See Claude L. Howe, Jr., "Significance of the Formation of the Triennial

Convention," in *Glimpses of Baptist Heritage* (Nashville: Broadman Press, 1981), pp. 54-58.

5. Frank Norfleet, "Constitution, Southern Baptist Convention," vol. 1 of *Encyclopedia of Southern Baptists* (Nashville: Broadman Press, 1958), pp. 311-12.

6. "The Southern Baptist Synthesis: Is it Cracking?" *Baptist History and Heritage*, vol. 16, no. 2 (April 1981): 2-11; also a good summary is found in Slayden A. Yarbrough, *Southern Baptists: Who are We?* (Oklahoma City: Baptist General Convention of Oklahoma, 1984), pp. 24-26.

7. David Benedict, *General History of the Baptist Denomination in America, and Other Parts of the World*, 2 vols. (Boston: Manning and Loring, 1813), vol. 2, pp. 42-43, quoted by Daniel H. Holcomb in *Our Heritage of Faith* (Nashville: Convention Press, 1983), p. 25.

8. McClellan, p. 16.

9. FMB, *Annual Report*, 1975, in SBC *Annual*, 1976, p. 105.

10. The process is reviewed in the article by Jesse C. Fletcher, to which reference was made in the introductory chapter ("Foreign Mission Board Strategy," *Baptist History and Heritage*, vol. 9, no. 4 [1974]: 210-22).

11. William L. Lumpkin, *Baptist Foundations in the South* (Nashville: Broadman Press, 1961), p. 94.

12. "Financial Reports from Religious Bodies in the United States—1982" (Table), *The Quarterly Review*, vol. 44, no. 4 (July, August, September 1984): 76.

13. "The Record of Southern Baptist Churches—1982–1983" (Table), *The Quarterly Review*, vol. 44, no. 4 (July, August, September 1984): 7.

14. SBC, *Annual*, 1921, p. 126.

15. The way independence and cooperation have complemented each other in Southern Baptist life is well illustrated in Albert McClellan's account of the founding of the Baptist Sunday School Board (McClellan, pp. 39-40). See also Howe, chapter 4, and Cecil Ray and Susan Ray, *Cooperation: The Baptist Way to a Lost World* (Nashville: The Stewardship Commission of the Southern Baptist Convention, 1985).

# 3
# Where Do We Stand Now?

*"Just at sunset,* when the green darkness began to envelop the jungle, a tall man stepped out of the tent. He removed his pith helmet, wiped the perspiration from his brow, and seated himself upon a campstool. When his ear caught the throb of distinct drums he murmured, 'The natives are restless tonight.' "

Ross Coggins commented that the scene he had described is admittedly overdrawn, but it is still the impression many people have of missions.[1]

Of course many missionaries do serve still in rather primitive surroundings, but many more are likely to be in well-developed towns or even in great cities. Stereotyped images of missionaries and their work are passed down unthinkingly from generation to generation and hinder understanding of modern missions. (Cartoonists still love to portray a missionary in a cannibal's cooking pot—though that picture is outdated by more than a century.)

Context is a crucial factor for mission work. Today's missions are projected from where we stand now—not from where we were yesterday, where we might have been if things had developed differently, or where we wish we were. The realities of the world today determine to a large degree both what can be done and what should be done in Christian missions.

Context, of course, does not have the primary or the final word in determining the nature of missions. Those words belong to God. The world sets the agenda for the church only within the larger agenda that has already been established by the will of God for his people.

Even so, context is so very important that any realistic understanding of missions and any effective preparation for missions must be thoroughly informed by current realities.

W. O. Carver began a series of addresses on "Christian Missions in Today's World" (presented at Hartford Seminary and at Southwestern Baptist Theological Seminary) with this axiom: "Christianity from its beginning has faced the world as its practical problem. Christianity, however, must approach the world not only as a practical problem, but also as an actual fact. Christians must set themselves to understand the world—as it is and as it might be. There must be realistic understanding of that for which Christianity has an idealistic program." He commented further, in line with the ultimate divine agenda of the Christian faith, that "Christianity comes to the world; it does not arise out of the world."[2]

Planning for Christian missions must be up to date. This means keeping up with whatever "megatrends" may be identifiable in the world at large and in Christian missions.[3] In missions, there can be the same danger that has been observable in national defense: the danger of preparing for the previous war.

(Similarly, a current best-seller on business management cites research showing "that companies often hold on to flagrantly faulty assumptions about their world for as long as a decade, despite overwhelming evidence that that world has changed and they probably should too."[4])

Ted Ward, Michigan State University professor, in a series of addresses to the Southern Baptist Foreign Mission Board in 1980, made the following summary comment: "God isn't necessarily always going to do things the way he has been doing them. . . . Your mission board faces a time when there are to be in the plans of God new modes of mission, new kinds of activity."

Awareness of world realities does not come automatically. It requires careful and continuing study. Every church member, not just missionaries and missions administrators, should give attention to world developments.[5]

The need not only to understand but also to accept world

realities is illustrated by the experience of a young missionary some years ago. She was having difficulty adjusting to the mission field and felt frustrated continually by her work situation. Finally (as she related it) one day during her personal prayer time, the Lord asked her, "Would you like me to make a special world just for you, according to your wishes?" Through that experience she came to recognize that mission work must be carried on in the real world as it actually is.

John Wesley summed it up in the line from one of his well-known hymns, "to serve the present age." General understanding of that "present age" in which our global mission will be performed is the purpose of this chapter.

## World Context

Seeing planet earth as it looks from outer space, probably more than anything else in our day, has pushed us toward thinking globally. From space, earth is seen clearly as a globe and as a unit. Divisions that separate humanity are not visible.

Though McLuhan's concept of "the global village" is an overstatement, it is increasingly true that events anywhere can have repercussions at the far end of the world. Global vision is important for Christians today.

Any brief review of world circumstances is possible only in general terms—and subject to all the hazards of generalization. However, adequate understanding of Southern Baptist world missions requires at least a general understanding of the world scene.

### Demographic

Reactions to the continuing growth of world population are not quite as frantic as a decade or so ago. Perhaps we are all becoming more accustomed to the idea of mushrooming population. The shock has worn off. Furthermore, the rate of population growth has declined some, and projections for the remainder of this century are not as frightening as earlier projections.

It took many thousands of years for world population to reach one billion. Then it doubled in about 125 years and doubled

again in about 50 years. At the current net annual growth rate of
1.7 percent, population doubles in only a little over 40 years.

Earlier some were projecting world population as high as 8
billion by the end of this century. By now, however, with a lower
annual growth rate, the estimate for AD 2000 is 6.1 billion.[6]

The rapid growth in world population in modern times is
caused primarily by reduced death rates, due to improvements
in sanitation and health services and to the discovery of effective
treatments for many diseases. Thus the population explosion is a
threatening by-product of valuable progress in world health.

Since population is growing so rapidly, especially in developing countries, there is an overload toward the younger end of the
age spectrum, with about 35 percent of world population under
age 15 (in spite of the relative "graying" of population in highly
developed industrial nations like the United States).

As more countries reach an advanced stage of economic development and as birth rates decline, the rate of world population
growth is expected to continue tapering off. Population stability
is expected about the middle of the next century, at perhaps close
to 10 billion persons.

Another major and highly significant demographic development in this century is the rapid pace of urbanization. At the
beginning of this century, only 13 percent of the world's people
lived in cities. The figure is now more than 40 percent and by the
end of the century it is expected to exceed 50 percent.[7] Alongside
our traditional image of the missionary pioneering somewhere
in "the bush," we need now to add another image of a missionary caught in a traffic jam in one of the world's great cities.[8]

As we become entangled in demographic data, we need to
keep reminding ourselves that they represent persons. It is easy
to start thinking of the world in other terms—as figures in a
population table, as dots on a map, as movements in society—
instead of thinking in personal terms. At current rates of population growth, with every minute that passes there are 152 more
persons in the world than there were before. This means an
increase of 9,120 persons per hour, nearly 220,000 persons per
day (equal to the population of a small city), and almost 80
million additional persons per year (roughly equal to the entire

population of Mexico). These global demographic factors have to play a major part in world missions planning.

### Technological

This century has seen not only a population explosion, but a "knowledge explosion" as well. New discoveries of science, applied through technology to almost every aspect of human life, have worked myriads of miracles—everything from the lifesaving wonder of a heart transplant to the transfixing sight of persons walking on the moon, to the mushroom cloud of atomic destruction.

In today's world, the achievements of science and technology are universally recognized and almost universally acclaimed. At the same time, there is growing realization that technological changes have raised complex new problems to which we do not yet have answers. Our systems for ethical analysis and social response have not functioned rapidly enough or well enough. Change has taken place so rapidly that we have had an overload of "future shock" (as explained in the book by Alvin Toffler).

Our era has been characterized as the atomic age, not only because of military uses of nuclear weapons but also because of other applications of atomic science—in production of electric power and in medicine, for example.

This has been characterized also as the space age. The term is appropriate in view of human forays into space, the space probes that have revealed more about Mars and Saturn, and also the communication satellites with their receiver dishes everywhere (including the top of the Southern Baptist Foreign Mission Board office building).

This age is characterized as the information age because of the marvels of electronic communication and data processing.[9] As computers have become more and more powerful, smaller, less and less expensive, and therefore common, those of us in technological societies are finding ourselves swamped with information and our lives increasingly adapted to the convenience of the computer. We become dependent upon electronic computerlike controls for our cars, our radios, even our cookstoves.

We are moving into a new era of genetic engineering: An

uncharted trail that may lead to solutions for many health problems but may lead also to new threats to important ethical and social values.

Most of the typical achievements related to the exploration of space, to nuclear science, to electronics, and to discoveries in genetics have primarily affected only the technologically developed societies up to now. But even the most remote areas of the world have been changed already by the achievements of modern science and technology in the fields of transportation and communication.

My grandfather, a farmer and pastor in central Kentucky, traveled mainly by horse and buggy. Occasionally he may have ridden a train as far as Louisville. My father, when I was a boy, had a Model T Ford. He could remember when he had first seen an airplane. In my own work with the Foreign Mission Board, I have traveled well over a million miles all around the world, mostly by jet plane. Persons in many less developed societies have become accustomed to airplanes even while they still move mainly on foot or by oxcart. Transportation patterns have changed radically and are still changing.

One of the most significant technological agents of change worldwide has been the transistor radio. A peasant from some unknown village, as he plants rice in a routine centuries old, is often now being introduced to the modern world through the transistor radio he carries. In other ways also, communication across the world has become simpler, quicker, and less expensive.

These scientific and technological advances have important and essentially unpredictable economic and cultural effects (as will be described in the following sections). They have important effects also on human ways of thinking and feeling. Naisbitt, in his analysis of megatrends, noted that high technology situations need some "high-touch" accompaniments, so that the human element may be retained in modern technological settings.

### Economic

Demographic and technological developments have combined to create an amazingly complex world economic situation.

Part of the world is industrialized, but many nations and societies are still, for practical purposes, preindustrial. Those peoples almost without exception desire the modern development that is based on science and technology. They see such development as the path to improvement in their individual lives. But the capital and the skills needed for modern development are not easy to acquire. And growth in population often outpaces economic growth, so that the net available is less per person rather than more.

In the meantime, the industrial societies are moving toward becoming information societies. Thus the gap between more developed societies and less developed may widen instead of narrowing.

Another problem of modern development is its effects on the environment. Growing concern for ecology has bred caution about industrial development. It is the already developed countries that have become concerned about ecology. Most of the so-called Third World[10] is still more concerned for development. However, both for ecological and for economic reasons, there has been movement toward what is sometimes called "appropriate technology"—that is, the use of less industrialized ways of social and economic improvement.

A major fact of economic life in much of the world is poverty. In many lands the gross national product per capita is less than $200 per year. In some nations, most of the people never have a chance to learn to read and write, and most never in a lifetime have the services of a trained physician.

Both the recent decrease in the rate of population growth and newly developed, improved agricultural methods (sometimes called the "green revolution") have moderated the impending crisis from world hunger. A decade or two ago some were implying that entire nations might simply have to be written off as hopeless, in an adaptation to the world economic situation of the triage approach of combat medical units. Nevertheless, starvation is still a serious threat in many parts of the world (such as the Sahel or sub-Sahara area of Africa).

Dire economic need is compounded among refugees. The number of refugees varies from time to time and from place to place, but usually includes 12 to 14 million people, who have fled with no more than they could carry in their hands and on their backs.

The energy problem is another important factor in the world economy. It cannot appropriately now be called an "energy crisis," but wars or adverse political developments could turn the situation into crisis very quickly. The much higher cost of energy today aggravates the economic problems of many nations, particularly the developing nations.

Growing population brings great pressure on even less sophisticated energy sources. Note, for example, the crucial lack of firewood needed for bare existence in some parts of the world.

Many local and national economies are so locked into the global economy that periods of recession cause major crisis. In recent years we have seen the domino effect of greatly increased energy costs, worldwide recession, massive national debts, runaway inflation, widespread unemployment, and grave economic and social disruption.

Unfortunately, in many lands public policies have been so directed toward managing the distribution of limited resources as to neglect actions needed to stimulate increasing production. In other countries, policies catering to local pride and prejudice have hindered production. Economic actions based on political considerations have often been counterproductive. In Indonesia, for example, an earlier government took a series of positions that led to twenty years of economic decline, before the present government turned the situation around and began to rebuild the national economy. Similarly, in Korea, the war in the early 1950s left such economic disruption that it was more than a decade before South Korea could reach the "economic takeoff point" and move on to its current level of economic strength. These and other examples show that the world's economic problems, though serious, should not be considered hopeless.

### Cultural

We live in a time of a developing world culture. This development grows from modernization, technical advances, and the spread of modern Western influence throughout the world.

In past centuries, cultures developed within limited settings, producing many different culture areas, each with its natural boundaries. Some interchange took place across those boundaries, but each culture area remained more or less self-sufficient, retaining its own inner unity. Now those boundaries are being broken down in the dawn of one worldwide civilization.

At some unknown future date, most things accepted as fundamental in one section of the world will be the same things accepted as fundamental in other sections. Obviously, this acceptance is far from an accomplished fact. But it is now taking place, as cultural boundaries break down and as differences between world areas decrease and likenesses increase. Already a newcomer does not feel as much a stranger in any part of the world as formerly, for so many things that are familiar have now been accepted across most boundaries.

The culture which developed in Western Europe and in the United States spread across the world during what is known as the Colonial Period and began to impinge upon other societies. Reactions to the impact of the West varied. In some cases there was ready acceptance; in other cases there was a strong reaction; in still other cases there was a reviving of local values and customs as a shield against the coming in of Western ways. Different lands display various stages of Westernization or of cultural revival, as the case may be.

Materialism and secularism have been almost universal responses to the introduction of Western culture. Wherever you may go around the world today, you are likely to find enormous pressure toward a materialistic and secular point of view. The Western imports that have been most rapidly adopted are elements of secular culture—material, physical, scientific, technological. Adoption of religious or other value elements from another culture takes place much more slowly. Thus we face a world that is becoming one world primarily in its secular aspects.

This process has reached a critical stage in many countries. The earlier culture, which had been unified and had formed the framework in which everyone lived, has begun to break down under the impact of influences from the Western world—yet no new ready-made culture moves in immediately to take its place. Many old standards have been eliminated but not replaced by generally accepted new standards. That problem can be seen especially in many large cities around the world.

From the viewpoint of Christian missions, some degree of cultural ferment is probably desirable. In fact (to use only one illustration), in a strong and tight-knit Muslim setting, until there is some erosion of the monolithic social structure there will be little freedom for individual acceptance of Christ and for the rise of a strong Christian movement.

However, if cultural change occurs too rapidly, the end result may be extremely dangerous. It is like an atomic chain reaction in a laboratory, started with the expectation that it will be under control. Sometimes something may slip, and the reaction may get out of control. Then comes an explosion. If cultural break-down and crisis take place more rapidly than the molding of a modern international culture, the result can be chaotic.

A survey in the South Pacific islands a few years ago revealed that people there had two very strong desires: One was for modernization, and the other was for the preservation of their traditional culture and its values. They did not seem to realize that the two desires move in opposite directions. Most of the world's peoples today probably feel the same conflicting desires. With one foot firmly planted in their own local cultures, they seek to plant the other foot in the developing modern culture— hoping meanwhile not to lose their balance.

### Political

Political forces, trends, and events are so closely related to the economic and cultural situation that it is hard to draw firm lines to separate them.

The central political fact of this century is revolutionary change. Its manifestations have been worldwide. Details have differed widely, but they express a common underlying force and direction. The pace of such change has accelerated signifi-cantly since World War II.

Back of the movement for change, and fueling the movement, are a new awareness of human needs and new concerns and struggles for the meeting of needs. Furthermore, "rising expec-tations" have been based on new belief that change is possible.

Persons whose parents assumed that life would go on as it had for generations are now, in this generation, deciding that things should be different and can be different—and they are determining to find some way to change things.

This century's revolution has been far-reaching, not limited to any one section of the world. It includes all aspects of human life: physical, material, economic, spiritual, social, political, esthetic, religious—all are undergoing change.

Americans may be tempted to interpret the thrust for revolutionary change as a result of communist agitation, but the two should not be equated. The revolutionary element in modern world history is far more fundamental than communism. In fact, I am convinced that radical change would have come even if Karl Marx had never lived and if there were no Marxist theories about social, economic, and political forces. Modern education and modern communication have made the world's masses aware of other patterns of life and have aroused hope for improvement in their own lives.

To a large extent, Christian missions has contributed to the desire for change, not only by the introduction of stimuli toward modern development (such as schools and hospitals), but also through such vital (and probably more important) concepts as the worth of every person and the desire of God that every person should have life "more abundantly" (John 10:10).

The acute human need from which revolutionary desires and pressures grow is summarized vividly by David Barrett.

> Some 46% of the world, 2.0 billion people, eke out a living in 26 countries each with a per capita income of under . . . $235 . . . per year. In the world's 172 less developed countries, 780 million live in absolute poverty, a clearly defined category that represents "a condition of life so characterized by malnutrition, illiteracy, and disease as to be beneath any reasonable definition of human decency" (World Bank, 1980). This total increases annually as the gap between affluence and poverty widens rapidly almost everywhere. Among the consequences are: permanently unsettled refugees, now 16 million, increase in number each year; 20% of the Third World, and 33% in several countries, suffer from severe protein-

calorie malnutrition; 40% remain without adequate shelter;
80% do not have access to adequate water supply; 850 million
have little or no access to schools; and 500 million exist on the
edge of starvation. Altogether, some 1.5 billion human beings
on earth are malnourished. A further consequence is seething
unrest, anger, hatred toward the affluent world, and revolutionary goals.[11]

Pressure for a better life, including a sense of human dignity,
expresses itself in many ways. One of the most prominent has
been nationalism. It has flourished in this century largely as a
negative movement—a struggle against colonialism, against imperialism, against exploitation, against anything which might
hold a people down. Historically, this was a conflict with the
kind of world inherited from earlier centuries.

From anti-colonialism it is only a short step to anti-foreignism.
It is not surprising that anti-foreign feeling has been common.
Such an attitude was almost inevitable if subject peoples were to
move toward freedom.

Though the United States was not so prominent as several
European countries in the accumulating of colonies, a good bit of
anti-foreign feeling has been directed from time to time against
America. This has been due to America's political and economic
strength and American involvement in so many international
political and economic developments. The existence of anti-
Americanism is a fact of the world context with which Southern
Baptist foreign missions has to reckon.

The world has now been substantially decolonized. Many of
the countries of Asia gained their independence in the 1940s and
1950s, and the countries of Africa in the 1960s and 1970s. Of
perhaps 223 countries in the world (the number reported in the
World Christian Encyclopedia), probably 96 have become independent since World War II.[12]

At the point of independence, nationalism usually suffers
growing pains. It is much easier for people to unite against
something they all resent than it is for all to agree on a positive
program after getting rid of the old colonial power. Brand-new
countries often exhibit considerable confusion: Political parties

multiply, and proposed plans are numerous, but the country for a time may seem unable to pull itself together. (That, incidentally, is the way our own nation was in the period just after the American Revolution.) Many new countries today have serious economic, political, social, racial, and linguistic problems, with national unity diluted by personal interests, party interests, and tribal or group interests. It may take some time for new nationhood to solidify.

Ironically, while the old colonialism has almost disappeared, a new form of colonialism has been imposed in Eastern Europe and in Indochina and more recently also in Afghanistan.

An ongoing struggle for human betterment is another major expression of today's world revolution. Concern for development brings political processes to the support of economic progress (as is demonstrated by the modernization priority of China's current leaders). Agitation seeking guarantees for human rights is a further example of the broad concern for human betterment. Even though repressive governments may for the time being clamp a lid on the aspirations of their people, there are powerful desires for effective participation in political life (as seen in the Solidarity movement in Poland) and for enjoyment of the benefits of economic progress.

Revolutionary pressures for change tend to stiffen the resistance of those exercising power. Such pressures also attract opportunistic groups which seek to manipulate the revolutionary process in order to gain control. Thus the world's developing nations find themselves caught in a polarization between authoritarian groups of right and left. In many cases, a moderate third force that might assure human liberties and democratic process has had difficulty in developing. The choice, at least for the present, has seemed often to lie between a repressive rightist regime and a totalitarian repression of the left that would make peaceful evolution toward democracy even less likely. Populations caught in armed struggle between the polarized forces would like to say, "A plague on both your houses."

Marxism has seemed at times to be advancing on the world scene and at other times retreating. In either event, Christians and Christian missions need to accept the challenge of witnessing and ministering for Christ in settings with differing ideologies.

The most threatening aspect of ideological polarization, of course, is the nuclear arms race. Christian missions is projected in a contemporary world under the threat of atomic destruction.

Another tension today is sometimes described as between the North and the South (referring loosely to the world's hemispheres). Perhaps it is more properly understood as representing the conflicting interests of the privileged and the underprivileged, the developed and the less developed nations of the world. The tension is basically economic, but it has resulted in political positions and actions which are expected to continue and probably to increase in intensity.

Since the improvements in quality of life being sought by multiplied millions are far from realized, the era of revolutionary change and the crises that it spawns are far from over. The famous British historian Arnold Toynbee predicted that there will probably not be a third great world war in this century, but that local brushfire conflicts, riots, and political disturbances will likely continue through the century. All hope that he is right about the first part of that prediction. I have no doubt that the second part is correct. Revolutionary change is continuing.

### Religious

In much of the world, the religious situation is unsettled—again largely through the impact of modern Western culture.

Primal (sometimes called primitive) religions have been losing their grip on their adherents. This is especially noticeable in Africa, where tribal peoples who formerly followed traditional African religions have been shifting in large numbers to Christianity or Islam or modern materialistic secularism.

This same encounter between traditional religious practices and the new values of Westernized culture can be seen in urban and university settings in many lands. In some places, a definite spiritual vacuum has resulted. (In Korea, for example, a survey some years ago reported 87 percent claiming no religious faith.)

Of course, in several lands communism has become in effect an official "religion"—with atheism officially promoted and religious faith at best only tolerated, with varying degrees of restriction.

In major centers of Western culture (especially in Europe, but also significantly in the United States) secular humanism has become more and more prevalent. The *World Christian Encyclopedia* shows the nonreligious element in Europe and North America growing at a rate of 3.8 percent each year. As a result of this shift and the pervasive decline in the influence of Christian values in Western culture, some interpreters refer to "post-Christian" civilization today in Western Europe.

In several countries the impact of Western culture has stimulated a resurgence of local religion, often as a touchstone for national identity. Thus there have been renewal movements within the major world religions (Hinduism, Buddhism, Islam).

The most impressive resurgence has made Islam a major new power bloc in world affairs. Wealth derived from rapidly escalated oil prices has been a major contributing factor. Another has been the emotional boost given to Islamic orthodoxy everywhere by the new fundamentalist Muslim regime in Iran.

In summary, the world context of Christian missions today is characterized by radical change and uncertainty. This inevitably makes Christian missions more difficult. Some years ago, when I was area director for Asia, I interviewed a missionary candidate who wanted to serve where he would not face disturbance and possible interruptions. I could not give him any guarantee about calm and stability in the lands of Asia, so he went to Nigeria— just in time for the Biafra war. I found that rather amusing. But I find it also symbolic of the uncertainties and difficulty of Christian missions anywhere today.

However, a disturbed world also means responsiveness. The very things that disturb the world plow up the hearts of people for the planting of the gospel. We have seen this demonstrated again and again. In Vietnam, in the closing months of Southern Baptist ministry there, people were so hungry for some word of love and encouragement that the response was amazing. The very time of greatest difficulty is likely to be the time of greatest opportunity for Christian missions.

Furthermore, this changing world poses a special challenge to

Christian understanding and love. Our own national revolution is two centuries in the past. Since we now already enjoy many of the privileges for which people in other lands are still struggling, we may have a natural tendency toward caution and conservatism. We need to understand and sympathize with the desire of the world's masses for a better life. We need to be channels for the expression and the demonstration of the love that Christ has for a world of persons "harassed and helpless, like sheep without a shepherd" (Matt. 9:36, RSV).

## Christian Context

For a generation, there has been speculation as to whether "the day of the missionary is over." A slightly different turn was given to the question in a major consultation at the Overseas Ministries Study Center in Ventnor, New Jersey, in May 1982. The theme was "The Role of North Americans in the Future of the Missionary Enterprise." Approximately 180 persons, representing a wide range of Christian missions agencies, considered the present status of Christianity worldwide and how North America as a base for international missions fits into the picture.

### Situation

Such discussions reflect an important reality: The Christian world situation is vastly different from what it was nearly two centuries ago when William Carey set the modern missionary movement in motion, or in the middle of the past century when the Southern Baptist Convention was organized. By now we see around the world the fruit of the modern missionary era.[13] Christianity has become by far the most universal religion in history.

The current status of Christianity is described comprehensively and in detail in the *World Christian Encyclopedia* (which since its publication in 1982 has become the standard reference for any comparative world religion statistics). Although there had been earlier surveys of world Christianity, there was nothing remotely approaching the scale of this encyclopedia. It was approximately 12 years in preparation; and its editor, David B. Barrett, visited most of the 223 nations covered by the research.

Most remarkable is the encyclopedia's comprehensiveness. It covers all branches of Christendom, and it places Christians in the world context of secular and political conditions and of other religious movements. In addition to extensive overview charts and analyses, there are detailed country-by-country treatments.

According to the *World Christian Encyclopedia*, Christians in 1985 constitute 32.4 percent of the world's population. It must be recognized that the encyclopedia uses the very broadest definitions for followers of the various religions. Any persons who consider themselves Christian in any sense, or would be so considered by others, are included in the total count of Christians. For example, Latin America is listed as 93.7 percent Christian.

The encyclopedia reports the percentage of Christians in the world as now decreasing slightly. Perhaps a high point was reached about 1900, with 34.4 percent of the world's people counted as Christian (by the broad definition used in the encyclopedia). The projection for AD 2000 is 32.3 percent. The decreasing proportion of Christians is due mainly to low birth rates and the trend to secularism in Europe and North America. Meanwhile, the percentage of Christians in both Africa and Asia is rising—and quite rapidly in Africa. (Incidentally, the 2 percent decline in the percentage of Christians in the world from 1900 to 1985 is more than accounted for by the decline in percentage of Christians reported for the Soviet Union.)

Barrett has no category of data to fit exactly the narrow definition of *Christian* which Southern Baptists generally have in mind when they use the term—that is, persons who have experienced the new birth through faith in Christ. Barrett does show "evangelicals" as 3.6 percent of world population and growing to a projected 4 percent by AD 2000.

Barrett also seeks to evaluate the extent to which the world has been "evangelized" (using again a very broad definition). He estimates that almost 70 percent of the people of the world have now been evangelized and that the percentage will grow to probably 80 percent by AD 2000.

The extent to which the world has been evangelized does not lend itself to easy calculation. Some still are saying that more than half the people of the world have never heard the name of Jesus. In 1985 that is highly doubtful. With improvements in education and communication, I believe it is probable that most of the world's people know that there are some persons called Christians who revere a man called Jesus. However, that is very different from having heard, in a culturally meaningful way, the good news of who Jesus is and of salvation available by grace through faith. I feel sure it is still true that more than half the people of the world have not yet heard the gospel. Ralph D. Winter, founder of the U.S. Center for World Mission, maintains that approximately half of the world's people are out of contact with Christians, living in people groups that do not yet include a nucleus of churches able to evangelize them.

A further caution regarding the data in the *World Christian Encyclopedia* is that the extent of Christianity in China was not known when the encyclopedia was being prepared. During the past several years, as information about religion in China has become more readily available, it has become obvious that Protestant Christians there are a much larger proportion of the population than they were when the communist government assumed power in 1949.

Religious statistics at best are slippery, and the results of even the most careful research can give only a very rough impression of the condition of world Christianity. However, even that limited information is of great importance as a background for understanding Christian missions today.

One strategic feature in current world Christianity is a shift in the center of gravity. The first major shift took place in New Testament times, as the church moved from being entirely Jewish to being predominantly Gentile. Later there was the shift from the Mediterranean world as the center of Christian strength to the continent of Europe. In this century, North America even more than Europe has been the main base for Christian missions outreach. Now, Christians in the Third World are beginning to outnumber those in Europe and North America. By the twenty-first century (if current trends continue) Latin America, Africa, and Asia will be the major centers of world Christian strength.

## Trends

A number of developments within Christianity and within the missionary movement are part of the context of Southern Baptist missions.[14] Some of the more prominent trends are worth noting.

1. *The "six-continent" concept.*—Since the meeting in Mexico City in 1963 of the Division of World Mission and Evangelism of the World Council of Churches, it has been commonplace to think of all the continents of the world as both a mission base and a mission field. This concept replaces an earlier view that tended to divide the world into Christian lands from which missionaries were sent and heathen lands to which they went. The new understanding reflects the realities that no land is fully Christian and that the church has been planted now worldwide.

2. *Constrained circumstances.*—Many lands impose restrictions and pressures on Christians, and such limitations often affect especially international missions. In 1980, according to the *World Christian Encyclopedia*, there were 25 countries closed to foreign missions and 24 partially closed. Eighteen others restricted missionary entry significantly. Those 67 countries together included almost three fourths of the world's population. Over 60 percent of all Christians were living in countries with limited civil liberties. As a result of such problems, there has been growing consideration of the possibility of nonprofessional or bivocational missionaries.

3. *Focus on the poor.*—What Roman Catholics have been calling the "option for the poor" is representative of Protestant and evangelical missions also. Special attention centers on ministry to persons in need. Closely related is increased concern for world hunger and for development projects. A kindred movement is the liberation theology which has developed in recent decades primarily in Latin America.[15]

4. *Charismatic renewal.*—Pentecostal churches have become more and more prominent in the missionary movement, with remarkable success in their missions efforts especially in Latin America. In addition, the modern charismatic emphasis has affected significantly a number of mainline denominations, including the Roman Catholic Church.

5. *Ecumenical developments.*—A number of processes have drawn denominations into increased contacts or closer relationship. After Vatican Council II, Roman Catholics began to relate more freely to other Christian groups. In addition to what is usually called the ecumenical movement, with its related organizations, there have been other less formalized interdenominational movements and conferences. A significant example is the Lausanne Movement, which has brought together in conference and in concern for evangelization a wide range of Protestant and evangelical Christians. The number of international and/or interdenominational conferences and programs has increased greatly. These conferences and programs reflect a wide range of doctrinal positions and specific concerns.

6. *Parachurch agencies.*—The number of nondenominational Christian organizations with sharply focused or limited special functions continues to multiply. There are also parachurch agencies which relate primarily to one denomination, including some that are Southern Baptist in orientation.

7. *Volunteerism.*—Large-scale involvement of laypersons from the United States in overseas projects has become an important part of the world missions scene.

8. *Makeup of missionary forces.*—In recent years there have been several major changes in the overall makeup of Christian missionary forces. A much smaller portion of those forces comes from mainline denominations, with a larger portion from newer and smaller agencies and from nondenominational mission organizations. The proportion of missionary forces that is short term has increased greatly. Missionaries have tended to be engaged largely in specialized work rather than basic evangelism and church nurture.

9. *Internationalization.*—Increasing emphasis is being given to the possibility of mission structures that will include persons from different national backgrounds.

10. *Transfer of leadership and responsibility.*—Missionaries more and more have a background role as helpers to strong national Christian leaders and national church organizations and programs. (The term *native* used in earlier generations is no longer considered acceptable. *National* is the preferred term—though it

is missionary jargon that may not communicate clearly to most church members. Whenever possible, a more specific term, such as *African* or *Zambian*, is better.) A related trend has been the increasing prominence of theologies developed in the Third World.[16]

11. *Third World missions agencies.*—Recent decades have seen an explosion of new missions agencies based in the non-Western world. By 1973 there were over 200 such agencies, with perhaps 3,000 missionaries. By now the number of missions agencies based in Asia, Africa, and Latin America has increased to about 400, with probably more than 15,000 missionaries.[17]

12. *Missiological concerns and emphases.*—Some of the most important developments in current missiology are expressions of the concerns or the emphases of different influential individuals. In many cases, schools of thought and writing have developed around the emphases. Prominent examples are church growth, unreached people groups, and major unevangelized population blocs.

13. *Modern technology.*—All kinds of technical improvements affect both missionary life-style and missions methodology. For example, convenience of transportation has facilitated volunteer involvement and has also brought changes in missionary furlough patterns. Electronic advances have made possible extensive broadcasting ministries. Computers are now being used in missions institutions and missions offices.

14. *Financial pressures.*—Inflation and recession, plus diversion of the attention of many Christians to more local concerns, have placed severe financial pressures on world missions.

### Southern Baptist Context

Following World War II, Southern Baptists embarked on almost twenty years of remarkable advance, climaxing with the Baptist Jubilee Advance and the meeting of the Southern Baptist Convention at Atlantic City in 1964.

Advance was evident in nearly every aspect of Southern Baptist life. Membership grew by 74.39 percent, from the 6,079,305 reported in 1946 to the 10,601,515 reported in 1964. Baptisms kept increasing steadily. The Sunday School slogan of "A Million

More in '54" was typical of the spirit of the denomination. Seminary enrollments grew rapidly. Home missions efforts spread to more and more states. In foreign missions, the vision of the advance program adopted at Memphis in 1948 was realized by 1964. With the Southern Baptist Convention Cooperative Program budget strategically structured for missions advance, 53 percent went to foreign missions in 1964.

Unfortunately, advance did not continue at the same pace. The late 1960s and early 1970s were a time of plateau or even sag in some aspects of Southern Baptist life. Growth in baptisms and in seminary enrollment tapered off. The Cooperative Program budget was restructured so that the advance section became less significant. A smaller proportion was allocated for foreign missions. Much Southern Baptist speaking and writing became introspective and analytical, if not actually pessimistic.

This to some extent reflected developments in American culture. The late sixties were a time of turmoil. There was growing disillusion with foreign involvements and a tendency toward new isolationism. Costly commitments became unpopular, as "cool" detachment became the ideal.

It seemed that both the American culture and Southern Baptists were seeking a sense of direction. Some Southern Baptist leaders said that a new missions challenge was needed to get the thoughts and feelings of Southern Baptists turned outward and upward again. That concern was picked up and brought as a proposal from a special "Committee of 15" that had been asked to survey the work of Southern Baptist agencies. In response to the committee's suggestion, the SBC Executive Committee recommended and the Convention adopted in 1974 a call for bold new plans. The action called for each of the mission boards to propose to the Convention plans for bold advance. Also, a special committee (later called the Missions Challenge Committee) was to consider the plans of the mission boards and call the Convention to commitment for the implementing of the new advance plans.

The carefully developed plans of the mission boards and the report of the Challenge Committee were adopted by the Convention at Norfolk in 1976. These plans for advance soon became identified as Bold Mission Thrust. They form the general framework for Southern Baptist planning for the final quarter of the century. The proposals included a stated purpose of world evangelization, which was adopted twice—once in the report of the Foreign Mission Board, and again in the report of the Challenge Committee.[18]

Although both the Foreign Mission Board report and the Challenge Committee report included many other supporting objectives, attention since that time has focused almost entirely on what was stated as the "great overarching objective: to preach the gospel to all the people in the world." This statement of Southern Baptist Convention purpose and the idea behind it seem to have caught the attention and kindled the imagination of Southern Baptists more than anything else in our denominational life in many years.[19]

In outlining specific long-range plans under the overarching purpose of world evangelization, the Foreign Mission Board was careful to state that it would continue its comprehensive missions strategy according to proven mission principles. Furthermore, nine definite intentions related to various aspects of missions were set as guides for continuing missions advance up to AD 2000. Several items include numerical challenge figures, which are now being used as measures to evaluate progress in bold missions. The figure which has become best known to Southern Baptists is the challenge of having 5,000 foreign missionaries by AD 2000.

After R. Keith Parks became Foreign Mission Board president in 1980, the Board moved toward development of a formal planning process. Along the way, the president and other appropriate staff members reviewed and reaffirmed the directions already established for the final quarter of this century. They also prepared a statement of mid-range projections to indicate levels of advance by 1990 that will be on course toward the target figures that have been adopted for the end of the century.

At this point in the foreign missions portion of Bold Mission Thrust, progress in most respects is moving at a rate that should meet the challenge figures. The one major exception is the most demanding of the challenges: that of tenfold multiplication of

## BOLD NEW THRUSTS
## in Foreign Missions 1976-2000

Ten selected highlights

1. Great overarching objective: To preach the gospel to all the people in the world.

2. One hundred percent increase in missionary staff—more than 5,000 by A.D. 2000.

3. Missionaries at work in at least 125 countries as God may lead.

4. Accelerated tempo of volunteer lay involvement overseas—up to 3,000 per year needed now, and up to 10,000 per year by A.D. 2000.

5. Greatly expanded efforts in evangelism—major thrusts in urban areas and among students and other young people.

6. Tenfold multiplication of overseas churches—with concomitant increases in baptisms and church membership.

7. Extraordinary efforts in leadership training—through strengthened seminaries, Theological Education by Extension, and lay leadership training.

8. Vastly increased use of radio, television, and publications on mission fields, and penetration by way of mass media of areas not presently open to missionary activities.

9. Accentuated attention to human need—through health care, disease prevention, benevolent and social ministries.

10. Vigorous, appropriate, and prompt responses to world hunger and disasters.

—Adopted by the Foreign Mission Board, January 13, 1976

churches within 25 years (with concomitant growth in church membership and baptisms). Even in that respect, progress thus far has been good, but it will need further acceleration if tenfold multiplication is to take place by AD 2000.

Another vital part of Bold Mission Thrust that has thus far lacked real boldness is financial fuel for the thrust. Southern Baptist giving for foreign missions through the Cooperative Program, the Lottie Moon Christmas Offering, and other special contributions has continued to increase in dollar amounts. But the increase has not been rapid enough to make up for inflation in the United States and overseas and still match the growth in number of missionaries and fund further bold missions outreach. This means that increased boldness in giving for foreign missions is needed if bold missions advance is to accelerate. (See the graph in Appendix 8, comparing growth in missionaries with growth in missions funds, adjusted for inflation.)

Boldness in world missions depends ultimately on what happens in the churches. The Foreign Mission Board is only a channel through which resources of missionary personnel and money flow from the churches to mission work around the world. At first, bold missions was primarily a concern in the minds of Southern Baptist leaders. After the Convention adopted the plans for Bold Mission Thrust, the idea began to be emphasized through all the denomination's communication channels. However, as J. B. Gambrell, Southern Baptist leader and writer of an earlier age, is quoted as saying, "It takes five years to say hello to Southern Baptists." Communicating any new vision is a slow process.

After four or five years, signs of more widespread concern in Southern Baptist churches for bold missions outreach began to appear. The number of new missionaries has increased in recent years. Many state conventions have increased the proportion of their Cooperative Program funds sent to Southern Baptist Convention and world needs. The percentage of Southern Baptist Cooperative Program funds being allocated for foreign missions has begun to turn upward, after seven years of decline in the late 1970s (several of those years coming even after the Convention had adopted the plan for Bold Mission Thrust). There has been an upsurge of interest in prayer for missions. Giving for world hunger continues to increase. More and more Southern Baptists are interested in participation in partnership evangelism and other partnership projects overseas, and many states have entered into partnership missions arrangements with specific overseas countries. Perhaps the great new thrust of Southern Baptist missions advance for which we have been praying is under way.

However, there are reasons to feel cautious. There is still much relativism, indifference, and missions illiteracy in the churches. And we run the risk of being distracted from our missionary purpose by controversy or simply by majoring on bigger churches with more buildings and more church staff for ourselves. Boldness in missions cannot be taken for granted.

The total context of Southern Baptist missions includes many favorable circumstances and many unfavorable. Ultimately our mission thrust is not dependent on circumstances but on God's purpose and our faithfulness. God will move ahead with His world purpose. What about Southern Baptists? Will we boldly move ahead with Him?

### Notes

1. Ross Coggins, *Missions Today* (Nashville: Convention Press, 1963), p. 3.

2. W. O. Carver, *Christian Missions in Today's World* (Nashville: Broadman Press, 1942), p. 1.

3. The term *megatrend* has been popularized by John Naisbitt through his widely acclaimed book *Megatrends: Ten New Directions Transforming Our Lives* (New York: Warner Books, 1982).

4. Thomas J. Peters and Robert H. Waterman Jr., *In Search of Excellence* (New York: Warner Books, 1984), p. 7.

5. See Sadie T. Crawley, *World Awareness* (Nashville: Convention Press, 1963). For specific overview of Christian context and world context, see chapters 2 and 4 in E. Luther Copeland, *World Mission and World Survival* (Nashville: Broadman Press, 1985).

6. The best readily available source for comprehensive up-to-date world population information is the World Population Data Sheet issued annually by the Population Reference Bureau, Inc. (2213 M Street, N.W., Washington, D.C.

20037). The data sheet is based primarily on published materials from the United Nations.

7. For data on urbanization, see *Patterns of Urban and Rural Population Growth* (New York: United Nations, 1980).

8. For further details on urbanization from the Christian missions perspective, see Larry L. Rose and C. Kirk Hadaway, eds., *An Urban World: Churches Face the Future* (Nashville: Broadman Press, 1984).

9. See Alvin Toffler, *The Third Wave* (New York: Bantam Books, 1981).

10. This term has been discussed considerably and some prefer not to use it. It is used in different ways by different authors. See for example Orlando E. Costas, *Christ Outside the Gate* (Maryknoll, N.Y.: Orbis Books, 1982), pp. 118-119; and Lawrence E. Keyes, *The Last Age of Missions* (Pasadena, Calif.: William Carey Library, 1983), pp. 9-10. The term is used here in its very general sense as representing those countries that are not part of the developed "Western" political and economic system or the Communist bloc.

11. *World Christian Encyclopedia* (London: Oxford University Press, 1982), p. 5.

12. For brief analysis of the question of the number of countries in the world, see Winston Crawley, "Horizons: How Many 'Countries' Should be on the List?" *The Commission*, vol. 46, no. 8 (October-November 1983): 73.

13. The results of modern missions can be reviewed from such sources as the summary section of Kenneth Scott Latourette's volumes on *The Great Century* and *Advance Through Storm* in his monumental seven-volume *A History of the Expansion of Christianity* (New York: Harper and Brothers Publishers, 1943, 1945); Ralph Winter's *Twenty-Five Unbelievable Years, 1945-1969* (South Pasadena, Calif.; William Carey Library, 1970); and Stephen Neill's *A History of Christian Missions* (Baltimore: Penguin Books Inc., 1964).

14. Gerald H. Anderson and Thomas F. Stransky have edited five volumes of essays under the title *Mission Trends* (published jointly by Paulist Press [New York] and Wm. B. Eerdmans Publishing Company [Grand Rapids] with publication dates from 1974 to 1981). The content is not strictly limited to new trends in missions, since many of the concerns dealt with have been matters of major ongoing discussion by missiologists for many decades.

15. See *Mission Trends No. 4: Liberation Theologies in North America and Europe.*

16. See *Mission Trends No. 3: Third World Theologies.*

17. See January 1983 issue of *Mission Frontiers*, the bulletin of the U.S. Center for World Mission.

18. The full reports are found in the SBC, *Annual*, 1976.

19. For an analysis of this stated purpose of world evangelization see Winston Crawley, "Is World Evangelization Really Possible?" *The Quarterly Review*, vol. 40, no. 3 (April, May, June 1980).

# Part II
# Systems

In recent years systems analysis has become a new specialty, and we have learned to pay increasing attention to systems. Though the term is used frequently in a narrow technical sense, systems analysis can also be understood more broadly as the "process . . . of studying an activity . . . in order to define its goals or purposes and to discover operations and procedures for accomplishing them most efficiently" (Webster's *New Collegiate Dictionary*, 1977).

Already we have considered who we are as Southern Baptists and where we stand now in the context of the modern world and of our own denominational development. Now we turn to the study of Southern Baptist foreign missions activity in terms of its purposes and its organizational operations and procedures—in other words, to examine the systems of Southern Baptist foreign missions.

Most simply stated, of course, the purpose is international Christian missions; and the structure which serves as the means to that end is the Southern Baptist Foreign Mission Board. But the matter is not nearly that simple. There are many different understandings (and some misunderstandings) of foreign missions. Also, the nature and manner of operation of the Foreign Mission Board are not widely known. Therefore, the two chapters in this section elaborate on what these systems actually mean as to purpose and structure.

# 4

# How Do We Understand Our Mission?

"Everybody ought to know who Jesus is." This simple line from the familiar gospel chorus is one way of expressing the conviction that is the heart of the Southern Baptist understanding of our world mission.

It is what we have believed that has made Southern Baptists "a missions people." This is not primarily a matter of doctrines, such as may be written in a creedal statement of faith. What really matters is not propositions to which we may give assent, but rather those things believed so strongly that they influence who we are and how we live. *Convictions* is perhaps a better word: Biblical convictions are the soil in which missions grows.

"Do Southern Baptists still believe that everyone should hear the gospel?" The question was asked by a missionary serving in a difficult and neglected mission field. For several years without success we had been seeking persons to reinforce the small missionary group there. Overburdened as they were with multiplied responsibilities, and surrounded by an ocean of people who had never heard the gospel message, it is easy to see why they might wonder about our commitment to share the gospel with everyone.

In this day it may be naive to assume that all Southern Baptists do believe deeply in world missions. There are indeed caution signals in Southern Baptist life that warn us to reexamine our missionary commitment. Southern Baptist churches as a whole have been using a gradually increasing proportion of their money for their local programs. Many churches are following a pattern of expanding building and program and staff, thoughtlessly letting that expansion come at the expense of world missions. New missionaries coming for appointment have increased, but not in proportion to the increase in seminary enrollments.

Without our knowing it, our thinking about world missions may have been affected by changes around us. For example, most major Protestant denominations have been reducing over-seas missionary forces for two or three decades. Questions are raised about the legitimacy or the importance of foreign missions. Perhaps unconsciously we are influenced by these and other trends in the wider Christian world.

Probably several factors lie behind the lukewarmness toward missions that is evident at times within our own Southern Bap-tist churches. One is a usually unexpressed feeling that people in other lands really do not need Christ—that "it doesn't matter what one believes, as long as he is sincere"; and that since persons in other lands already have their own religions, we should not urge ours upon them. This religious relativism (equivalent almost to Hindu doctrine) is probably more wide-spread than we have realized.

Many persons who believe deeply that everyone should know Christ wonder today to what extent it is possible or appropriate for the message still to be carried by "foreign missionaries." Some writers have speculated that "the day of the missionary is over." Doors to a number of countries are definitely closed. Strong nationalism is a major factor in today's world. The church has already been planted in nearly every land, and local Chris-tian leadership is rising to take initiative in the spread of the gospel.

A less obvious (and entirely unintended) reason for slacking off of the overseas mission effort has been the focus of attention in recent years on the total mission of the church to the world, in contrast with the earlier focus on specific missions to so-called pagan lands. Emphasis on the biblical truth that "all are called" has seemed to diminish the concern for specific persons to go out as missionaries to places of special need.

Furthermore, the recent American psychology of withdrawal

from a world that is confusing and from international commitments that have sometimes seemed overextended apparently
has also affected the thinking and feeling of church people about
worldwide Christian efforts.

If Southern Baptists now drift away from missionary zeal and
lose the compelling vision of outreach to the whole world, we
will become just another institutionalized and formalized
church body, with Ichabod ("the glory is departed") as our
fitting symbol.

"Everybody ought to know who Jesus is." We have believed
that this is our Lord's expectation of us—for us to devote ourselves to making it possible for everybody everywhere to know
Jesus. It has been said that "no one has the right to hear the
gospel twice until everyone has heard it once." In actuality that
is an impossibility, but the statement has much truth in it. Many
persons in favored places hear the gospel scores or even hundreds of times, while countless multitudes never hear at all. This
is far from our Lord's intention. In fact, the contrast would be
ridiculous except that it is so tragic.

To spell out in full detail how we understand our global
mission would require an entire volume on the theology of
mission and another related volume expounding our philosophy
of missions. (Of course, there are already many books dealing
with both subjects or with the two together, and from many
different perspectives. Some of the more prominent ones are
listed in the Bibliography.) In this chapter I am undertaking a
summary of major elements in what I believe is our commonly
accepted Southern Baptist theology of mission and philosophy
of missions—without attempting to make any strict separation
between the two. Our convictions that are essentially theological
find expression in principles that control our missionary purposes and practice.

The Foreign Mission Board does have a very brief statement of
its operating philosophy, adopted in June 1978, which is included as Appendix 1. In some respects, that statement moves
on into strategy considerations. Philosophy of missions deals
with the question of what we do and why, whereas strategy asks
how. It is the why question, of course, which is rooted more

deeply in the theology of mission. All of these elements interrelate to such an extent that the divisions used for the following analysis are inevitably somewhat arbitrary.

### Rationale

Why are we involved in a world mission? The answer lies in our understanding of God as revealed in the Bible.

In the oft-quoted words of W. O. Carver, the origin of missions is ultimately to be found "in the heart of God."[1] Hugo Culpepper summarized Carver's expansion on that theme: "No thought of God is true to His revelation of Himself that does not rest on the fact that He 'so loved the world that He gave His only begotten Son' that by believing in Him 'the world should be saved through Him' . . . this attitude of God is eternal and is determinative in all His dealings with men."[2]

The comment of Robert E. Speer was similar to that of Carver. "It is in the very being and character of God that the deepest ground of the missionary enterprise is to be found. We cannot think of God except in terms which necessitate the missionary idea."[3]

Luther Copeland commented on the ultimate authority for the Christian mission. *"The authority for the Christian mission is the revelation of the living God in Jesus of Nazareth. Or, to put it slightly differently, the authority for the Christian mission is Jesus Christ, viewed in the full orb of the biblical revelation."* He then quoted James S. Stewart. "The concern for world evangelization is not something tacked on to a man's personal Christianity, which he may take or leave as he chooses: it is rooted indefeasibly in the character of the God who has come to us in Jesus." Copeland further commented: "There may be many secondary authorities, but the ultimate authority is the living God who has revealed himself to us in Christ and has given us the privilege to share his mission."[4] J. Herbert Kane wrote similarly.

> The Christian mission is part of God's sovereign activity in the realm of redemption. From first to last, the Christian mission is God's mission, not man's. It originated in the heart of God. It is based on the love of God. It is determined by the

will of God. Its mandate was enunciated by the Son of God. Its
rationale is explained in the Word of God. For its ultimate
success it is dependent on the power of God.[5]

R. Pierce Beaver related Christian missions to "the creative,
revelatory, and redemptive work of God."[6]

The words *mission* and *missions* are not in the earlier standard
translations of the Bible. But the central concept of sending or
being sent, which is the root of both terms, is so prominent
throughout the Bible that it has been taken as the keynote of the
new book interpreting the theology of mission by Francis Dubose, *God Who Sends*. Dubose emphasized sending as a basic
element in the nature of God.

This means further that the Christian mission is God's undertaking, belonging to Him and under His control. That concept
has been popularized by Georg F. Vicedom. "The mission is
work that belongs to God. This is the first implication of *missio
Dei*. God is the Lord, the One who gives orders, the Owner, the
One who takes care of things. He is the Protagonist in the
mission."[7]

Our understanding of God sees mission (sending) not only as
basic in His nature, but also as the clue to His purpose in human
history. W. O. Carver expressed this concept in the phrase "the
plan of the ages"—a literal translation from Ephesians 3:11—and
incorporated into the title of his seminal book, *Missions in the
Plan of the Ages*. We have now seen that plan unfolded across
many centuries, validated by the historical expansion of the
Christian faith to "the ends of the earth."

All this is to say that we are convinced that Christian missions
is not a human enterprise. It is not the religious aspect of the
historical expansion of Western culture. It is not something
invented by churches or missionary organizations as a romantic
outlet for the energies of modern Christians. We are convinced
that Christian missions is grounded in the very nature of God
and is expressive of His eternal purpose.

## Revelation

We are able to understand God's nature and His purpose
because He has revealed Himself.

God's love is revealed supremely through the sending of His unique Son into the world (John 1:18; John 3:16; 1 John 4:9; John 14:7; Heb. 1:1-2; Col. 1:15,19). We understand and believe in Jesus as the perfect revelation of God, intended for all humanity ("everybody ought to know").

Before God revealed Himself fully and finally in Jesus, He was already revealing Himself "in many and various ways" (Heb. 1:1). After the resurrection and ascension of Jesus, God continued to reveal Himself to and through the apostles. We have the Bible as the written Word of God, the record and interpretation of God's revelation centering in the living Word, Jesus Christ.

We understand and believe in the Scriptures of the Old and New Testaments as authoritative.

There has been a tendency throughout the modern missionary movement to base foreign missions primarily on the Great Commission, as found in Matthew 28:18-20. William Carey began there by inquiring whether the commission of Christ to the apostles is still binding on His followers today. However, we understand the missionary theme as running through the entire Bible.

Cornell Goerner recalled the question with which W. O. Carver used to begin a seminary course in missions. "What is the Bible all about?" Is it simply 66 scattered books with various themes, or does it have some central unifying element? We are convinced that the universal, loving, and redemptive purpose of God is the basic theme of biblical revelation. The process of divine sending which we call missions is indicated in the Bible as God's way of accomplishing His purpose. Jesus described the ongoing mission in terms of His own mission: "As the Father hath sent me, even so send I you" (John 20:21).

Carver interpreted the entire process as God's "plan of the ages" (expounded in Eph. 3). God intends to demonstrate through the church the manifold wisdom of his plan for incorporating all peoples ("the Gentiles") into the people of God. (Compare also Acts 15:13-18.)

This is what God is doing in human life and human history: He is bringing persons from all nations into vital relationship with Himself through Jesus Christ. Of course, God is active also in the forces of nature and of so-called "secular" history; but the process of redemption is at the heart of His plan for humanity. The Great Commission refers to it as "discipling all nations."

God doubtless could have chosen some other way to accomplish this purpose of discipling the nations. Presumably He could have sent angels to proclaim His message to everyone. Conceivably He might have put a public address system in the skies or might have broadcast the message, as it were, on a special wavelength to some appropriately tuned receiver in each heart. Instead, in the mystery of His providence, He has chosen to use human instruments for the discipling of the nations. In other words, His plan is to do it through missions.

This is not the place for a thorough examination of the biblical basis for missions. Many books or portions of books are readily available. A selected list is given in the Bibliography. A few brief paragraphs can summarize our understanding of the biblical basis of missions.

The Old Testament reveals God's intention to use His covenant people as His witness to all the world's peoples. In the beginning, the purpose was stated only in very general terms (Gen. 12:1-3). But as the history of Israel proceeded, God gradually further revealed His plan for His people. The Chosen People's understanding of their mission was far from adequate and the carrying out of the mission even less satisfactory—to the point that one of God's prophets said, "Who is blind, but my servant? or deaf, as my messenger that I sent?" (Isa. 42:19). The tension between the missionary purpose of God and the lack of missionary vision and compassion on the part of God's people is well illustrated by the prophet Jonah.

The "event of Jesus Christ" (in the phrase sometimes used to summarize incarnation, atonement, and resurrection) instituted the new covenant, with its new covenant people (see Matt. 21:33-43 and 1 Pet. 2:9-10). Jesus was proclaimed as both Messiah and Lord (Acts 2:36). This news is for everyone, without distinction ("everybody ought to know") and is to be carried by messengers sent out to preach good news, as Paul explained in Romans 10:9-17.

God's purpose is set in its broadest context in such passages as

Romans 8:18-23, Ephesians 1:9-10, Ephesians 3:20-21, Colossians 1:15-20, Philippians 2:9-11, and Revelation 7:9-12.

Though the missionary mandate issues from biblical revelation as a whole, and not just from any isolated passage, the Great Commission still receives and deserves special attention. As missiologist Johannes Verkuyl expressed it, in comparison with the commissions of the risen Christ recorded in the other Gospels and in the book of Acts, the closing verses of Matthew's Gospel express the "mandate for engaging in worldwide mission . . . the most forthrightly." He continued: "Not only is the conclusion to Matthew's Gospel extremely powerful compared to the others, but the final verses form a climax and present a summary of what was written before. They are the key to understanding the whole book."[8]

The core of the Great Commission is a command to bring every people group in the world into discipleship to Jesus. In the original language, this does not include a command to go. The word for *go* is a participle, *going*. This means that the going is secondary to the main thrust—though in many cases essential to the reaching of specific people groups. On the authority of Jesus, His followers are to make whatever concentrated effort is necessary to carry the gospel to every people group in the world.[9]

The formal philosophy statement adopted by the Foreign Mission Board in June 1978, in a list of sources for the Board's philosophy of world missions, mentions first the Bible. It encapsulates the missionary message of the Bible in two sentences. "God has an eternal purpose, expressive of His love for mankind, and missions is an integral part of God's plan for the achievement of that purpose. . . . The Great Commission makes the overseas task the responsibility of each Christian and each church."

Occasionally Christians may be heard to comment, "I don't believe in missions." This is an extremely strange statement to come from a Christian, for it amounts to saying, "I don't believe in God's plan for accomplishing His purpose in the world." At the very least, such a statement reflects a woeful ignorance of God's plan. Many Southern Baptist church members are not aware of what the Bible is all about. Obviously the biblical basis of missions needs to be given a central place in Southern Baptist curricula.

## Purpose

The "why" question can be understood in various ways. Sometimes it is an inquiry about causes. We have examined the why of Southern Baptist foreign missions in that sense: The cause (or rationale) is our understanding of God and His self-revelation. In that sense, the question is examined from the perspective of the past—it means that we are missionary because of who God has always been and what God has already done and said.

Another perspective on the why question considers purposes. It looks from current realities toward the future. In that sense, we understand our mission in terms of our commitment to Christ: His kingdom, His gospel, and His church.

This examination of purposes will be hard to keep separate from the "what" question that deals with the objectives of missions and begins to move into the realm of strategy, rather than philosophy. In this chapter an attempt will be made to stay more in the realm of our philosophy of missions.

Many of the major issues that divide missiologists and other Christians today, and probably most of the more serious issues, are related to the purposes of the Christian world mission. (When matters are identified as "issues" that almost automatically means polarization, though there usually is truth in each differing perspective. For that reason I generally prefer to think of "concerns" instead of "issues"—thereby holding open the possibility of some harmonizing of differing viewpoints.)

### The Kingdom

God's intention is a world in which Christ rules as King in the hearts and lives of all people everywhere. In our Lord's model prayer, we are instructed to make this a part of our personal praying: "Thy kingdom come. Thy will be done . . ." (Matt. 6:10). This concern for God's kingdom and for the doing of God's will is supposed to be at the heart of the yearning of every Christian. The more we understand the Bible, the more we see that God's kingdom and God's will are of central importance in human life.

Even in comparison with such basic matters as the material necessities of life, Jesus said, "Seek ye first the kingdom of God" (Matt. 6:33). We face always the risk of preoccupation with many other concerns (even in the projecting of Christian missions), but nothing else can possibly be as important as commitment to God's kingdom.

Luther Copeland, in inquiring as to the ultimate goal of mission, concluded: *"The reality most consistently set forth in the Bible as the ultimate goal of God's mission is the kingdom of God or the kingdom of heaven."* In a document interpreting the scope of the responsibility for teaching missions in the Southern Baptist curriculum, Copeland expounded the relationship between the kingdom of God and the mission of the church.[10]

This theme had also been emphasized by W. O. Carver 40 years earlier. In a lecture on "Christianity Redefining Its Function," he stated:

> First of all, and always, the point of reference must be the ultimate objective. Jesus stated it for us in a number of terms all reflecting one comprehensive purpose and passion.
>
> His constitutive concept from first to last was the kingdom of God, or kingdom of heaven. To proclaim the reign and win obedience to the rule of God was to discharge the first duty to God and to serve the complete good of man. . . .
>
> *The proximate tasks* of Christianity—individual and church— are to be determined by reference to this supreme objective. The function of the Christian—individual and organization— is to lay hold of every situation for the kingdom of God and relate it in whatever way and measure are possible to the whole undertaking. We are always in danger of seeing our problems and setting our tasks in too limited a context. . . .
>
> This objective before Christians—individuals, and groups, every group large or small, and the very grouping itself—will lead us to seek the methods appropriate to that end. The end must determine the means or means will determine the end.[11]

The lordship of Jesus is closely tied to the concept of the

kingdom. Jesus Christ is the victorious Lamb who "is Lord of lords, and King of kings" (Rev. 17:14).

Much attention has been given in recent years to the kingdom of God as the key to understanding the mission of the church. Some examples are the little book of lectures on missionary motivation by James S. Stewart, with the title *Thine Is The Kingdom*,[12] and a chapter by D. T. Niles on "The Kingdom of the Father is Fulfilled," in his book on the mission of God and the missionary enterprise of the churches, *Upon the Earth*.[13] Lesslie Newbigin in *The Open Secret*, subtitled "Sketches for Missionary Theology," used the doctrine of the Trinity as a basis for interpreting mission and included a chapter on "Proclaiming the Kingdom of the Father."[14] From a distinctively evangelical perspective, Arthur F. Glasser treated the Kingdom of God as the unifying theme in a chapter on "The Whole-Bible Basis of Mission."[15]

Verkuyl's comprehensive work, *Contemporary Missiology*, posited the kingdom of God as the ultimate goal of the *Missio Dei* in words similar to those used by Carver and Copeland.

> In both the Old Testament and the New, God by both his words and deeds claims that he is intent on bringing the kingdom of God to expression and restoring his liberating domain of authority. From the countless biblical images and symbols which describe God's intentions I select this one as the clearest expression of God and his purposes. . . .
>
> The whole of the church's deep and wide mission agenda must receive its focus and orientation in this kingdom perspective. . . .
>
> The first three petitions of the Lord's Prayer summarize so well the deepest and ultimate goal of mission: 'Hallowed be Thy name; Thy kingdom come; Thy will be done on earth as in heaven' (Matthew 6:9-10).[16]

The 1980 meeting at Melbourne, Australia, of The Commission on World Mission and Evangelism of the World Council of Churches took as its theme "Your Kingdom Come." The preparatory documents and the reports from that conference interpret the relation of the kingdom to the mission of the church from the more liberal perspective.

Though a number of Southern Baptists (such as Carver and Copeland) have stressed the relationship between commitment to God's kingdom and the mission of the church, most Southern Baptists have not given such prominent attention to the kingdom. The Foreign Mission Board in its formal statement on missions philosophy (which of course is not intended as a theological document) does refer twice to "kingdom extension" as an element of the purpose of Southern Baptist missions.

For about 30 years, in orienting Southern Baptist missionaries to the missions philosophy of the Foreign Mission Board, I have explained the general long-range objective of Southern Baptist missions as being summed up in the phrase "the kingdom of God." This means that our ultimate hope and aim are for God to rule through Jesus Christ in the heart and life of every person in the world. We are not concerned for only a portion of the world or for merely superficial Christianization. Our ultimate desire is for God's will to be done as fully on earth as it is in heaven.

We recognize, of course, that we cannot by our own efforts "bring in the kingdom." But we recognize also that God has chosen to use human instruments in the extension of His kingdom, as more and more persons are helped to understand and experience the new birth without which one "cannot see the kingdom of God" (John 3:3) and to become "fellow-citizens with the saints" (Eph. 2:19) in the kingdom of God. We understand our foreign missions efforts as an instrumentality of God toward the ultimate aim of the universal reign of King Jesus.

### The Gospel

Southern Baptists are evangelicals—perhaps not entirely in the sense in which the word is sometimes used with a capital E, but in the broader and more important sense of our absolute commitment to the gospel. We believe in and proclaim God's good news of salvation by grace, based on the finished work of Christ in His death and resurrection, and received through faith (Rom. 5:10; Eph. 2:8). We understand our world mission in terms of proclaiming a gospel story which "everybody ought to know."

By its very nature, the gospel is "a story to tell to the nations." If its relevance is not universal, it has little ultimate meaning or value anywhere. Some would argue that persons in other lands do not need Jesus, since they are sincere and devoted followers of their own religions. That viewpoint implies that Jesus and the gospel do not matter very much.

If it makes no difference whether a person knows Jesus, then Christian missions is at best a sort of interesting hobby, and at worst probably an arrogant impertinence. However, the common modern argument against missions, if applied with logical consistency, would argue also against Christian witness and evangelism in our own communities—and would have argued against the preaching of Jesus and the missionary ministry of Paul.

We are convinced that what a person believes does make a tremendous difference. For example, Hitler apparently believed quite sincerely a doctrine of racial supremacy; and what he believed brought tragedy not only to himself but to millions of other persons.

We believe further that all persons, of whatever culture, are made in the image of God and are essentially alike in spiritual nature and spiritual needs. We are convinced that God did something in Jesus Christ and does something through Him in human life that is of infinite importance for any person anywhere. We have "complete confidence in the gospel; it is God's power to save all who believe," of whatever nationality or culture (Rom. 1:16, GNB).

Until about 60 years ago the biblical understanding of the gospel, along lines very briefly stated above, was one of the foundation assumptions in foreign missions. Evangelicals generally have stayed with that understanding of the gospel. But more recently others have raised new issues which have been discussed sometimes rather heatedly. These issues touch in various ways the meaning and the significance of the gospel. Southern Baptists have not been involved much in the controversies, but do need to be familiar with them in order to communicate clearly our own understanding of our gospel mission.

1. *The nature of the missionary message.*—In the several inter-denominational missionary conferences that were held from 1854 through 1910, no serious question was raised about the nature of the missionary message. That message was assumed to be the gospel, expressed in biblical terms.

The meeting of the International Missionary Council at Jerusalem in 1928 was different. There the nature of the message was the main concern. Participants could agree upon a statement defining the missionary message only by compromise between strongly held opposing views. The compromise statement was worded in very general terms to allow room for differing interpretations. W. O. Carver described the result:

> Then it was proposed to accept the Jerusalem statement, "The Message is Christ," leaving the reader large freedom in interpreting the terms. The Jerusalem deliverance amplified the central thesis in terms in which the conservative majority could easily read the historic orthodox definition of the person and the function of "Christ," but which the "liberal" Christians could construe according to their humanistic definitions.[17]

The tendency to redefine the Christian message was further expressed in a book published in 1932. A special commission of appraisal had sent researchers to foreign mission fields, under the auspices of the Layman's Foreign Missions Inquiry. Their findings were reported under the title *Rethinking Missions*. A representative viewpoint was that "ministry to the secular needs of men in the spirit of Christ is *evangelism*, in the right use of the word."[18]

More recently, prominent theologians have tended toward universalism (examples are Rahner among Roman Catholics and Braaten among Protestants), and their views have had an impact on concepts of the Christian message. To the less theologically sophisticated, the view seems to suggest going across the world to inform people that they are all already saved and to encourage them to rejoice in that salvation.

2. *The meaning of evangelism (and evangelization).*—Since our English word *evangelism* is based on the Greek word for gospel

(good news), it is obvious that reexamination of the nature of the gospel would include also taking a new look at the meaning of evangelism.

In common Southern Baptist usage, *evangelization* is a general term that incorporates all the many ways in which persons may become aware of Jesus and the gospel. *Evangelism* is generally used for intentional proclaiming of the gospel with an expectation of decision. The wider world of Christendom does not always distinguish the two terms in that way. (Gerald H. Anderson and Thomas F. Stransky, in the foreword to *Mission Trends No. 2*, point out that " 'evangelization' is now used in all Christian traditions, while 'evangelism' seems largely confined to the Protestant."[19])

The meaning of evangelism, or evangelization, has been widely discussed in the international and interdenominational missionary conferences of the past two decades. The discussions have generally been polarized, with some stressing the importance of evangelism through witness and others pointing out the urgency of ministry. It has been easy for those who have focused on ministry to accuse others of superficiality in merely verbal expression of the gospel. Meanwhile, those committed to witness have in turn denounced a "social gospel" which may obscure the historic gospel message. The appropriateness of Christian "presence" apart from specific witness and the place of "dialogue" in evangelism have been added elements in the discussion.

The importance of questions about the meaning of evangelism in recent missiological discussion is affirmed by the fact that the entire second volume in the mission trends series edited by Gerald Anderson and Thomas Stransky, published in 1975, deals with evangelization. Interest in the matter is widespread, and the topic is considered central to the mission of the church.

In Roman Catholicism, a bishop's synod which was held in 1974 as part of the follow-up to the Second Vatican Council concentrated on "Evangelization in Today's World."

In Protestantism, the same year at Lausanne, Switzerland, an International Congress on World Evangelization—which has developed into an ongoing movement, loosely known as the Lausanne movement—emphasized world evangelization.[20]

The Lausanne movement has been unusually broad in scope, bringing together church and mission leaders both from the evangelical wing of Protestantism and from the mainline denominations which are part of the ecumenical movement. (These two groups, the conciliar and the evangelical, have otherwise tended to go their separate ways in missiological thought and action.) Furthermore, the movement, with its focus on evangelization, has included in its general meetings an unusually wide range of world representation.

3. *The meaning of salvation.*—Since the good news relates to salvation, it is natural that any reexamining of the gospel has also included asking anew what it means to be saved. This theme has been included in several international Christian conferences in recent decades, but it was especially the focus of the 1973 Bangkok meeting of the Commission on World Mission and Evangelism of the World Council of Churches. The conference theme was "Salvation Today." The tendency in such conferences has been to redefine salvation in terms of "humanization" or other related terms (such as liberation).

It is important to recognize that the concern for quality of life which has been emphasized in conferences and in numerous publications is an appropriate biblical and Christian concern. Problems and controversy have been caused by attempts to substitute those concerns for other important biblical and Christian concerns, instead of recognizing that the different concerns and emphases can be complementary.

One great value of the emphasis on humanization is a reminder that salvation is intended to be more than simply right standing with God. It is intended also to be wholeness *(shalom)*—the "life . . . more abundantly" that Jesus promised (John 10:10).[21]

Humanization had already been emphasized in the Fourth Assembly of the World Council of Churches at Uppsala, Sweden, in 1968. Donald McGavran pointed out the following representative statements: "We have lifted up humanization as the goal of mission. . . . In another time the goal of God's redemptive work might best have been described in terms of man turning toward God. . . . The fundamental question was that of the true God. . . . Today the fundamental question is much more that of the true man."[22]

4. *The concept of conversion.*—There has been a tendency to dilute the generally understood meaning of conversion to faith in Christ, or to minimize its importance. This change—like the others related to the Christian message, evangelism and salvation—has characterized especially speakers and writers representing the mainline denominations and the councils of churches. The result has been some estrangement between the conciliar element of current Christian leadership and the openly evangelical element. As discussion between the two elements has continued, each apparently has been helped some by the emphasis of the other. As a result, there are signs of increased attention from the conciliar wing to traditional biblical concerns in missions, and there are indications of increased commitment of the evangelical wing to the equally biblical concerns for social justice and human welfare.[23]

A parallel development of considerable importance in current evangelism and missions is a new and intense emphasis on discipleship.

There is at present some confusion of terminology about discipleship. Many persons have started using the term *to disciple* in a narrow technical sense to describe a training process by which a Christian leader helps persons (individually or in small groups) to develop spiritually in attitudes, skills, and habits—usually according to a formal "discipleship" plan. Such programs (MasterLife is a Southern Baptist example) can be helpful tools for implementing the follow-up portion of the Great Commission: "Teaching them to observe all things whatsoever I have commanded you" (Matt. 28:20). However, using the term *to disciple* exclusively in reference to such a process tends to obscure the basic thrust of the Great Commission, which calls for the "discipling" of all peoples.

In the Great Commission, the term refers to bringing persons into a saving relationship with Jesus as their Savior and Lord. It is one of many New Testament terms describing that relationship. It assumes that the believer will continue to learn more and more of what it means to follow Jesus.

In our American churches, we have often spoken almost entirely of Jesus as Savior, without appropriate emphasis on His lordship. Many persons have not been aware that believers in Jesus are disciples—that is, continuing learners and followers.

General practice in churches overseas, where our missionaries serve, has given more emphasis to the lordship of Jesus, to distinctive Christian life-style, and to church discipline. Furthermore, in many societies there is little or no temptation for anyone to be a nominal Christian. Even so, on many mission fields the new discipleship programs are proving to be very helpful and effective tools for Christian training.

5. *The gospel and world cultures.*—Culture is a fundamental concern in foreign missions. By definition, the sharing of the gospel by a foreign missionary is cross-cultural communication. Greater awareness of and sensitivity to cultural differences have become an important part of today's world mission.

All persons become conditioned by their own surrounding culture as they grow up—without any awareness of culture except as they may encounter "strange" persons who think, speak, and act differently. The individual naturally assumes that his own culture is normal or even normative. This is true in religious experience also. The American Christian who becomes a foreign missionary has had many years of experiencing certain ways of thinking, talking, and acting as normal Christian ways— without recognizing that those ways are conditioned by American culture.

The shift to cross-cultural communication of the gospel is a difficult one. More and more the insights of cultural anthropology have been brought to the aid of Christian missions. For example, the current quarterly journal *Missiology* is the successor to an earlier journal, *Practical Anthropology*, which had the specific intent of illuminating Christian missions through anthropological insights.

A common current word—almost a fad word—in missiology is contextualization. It emphasizes the importance of appropriate cultural expression of the gospel. Concern for contextualization in missions has been controversial because many have feared that the gospel itself will be watered down in the process of expression in unfamiliar cultural forms.

The entire question of the relationship of gospel and culture is extremely complex. How is the essence of the gospel to be understood, free from any cultural trappings? We can understand things only through the forms of thought and language that are part of our cultural heritage. The New Testament reflects the Jewish and Greek cultures of the first century. At best, our attempts to identify the essence of the gospel apart from cultural trappings will apparently be imperfect.

Of course, many theologians and missiologists have wrestled with the question of the relationship between gospel and culture. A classic earlier treatment of the subject is Niebuhr's *Christ and Culture*.[24] A helpful recent booklet prepared from an evangelical and missiological perspective came out of the Lausanne movement. It was developed in a consultation on "Gospel and Culture" sponsored by the theological working group of the Lausanne Continuation Committee.[25]

Since the modern missionary movement originated in the Western culture of Europe and North America, Western cultural forms have tended to characterize church life that has resulted from missions in the rest of the world. That cultural "overhang" has been a serious hindrance to the spread of the gospel. But the situation is not easy to change. After wrestling with the problem in his book *The Open Secret* Lesslie Newbigin concluded:

> It is the urgent need of the hour that the ecumenical fellowship of churches should become so released from its present dependence upon one set of cultural forms that it can provide the place wherein we are able to do theology in the only way that it can be done properly—by learning with increasing clarity to confess the one Lord Jesus Christ as alone having absolute authority and therefore to recognize the relativity of all the cultural forms within which we try to say who he is.[26]

Missiological writings and discussions during recent years have dealt with a closely related topic—the "homogeneous unit principle." Its basic concern is that persons be able to become Christian within their own cultural framework. The principle and the controversy surrounding it will be analyzed in chapter 9.

We are convinced that the gospel is universal. It transcends all cultures yet is relevant to any culture. Therefore, we are committed to the sharing of the good news of Jesus Christ in appropriate cultural forms with all peoples.

6. *The gospel and the world religions.*—For more than half a century, at least from the time of the Jerusalem Conference of the International Missionary Council in 1928, the relationship between the gospel and the world's religions has been a central missiological concern. In preparation for the IMC conference at Madras, India, in 1937, Hendrik Kraemer presented a thorough and definitive statement, *The Christian Message in a Non-Christian World.*[27] From the conference itself, the first volume of the findings dealt with "The Authority of the Faith."

More recent examples of attention to this subject are the section on "Trends in the Theology of Religions" in Verkuyl's *Contemporary Missiology;* Part Three of *The Theology of the Christian Mission,* edited by Gerald H. Anderson and published in 1961; and the entire relatively recent *Mission Trends No. 5* with its subheading "Faith Meets Faith."[28]

The plurality of world religions is a "given" in missions today. (This has become true even of home missions.) Though secularism and irreligion have spread in this century, especially in urban and university settings, and most notably where Marxism is dominant, and though much religious belief and practice may be superficial, historic religions are still held with tenacity in much of the world. Many places experience religious resurgence (as described in chapter 3).

The relationship between the Christian faith and the world of religions is far too large and complex a subject for analysis here. As pointed out earlier, a recent tendency in much of Western Christianity has been toward religious relativism or syncretism. Prominent theologians state their positions in sophisticated concepts and terminology, often explicitly denying syncretism as a goal; however, the end result is often relativist.[29]

A helpful brief summary of common views regarding the relation between Christianity and other religions is given by Asian theologian D. T. Niles.[30] In passing, he referred to the fairly common proposal that conversation (or, in the more usual jargon, "dialogue") is the appropriate Christian approach to persons of other faiths. Central for Niles, however, whether through dialogue or through some other form of interpersonal contact, is "the task of Christian witness" which is "at the heart of Christian obedience."[31]

Our essential position is that the gospel is intended for all persons everywhere. The religions of the world obviously have many good and valuable elements in them, but they have in them nothing comparable to Jesus Christ. They do not know of a holy and righteous God who so loved the world that He sent His Son to provide deliverance and life through His marvelous death on a cross. The difference is well stated in the title of a little book by Christopher E. Storrs, *Many Creeds, One Cross* (New York: The Macmillan Company, 1945). Jesus Himself stated it in His prayer recorded in John 17: "O righteous Father, the world hath not known thee" (v. 25). "And this is life eternal, that they might know thee the only true God, and Jesus Christ, whom thou hast sent" (v. 3).

We are convinced that being in Christ makes an immeasurable and eternal difference; it means "a new creation; the old has passed away, behold, the new has come" (2 Cor. 5:17, RSV). It means passing "from death unto life" (John 5:24), and "out of darkness into his own marvelous light" (1 Pet. 2:9, RSV).

Actually we present Christ to persons in all lands for exactly the same reasons we present Him to people in this land. Our witness is to persons because they are persons, and not to believers in some particular religion. It is not a question of whether they are agnostics, or communists, or materialists, or adherents of some world religion, or even nominal Christians. In any case, they need to know Jesus Christ as personal Savior and Lord. D. T. Niles illustrated that principle: "The basic truth remains that it is man whom the Gospel addresses. William Ernest Hocking is reported as having asked C. F. Andrews, 'How do you preach the gospel to a Hindu?' to which Andrews replied, 'I don't; I preach the gospel to a man.' That is a profound answer. The Christian message is not addressed to other religions, it is not about other religions: the Christian message is about the world."[32]

It is not enough to say that other persons have their own religions. Nicodemus was a man who had a very lofty religion. He was a man of high culture and of the finest morality. But Jesus said to him, "You must all be born again" (John 3:7, GNB). The availability of this new birth through Christ is the universal gospel to which we are committed.

### The Church

Commitment to Christ includes allegiance not only to His kingdom and His gospel but also to His church. We are convinced that the church is the divinely appointed agency for world evangelization and that the planting and maturing of churches is the expected result of such evangelization.

The famous statement of Emil Brunner that "the church exists by mission, just as a fire exists by burning" is usually interpreted to mean that the nature of the church can only be understood in the light of its mission. However, the reverse is also true: The meaning of missions is properly understood only in relation to the church.

The philosophy statement of the Foreign Mission Board affirms that "churches exist and cooperate for the purpose of world outreach and kingdom extension." It further affirms that "the board was created to be a channel for the missionary efforts and resources of the churches."

As to the results of mission efforts, the philosophy statement indicates that "New Testament churches, interdependent and autonomous under the lordship of Christ, are to be established and multiplied as the basic units for Christian nurture and kingdom extension."

Several considerations related to the place of the church in our understanding of our mission deserve special attention. Most fundamental is the *nature of the church,* conceived in terms that are dynamic and not institutional. As stated in the Southern Baptist Inter-Agency Council document, *A Basic Understanding of Southern Baptist Missions Coordination,* the church "is the Body of Christ (cf. Col. 1:24; Eph. 3:10; 4:12,15-16), the people of God (cf. 1 Pet. 2:9-10), led of God in redemptive activity for his glory." The document goes on to state that "a church is the church in a given place and time. . . . A church, therefore, is the Body of Christ in a historical setting, constituted of those who believe on the Lord Jesus Christ (Acts 16:31) and through whom God is realizing his redemptive purpose which is centered in Christ Jesus (Eph. 3:10-11)."[33]

Another way of stating the nature of the church is as a "witnessing community."[34] This description of the church implies fellowship and mission as constituting the essence of the church. These correspond roughly to the rhythm of "come" and "go" in the life of the church, the distinction between "the church gathered" and "the church scattered," the alternation of coming together for worship and fellowship with going out for witness and ministry to the world.

This organic spiritual concept of the church means that churches planted in varying cultural settings obviously and naturally will not be institutional replicas of churches in America. Our commitment is to the church in its essential nature as the body of Christ, as a witnessing community, and not to any particular institutional form the church may take under the influence of a particular cultural context.

(This is not the place for an exposition of Baptist ecclesiology; however, it is relevant to point out that in these paragraphs and frequently in Baptist usage the church refers to the entire mystical body of Christ. W. O. Carver explained the concept: "The Church in Ephesians and in Colossians is the spiritual Body of the Christ, constituted of all who are children of God through the calling of God and by their 'faith in the Lord Jesus.' This Church is conceived as organic with the Christ, his Body in the world, in the process of redemption, in the unfolding of history. In this sense the Church is not organized, has no human head or headship."[35] A church and churches refer to local congregations. Southern Baptists do not use the term *church* to mean a collective church organizational structure. In other words, we would not refer to our denomination as the "Southern Baptist Church.")

Emil Brunner, in what is probably his best-known statement, said, "The church exists by mission, just as a fire exists by burning. Where there is no mission there is no church; and where is neither church nor mission, there is no faith."[36] This same idea has been expressed by Georg Vicedom, who wrote: "There is no participation in Christ without participation in His mission. . . . Hence the church is not called on to decide whether she will carry on the mission. . . . She can only decide . . . whether she wants to be the church."[37] Since the church is God's appointed agency for world evangelization, with missions as an integral part of its nature, any church which fails to be missionary is not truly a New Testament church. Lesslie New-bigin wrote, "We must say bluntly that when the Church ceases to be a mission, then she ceases to have any right to the titles by which she is adorned in the New Testament."[38]

An important concern commonly and biblically involved in the relationship of the church and mission is *Christian unity*. That concern is grounded most fundamentally and most clearly in the high priestly prayer of Jesus in John 17: "The glory which thou hast given me I have given to them, that they may be one even as we are one, I in them and thou in me, that they may become perfectly one, so that the world may know that thou hast sent me and hast loved them even as thou hast loved me" (vv. 22-23, RSV).

The oneness described in the prayer of Jesus is spiritual oneness ("I in them and thou in me"). Southern Baptists have maintained that it does not prescribe organizational unity. (The question of Southern Baptist relations with other Christian bodies will be discussed later, in chapter 10.) However, sadly, Southern Baptists have been troubled from time to time by inner dissension that has been a distraction from our mission and has failed to reflect glory on the name of Christ. Furthermore, we have often failed to pursue biblical unity in spirit with others who know, love, and serve the Lord Jesus.

Paul in Ephesians follows his emphasis on the mission of the church (chapter 3) by urging the unity of the church in the first half of chapter 4. Biblically, mission and unity belong together.

Another quite prominent aspect of Christian missions today is the development of hundreds and perhaps thousands of *para-church missions organizations*. They are organized on the society principle, with participation and support from individuals who are interested in the special emphasis of each particular organization. Most such organizations are nondenominational, with supporters from many different Christian groups. Some of them seek supporters from within a single denomination. Many individual Southern Baptists are involved in foreign missions as missionaries or supporters of parachurch groups.

By contrast, as pointed out already in chapter 2, Southern Baptist work is established on the convention principle, with the Convention and its agencies as channels for the cooperative efforts of all Southern Baptist churches. To be sure, there is a sense in which even an association or state convention (or an agency of the Convention) is a "parachurch" organization, but the term usually refers to organizations which have no formal ties with denominational bodies—and there is an essential difference between the two.

Southern Baptist foreign missions is a cooperative effort of Southern Baptist churches through Southern Baptist channels. This means that we understand our mission as a comprehensive one. The work of a parachurch organization is often limited to one aspect of Christian missions. The work of the Southern Baptist Foreign Mission Board includes a wide range of missions activities and seeks to provide a channel for expression of the missions concerns of all Southern Baptists. It represents the many churches which have joined in forming the Convention, not just the special interests of groups or individuals.

One further consideration is vital for an understanding of the relationship of Southern Baptist foreign missions to the church. *The calling of a missions agency* is not the same as the whole calling of the church. Mission is integral to that calling, but it is not the whole. Mission is the responsibility of the church for witness and ministry to the world. The church is called also to worship and to the nurture of its inner spiritual life. Foreign missions is an even more limited portion of the full mission of the church. Therefore, foreign missionaries and a missions agency should not be expected to do everything that might be involved in the total responsibility of the church.

This principle of different gifts and different roles in the church is expressed clearly and in detail in 1 Corinthians 12. However, there are still many persons who want to insist that a missions agency exercise every role. In our denominational life, we have expressed the principle of differing functions by creating a family of agencies. The Foreign Mission Board can therefore devote itself to its assigned responsibilities in confidence that other appropriate concerns of the church are being expressed through other agencies with different assignments.

Interestingly, Bishop Lesslie Newbigin agrees with Donald McGavran on this point (though they doubtless disagree on many other missions issues). With reference to McGavran, Newbigin has written:

> He is right in insisting that the missionary has a specific task— not the whole task of evangelism, nurture, prophetic witness, and action for justice and compassion, but the more limited task of "discipling." This is not to deny that the others named and many more must be included in any full statement of the church's calling; it is only to insist that within the broader spectrum of the church's calling the missionary has a specific and more limited calling. He is to "disciple the nations." The other things must not be left undone, but they must not deflect the missionary from the essential thing to which he is called—to bring "the nations" into allegiance to Jesus Christ.

Further, interpreting the preaching and practice of Paul, Newbigin commented:

> His task as a missionary is clear, limited, and—literally— fundamental. He is sent to lay the foundation stone of the church, and that stone is Christ. The result of his work, in other words, will be a community which acknowledges Jesus Christ as the supreme Lord of life.[39]

### Motivation

Motivation is another element in our understanding of our mission. Motives for mission are related to rationale and purpose, but they answer the "why" question in a different way— on the basis of spiritual qualities that actually impel individual Christians or churches to be missionary.

We all no doubt act from very mixed motives. Some possible

impulses to participate in missions are more selfish than Christian. Even among the higher and better motives, there is still no obvious single true motive for Christian missions.

Johannes Verkuyl in his definitive book *Contemporary Missiology* included a chapter on "Motives for Fulfilling the Missionary Task." He separated these into pure and impure motives.[40] Creighton Lacy detailed a longer list of possible motives (in an article, "Motivation for Mission," in *The Outlook*, quarterly journal of Southeastern Baptist Theological Seminary). Luther Copeland in his recent book *World Mission and World Survival*, after referring to Lacy's survey and conclusions, suggested "a basic understanding of motive which can embrace individual variations on the same theme." He proposed "the basic motive of the Christian mission as grateful, loving response to the living God who has revealed himself to us graciously in Jesus Christ."[41]

A fairly common summary of essential motivations for world missions classifies them as external, internal, and eternal reasons.

The *external* reason for missions lies in the tremendous, pathetic needs of humanity. Missionaries minister to all kinds of human need, and there are concentrations of need around the world far more acute than we can readily imagine. Appropriate Christian concern for the meeting of dire human need is an urgent motive for foreign missions.

Everywhere, regardless of material or social circumstance, there is the spiritual plight of lost mankind. Today's multitudes, without a saving knowledge of Jesus Christ, are still "like sheep without a shepherd" (Matt. 9:36, RSV). Appropriate Christian concern for the spiritual need of persons who do not know Christ impels us urgently to world missions.

As long as the proportion of Christians in our own land is so large and we have so many resources, and while both physical and spiritual need is so great in other lands, our stewardship debt to the world calls for us to do as much as we possibly can in missions around the world.

The *internal* motive for missions is the love which is the natural expression of the truly Christian heart. Even if we did not have other reasons for being missionary, the love that characterizes us when we are most truly Christian would lead us to reach out to others, without being limited by boundaries of race or nation. When Jesus saw the distressed multitudes, He was moved with compassion. Motivated by such compassion, we cannot help sharing with others the blessings we have received in Christ.

The third motive for foreign missions is more fundamental than either human need or Christian love. It is the *eternal* motive of faithfulness to the will to God. Regardless of whether we pay attention to human need or whether we feel like helping, it still remains the will of God for every person everywhere to have a chance to know Jesus.

The philosophy statement of the Foreign Mission Board includes these three central motives for missions and adds a fourth which expresses even more profoundly the essence of missionary motivation. The statement is, "Mission ministries are motivated by Christian love, concern for human need, the impelling of the Holy Spirit and the revealed will of God."

I am convinced that the *indwelling Holy Spirit* is the true source of missionary motivation. Our experience of the Holy Spirit stands alongside our understanding of God and His revelation and our commitment to Christ as a fundamental element in our understanding of our mission. The major elements in missionary motivation are mediated to us through the Holy Spirit: He makes us sensitive to human need; He plants God's love in our hearts (Rom. 5:5; Gal. 5:22; 2 Cor. 5:14); and He impels us to carry out the universal redemptive purpose of God.

Space does not allow full treatment of the place of the Holy Spirit not only in motivation but also in other aspects of Christian world missions. The Holy Spirit is so prominent in the Acts of the Apostles that the book might well be called the Acts of the Holy Spirit.[42]

The most thorough and influential treatment of the Holy Spirit in missions is that of Harry R. Boer in *Pentecost and Missions*.[43] The importance of the Holy Spirit to the Christian mission is clear from the prominent place given to the Holy Spirit in connection with the commissions of the risen Christ (see Luke 24:47-49; John 20:21-22; and Acts 1:8).

Several vital aspects of the role of the Holy Spirit in missions, along with the motivating of missions, are the bestowing of appropriate spiritual gifts (1 Cor. 12), the providing of spiritual power, and the giving of leadership and direction.

It seems strange that the modern charismatic emphasis has focused so much on inner personal experience, whereas the presence and the filling of the Holy Spirit in the New Testament are linked so prominently with witness to outsiders, the spread of the gospel and the planting of churches, and the mission to all nations. As our experience of the Holy Spirit becomes more biblical, the hope of Bold Mission Thrust will become more realistic (Acts 4:31).

### Concern

Our understanding of our Christian mission is conditioned by involvement in and with humanity. We are concerned that the mission be carried out in ways that are harmonious with that involvement.

We recognize that this concern is secondary in Christian missions. We understand our mission primarily in terms of our relation with the Triune God (as described in the first three sections of this chapter). The command to love one's neighbor is secondary to the first and great command to love the Lord our God. But Jesus did not separate the two commands or place them in opposition to each other. He treated the second as the natural expression of the first. They are integrally related.

Some in recent years have suggested that the specific needs of the world should set the agenda for the church. We do not see it that way. We are convinced that the agenda of the church is already set within the *Missio Dei*. However, the church deals with that agenda in a real world, and the way in which the agenda is handled must reflect the realities of the human condition and human needs. Much more will be said along that line in later sections discussing objectives and strategy, but it is part of our basic philosophy of missions that we are engaged with a real world.

We are convinced of the essential oneness of humanity. Cultural differences are real, and they do matter; but they are not ultimate. The same is true of differences of race, language, religion, age, sex, and social condition. Beneath and beyond all such differences, the human race is one race, created in the image of the one God, created with a common spiritual nature that makes possible fellowship with God.

We are convinced, further, of the essential lostness of all humanity, for "all have sinned and come short of the glory of God" (Rom. 3:23). This is true for all social conditions. The privileged person is not protected from lostness by his privilege, and the needy person is not exempted because of his deprivation. It is to this universal lostness that the gospel is addressed.

Many Christian leaders today are giving unusual attention to material needs. The Roman Catholic church has defined this as an "option for the poor"—apparently partly as a corrective for what was perceived in some settings as an alliance between the church and the power structures of society. In all denominations, including our own, there is increased awareness of the strong biblical emphasis on compassion for and identification with the poor. This emphasis has many ramifications (including relief and development ministries, action for social justice, liberation theology, attention to the structures of society, and so forth) which will be discussed in detail in chapter 13.

In Southern Baptist foreign missions, there has never been any social "gospel" as a rival to the spiritual gospel of salvation in Christ, but there has been a great deal of social concern and action to meet physical, material, and social needs. Witness and ministry are not polarized; they are considered complementary. The Foreign Mission Board philosophy statement puts both in one paragraph: "The task of missions supremely and imperatively is to make disciples, to baptize them, and to teach them to observe all that Christ commanded. . . . The task of missions is also to minister compassionately to those who are hungry, thirsty, strangers, lack clothing, sick, imprisoned, etc."

Currently the term *holistic* is used to describe this understanding of our mission intentions. We seek to express concern for the whole person. Chapter 13 will explain this holistic approach.

Another important part of our involvement with humanity is the servant role of the missionary (2 Cor. 4:5). This is difficult to maintain, not only because of the egotism that is endemic in human nature, but also because our American culture emphasizes competition and leadership rather than servanthood. We recognize, though, that servanthood is required by the incarnational principle (Phil. 2:5-8) which will be described further in chapters 6 and 7.

## Concepts

Our interpretation of several common concepts in recent missiological thought and writing should be explained. Terminology that we use—or do not use—helps to illumine our understanding of our mission.

Communicating the meaning of words and phrases with clarity is not easy. Any term that is used may have some disadvantages. Many words can be used with a variety of meanings. Most of us already have some built-in assumptions as to what particular words or phrases mean. However, what follows represents roughly the usage that is common in Southern Baptist foreign missions.

### Missions

Christian outreach with the gospel into new areas has been identified for generations by the word *missions*. Most Southern Baptist church members have a rather clear and consistent idea as to what they mean by the word. But the word is not entirely free from problems.

On the one hand, many persons, especially in the Third World, have come to feel that "missions" implies condescension. A common European perspective has tended to identify missions with the spread of civilization. Therefore, many persons in other countries and in other denominations avoid using the word. But words that may be substituted also have their own problems, and giving up the term seemed in many cases to result in diminishing or even abandoning the very concept of missions.

On the other hand, among Southern Baptists the word has had such strong and favorable emotional overtones that there has been a tendency to stretch its meaning. Churches, conventions, and denominational agencies have wanted to expand the category of "missions" to include as much of what they are doing as possible. Some have even said in effect that all we do as churches and as a denomination is missions. The result of such stretching is to rob the word of any real meaning, while deceiving both ourselves and others as to how much we are actually doing in missions.

When the Southern Baptist Convention began to develop formal program assignments for its agencies, the process called for defining significant programming terms. Those involved in the process (and eventually scores of persons in Southern Baptist leadership became involved) found it difficult to agree on a definition of missions. The process involved tension between persons who wanted a very broad definition, to make sure their own work assignments were called missions, and others who wanted a narrower definition retaining the historic and commonly understood focus of the word on outreach to new groups or areas. Ultimately that sharper focus was retained.[44]

The definition of missions as approved by the Inter-Agency Council and included in the SBC Program Planning Glossary is: "What the churches do in keeping with the Great Commission of their sovereign Lord to extend their witness and ministry beyond themselves to bring all persons to Christ and to glorify God."

Another definition of missions in current use among Southern Baptists is that given in the Missions Education Council curriculum scope document on missions. *"Christian missions are specific divine commissionings of individuals and groups, ordinarily with churchly sanction, for the implementation of the church's mission to communicate the gospel of Christ."*[45]

The Foreign Mission Board operates on the assumption that the concept of missions is an important biblical concept and that there is no other word which expresses it as well as the word *missions*. Therefore, though there are admittedly some problems and a possibility of misunderstandings, the word is retained as a summary word for Christian outreach activities of witness and ministry.

### Mission and Missions

In recent decades the singular form *mission* has come into prominence, often displacing the use of the plural form *missions*. This trend *From Missions to Mission* became the title of a brief book by R. Pierce Beaver.

The main point intended by the phrase *from missions to mission* is both true and vital. It implies that formerly the spread of the gospel was understood in terms of the responsibility of a few people (missionaries) to go from a few lands which were thought of as Christian to other lands which were considered heathen. We understand now, however, that all of the people of God are involved in the mission of the church; that Christian faith and Christian churches are spread throughout the world; and that the entire world is a mission field. As Beaver pointed out, we now have "a vision of one world mission of the one Church of Christ to the whole inhabited earth, with lines of witness running through every nation to all frontiers where Jesus Christ is not recognized as Lord." On the basis of that vision, he says, "the term *mission* has come very widely to replace *missions*."[46]

Though the point intended by the phrase *from missions to mission* is both valid and valuable, the phrase needs careful understanding or it can become quite misleading. We do need to retain also the use of the word *missions* and to understand clearly the way in which mission and missions are related.[47]

Substitution of mission for missions is an example of the polarizing tendency in human nature, which sets over against each other things that really belong together. This polarizing tendency usually is compounded by pendulum swing from overemphasis on one aspect of a matter to overemphasis on a complementary aspect. *From mission to missions* expresses well the fact that an earlier day overemphasized missions and neglected the whole mission of the whole church to the whole world. Now emphasis centers on that more general responsibility of the church, with resulting neglect of specific outreach with the gospel.

The word *mission* expresses a general principle. Missions stands for specific actions as practical expressions of that principle. The two need to be kept in dynamic relationship with each other.

The relationship of mission to missions is similar to the relationship of the general principle of giving to actual gifts. The concept of gifts does not have to be abandoned in order to emphasize the spirit of giving. Rather, that spirit is actualized through gifts. Similarly, instead of discarding the word *missions,* we continue to think in terms of mission expressed through missions. The general mission of all God's people to all the world must be made concrete and effective through many specific sendings of specific people to specific places—that is, through missions.[48]

### Foreign Missions

"The field is the world" (Matt. 13:38). In the broadest and most fundamental sense, the field of all missions is the entire world. God's saving purpose and the mission of the church are universal. On the basis of that spiritual truth, a number of denominations have chosen not to speak any longer of "foreign" missions, but to refer instead to the world mission of the church and to structure their mission activities through a unified "world" or "global" mission board.

The concept of Christendom is no longer operative. It is the old term for "the portion of the world in which Christianity prevails."[49] Although the *World Christian Encyclopedia* does list countries in which Christianity is the majority faith, many of those countries are largely secular in culture. Furthermore, there are large and vigorous Christian groups in many countries where Christians are still a minority of the population. In other words, any division of the world's nations into Christian lands and heathen lands would be highly misleading. Both Christian faith and paganism can be found worldwide, regardless of national or cultural setting. (Incidentally, the terms *heathen* and *pagan* must be used with extreme caution if at all, in respect for the sensitivity of many who consider the terms offensive.)

Since 1963, the phrase "Mission on Six Continents" has been a widely used summary of the oneness of the worldwide Christian mission.[50] However, those denominations which have most emphasized this truth and have restructured their mission efforts to reduce distinctions between homeland and international missions have ended up doing less and less in missions overseas.[51]

Areas outside our own homeland differ from our own in so many ways that effective witness in their cultural settings requires specialized understandings and many kinds of adjustments. There are sound and strong reasons for foreign missions to constitute a logical practical subdivision of the total task of world missions. Therefore, Southern Baptists continue to organize for home and foreign missions separately. As G. Thompson Brown pointed out:

> How a denomination engages in mission in relationship to its own judicatories and congregations is quite different from the way in which it ought to do mission with independent and autonomous churches. What might be appropriate and helpful action at home may be viewed as neo-colonialism when practiced abroad. The assumption that mission is one and the same leads too easily to the assumption that what are high priorities for my church are the same priorities for churches in other lands.[52]

The division between home and foreign missions is only a practical working division. It is not a theological or biblical division (though it is sometimes treated as roughly in harmony with the geographic distinctions in Acts 1:8). But the practical reasons for the distinction are compelling. The possibility of focusing planning and strategy sharply on the realities of international and cross-cultural work is one of the great strengths of Southern Baptist missions.

### Foreign Mission Board

At times the Foreign Mission Board considered the possibility of changing its name. It is sometimes suggested that the name sounds archaic or that it may cause problems in some overseas setting where there may be local bias against the word *foreign* or the word *mission* or both. Some future change is possible; but up to now, after careful study, no change has seemed advisable.

Other denominations now have a board of global missions or a board of international ministries. As a substitute for *foreign*, *international* would probably be our best choice. *Global* or *world* could imply a comprehensive board combining home and foreign missions. *Overseas* would not be literally accurate (though we do use the term frequently as a synonym for foreign). *External* or *abroad* would be awkward to use. We continue to use *foreign*, but without any qualitative connotation; it means simply in countries other than our own.

Any possible problem in the term is reduced by the fact that the board's name is translated into other languages in many overseas settings. Any potential advantage in changing from foreign to international might well be outweighed by the expenditure of time, trouble, money, and the legal complications of a name change.

Mission is a concept we do not want to weaken. If some other word—even a good word like *ministries*—were substituted for mission, it might seem to represent a shift from our central mission purposes.

Some boards of other denominations have reinterpreted their purposes in terms of fraternal relations or interchurch aid. These can be valuable parts of what we do in relation to Christian work in other lands—but we see them as supportive of the purposes of missions and not as a substitute for those purposes. Retaining the term *mission* in the board's name helps keep our purposes in clear perspective.

Furthermore, we are making no attempt to hide the nature of our organization and its work from persons in other lands. The name of the Foreign Mission Board is a frank statement of what we believe in and what we are undertaking to do.

### Missionary

We have seen no reason to change to another term to describe the missionary. To be sure, in some overseas settings where the term would cause major problems, we avoid using it. But we have not shifted in general usage to *fraternal worker* as some have.

It is our conviction that the term *fraternal worker*, though in itself true and appropriate, tends to obscure the central thrust of missions. That central thrust is toward the world, not toward the body of believers. We do relate fraternally to them and work alongside them in the mission thrust toward the world. Continuing to use the term *missionary* says something important about our understanding of our mission.

One reason Southern Baptists have had no serious problem with the term *missionary* is that we have never thought of missionaries only in terms of persons going from our cultural setting to some place in the "less developed" world. We have always recognized the value of having missionaries in our own nation, in our own states, in our own cities and communities. This has not automatically protected us from condescension, since it is always possible to think of community missions as taking place "across the tracks," in some less privileged section of our community. But certainly in principle it has kept us open to the idea that missionaries might come from other places to serve among us—and that it would not be an insult to us for them to do so.

Many in recent years have referred to missions as "a two-way street." This is a way of emphasizing the six-continent view of missions. Spiritual need is not a matter of geography. Missionaries to the United States from other lands are welcome and can make a valuable contribution to the evangelizing of our nation. It happens that most of what has taken place under the "two-way street" banner has been interchurch relations rather than missions. It has often been American churches bringing Christians from other lands to speak in our churches and conventions at our expense. It has seldom been the sending of missionaries by Christians in other lands to share the gospel with unbelieving Americans. It would be more appropriate to describe what usually happens by saying "interchurch relations are a two-way street."

Another complication about the term *missionary* arises from the needed emphasis in recent years on the involvement of all believers in the mission of the church. It is sometimes said that every Christian is a missionary. Some years ago the Foreign

Mission Board released a film with the title "All Are Called." Volunteerism in modern American church life has produced thousands of short-term "missionaries" going on projects of a few days to a few months. In the main, however, Southern Baptists have continued to use the word *missionary* primarily for those persons with a long-range assignment that involves the crossing of some frontier or barrier (national, ethnic, linguistic, religious, economic, or social), either in this country or abroad.

### National

This term is part of the current jargon of Christian missions—probably not too readily understood by many persons in our churches and by most of the general public. About a generation ago it replaced the term *native*, which had been associated so frequently with condescending attitudes and statements that it became offensive to most of the world.

In itself, the word *native* is a fine word. All of us are natives of one place or another. I am a native of the United States and of East Tennessee. But multiplied references to "the natives," often from colonial perspectives (such as the cliché "the natives are restless tonight"), made the term undesirable.

The term *national* is ambiguous unless used very carefully. All of us are nationals of one country or another. I am a national of the United States. Of course, when I serve as a missionary in another country, I become an expatriate, living and working among the "nationals" of that country. But if we refer simply to "national Baptists," this may seem to be a reference to the black Baptist conventions in our own nation. And if we refer to Baptist leaders in other countries as "national leaders" without adding the word *Baptist*, many hearers might think we are talking about political leaders.

In effect, our jargon has given the term *national* a special definition as "persons of countries other than the United States." We do better to avoid the use of jargon as much as possible, using whatever specific term is applicable (we relate to African people, we work alongside Nigerian Baptist leaders, and so forth). Not only does this way of speaking and writing communicate more clearly; it also helps to avoid the likelihood that after a time *the nationals* may become as unacceptable a term as *the natives*.

Some other terms that have been common missions jargon have not been used much by Southern Baptists. For many years, it has been usual in some church circles to refer to "older and younger churches" or to "sending and receiving churches." The implication has been that the "older churches" of Europe and North America send missionaries who are then received by the "younger" churches of the Third World.

One reason we have not used the terms very much is that they really refer to denominational groups rather than congregations, whereas when we speak of "churches" we mean congregations. I am a member of a "younger church." It was constituted as a church about 20 years ago. In Nigeria or Brazil or Japan, there are many churches older than that. For Southern Baptists, the terms do not communicate clearly.

Another problem is that the terms easily lend themselves to an attitude of condescension: The younger should look up to the older, and the receiver should be grateful to the sender. We are probably fortunate that the terms have not fit readily into our usage, since there is more than enough temptation to pride and ethnocentrism anyway.

Still a further problem with the terminology of sending and receiving is that it distorts the concept of missions and the partnership of churches in missions. It seems to say that missionaries are sent to the churches in some other country and that these churches are simply receivers. Our understanding of missions, however, is that missionaries are sent to the world and that we are partners with churches in other lands in the process. They send their own missionaries or other Christian workers to the world around them, and our missionaries work alongside them.

A better recent term is *sister churches,* but it still is used mainly with reference to denominational bodies rather than con-gregations.

Unfortunately, we do not have any clear, brief, and suitable term to use. We refer to the Baptist churches and conventions in other lands with which our mission work is related—or we use some variation of that explanatory phrase. Since people in general (including editors) prefer brevity, we easily fall into the trap of referring to all that is being done as "our work," to each part of the work as "our seminary" or "our hospital," and perhaps even "our church"! The reality is that Baptist churches in another land have their convention, their leaders, their seminary or hospital, and their work. We are privileged to relate to them in partnership and to help in various ways in their work.

Obviously, terminology in missions is a problem that may reflect old prejudices or new fads. Many terms are more likely to be misunderstood than to be understood. No available terms are perfect. Different Christian groups may use different terms because they seek to make different emphases. Southern Baptists have sought to stay with terminology that reflects who we are as Baptists and how we understand our mission.

## Challenge

Bold Mission Thrust (as explained earlier) is the plan by which we currently understand and interpret the challenge that faces Southern Baptists in world missions. The outlook for Bold Mission Thrust in the years ahead will be examined in chapter 16. But some interpretation of the concept is needed here.

Much of the attention to Bold Mission Thrust has centered on the great overarching objective of preaching the gospel to all the people in the world. At times that statement has been used in ways that seem to imply that it is the sole objective set forth by the Foreign Mission Board for Bold Mission Thrust. Actually there are ten stated emphases, and they are to be understood in the context of the basic principles of missions that are outlined in the Bold Mission Thrust document "Foreign Missions Looks Toward AD 2000." If only the overarching purpose is given attention, and if it is not seen in the context of the basic principles, what the Board is undertaking and what our missionaries across the world have in view will not be understood correctly by Southern Baptists. The overarching purpose, if taken literally and taken alone, would lead to almost exclusively a seed-sowing endeavor. It would lead also to the spreading of ourselves so thin that very little might really be accomplished.

The actual idea is so to accelerate and to focus all parts of our mission effort that we will multiply astronomically the part we play in full evangelization of the world in this century.

The challenge of the unfinished task is staggering, as was noted in the previous chapter; but Bold Mission Thrust assumes that it is finishable by the miraculous power of God.[53]

Some see the very idea of Bold Mission Thrust as an expression of *triumphalism*. This term is commonly used today to criticize any note of apparent human boasting about the spread of the gospel or the growth and influence of the church. It is a valuable reminder that the church does not exist to glorify itself, but for service to Christ and to others.

Unfortunately, the criticism of triumphalism sometimes tends to dampen any enthusiasm for facing the challenge of world evangelization, diminish the hope of the growth of God's kingdom within history, and obscure the victory of Christ as Lord of history.[54]

It is our conviction, centered in the revealed purpose of God in Christ Jesus, that the mission of the church will continue until the end of history. It is our conviction further that God challenges His people to share the good news of Christ Jesus with every human being. The forms of missions are sure to change, and the extent to which the challenge will be fulfilled is uncertain. We realize that God does not intend to use Southern Baptists alone in evangelizing the world—that our part, indeed, is only a small part of what God is doing through all who know, love, and proclaim the Lord Jesus. But we acknowledge a stewardship responsibility that challenges us to do a far, far larger part in world evangelization. We accept, therefore, today's challenge to unprecedented boldness in world mission thrust.

On the one hand, there is the danger that we may become triumphalists, assuming that we can evangelize the world in our own strength. But the more likely danger is that we will adopt Bold Mission Thrust in theory only, claiming the underlying doctrinal convictions and repeating the appropriate world missions themes but with little actual commitment or boldness.

Understanding one's mission does not automatically mean the fulfilling of that mission. To sing "Everybody ought to know who Jesus is" is not enough. What matters is believing and caring so deeply that our entire lives and the full resources of our churches are devoted to helping make it possible.

## Notes

1. W. O. Carver, *Missions in the Plan of the Ages* (New York: Fleming H. Revell Company, 1909; reprint Nashville: Broadman Press, 1951), p. 12.

2. *A Basic Understanding of Southern Baptist Missions Coordination* (Nashville: Inter-Agency Council, SBC, 1972), p. 6.

3. Robert E. Speer, *Christianity and the Nations* (New York: Fleming H. Revell Company, 1910), p. 18.

4. *MEC Curriculum Scope Document, Task: Teach Missions* (Nashville: Missions Education Council, SBC, 1984), pp. 27-28; James S. Stewart, *Thine Is the Kingdom* (New York: Charles Scribner's Sons, 1956), p. 14; and also E. Luther Copeland, *World Mission and World Survival* (Nashville: Broadman Press, 1985), pp. 134-37.

5. J. Herbert Kane, *Understanding Christian Missions*, rev. ed. (Grand Rapids: Baker Book House, 1978), p. 87.

6. R. Pierce Beaver, *The Missionary Between the Times* (Garden City, New York: Doubleday and Company, Inc., 1968), p. 8.

7. Georg F. Vicedom, *The Mission of God: An Introduction to a Theology of Mission*, trans. Gilbert A. Thiele and Dennis Hilgendorf (St. Louis: Concordia Publishing House, 1965), p. 5.

8. Johannes Verkuyl, *Contemporary Missiology*, trans. and ed. Dale Cooper (Grand Rapids: William B. Eerdmans Publishing Company, 1978), p. 106.

9. For fuller discussion of the meaning of the Great Commission, see Winston Crawley, "Horizons: Clarifying the Command in the Great Commission" in *The Commission*, vol. 46, no. 5 (June-July 1983): 73; the extended passage by Verkuyl to which reference has been made; and Karl Barth, "An Exegetical Study of Matthew 28:16-20," trans. Thomas Wieser, in *The Theology of the Christian Mission*, ed. by Gerald H. Anderson (New York: McGraw-Hill Book Company, Inc., 1961), pp. 55-71.

10. *MEC Curriculum Scope Document, Task: Teach Missions*, pp. 29-31. See also Copeland, *World Mission and World Survival*, pp. 139-45.

11. W. O. Carver, *Christian Missions in Today's World* (Nashville: Broadman Press, 1942), pp. 61-63.

12. Stewart, 74 pages.

13. D. T. Niles, *Upon the Earth* (New York: McGraw-Hill Book Company, Inc., 1962), pp. 80-98.

14. Lesslie Newbigin, *The Open Secret* (Grand Rapids: William B. Eerdmans Publishing Company, 1978), pp. 32-45.

15. Arthur F. Glasser and Donald A. McGavran, *Contemporary Theologies of Missions* (Grand Rapids: Baker Book House, 1983), pp. 30-46.

16. Verkuyl, pp. 197-98.

17. Carver, *Christian Missions in Today's World*, p. 73.

18. William Ernest Hocking (Chairman of the Commission of Appraisal), *Rethinking Missions: A Laymen's Inquiry After One Hundred Years* (New York: Harper and Brothers Publishers, 1932), p. 68.

19. Gerald H. Anderson and Thomas F. Stransky, eds., *Mission Trends No. 2: Evangelization* (New York: Paulist Press and Grand Rapids: Wm. B. Eerdmans Publishing Co., 1975), p. 1.

20. See appendixes to Anderson and Stransky, eds., *Mission Trends No. 2*, pp. 239-48. See also J. D. Douglas, ed., *Let the Earth Hear His Voice* (Minneapolis: World Wide Publications, 1975), the official report volume from the International Congress on World Evangelization, Lausanne, Switzerland.

21. For evangelical interpretations of the recent "salvation" discussions, see John R. W. Stott, "The Biblical Basis of Evangelism," in *Mission Trends No. 2*, pp. 4-23; J. Herbert Kane's chapter on "Humanization or Salvation?" in *The Christian World Mission: Today and Tomorrow* (Grand Rapids: Baker Book House, 1981), pp. 155-71; and Donald McGavran, "New Mission: A Systematic Reinterpretation of the Concepts of Mission," in Glasser and McGavran, pp. 47-61. (Stott also dealt with "conversion.")

22. Quoted by McGavran in *Contemporary Theologies of Mission*, p. 20, from Drafts for Sections: Uppsala '68 (Geneva: International Review of Mission, 1968), p. 34.

23. As an example see Waldron Scott, *Bring Forth Justice: A Contemporary Perspective on Mission* (Grand Rapids: William B. Eerdmans Publishing Company, 1980).

24. H. Richard Niebuhr, *Christ and Culture* (New York: Harper and Row, Publishers, 1951; Harper Torchbooks, 1956).

25. Robert J. Coote and John Stott, eds., *Down to Earth: Studies in Christianity and Culture*, The Papers of the Lausanne Consultation on Gospel and Culture (Grand Rapids: William B. Eerdmans Publishing Company, 1980).

26. Newbigin, *The Open Secret*, p. 180.

27. Hendrik Kraemer, *The Christian Message in a Non-Christian World* (Grand Rapids: Kregel Publications, 1963).

28. Verkuyl, pp. 341-72; Anderson, ed., pp. 135-228; and Gerald H. Anderson and Thomas F. Stransky, eds., *Mission Trends No. 5: Faith Meets Faith* (New York: Paulist Press and Grand Rapids: Wm. B. Eerdmans Publishing Co., 1981).

29. James Leo Garrett, Jr., in an unpublished paper prepared in 1971 at the request of the Mission Support Division of the Foreign Mission Board, analyzed the positions of historian Arnold Toynbee, in *Christianity Among the Religions of the World* (New York: Charles Scribner's Sons, 1957); of Paul Tillich in *Christianity and the Encounter of the World Religions* (New York: Columbia University Press, 1963); and of John Macquarrie in *Principles of Christian Theology* (New York: Charles Scribner's Sons, 1966). He found that each defined true religion

"in terms of his own personal religio-philosophical postulate" and that "in each case, true religion is definable without reference to Jesus Christ."

30. Niles, pp. 227-30.

31. Ibid., p. 246.

32. Ibid., p. 235; also Copeland, *World Mission and World Survival*, pp. 129-32.

33. *A Basic Understanding of Southern Baptist Missions Coordination*, p. 9.

34. J. Herbert Kane in *The Christian World Mission: Today and Tomorrow* (Grand Rapids: Baker Book House, 1981), includes a chapter on "The Church: A Witnessing Community," pp. 45-56. Dean S. Gilliland in *Pauline Theology and Mission Practice* (Grand Rapids: Baker Book House, 1983) has an entire section entitled "The Church: A Witnessing Community," pp. 179-256.

35. W. O. Carver, *Ephesians: The Glory of God in the Christian Calling*, paperback ed. (1949; reprint, Nashville: Broadman Press, 1979), p. 33.

36. Emil Brunner, *The Word in the World*, 2nd ed. (London: CSM Press, 1931), p. 108.

37. Vicedom, p. 6.

38. Lesslie Newbigin, *The Household of God* (New York: Friendship Press, 1954), p. 163.

39. Newbigin, *The Open Secret*, pp. 142-43.

40. Verkuyl, Chapter VI, pp. 163-75.

41. Copeland, *World Mission and World Survival*, p. 138.

42. Carver, *Missions in the Plan of the Ages*, p. 215.

43. Harry R. Boer, *Pentecost and Missions* (Grand Rapids: Wm. B. Eerdmans Publishing Co., 1961).

44. For a brief description of the process and some of the considerations involved, see *A Basic Understanding of Southern Baptist Missions*, pp. 43-44.

45. *MEC Curriculum Scope Document, Task: Teach Missions*, p. 5.

46. R. Pierce Beaver, *From Missions to Mission: Protestant World Mission Today and Tomorrow* (New York: Association Press, 1964), p. 79.

47. For further discussion of this topic pro and con, see articles in *The Commission:* Francis M. DuBose, "From 'Missions' to 'Mission,' " vol. 32, no. 7 (July 1969): 8-9; and Winston Crawley, " 'Mission' and 'Missions,' " vol. 25, no. 8 (August 1972): 12-13.

48. An interesting commentary on this point is the suggestion of the term *missiones Dei* offered by Johannes Aagaard, "Mission after Uppsala, 1968," in Gerald H. Anderson and Thomas F. Stransky, eds., *Mission Trends No. 1: Crucial Issues in Missions Today* (New York: Paulist Press and Grand Rapids: Wm. B. Eerdmans Publishing Co., 1974), pp. 15-21. See also G. Thompson Brown, "Rethinking Some Modern-Day Missionary Shibboleths," in *Missiology*, vol. 12, no. 1 (January 1984): 87-95.

49. *Webster's Third New International Dictionary of the English Language Unabridged* (1976), s.v. "Christendom."

50. The phrase was the theme for the 1963 meeting at Mexico City of the Commission on World Mission and Evangelism of the World Council of Churches.

51. Brown, pp. 90-91.

52. Ibid., p. 91.

53. In a little book, *Myths about Missions*, by Horace L. Fenton, Jr. (Downer's Grove, Ill: InterVarsity Press, 1973), there are interesting chapters on "The Myth of the Finished Task" and "The Myth of the Unfinishable Task."

54. For expansion on these themes, but without specific reference to the concept of triumphalism, see the closing chapters of James S. Stewart, *Thine is the Kingdom*.

# 5
# How Do We Operate?

*Southern Baptist missions is faith missions.* In common usage, the term *faith missions* applies to a system under which missionaries are responsible for arranging their own support from individuals and churches. However, that use of the term is too narrow. The difference between that very common missions arrangement and Southern Baptist missions is a difference of system, not a difference in faith.

As an illustration, a farmer may decide to work by himself, arranging his own financing for his work and making his own decisions about the details of his work. He looks to God in faith, both for the provisions he needs and for the anticipated harvest. Another farmer may be part of a partnership arrangement in which he is involved with others. They develop together their arrangements for financing their work, and they make decisions together about how to do the work. But they still look to God in faith for the provisions needed and for the harvest. The difference between the two operations is a difference of system, not a difference in faith.

Actually any farmer or any missionary, regardless of the system used, may be tempted to trust his own efforts or to trust the system instead of exercising faith in God.

Any human undertaking, no matter how divinely inspired and led, will have some kind of system. And any human system has both advantages and disadvantages. Southern Baptists are convinced that the way we operate in world missions came into being through the guidance of God and is God's continuing will

for us. We believe it fits who we are—with our understanding of
the Bible and of the nature and mission of the church. From our
generations of experience with this Southern Baptist system, we
know that it has great strength and effectiveness. We continue to
use the system with faith in the guidance, the power, and the
blessing of God.

### Partnership

Southern Baptist foreign missions is cooperative missions.
The principle of working together (teamwork) applies
throughout. This is a difference between Southern Baptist
missions and independent missions. For happy and effective
service in Southern Baptist foreign missions, a person needs to
be able to work effectively as a team member.

This partnership in missions was predetermined by the decision of Southern Baptists in 1845 to organize for missions as a
convention, rather than in the society pattern that was usual
previously. The society pattern, by implication, left foreign
missions to individuals who would participate by personal
choice. The convention arrangement assumes that all the
churches are committed to a continuing partnership in world
missions. The Convention itself exists as an organizational expression of that partnership. The Convention and its boards
make it possible for churches to do in missions as partners what
no one of them would be able to do alone.

The Cooperative Program is an entirely fitting name for the
financial plan developed by the Convention to sustain its
missions outreach. In fact, the Convention itself and all its endeavors are a "cooperative program."

Partnership is an even broader and deeper word than cooperation and therefore even more appropriate as a description of the
Southern Baptist missions system. Partnership is an important
biblical concept. Paul expressed appreciation to the church at
Philippi for "partnership in the gospel" (Phil. 1:5, RSV). The
King James Version had generally translated the Greek word
*koinonia* as *fellowship*. By now, that English word communicates
to most persons mainly the emotional aspect of a relationship
(whereas *cooperation* usually communicates mainly the work as-

pect). Partnership represents the broad range of meaning in the Greek word. The root meaning of both *koinonia* and *partnership* is sharing, which includes sharing in both the privileges and the responsibilities of a relationship.[1]

In connection with world missions, partnership has been a major emphasis in interdenominational circles for over a generation. After World War II, when the International Missionary Council met at Whitby, Ontario, in 1947, "Partners in Obedience" was one of the sectional themes. That section dealt specifically with ties between what were then often called "older" and "younger" churches. Discussion centered on ways church groups in various parts of the world can work together effectively. Specific concerns were partnership in personnel, finance, policy, and administration. The Whitby Conference produced a formal statement acknowledging a real partnership between "older and younger churches" based on common faith and on common responsibility for an immense and unfinished task.[2]

From the time of the Whitby Conference, "Partners in Obedience" has been a commonly accepted and often repeated expression of Christian responsibility for world mission.[3]

Though the partnership concept is biblical, until fairly recently Southern Baptists have not used the word as prominently as have other denominations. Fellowship, participation, involvement, and cooperation have been more common words in our speaking and writing. Now *partnership evangelism* and *partnership missions* have become special terms in our foreign missions vocabulary. More and more now we are using the word *partnership* as a broad and deep expression of a vital biblical principle.

There are three major ongoing partnerships in Southern Baptist foreign missions. Other more limited types of partnership operate within the context of those broader partnerships.

First comes the partnership of Southern Baptists through which the world mission effort is projected, as described already. Since 1845 the expressions of our partnership have expanded and become more complex, but the basic commitment to mission and to partnership remains, with the Foreign Mission Board representing that partnership in outreach to the whole world.

A second Southern Baptist partnership in missions links foreign missionaries with one another and with the supporting constituency through the Foreign Mission Board and its staff. This is a faith partnership which enables missionaries to function as a team, confident of the backing of all the rest of us who are their partners.

The third ongoing partnership is that with churches and Baptist conventions in mission areas abroad. This basic element in Southern Baptist foreign missions will be considered in depth in Part IV and especially in chapter 10.

One great strength in the cooperative missions plan of Southern Baptists is the saving of large amounts of time, money, and energy that are invested in fund-raising under other systems. Most parachurch organizations spend a much larger proportion of their total funds for overhead expenses. Many independent missionaries spend a significant portion of their workday in writing to their supporters to assure continued support. Southern Baptist missionaries can devote that additional time and energy to the work for which they have been sent.

Another advantage is that strategy planning is more readily possible when teamwork and coordination of effort are basic ground rules.

Furthermore, our system yields much greater continuity of effort than is possible in more independent and individualistic missions approaches. The team adapts its plans to provide for the ongoing work of a team member who may be on furlough or may have had to withdraw from missionary service.

Probably the greatest strength in the partnership system is that it facilitates transfer of responsibility to maturing Baptist churches and conventions overseas (as will be discussed more fully in chapter 9), and models the kind of partnership which hopefully such emerging Baptist denominations will embody in their own common life.

## Channels

Many persons in Southern Baptist churches, or even leaders in denominational life, seem to think of the Foreign Mission Board as an organization seeking support from Southern Baptists for its own programs. When the Foreign Mission Board, its staff, and its missionaries urge the sharing of the gospel with the whole world, they hear it as a plea to "help us with our work." It is not easy to shift perspective and realize that foreign missions is the outreach of churches to the world, with the Foreign Mission Board and its staff as servants of the churches and their members.

Nothing in the Bible lays responsibility for world evangelization on a mission board. One of the basic principles stated by the Foreign Mission Board in its Bold Mission Thrust document is: "The 'Great Commission' makes the overseas task the responsibility of each Christian and each church. Churches exist and cooperate for the purpose of world outreach and Kingdom extension."[4]

This principle seems both simple and self-evident. It expresses a basic conviction of Southern Baptists about the nature and mission of the church. It means, therefore, that the Foreign Mission Board is simply an instrument, a channel created by Southern Baptists to expedite the missionary calling and responsibility of the churches. In fact, even the Southern Baptist Convention itself was formed as a channel for that same purpose.

Although the Bible says nothing about conventions or mission boards, some form of organization through which churches can express their partnership in missions is essential—"to be a point of concentration and commitment whereby the whole people of God is kept aware of itself as mission, and whereby that mission is given concreteness and particularity and is preserved from being dissolved in abstraction or imprisoned in local or temporary particularities."[5]

In setting up channels for missions, the Southern Baptist Convention has assigned responsibility to the Foreign Mission Board for all Southern Baptist cooperative mission efforts outside the United States and its territories. This includes responsibility for countries to which missionaries are assigned (105 at the end of 1984) and for all other foreign countries as well. The Board projects its strategy on the basis of the *entire world* outside our national borders (with the Home Mission Board and other Southern Baptist Convention agencies having various assignments in the United States).

This principle is clear in the program statements by which the Convention has defined the tasks of the Foreign Mission Board. The scope of the Board's concern is stated as "other lands around the world." Each specific program (such as for evangelism, for publications, for medical care, and so forth) is defined as in "foreign lands." Thus the Foreign Mission Board is in a position to help and to correlate any overseas project with which any Southern Baptists may be involved.

The assignment of the Foreign Mission Board in foreign lands is *comprehensive*, embracing every kind of functional ministry that might be exercised by churches and conventions in the United States. Included are the ministry concerns of all the other Southern Baptist Convention agencies and many of those handled in this country by state convention agencies.

Sometimes comparisons are made between the Foreign Mission Board and the Home Mission Board, as if the scope of ministries of the two were quite similar. It is more relevant to compare foreign missions with all the combined mission efforts in the homeland (through the Home Mission Board, the Radio and Television Commission, seminaries and other SBC agencies, the state conventions, the associations, and the direct mission outreach of the churches).

One aspect of the Foreign Mission Board's service as a Southern Baptist channel involves missionary *personnel*. Our concept of the calling of God makes the role of the Foreign Mission Board secondary or even tertiary. Primarily, missionaries are called and sent out by God himself. Secondarily, they go out as missionaries of Southern Baptist churches, in partnership through the Southern Baptist Convention, if they feel led to do so. The Foreign Mission Board represents the Convention in commissioning them and sending them out, if the Board feels led to do so. They then become missionaries of the Foreign Mission Board (and, in a sense, its "employees"). However, they remain primarily missionaries of the Lord Jesus.

In this process, the Foreign Mission Board obviously serves only as a channel. It does not create missionaries. Many times an area director may wish that there were some machine in the Foreign Mission Board offices which, when the right buttons are pushed, would produce a missionary with certain desired qualities. The Board actually cannot even advertise for and employ persons with needed qualifications as a business would. Instead, missionaries come from the churches at the impelling of the Holy Spirit.

Other intermediate channels are involved in the lives of missionary candidates—a wide range of channels which help to prepare persons for effective service, most notably the Southern Baptist seminaries for formal training and the churches themselves for ministry experience.

Similarly, the Foreign Mission Board serves as the channel established by Southern Baptists for *financial resources* for the "discipling of the nations." As with missions personnel, the board does not create missions funds. The United States Government would not allow a printing press in the Foreign Mission Board offices to print money for use in missions. Money flows from individual donors and the churches to mission work overseas through the channel of the Foreign Mission Board.

The main intermediate channels for Southern Baptist foreign missions funding are the Cooperative Program and the Lottie Moon Christmas Offering.

The Cooperative Program as a plan for Southern Baptist partnership in supporting missions and benevolences was adopted by the Convention in 1925. It relates state conventions and the Southern Baptist Convention cooperatively with the churches. Each church determines the amount or proportion of its resources that will be channeled through the Cooperative Program. The state convention receives money contributed by the churches and determines amounts that will be used for various needs within the state and the proportion that will be forwarded to the Southern Baptist Convention. (In recent years that proportion has averaged about 38 percent.) The Southern Baptist Convention then determines amounts or percentages to be allocated for the different programs of work of the Convention (including in recent years about 48 percent for foreign missions). This means that about 18 percent of the entire Cooperative Program amount coming from the churches is used for foreign missions.[6]

The Cooperative Program is frequently called the "lifeline" of Southern Baptist foreign missions. Missionaries look to it as their basic financial backing for their own support and for the work to which Southern Baptists have sent them. It is always subject to the possibility of misunderstanding and neglect and is subject at times to criticism, but it is still vital to Southern Baptist foreign missions.[7]

Most or all major denominations have a channel for missions giving that is roughly comparable to the Cooperative Program, but no other Christian group has anything like the Lottie Moon Christmas Offering, at least in its size and importance. The offering, taken during the Christmas season every year specifically for foreign missions, was suggested by Charlotte (Lottie) Moon, missionary to North China. It began in 1888 with an offering of about $3,000. In the most recent year for which figures are available, the offering amounted to nearly 60 million dollars. This is surely the largest offering given at any one time by any group of Christian people for any single purpose. Because it gives opportunity for an outpouring of Christian love and Christian gratitude at Christmastime, it has a special place in the hearts of Southern Baptists. For many years the Lottie Moon Offering has provided about half of all Southern Baptist giving to world missions through the Foreign Mission Board.

Through the years Southern Baptists have made designated gifts for foreign missions that have not gone through the channels of the Cooperative Program or the Lottie Moon Christmas Offering. As the Christmas offering grew in earlier years, the relative size and importance of special donations decreased.

More recently, as an outgrowth of desire for direct personal involvement, special gifts have increased again. That same desire has produced a large flow of short-term volunteer personnel for projects overseas. Since the Foreign Mission Board is intended to serve as a comprehensive channel for Southern Baptist outreach to other lands, the Board seeks to facilitate these expressions and make them as effective as possible, alongside the basic channels for the regular flow of missionary personnel and missions funding.

The Board is a channel also for a current that goes the other direction: the flow of *information* about missions work from the fields back to the churches. That is of great importance, since the stimulus of knowledge about missions affects the offering of lives and money for missions.

There are intermediate information channels in Southern Baptist life identified by the term *channeling*, which refers to the role that church program organizations and Baptist communications media play in telling the story of missions.

A prominent characteristic of American Christianity today is the proliferation of parachurch agencies—organizations developed by individuals, without formal church or denominational sponsorship, to focus on specific Christian purposes. There are said to be more than 10,000 such organizations in the United States. Many of them engage in some aspect of overseas missions.

A parachurch organization usually concentrates on one limited phase of missions—perhaps one geographical area or one type of mission activity or both. It presents a strong emotional appeal to persons who constitute its special interest group. It is usually aggressive in publicizing what it is doing and in raising funds through direct approaches to individuals and churches.

Of course, there will always be independent mission agencies. The work they are doing is in most cases good work. There will always be some Southern Baptists who give to the support of those agencies. That is one of the facts of life in a spiritual democracy. However, Southern Baptists have the Foreign Mission Board as a channel through which contributions for special purposes can be made as part of a comprehensive and coordinated missions effort, which can focus all resources for greatest effectiveness.[8]

With the many opportunities now open to Southern Baptist individuals and churches for involvement in missions, continuing commitment to partnership through the Convention's channels will be of major importance to the future of our Convention and its foreign mission work.

## Support

The concept of support for missions is much broader than just financial support or even finances and personnel reinforcements combined. For twelve years (from 1968 to 1980), the Foreign Mission Board had a main administrative unit called the Mission Support Division. The interests of that division included all the ways in which the Foreign Mission Board is involved with its Southern Baptist constituency. The purpose of the division was to seek from Southern Baptists every kind of support neded for overseas missions. Organizational arrangements now have changed, but concern for mission support is still valid.[9]

The idea of mission support is sometimes expressed by the term "representative missions." There are many parts of the world mission of the church in which I cannot participate personally (no one person can do everything), but of which I should be fully supportive. The ones who do participate personally in those efforts represent me, and I share in those efforts through my support of them. The cooperative mission work of Southern Baptists through denominational channels is representative missions, with all Southern Baptists (at least in principle) involved in the mission support role.

Through discussions at a national seminar on support of missions in 1975, I became aware that *mission support* is a disconcerting term to some persons. Especially for theologians and others so oriented, the term can seem to have implications that are unbiblical and undesirable. Those implications are sometimes labeled "missions by proxy"—a perception that a few persons are really personally involved in missions, while the rest are spectators who do nothing but pay the bills. Unfortunately, that caricature of the mission support concept may state the true extent of involvement many believers have had in missions.

Biblically and theologically, of course, the whole church unquestionably is to be fully involved in world missions. That is essential to the very mission of the church. One suggestion made at the seminar was that the term *mission involvement* might express this truth better than *mission support*.

Here again we encounter the danger of the current emphasis on the broad general concept of mission. It needs to be augmented by emphasis on missions (definite outreach to areas of unusual need) and mission support (the personal responsibility of other believers to give backing to such outreach). The differences of gifts and functions in the church that are expounded in 1 Corinthians 12 need to be kept in view.

Recently many church members have sought increased personal participation in missions—usually in brief projects. The vital contribution of concern, prayer, and sharing in the mission cause on a long-range basis has seemed less satisfying to many people. But a project approach runs the risk of reducing missions to what is most natural or easiest, perhaps because it is close at hand, instead of what is most needed. There is a further risk of majoring on types of mission involvement that are emotionally appealing—the current fad, the glamorous, the less culturally demanding situation.

If the church is to fulfill its mission, it cannot afford to reduce its understanding of that mission either to a general blur of good intentions or to a series of relatively easy or relatively appealing projects. It will need continuing and intensive outreach to all persons who will not be included automatically in "what comes naturally"—that is, to those areas and those persons who are quite different from us, are outside our normal contacts, and are relatively unreached.

Practically speaking, for all of us to keep on caring about and making possible gospel ministries to the most needy parts of the world with long-range effectiveness will be possible only through what we normally think of as "mission support": through educated interest, compassionate concern, prayer, sacrificial giving, and perhaps occasional direct contacts of one sort or another. At a time when emphasis has centered on the very general mission of the church and of all believers and on personal involvement on a project basis, fresh new emphasis is now urgently needed on the additional truth that mission support is real involvement in mission.[10]

A major part of the concept of mission support is providing appropriate *backing for missionaries*. This includes financial support, but it also involves other aspects of a total support system, such as upgraded training for specific mission assignments, aid in strategy planning, administrative guidance, and pastoral care.

In staffing and in budget allocations, the Foreign Mission

Board has given priority to the needs of missionaries. The underlying principle is that the missionary is central in the Southern Baptist contribution to world evangelization. The Board would send out and support missionaries even if funds were not available for other missions needs. (That was indeed the case in earlier periods of severe financial stringency, such as the Depression years.)

Periodic furloughs are a regular part of missionary responsibility and are fully supported, just as are the periods spent on the field of work. Timing and length of furlough are based on a flexible formula which the missionary, in conference with colleagues, can adjust to meet the needs of the work and special family needs. Reporting to Southern Baptist churches about missions is the missionary's main furlough work assignment.

This reporting to the churches is an integral part of another major element in mission support, the element of *missions education*. The Foreign Mission Board does not have a specific assigned responsibility for missions education in the churches (that role is assigned to Woman's Missionary Union and Brotherhood). But the Board does have a heavy responsibility to provide realistic content for materials for use in the churches and to help keep Southern Baptists informed through other communications channels. More recently the channels have increasingly used audiovisual and not merely print media.

The philosophy statement of the Foreign Mission Board notes this responsibility in missions education: "The board recognizes that it has responsibilities in homeland cultivation. This is one of the paradoxes in Southern Baptist life. The board was created to be a channel for the missionary efforts and resources of the churches, which the Convention elicits, combines, and directs. Yet the people in the churches look to the board for information, inspiration, motivation, and leadership."

The Board participates with other Southern Baptist agencies (specifically the Home Mission Board, Sunday School Board, Brotherhood Commission, and Woman's Missionary Union) in the Missions Education Council, which develops coordinated plans for promotion of missions education in the churches.[11]

*Stewardship* also is intimately related to missions support. The

Stewardship Commission of the Convention sponsored the special conferences on mission support that were held in 1975 and 1976. The Foreign Mission Board maintains close contact with the Stewardship Commission and with persons in state and associational offices who have significant influence on the stewardship of Southern Baptists.

The current Convention emphasis on Planned Growth in Giving, just now in its introductory stages, offers great hope for deepening of stewardship and resultant strengthening of Southern Baptist world mission outreach.

Foreign missionaries with one voice mention *prayer support* as their main need from Southern Baptists. At the meeting of the Southern Baptist Convention at New Orleans in 1982, the Foreign Mission Board initiated a continuing deepened emphasis on intercessory prayer for foreign missions, challenging Southern Baptists to make a commitment to daily prayer, offering special prayer pins for those who would do so, and promising to send information about specific prayer needs to interested persons.[12]

Prayer ultimately is the most vital element in mission support. All of the other elements and all of the mission efforts being supported are empowered only as persons in our churches are faithful partners in prayer for God's world purpose.

## Administration

Foreign missions is no exception to the general truth that any continuing undertaking will have some kind of operational system. (Even Christian groups that do not believe in mission boards usually have persons who fill the same function, but without being called a board.)

The specific system used in Southern Baptist foreign missions reflects at many points the congregational and democratic elements in Southern Baptist polity. For example, whereas some other missions agency may have a chain of command, Southern Baptists work through chains of responsibility. Delegated responsibility can be traced from the churches to the Convention, on to the Foreign Mission Board, and then to missionaries and mission organizations on the fields. In one direction the chain represents a delegation, and in the other direction it represents accountability.

Another fundamental premise of our system is that foreign missions takes place in an exceedingly complex cultural, political, and economic setting. Administration of missions amid such complexities calls for a high degree of specialization. Administrators need to be knowledgeable missiologists. Administration must encourage variety in missions approaches and methodology and flexibility to meet changing conditions.

A third fundamental premise in Southern Baptist foreign missions administration is projection of work on a geographic basis. This is stressed in the board's philosophy statement: "The board has considered its responsibility in geographic and functional terms, and has decided that the geographic element is basic and fundamental from the standpoint of administrative outlook and organizational arrangements. This is justified because of the nature of our world and the character of our Baptist polity."

This approach combines all mission efforts, regardless of functional or methodological differences, into a unified thrust.

Recent decades have brought pressures toward a basic functional approach to foreign missions administration, rather than the geographic approach. Under a functional system, each type of mission ministry would be administered worldwide by an officer with that particular program leadership assignment. For example, there might be an administrator for medical ministries, another for publishing ministries, one for broadcasting ministries, and so forth. At first glance, the functional approach may seem to offer many advantages, and it would match the way both business and religious organizations generally administer activities in this country.

About fifteen years ago the Southern Baptist Convention Executive Committee, at the instruction of the Convention, studied a proposal that all broadcasting worldwide should be treated as a functional unit and assigned to the Radio and Television Commission to administer (as might be logical if the approach were functional). After three years of study, the Executive Committee recommended and the Convention approved the concept of inclusive united work through the Foreign Mission Board, rather than the functional arrangement.[13]

One complication is that Southern Baptist Convention program statements define the assignments of the Foreign Mission Board under six functional programs: Missionary Support, Evangelism and Church Development, Schools and Student Work, Publication Work, Hospitals and Medical Care, and Benevolent Ministries—all identified as applying in foreign lands.[14] (Actually these broadly stated programs include any and every type of Southern Baptist mission effort in all lands beyond our own borders, such as agricultural work, radio and television evangelism, theological seminaries, orphanages, relief work, and a wide variety of other specialized ministries.) These formal functional programs are followed as a convenience in budgeting and in reporting to the Convention. This is done, however, with the understanding that mission work overseas is not administered functionally. On the fields the various "programs" are united in one mission program for each geographic unit.

Either the geographic or the functional approach must be predominant. The line of administrative responsibility must run through one system, with the other in a supportive role.

The major reasons for the geographic approach (which places area directors in the line of administrative responsibility, with consultants for functional concerns) relate to effectiveness in fulfilling mission purposes. Coordination of all kinds of mission efforts is vital. A united program simplifies relationships with Baptist churches and conventions overseas and facilitates transfer of responsibility from missionaries to those churches and conventions. A pattern of Baptist life in which all functions interrelate within a larger unity is modeled. As a matter of strategy, the exact combination of types of work needs to vary from country to country to suit the special circumstances of each country. (The relevance of these considerations will be clear in the light of later treatment of objectives in Part IV.)

### Home Office Administration

The Foreign Mission Board is a body of trustees elected by the Southern Baptist Convention. There are 84 Board members, representing various states according to a formula determined by the Convention. The Board meets six times a year. It does most of its work through committees (see Appendix 4 for the Board's organization chart).

The Board itself establishes basic directions, principles, and policies and delegates administrative responsibility to a staff that now numbers more than 400 persons. The roles of trustees and staff and the relationships between the two are those that are normal in Southern Baptist life.

The staff is organized into offices with responsibility for major administrative systems. The Office of Overseas Operations administers mission work on the fields. The Office of Human Resources seeks, recommends, and prepares personnel for overseas service. The Office of Communications informs Southern Baptists about foreign missions. The Office of Finance handles all matters related to funding for the home office and the fields. The Office of Administration provides logistical and other types of assistance needed in the missions operation. The Office of the President, the chief executive officer, is related to the Office of Administration. Denominational relations, planning, development, and prayer are special functions attached to the Office of the President. The president and persons responsible for these several offices and functions constitute an executive management group that deals with matters of general concern (see Appendix 5 for staff organization chart).

After more than a century of less formal planning, the board developed a comprehensive coordinated planning system which became operational in 1982. Already the Office of Overseas Operations was implementing more formal planning processes overseas. Other major advances have been made in strengthening missionary recruiting and arrangements for volunteer involvement—in video communications, in improved financial management, in use of data processing, and in research as a tool for administration. Recent opening of a Missionary

Learning Center in the Richmond area, adding a development office, and increased emphasis on prayer are other notable forward steps in home office administration.

In administering foreign missions, both the Board and the staff seek to keep several important concerns in view. One is that the entire operation has a spiritual purpose. The way the home office functions is intended to reflect that purpose. Nearly all the management and professional staff are persons who understand their work with the Foreign Mission Board as a calling. And this is true also of many in secretarial or other supportive positions.

Another concern is that the Board itself maintain a low profile. Prominence and visibility belong to the mission work itself, not to the home office machinery that supports and facilitates the work.

Closely related is another concern—for stewardship in use of resources, to keep overhead costs low and preserve as much of available funding as possible for actual work on the fields. For many years, the Board has thought in terms of no more than 10 percent of total expenditures to cover all expenses of the home office operation, including communication and missions education functions. Recently, because buying power of Southern Baptist foreign missions giving has not kept up with growth in missionary staff, and because of new expectations of increased Foreign Mission Board services, the percentage has been slightly higher; but it is being reduced by careful economies. By comparison with most other organizations with similar functions, including independent missions organizations, the overhead cost percentage is quite low.

### Field Administration

The line of delegated responsibility in foreign missions runs from the Foreign Mission Board through the president to the Office of Overseas Operations. The area director (formerly known as area secretary) is the administrative officer with direct oversight of the work on the fields. The area director also presents to the Board the needs of missionaries and mission work in his area. Therefore, the area director has a key responsibility, and an especially heavy one, in relation to the work of the Board.

Consultants, as indicated earlier, have advisory and supportive roles. Theirs is a staff function, whereas the area director is the line officer. The area office is the nerve center for relationship with the missionaries and the work in its area.

The administrative approach rests on several basic assumptions. One is an assumption of the availability of the Holy Spirit's guidance. We understand that guidance as available to each Christian, without having to come through some human mediator. Therefore, each missionary can receive direct leading from the Holy Spirit. But we believe also that the Holy Spirit gives guidance to groups of believers, as well as to individuals. It is possible to misunderstand the Spirit's leadership. Therefore, an individual's sense of the Lord's leading often needs to be confirmed by a larger community of believers.

This understanding that the missionary's impression of the Lord's will is confirmed by his group operates throughout our entire foreign mission undertaking. We are familiar with a similar understanding applying to church life in our own country. For example, an individual's impression that he should become pastor of a particular church is confirmed by the impression of the church members.

Another basic assumption relates to the unity needed for cooperative missions. There is great diversity among Southern Baptists. Differences grow out of regional tradition, social setting, educational background, or individual experience.

Southern Baptists have agreed to disagree (without making one fixed position a condition of fellowship) on eschatology, on details concerning the ordinances, on charismatic expressions in church life, on ways of explaining the inspiration and authority of the Scriptures, and on various other matters. The Foreign Mission Board is the foreign missions agency for all Southern Baptists. It does not make a particular view on these debatable matters a qualification for missionary appointment. Therefore, missionaries who work together overseas have differences of personal approach, viewpoint, and emphasis. With these differences, we assume that there is essential unity of shared convictions and purposes to make united effort possible. Our mission work overseas is not held together by an enforced external unity but by inner spiritual unity.

A third basic assumption is that a group of missionary co-workers can become a fellowship of mutual emotional and spiritual support. Such a group does not require a father figure, a person assigned to function officially as counselor. Rather, the group of believers, in mutual acceptance, can help each other, support each other, become counselors and confessors to each other. This kind of relationship goes far beyond mere formal task-oriented cooperation.

Against the background of those assumptions, three main principles characterize Southern Baptist foreign missions administration.

Foreign Mission Board administration is intentionally *decentralized*. This means that mission strategies (including decisions about methods to be used and about allocation of resources) are worked out primarily on the fields. The Foreign Mission Board outlines general directions but does not seek to control details of mission work by directives handed down from the home offices. In other words, contrary to the impression many persons seem to have, foreign missions is not administered by the pushing of buttons in Richmond to cause things to happen on the fields. Instead, the administrative process responds to requests and recommendations from the fields.

There are strong reasons for this decentralized administration. One is a basic conviction about the nature of the missionary calling and the relationship of the Board to the missionary. The missionary goes to the field, not at the call of the Board but at the call of the Lord. The Board exists as a channel through which Southern Baptists can provide the backing needed by the missionary and his work. His ultimate responsibility is not to the Board but to his Lord. As a matter of fact, in a very profound sense the Board itself and its administrative officers and arrangements exist for the sake of the missionaries and the work they do, instead of the other way around.

Administrative arrangements should provide a maximum of freedom for missionaries as they seek the direct leading of the Holy Spirit. Through its area directors, the Board encourages individual initiative and creative thinking on the fields. This is consistent with our understanding of the missionary calling.

In addition, there are very practical reasons for decentralized administration. The realities of mission work in complicated situations make it most unwise for actions to be determined by persons thousands of miles away. Also, as modern experts in management principles repeatedly point out, effective management calls for decisions to be made with maximum participation by the persons who will implement the decisions. We are convinced that locating decision-making responsibility in the actual work situation is the most fruitful way of carrying on foreign missions.

Still another fundamental reason for a decentralized approach is that from the very beginning, and increasingly as work matures, churches and developing Baptist conventions on the fields are involved in plans that are being made. It would be most inappropriate for decisions to be made for those Baptist churches and conventions at a foreign headquarters. Local Baptists can assume their rightful responsibilities in the cooperative decision-making process only if that process is centered on the fields.

In addition to being decentralized, our administrative approach is *democratic*. This characteristic reflects the fact that our mission effort is a cooperative, team effort. Teamwork requires some way of arriving at decisions applicable to the team as a whole. The system used is an organization of our entire missionary group in a particular country or region, called a "mission." It chooses its own leaders and determines how much authority each will have. It makes plans for the work, in cooperation with local Baptist entities.

The mission differs in nature and role from patterns which are familiar in church life and work in the United States. It differs also from systems that are common in the foreign mission work of many other denominations or independent organizations. Other common systems include (1) independent missions, with each missionary functioning separately from others; (2) a "chain of command" organization administered from the top down; and (3) merging of individual missionaries organizationally into church and denominational structures on the field.

Any organizational system has both advantages and disadvantages. The mission, in contrast with other systems, is essentially a plan for cooperative action. The intention is to combine, insofar as possible, the values of individual autonomy and group collaboration and to facilitate decisions in the actual field situation. No one of the other systems lends itself as well to this combination of concerns as does the mission.

In our plan, the mission functions through democratic process (which means that it has both the values and the possible problems of democracy). It generally does not operate as a pure democracy, but through delegation of responsibilities. The larger and more mature a mission becomes, the more it tends to delegate, often to a mission administrator. The great strength of the mission is the value and effectiveness of group process. Its major complication is that a fairly small group may have to deal with a very wide range of concerns. In this respect, the mission differs obviously from Baptist structures in the United States. Even so, the use of democratic process is still most appropriate to the Baptist way of doing things.

Conceivably, in any country the mission could be disbanded, but that is not the general intention of the Foreign Mission Board. In earlier years, experience in some situations with no mission organization and in others with a "field secretary" who was not responsible to a local mission led to the conclusion that the mission has values that justify its continuation.

Precisely because of its unusual nature and function, the mission offers a unique opportunity for a most rewarding relationship—one that combines individual creativity, effective personal influence, and interdependence. The missionary finds himself living and working not in "glorious isolation" nor as "a pawn in a chain of command," but in vital and dynamic Christian community.

The third characteristic of foreign missions administration is that the decision-making process is *directed* through channels established by the Foreign Mission Board. The Office of Overseas Operations and especially the area director represent the Board. They do not hand down orders to missionaries and the mission, but they do offer direction.

Part of that direction comes in the form of general principles and policies determined by the Board itself. Part is guidelines and strategy directions determined within the home office staff. Part is the practical counsel of the area director. He and any associates or consultants who are part of his area staff share in the decision-making process of the missions.

A football game may offer a helpful analogy. The purpose, rules, and boundaries of the playing field have all been determined. The role of the Foreign Mission Board in establishing principles and policies is comparable. The football coach, on the sidelines, has shared in the developing of a game plan, has helped prepare the players for the game, and may offer suggestions during the game. The role of the area director is comparable. The football team on the field faces immediate circumstances that affect decisions as to what plays to use—involving sometimes even the calling of an "audible" change of play at the line of scrimmage. This is roughly comparable to the mission and its leaders developing strategy in a real and changing context.

There are some inevitable tensions in this type of field administration. There is tension between planning done on the fields and the directions taken by area or worldwide planning in the home offices. There is tension between long-range commitments and new or current concerns and emphases. There is tension between missionary planning (following American patterns) and the ways of working of church and convention life in local field cultures.

Obviously there would be other possible ways to administer mission work, each with its relative merits. And of course there are ways in which the functioning of Southern Baptist missions administration can and should be strengthened. However, the Board and its staff have continued to believe that our administrative approach, in its essential principles, is true to the Baptist genius and is ultimately the most effective way.

## Conclusion

The principles of operation of the Foreign Mission Board and the structures that embody those principles are consistent with the purpose of the Convention for "carrying into effect the benevolent intentions of our constituents, by organizing a plan for eliciting, combining, and directing the energies of the whole denomination in one sacred effort, for the propagation of the gospel."[15] Support is elicited. It is combined through appropriate channels. It is directed through administrative process. And it is all done within the partnership of Southern Baptists for world evangelization.

The main principles involved have continuing validity and worth, grounded as they are in our understanding of Scripture and in who we are as Southern Baptists. Forms are constantly changing to meet new challenges. Thus the content of this chapter should be understood as one frame in a sequence that tells a continuing story. Keith Parks, Foreign Mission Board president, commented in a management luncheon in February 1984: "I see change not as a criticism of the past, nor as a determination of the future, but as a maximizing of the present." The way we operate today in Southern Baptist missions is designed to maximize the present. Any changes that are made tomorrow will be made within the context of general continuity and will be designed to maximize tomorrow's opportunities.

### Notes

1. The article on "Fellowship" in Alan Richardson, *A Theological Word Book of the Bible* (New York: The Macmillan Co., 1950), pp. 81-83, is helpful and stimulating.

2. C. W. Ranson, ed., *Renewal and Advance* (London: Edinburgh House Press, 1948), pp. 173-84.

3. This theme is explored in detail in an informative book by Max Warren, a prominent world missions leader, *Partnership: The Study of An Idea* (London: SCM Press, 1956).

4. "Foreign Missions Looks Toward AD 2000" (the Foreign Mission Board's long-range planning document, adopted by the board in January 1976 and by the Southern Baptist Convention in June 1976), SBC, *Annual*, 1976, p. 112.

5. R. K. Orchard, *Missions in a Time of Testing* (Philadelphia: The Westminster Press, 1964), p. 146. Note the theme of the entire chapter from which this quotation is taken: "Organization: Master or Servant?" As a matter of parallel interest, note also the July 1969 issue of *International Review of Mission* (vol. 58, no. 231), on the theme "The Role of the Mission Agency."

6. See tables in appendixes for foreign missions personnel and financial data.

7. Among many available materials describing the Cooperative Program and its importance, see for example two statements by Winston Crawley: "The Cooperative Program Is Vulnerable," *The Baptist Program*, November 1978, p. 14, and "Horizons: A Personal Debt" in *The Commission*, vol. 47, no. 7 (September 1984): 7.

8. For further information, see for example an article by Winston Crawley, "Let's Help Our Missionaries," in *The Commission*, vol. 138, no. 12 (December 1975): 23.

9. For an extensive treatment of this aspect of missions from the perspective of another denomination, see the chapter on "Crucial Issues at the Home Base" by T. Watson Street, *On the Growing Edge of the Church* (Richmond: John Knox Press, 1965), pp. 99-111.

10. Compare the brief statement on missions by proxy, representative missions, and mission support in *A Basic Understanding of Southern Baptist Missions Coordination* (Nashville: Inter-Agency Council, SBC, 1972), p. 44.

11. For details see the *MEC Curriculum Scope Document, Task: Teach Missions*, (Nashville: Missions Education Council, SBC, 1984), especially pp. 11-12 and the appendixes.

12. See "Horizons: Pins for Prayer" by Winston Crawley in *The Commission*, vol. 45, no. 7 (September 1982): 59.

13. SBC, *Annual*, 1971, p. 56.

14. SBC, *Annual*, 1966, pp. 60-67.

15. "Preamble and Constitution of the Southern Baptist Convention," SBC, *Annual*, 1845, p. 3 (cf. SBC, *Annual*, 1983, p. 4.)

# Part III
# Personnel

Bill Burkhalter, now a missionary in Bangladesh, was there for a summer several years ago, sent by the Baptist Student Union. He tells of traveling with missionary R. T. Buckley by motorcycles from Comilla to Sylhet. They paused for a while midway and, while resting, looked around them at village after village dotting the plains. As they started on their way again Buckley commented, "Just think: all those people—and nobody to tell them about Jesus."

Since "everybody ought to know who Jesus is," persons to tell the story are a primary requirement. "How shall they believe in him of whom they have not heard? and how shall they hear without a preacher?" (Rom. 10:14).

With the multiplying and the improvement of mass communication media in our day, some have wondered whether missionaries who live in other lands among people of other cultures are still needed. The comments of R. K. Orchard on this point are highly relevant.

> Knowledge of the Christ-event is personally conveyed. One may know the facts about the historic person, Jesus of Nazareth, from a written record. But any knowledge of the Christ-event as the decisive event in history, still more any awareness of its critical, decisive meaning for my personal history, depends upon the testimony of persons. Each of us has received the gospel in this sense from other persons: each of us is dependent on others for our hearing of this Word.
>
> The clear recognition of and emphasis upon this personal communication of the Gospel was one of the strengths of foreign missions in the nineteenth century. They were primarily and distinctively concerned with the sending of persons to proclaim the name of the Redeemer where it was not known. In so doing they expressed an essential insight into the character of God's redemptive act, that it was done in a Person—indeed through *the* Person who is the ultimate standard for our understanding of the meaning of personal existence—and that it spoke to persons in the center of their being as persons . . .

If we forget or lose this conviction that the Gospel is personally conveyed, we shall have lost something which is central and essential to the Christian mission.[1]

The philosophy statement of the Foreign Mission Board expresses this same conviction about the importance of persons to tell the story: "The enlisting, appointment, sending, and support of an ever-increasing number of God-called, and otherwise qualified, missionaries is the priority responsibility of the Foreign Mission Board. If nothing else could be done in foreign missions, the one indispensable thing would be the sending and supporting of missionaries."

**Note**

1. R. K. Orchard, *Missions in a Time of Testing* (Philadelphia: The Westminster Press, 1964), pp. 163-64.

# 6
# Why Career Missionaries?

Historically, the term *foreign missionary* has meant to most Christians a person going to some other land for long–range ministry, presumably for life (or until normal retirement age).

Two recent developments have tended to change the connotation of the term. One is use of the word *missionary* in a very general sense to express the involvement of every Christian in witness to the gospel. Thus any Christian living or traveling in some foreign area might be in a sense a missionary to that area. Further, and perhaps more tellingly, plans for limited involvement in overseas missions through specific projects or assignments have mushroomed. Most of the projects extend from a few days up to a few weeks in the overseas setting. "Short-term assignments" involve anything from a few months up to about two years.

A larger and larger proportion of the missionaries reported by missions agencies are short-term missionaries. A number of newer parachurch organizations send out only short-term personnel. Even some of the major mission boards have downplayed long-range missionary involvement.[1]

In the meantime, the Southern Baptist Foreign Mission Board has continued to emphasize long-range commitment and service, including in its philosophy statement an assertion that "the board regards as basic the concept of the career missionary." This chapter undertakes to explain why.

## Missionary Gifts and Calling

It may be helpful at this point to examine further the meaning of the term *missionary*. The term itself is not found in most translations of the Bible, but it is exactly the same in root meaning as the Greek word *apostolos,* which is common in the New Testament. (Both missionary and apostle have the root meaning of being sent, one from Latin and the other from Greek.) Translators have usually transliterated the Greek word as "apostle" instead of translating it into everyday English.

Sometimes in the New Testament *apostolos* is used in a special technical sense such as we usually associate with the term *apostle*. At other times it is used in a more general sense and would better be translated as *missionary.*[2] In either case, New Testament usage seems to apply the term to persons with a special continuing function in the spread of the gospel, not simply to the witness of all believers or to brief projects or assignments.

The term *missionary* is now commonly used to express the biblical truth that all are called to be obedient to Christ and to be witnesses for Christ. In earlier years, there had been a danger of expecting the gospel to be shared by only a few people— preachers and professional missionaries—whereas now there is better understanding that all believers have a "missionary" responsibility. Unfortunately, some have concluded that missionaries in the specialized sense are not needed anymore, that for world evangelization it will be sufficient simply for each Christian to be a witness wherever he is.

There seems to be a polarizing tendency in human nature which separates and contrasts truths that ought to be complementary. This polarizing is then compounded by a pendulum swing from overemphasis on one of the truths to overemphasis on the other. Recent stress on the importance of every Christian being a "missionary" has involved the danger that few will be sent out with a specific apostolic gift and calling.

R. K. Orchard again stated the point well.

> The basic form of this personal communication of the Gospel is that in which every Christian shares, in his speaking of

Jesus Christ to those with whom he has continuing personal relationships. But to draw from this the conclusion, as is sometimes done, that "we are all missionaries now" is an unwarrantable oversimplification. It ignores the differentiation of gifts and functions within the body of which the New Testament speaks, and thereby destroys the possibility of particular callings of Christians to engage especially in one particular form of service. It ignores the fact that there are groups of people and areas of life in which the Christ-event will not be proclaimed unless some Christians are specially set aside and specially equipped to live amongst those groups or within those areas for the purpose of bearing witness within them to the Christ-event.[3]

The better course is to retain the primary biblical and historical meaning of the word *missionary* as relating to persons commissioned and sent for special continuing responsibility in the spread of the gospel to new places and new groups. Secondarily the word may sometimes be used more broadly, to refer to the general mission of the church and of all believers, but with the recognition that this use does not take the place of the primary meaning of the word. The two concepts are complementary.

Christ "gave some to be missionaries," as one of his gifts to the church (Eph. 4:11; 1 Cor. 12:28). In recent missions literature, the idea of a special "missionary gift" has been explored. It has generally been interpreted as a specific endowment for working in cross-cultural settings. Sometimes the question is linked with that of a special missionary calling or "vocation." Historically, of course, the idea of a special "call" to missions has been generally recognized.[4] (The question of the "call to foreign missions" will be considered in the next chapter.)

Regardless of technical questions that may be raised about the "missionary gift," there obviously are some persons who have spiritual gifts that make them especially suited to service within another cultural setting. And regardless of technical questions about the nature of a "missionary call," clearly the spirit of God does call out some believers for missionary ministry in other lands. Such persons fit what we understand as the biblical concept of missionary.

## The Incarnational Principle

There is no quick, simple, easy, or painless way to evangelize the whole world. The biblical analogy of grain falling into the earth and dying (John 12:24) is still relevant. It is comparable to the "emptying" described in Philippians 2 as characterizing the incarnation of Jesus. Of course, this principle applies to all Christian living, but it has special importance in relation to cross-cultural sharing of the gospel.

The position of the Foreign Mission Board, set out in its philosophy statement, is clear: "The board regards as basic the concept of the career missionary. The board is committed to the use of short-term and volunteer personnel, but the overwhelming, long-term need is for career missionaries who are committed to the truth of the incarnational principle—'the Word became flesh and dwelt among us'—dwelling among the people of some other land on a long-term basis."

Foreign mission leaders have set forth this position consistently. M. Theron Rankin, executive secretary of the Foreign Mission Board, 1945-53, wrote:

> If God could have saved the world by remoteness, by remaining separated from men, would he have incarnated himself in human form and become in fashion as a man to live among men as one of them? . . .
>
> We have never made an approach to the world that can be more convincing than the sending of missionaries who, in the name of Christ, will lose themselves and bury their lives among the people to whom they go; missionaries who live and serve along with the people, who speak their language, who acquire the capacities of sympathy for their miseries and human hungers, and who learn to love them personally and individually.[5]

R. Keith Parks, current Foreign Mission Board president, reporting to the board in October 1980, identified areas of challenge for the 1980s and principles of response. One element of response was stated:

There will be an ongoing emphasis on the necessity
for the people called of God to go forth to incarnate the
gospel in a needy world. This will require on the part of
those who respond a commitment of unlimited length
which enables one to learn the language, become familiar with the culture, and communicate the gospel in a
way acceptable to the people of a particular culture.
People with this kind of commitment are career missionaries.

Many observers of today's world note (quite correctly) that
foreign missionaries in the technical sense of the term are not
necessary for the spread of the gospel. They cite, for example,
the remarkable increase in Christianity in China during these
decades when foreign missionaries could not be present. In
other words, God can accomplish his purposes without us.

A complementary biblical truth is that God does desire to use
his people as instruments of his purpose. An observable reality
is that churches are planted and helped to become strong by the
presence of missionaries where that is possible. Southern Baptists have considered it axiomatic that sending missionaries is the
best help we can give in world evangelization. The presence of a
missionary may not do the job (or sometimes may even hinder
it)—but without a missionary in many cases the job will simply
not be done. The area or group of persons will remain unevangelized.

Sharing the gospel is essentially personal. Television and
other methods of mass communication can be highly valuable
supplemental evangelistic approaches (though often with serious limitations as to adaptation of language and culture). Even
in America, where most people have television sets and have
much background for understanding the gospel, would anyone
suggest a televised Sunday morning broadcast as an adequate
substitute for the local pastor and the ministries of other Christian workers? Overseas the need for the personal gospel messenger is far more acute. M. Theron Rankin, speaking in a
seminary chapel, insisted that a "loudspeaker" on a cross will
never win the world; there must be a man on the cross.

The Foreign Mission Board was established initially and primarily as a channel for sending out and supporting missionaries. This has been its primary function throughout its history. Only in more recent decades has it become possible for the Board to add many other services.

In spite of the trend in many denominations mainly to short-term missionaries, the Southern Baptist Foreign Mission Board continues its central emphasis on career missionaries. The term *career* is a problem in two ways. One is that some persons perceive it as a secular concept—that is, a person making his own plans for a lifework that will be personally rewarding. Others are disturbed by the implication of permanence and perhaps unchangeableness, with no way out until retirement (or death). Everyone should be aware, however, that many persons sent out as career missionaries do not remain on the mission field all their lives (myself included). Even though the term is subject to possible misunderstanding, the Foreign Mission Board still finds it useful to designate its main body of missionaries.

The most effective missionary service is possible only through an incarnational type of ministry. In cross–cultural missions, such ministry is not possible by brief or superficial contact. It requires long-range depth involvement. Languages take time to learn. Adaptation to culture also requires time. Both call for strong motivation. Development of warm personal relations with those of another culture is possible only from an incarnational attitude. All of these considerations must rest in an open-ended commitment. Whatever terms may be used (*career, long-range, open-ended,* or some other term), the Foreign Mission Board is convinced that in cross-cultural missions this kind of missionary is essential.[6]

For some decades, this continuing strong Foreign Mission Board emphasis on an increasing number of career missionaries has meant swimming against the current of several trends in American church life. Availability of missionary candidates and continuity in missionary service have been affected by those trends.

For about twenty years, American culture has encouraged

temporariness of personal direction. It has been expressed sometimes as "doing one's own thing"—that is, following the feelings and impressions of the present, not necessarily the intention or the commitment of the past. And so we have seen much changing of careers, much instability in marriages, many popular songs and movies that play up the "easy rider"—the person who is here today, but may not be here tomorrow. A prominent cultural value is being "cool," which means de-tached—and detachment is the opposite of commitment. There-fore, it is not surprising that many persons have hesitated to make a long-range commitment to missionary service.

Another major cultural emphasis, self-fulfillment through ex-panded personal experience, has contributed to a growing de-sire for personal involvement in missionary projects. Attention to the general mission of the church and the general calling of all Christians has supported this trend. Many have pointed out (correctly, as mentioned already in chapter 4) that in the Great Commission of Matthew 28:18-20, the word *go* in the Greek is not an imperative form, but a participle—*going*. Some persons have then translated it "as you go" and have interpreted it to mean, "wherever you happen to go, make disciples." The problem is that the central command to disciple all the nations cannot be fulfilled just by the witness of persons who "happen to go." There are many places which will be evangelized only as Chris-tians go there intentionally and stay long enough for an incarna-tional ministry. The Great Commission really is not saying, wherever you happen to go, make disciples. Though that is a Christian principle, it is expressed in other Bible passages. What the Great Commission says is, by going as may be necessary, disciple all the nations.

At times there have been suggestions that the trends toward volunteer projects and short-term assignments represent the current "shape of missionary support," with the implication that Southern Baptist overseas missions should be adapted to that shape. However, simply to accept the situation, with no attempt to influence or change it, would be comparable to the "hard-shell" view about individual salvation that was held by extreme Calvinists in earlier days: that the Holy Spirit would bring persons to conviction of sin and faith in Christ when He chose, without any need for evangelistic proclamation and persuasion. Southern Baptists have rejected the hard-shell view about individual salvation, and the Foreign Mission Board has rejected any hard-shell view about the shape of missionary support. It is convinced that the biblical principle of incarnational ministry and the cultural realities of the world call for career missionaries and that appeals should be made for commitment to such long-range, open-ended service.

Not only the principle of incarnation, but also the principle of the cross in the life of the Christian is actually involved here. More superficial approaches in missions can never take the place of the life truly "planted" for Christ, that it may bear "much fruit." Christ enunciated that principle in relation to his own death on the cross. Philippians 2 links the principle of incarnation with the principle of the cross. That quality of long-range unconditional self-giving to the world mission cause is as urgently needed as ever.

## Supplementary Personnel

The Foreign Mission Board does serve as a channel for overseas involvement of many other Southern Baptists, alongside career missionaries. As is the case with other aspects of missions strategy, the approach is "both-and" rather than "either-or." As to missionary personnel, this means both career missionaries in the primary role and many other persons in supplementary roles.

The missionary associate category was created in 1961. It makes possible missionary service by persons who may not qualify fully for career appointment, including especially persons too old for appointment (the career age range extends to age 45; the range for associates is 35-60). A missionary associate goes to the field committed to a four-year assignment. If all goes well and by mutual agreement with the Board, the term for the associate is repeatable up to retirement age. After two full terms, if specified conditions are met, an associate can be transferred to career status. Both career and associate staff are now included in the broad category of "missionary" personnel.

Another broad category of "auxiliary" personnel includes journeymen (a program initiated in 1967, providing two-year assignments for young college graduates up to age 27); special assignment (an extended term arrangement for four months to two years of overseas service); Mission Service Corps (a plan instituted in 1977 for special assignment at personal expense or at the expense of a sponsor); and specialized brief arrangements for service by Baptist Student Union summer and semester personnel and by medical receptors or residents. (A chart of personnel categories is in Appendix 6.)

All career and associate missionaries and those with two-year assignments at Foreign Mission Board expense (journeymen or special assignment) are included in the "missionary count" that is reported to the Southern Baptist Convention. A general guideline for many years has sought to maintain that count at a ratio of approximately 90 percent career missionaries and 10 percent in the other supplementary categories. At the end of 1984, the career ratio was 88.9 percent.

In addition, volunteers by the thousands go overseas each year to help the mission cause in a wide range of ways. The volunteer projects usually require only a week or two, but some may last as long as several months. (Some specialized project arrangements are described in chapter 10.)

The number of volunteers serving overseas through Foreign Mission Board channels has averaged about 5,000 per year in recent years and is expected to increase. In the Foreign Mission Board's long-range plans looking to AD 2000, volunteer involvement has been anticipated at the 10,000 per year level—with the probability of that level being reached some years sooner, perhaps as early as 1990.

When the desire for volunteer participation overseas expanded so rapidly about 15 years ago, it took a while for missionaries and the Baptist churches and conventions on the fields to learn how to use so many volunteers constructively. At the same time, financial pressures kept the Foreign Mission Board from enlarging its home office staff as rapidly as the volunteer interest was expanding. Thus there were several years of frustration for all concerned. By now, however, volunteers who allow adequate time and adequate flexibility for fitting in with real needs on the fields can find through the Foreign Mission Board opportunity to participate in useful and rewarding overseas ministry projects.

Southern Baptists who live or travel overseas in the normal course of their lives are another very valuable source of informal supplementary personnel to help in world evangelization. The impression made by Americans overseas is extremely important to the Christian cause. Most persons in other lands have not learned to distinguish between those Americans who are Christians and those who are not. They often assume that all Americans are Christians, then judge Christianity by what they see in the lives of Americans. This is of vastly increased importance today because both travel and residence abroad are common.

Even devoted Christians who live or travel abroad may need help if their Christian witness is to be most fruitful. They can be especially valuable if their efforts are linked with ongoing Southern Baptist mission programs, so that they can serve as unofficial colleagues to the missionaries. To facilitate this, the Foreign Mission Board has a program of Laity Abroad, which provides contacts and helps to interested Southern Baptists who will be traveling or living overseas.

In many places, there are English-language Baptist churches, developed with the help of the Foreign Mission Board, to minister to American and other English-speaking communities. In other places (Bangladesh and Mali are two examples), devoted lay-Christians were forerunners who helped in the beginning of Southern Baptist foreign missions work.

In his projection to the Foreign Mission Board about the continuing importance of career missionaries, Board President R. Keith Parks went on to say that such missionaries "become the foundation for the ministry of auxiliary forces of short-termers who will go in increasing numbers to work alongside them. . . . Career missionaries and short-term workers are mutually strengthening; but without the career missionary as the base the short-term ministries could hardly take place."[7]

## Conclusion

In relation to the spread of the gospel, the New Testament describes several models, all with evident validity and all mutually complementary. Individual believers witnessed in the natural course of their movements from place to place (Acts 8:4; 11:19-20). Some persons went on brief special missions—by invitation (Acts 10:23-24), or sent by a church (Acts 11:22-23), or at the direct leading of the Holy Spirit (Acts 8:26). Paul and Barnabas (and others later) were involved in longer-range mission undertakings. These models are roughly comparable to today's concepts of laity abroad, volunteers, and career missionaries.

Though the New Testament does not prescribe methods for modern missions, the spiritual principles that were operative in the New Testament churches are operative today in forms appropriate to the modern world.

Formal classifications of missionary personnel differ from time to time, and the role of missionaries continues to change; but the basic concept remains: a person in whom the gospel is embodied, in loving relationship with others across barriers of race, nation, language, and culture, to make Christ known as Savior and Lord and to initiate living fellowships of believers.

The Foreign Mission Board serves as a sort of pulpit committee, representing millions of persons who do not know that they need to hear the message, and thousands of churches needing leadership and nurture but with so few laborers. In response, at the leading of the Holy Spirit, persons devote their lives to a nation or to a people, just as the life of Paul was devoted to the Gentiles of the Roman Empire. We are convinced that this sort of incarnational dedication is still a vital part of God's plan for the telling of the story to the nations.

### Notes

1. For a summary and analysis of this trend, see Samuel Wilson, ed., *Mission Handbook: North American Protestant Ministries Overseas*, 12th ed. (Monrovia, Calif.: Missions Advanced Research and Communication Center, 1979), pp. 25,31–34.

2. For a helpful discussion of this New Testament terminology, see E. Luther

Copeland, *World Mission and World Survival* (Nashville: Broadman Press, 1985), pp. 145-46.

3. R. K. Orchard, *Missions in a Time of Testing* (Philadelphia: The Westminster Press, 1964), p. 164. See also more extended and very helpful treatments of this question by R. Pierce Beaver, *The Missionary Between the Times* (Garden City, N.Y.: Doubleday & Company, Inc., 1968), pp. 28–30, and J. Herbert Kane, *Understanding Christian Missions*, rev. ed. (Grand Rapids: Baker Book House, 1978), pp. 27–30.

4. For a rather rigid treatment of gifts and call, see the chapter on that topic by C. Peter Wagner, *Frontiers in Missionary Strategy* (Chicago: Moody Press, 1971), pp. 68–86. Beaver, pp. 30–33, and Kane, pp. 38–49, also deal with these concepts.

5. M. Theron Rankin, "Nothing But the Cross," *The Commission*, vol. 15, no. 6 (June 1952): 9.

6. For a more extended treatment of this theme from a similar perspective, see the chapter on "The Incarnational Life" in T. Watson Street, *On the Growing Edge of the Church* (Richmond: John Knox Press, 1965), pp. 83–98, especially pp. 92–93.

7. R. Keith Parks, in his October 1980 report to the Foreign Mission Board, SBC, attached to the Board minutes.

# 7
# What Kind of Missionaries?

People have strange notions about missions and missionaries. One common view of missionaries can be called the "halo concept." Many people think of missionaries as persons of almost angelic saintliness. Ordinary human beings with ordinary human weaknesses often feel that being a missionary is entirely beyond their reach.

An opposite idea is that missionaries are persons who were unsuccessful or frustrated in their chosen fields of work at home and found the mission field an avenue of escape. This point of view is often combined with an idea that people in other lands are inferior. Thus some feel that it would be a terrible waste for a person of real abilities to bury his life overseas.

Another fairly common impression about missionaries is the "martyr concept." This is the idea that the missionary life entails unusual sacrifice and great suffering. Many people expect a missionary to live in a grass hut and wear drab cast-off clothing. Actually Southern Baptists support their missionaries at a reasonable level of comfort and economic security. Missionaries do not want people feeling sorry for them, as they consider their lives to have joy and fulfillment in the center of God's will.

There is also a romantic view of missions. It imagines the life of a missionary as a thrilling succession of glowing experiences in exotic surroundings, with an unbelievable response to the message, and none of the drab everyday problems encountered in Christian work in America. Persons who go to the mission field with that notion experience a rather rude awakening.

What kinds of persons are missionaries? And what kinds of lives do they lead?

In a Southern Baptist missionary home overseas, the household helper was sick. The missionary wife took her helper to the doctor and paid the cost of treatment. For about two weeks the helper was not able to work, but at the end of that time she was given her usual pay—even though the missionary had been doing the housework herself. The helper was greatly surprised by such treatment and protested that it must be an error. When assured that it was not, she impulsively threw her arms around the missionary, saying warmly, "I love you very much."

That missionary had not intended to teach a spiritual lesson. She was simply doing what was natural to her, because "the love of God is shed abroad in our hearts" (Rom. 5:5). Even without intending it, she was demonstrating qualities of heart and life that make a missionary.

A famous old saying expresses it well: "You would not take to China a lamp that does not burn at home in America." Sharing the love of God with the world's people is an overflow from the abundant experience of God's love in the lives of those who become missionaries.

### The Missionary Call

It is expected that persons serving in Southern Baptist foreign missions will be "God-called." The Foreign Mission Board's philosophy statement indicates that "the enlisting, appointment, sending, and support of an ever-increasing number of God-called, and otherwise qualified, missionaries is the priority responsibility of the Foreign Mission Board."

Throughout their history, Southern Baptists have believed in a personal call to foreign mission service. Without attempting to define the term, most Southern Baptists have had a general understanding of what they have meant by *call*. But interpretations have varied widely. At times the presumption has been that a Christian worker should serve overseas unless there is some compelling reason for remaining in the homeland. Others have assumed that none should go as missionaries without such a strong compulsion that they could not happily remain in their own country. Most interpretations have avoided both extremes, but all have included an assurance of overseas ministry as the will of God.[1]

Many in more recent years have objected to the concept of a special call to foreign missions (and even to pastoral and other ministry roles in the church). Such objection is based on new awareness that the call of all believers to discipleship and ministry is the central biblical concept of calling.[2] Though some have recognized other biblical uses of the term *call*, the general tendency has been to downplay any other uses and to emphasize the truth that "all are called." As a result, any reference to a foreign missionary call has become a problem to some persons.[3]

Obviously the Foreign Mission Board does not agree with J. Herbert Kane that "the term *missionary call* should never have been coined."[4] The reference to "God-called" missionaries in the Board's philosophy statement almost certainly means called into foreign missionary service, and not merely called to Christian discipleship or even (as Kane would allow) called to "the service of God on a full-time basis."[5]

I believe, with probably almost all Southern Baptists, that biblical concepts and terminology include secondary callings to special roles in the work of Christ, alongside the primary calling to Christian discipleship and ministry. Paul certainly felt that God's will for him personally was to commit his life to the sharing of the gospel with other peoples (Gentiles)—a role generally comparable to that of foreign missionary in today's setting. (See, for example, such passages as Acts 26:17–18; Gal. 2:7; and Eph. 3:8.) The relevant phrase in Romans 1:1 can reasonably be translated "called to be a missionary"—following the general meaning of the Greek word.

However, terminology is not the main concern. If the word *call* is a problem to some persons today, other words can express the same reality. Some common terms include *motivation, sense of direction, sense of mission,* or *assurance of God's leading.* What matters is that persons be convinced that overseas missionary ministry is God's purpose for their lives. This is what the Foreign Mission Board means by the missionary call, and the Board expects candidates for missionary appointment to manifest this essential conviction.

Strong assurance of God's leading is vital for continuing and effective foreign mission ministry. The separations, the strangeness, and the stress experienced in long-range cross-cultural ministry require a profound assurance of God's direction. If motivation is based only on personal desire or some other lesser consideration, the missionary will not be able to carry through on his commitment. When the difficult times come (as they will), the missionary must be able to say with confidence, "God put me here and He can see me through to the fulfillment of His purpose."

Experience has shown that, in the case of married couples, both husband and wife need an assured missionary call. It is not enough simply to go along because the marriage partner feels called.

To ask how one can be sure of being called is about like asking how one can be sure of being in love and ready for marriage. The assurance comes in many ways because personalities and individual experiences differ so widely. Many human influences are used as means to awaken a sense of calling. Some persons have mistakenly awaited a dramatic experience like that of Paul on the road to Damascus, not realizing that God might speak to them instead through a still, small voice. The process is secondary. The resultant conviction is essential.[6]

There is indeed a general call that comes to all Christians—the call of God's unchanging purpose for the discipling of the nations, as revealed throughout the Scriptures and made explicit in the Great Commission; the call of enormous and acute human need; and the call implied by stewardship of privilege. But this general call must become personal through the inner voice of the Holy Spirit. It also finds confirmation through the backing of God's people.

The analysis made by Richard Niebuhr in relation to call to the Christian ministry is relevant. He suggested four elements: (1) the call to be a Christian, or the call to discipleship; (2) the secret call, or the inner summons from God; (3) the providential call, or the call of talents and preparation; and (4) the ecclesiastical call, which in the case of a pastor would be the call extended by a local church.[7]

Many persons readily assume that anyone who feels called to

foreign missionary service should automatically be sent by the Foreign Mission Board without any other requirements. However, the Board has the responsibility of judging whether it is led by the Holy Spirit to appoint and support the particular individual under consideration. This is simply another example of a principle that is common throughout Baptist church and denominational life—an individual's impression of the leading of the Holy Spirit is confirmed by the impression of the group.

Persons who might be qualified for foreign missionary service sometimes say that they have never considered it because they have not felt called. That is putting the cart before the horse. Assurance of call comes at the end of a process of consideration. Those who care about a lost world and who can perhaps share personally and directly in its evangelization (because of gifts and opportunities that the Lord has provided) should consider earnestly and prayerfully whether missionary service is God's will for their lives. After all, not every person called by the Lord has to be a draftee, surrendering after a struggle as Moses did; some can be volunteers, saying with Isaiah, "Here am I; send me" (Isa. 6:8).

## Selection

The philosophy statement of the Foreign Mission Board refers to the appointment of "God-called, and otherwise qualified, missionaries." This implies a selection process that will examine both the sense of call and the other qualifications of missionary candidates.

Many and perhaps most persons, on considering the realities involved in possible missionary service, are inclined to ask, "Who is sufficient for these things?" (2 Cor. 2:16). They may recognize further, with the apostle Paul, that "our sufficiency is of God" (2 Cor. 3:5). Both the call and the qualifications must come as gifts from God.

### Gifts and Roles

Some have speculated that there may be a special "missionary gift" which would qualify a person especially for cross-cultural ministry. However, since conditions and requirements of missionary service vary so greatly in different times and places and in different roles, it seems more reasonable to understand God's many gifts as equipment for differing mission ministries.

In earlier generations, overseas missionary personnel consisted almost exclusively of preachers, teachers, doctors, and nurses. Since World War II, with the rapid expansion of Southern Baptist foreign missions, specialized types of missionary service have expanded greatly. There are now more than 80 classifications, including such widely differing ministries as music, pharmacy, agriculture, business management, broadcasting, and even a limited number of airplane pilots.

Amid the many roles of modern missionaries, by far the dominant need still in Southern Baptist missions is for persons devoted to preaching ministries. These are sometimes called general evangelists. A term growing in popularity has been *church planter.* Perhaps the most descriptive name for the assignment is *evangelism and church development,* but that is a rather awkward term. Other terms (such as *church development consultant*) are sometimes used, but no entirely satisfactory wording has been discovered. The assignment is essentially that of seeking to evangelize a region through planting, multiplying, and strengthening churches.

It is puzzling that requests for specialized categories of missionary personnel can usually be filled more readily than urgent general evangelism requests. Perhaps the Foreign Mission Board has not communicated clearly enough the critical need for missionary church planters and developers, or the special challenges and rewards related to that kind of ministry.

Perhaps some are turned away by the general nature of the task—when they prefer to be specialists. The general evangelist is indeed a specialist, with special commitment to and expertise in several fundamental concerns of Christian ministry. He specializes in relating to and working with persons; in communicating the gospel; in leadership, motivation, and training; and in the nurturing of living Christian fellowships. The rather bland term *general evangelist* stands for human needs and mission opportunities that challenge the very best that one can bring to the task.

### Personal Qualities

All missionary specialists require a central core of personal qualities. The profile of those qualities defines the essence of the kind of missionary needed overseas. They can be summed up under several headings.

1. *Health.*—Both physical and emotional health are required for effective missionary service. In the modern world, however, some health problems which formerly prevented persons from serving overseas can now be handled, at least in many locations. A common health problem, typical of America's affluent society, which must frequently be brought under control before missionary appointment, is excess weight. One of the earliest stages in consideration of persons for possible overseas ministry is a preliminary health check through the services of the Foreign Mission Board's Personnel Selection and Medical Services Departments.

2. *Spirituality.*—Vital personal spiritual experience is an absolute essential for the missionary. This includes clear assurance of salvation and call; abiding trust in God; biblical convictions; development in both personal and group worship and devotional life; active witness and ministry; and ethical sensitivity. Trust in God is especially important. The element of trust makes it possible to be relaxed rather than uptight about difficulties experienced. Thus the missionary can ride the waves of change instead of being swept under by them. Attention and concern are freed from self, so the missionary can look outward in care for others.

3. *Maturity.*—Development of a mature personality is reflected in such qualities as self-understanding and self-acceptance and in good interpersonal relations, including charitable acceptance of other persons.

4. *Flexibility.*—This is an especially important missionary quality, since it implies being able to adapt to new situations without losing one's own direction. A fitting illustration of the needed flexibility is the tensile strength of fine steel which is tough enough to bend under pressure instead of breaking. The toughness of the missionary is that of tempered steel—sensitive, flexi-

ble, but strong. He is not broken or rendered ineffective by troubles. There is a tenacity that keeps him an idealist and keeps him present and active, in spite of any limitations or the downward drag of reality.

5. *Love.*—This is the "more excellent way" (1 Cor. 12:31), exceeding in importance all the various gifts. Love is the absolutely indispensable missionary quality. To be constrained by the love of Christ (2 Cor. 5:14) means that Christ's love is the main moving and controlling force in one's life. The universal, impartial, sacrificial love of Jesus experienced and expressed in heart and life makes one a true missionary.

### Appointment Requirements

In addition to the personal qualities needed for overseas missionary ministry, there are technical requirements. The Southern Baptist Convention, for example, requires that all persons appointed as missionaries by the Foreign Mission Board be members of Southern Baptist churches. The Board has established age limits for missionary appointment and other requirements related to educational preparation and professional experience. Other mission boards and agencies have somewhat similar requirements.[8]

One part of the selection process is a psychiatric interview. The Southern Baptist Foreign Mission Board pioneered in this type of evaluation, making it part of the selection process in 1937.

The general outlines of appointment requirements have remained unchanged for many decades, since the requirements reflect the nature of the task to be accomplished and the stressful realities of missionary service. Policy details change from time to time. A statement of all current requirements is available on request from the board's Personnel Selection Department.

A matter of special current interest is the place of women in foreign missions. Both opportunities for and contributions of women have been and are great. An early Southern Baptist missionary hero is Henrietta Hall Shuck, who began the first school for Chinese girls at Hong Kong (prior to her early death, shortly before the Southern Baptist Convention was organized).

It is appropriately symbolic that the best-known Southern Baptist missionary is a woman, Lottie Moon. Certainly through most of Southern Baptist history, and probably also today, women have had wider opportunities of service in foreign missions than in any other part of Southern Baptist life.

At first mainly married women were sent overseas by Southern Baptists. The first single woman, Harriet Baker, was appointed as early as 1849 for South China.[9] But single women were still rare among Southern Baptist missionaries when Lottie Moon went to north China in 1873.

Gradually over succeeding decades the proportion of single missionaries increased. By the middle of this century, Southern Baptist missionaries included as many single women as married couples. Therefore, women constituted approximately two thirds of all Southern Baptist missionaries, since single men were very few. (The Board formerly for some years refused to appoint single men as missionaries.)

Within the past 30 years, the proportion of single women in the Southern Baptist foreign mission force has decreased markedly to about 7 percent of all career and associate missionaries. Presumably this is due to enlarged career opportunities for women in American life.

The Board now has no restriction on appointment of single men or single women—though it recognizes the increased difficulty such persons are likely to face, both because of cultural considerations in some overseas settings and because of the possible extra burden of loneliness to add to the other stresses of missionary service.

Many married women are assigned primarily to missionary ministries through their homes and in their churches, especially during child-rearing years. The term *home and church work* to describe that assignment is less than fully satisfactory, but it is descriptive of the role being filled; and no other better term has been readily available. Women missionaries, whether married or single, are considered for mission field assignments in the same way as men. Even during the years when a married woman has home and church work as her primary assignment, she often uses her professional background and training in a secondary assignment—which then becomes primary as children grow up and leave home.

For decades and probably longer, there have been tensions related to the work of married women missionaries. Earlier there was a feeling (whether justified or not) that single women missionaries did not regard very highly the work being done by married women who had home responsibilities. Therefore, the Foreign Mission Board sought to emphasize the fully missionary role and the importance of the missionary with a home and church assignment. More recently many married women have seemed unhappy with the concept of ministry through the home and in the church and have eagerly sought some more specialized professional assignment. (Men have felt similar tension between home needs and assignments away from home, but less acutely.)

As in other matters of tension between valid principles, the Foreign Mission Board follows a "both-and" approach. It aims to provide opportunity for professional ministry for those women who feel so led and are so qualified, while at the same time maintaining the validity and importance of the home and church ministry for women who see that as their calling, at least in their present stage of life.

The personal qualities of the missionary, as emphasized in this section, are undoubtedly idealized. Actually, the missionary is entirely human—neither superman nor sub–par. Neither the halo concept, with its glow of exalted spirituality and success, nor the martyr figure, with its shadow of heroic suffering, gives a true picture. The missionary has a normal human quota of weaknesses and strengths, failures and successes, hardships and joys. The missionary selection process seeks to evaluate a real person in relation to some real situation of need and opportunity overseas and match them appropriately.

### Preparation

Having an orientation program for new missionaries implies that missionaries at the time of appointment are not really what the Foreign Mission Board wants them to be. The Board does want them as missionaries. Their appointment testifies to that.

But the Board wants them *plus* all the growth that will be possible through orientation and other specialized training and through years of missionary experience. Missionaries, like the rest of us, are still "under construction."

The seminary training that is an academic requirement for missionary appointment is an important part of missionary preparation. Those who will have church development assignments are expected to have full seminary training. Specialists in other fields such as medicine or agriculture get a semester or a year in seminary. Increasingly, the Southern Baptist seminaries are seeking to provide courses of study that will be especially fitting as preparation for missionary service overseas.

The professional experience that is another requirement for missionary appointment is also an important element in missionary preparation. The academic preparation that has been received in seminary or other professional training is applied in and supplemented by at least two years of solid, practical experience in the work place.

Following appointment, new missionaries receive special orientation provided by the Foreign Mission Board. The Board's first formal orientation conference for new missionaries was held in the summer of 1954. For several years such conferences lasted no longer than a week and a half. That was about as long as new missionaries could reasonably be away from their families. Any longer program could be possible only on a resident basis. A program lasting several months was initiated in September 1967, first at Ridgecrest and then from 1969 at Callaway Gardens, Pine Mountain, Georgia.

Early in 1984 the Foreign Mission Board opened its new learning center near Richmond, Virginia, where the Board's home offices are located. The philosophy and program have been refined through these years of experience, and the orientation period for career and associate missionaries is now eight weeks.

The more important orientation for missionary service takes place on the mission field. Pre-field preparation is hampered by the limited understanding and readiness for learning that are due to lack of field experience. The Foreign Mission Board has worked with its mission organizations to develop effective field orientation for new missionaries.[10]

Language study is usually the first major responsibility of new missionaries when they arrive overseas. In some cases, language study precedes arrival on the actual field of anticipated service. (For example, most missionaries for Spanish-speaking Latin America have received language training in recent years in Costa Rica before proceeding to their assigned countries.) Communicating the gospel is basic in missions, and language is basic to communication. Therefore, effective command of the local language (or languages) is extremely important.

Because language learning is difficult, new missionaries are tempted to turn toward witness or ministry possibilities that are available to them in English, or to level off too soon in acquiring the new language. Those temptations must be resisted, since the language is to be the tool for a lifetime of ministry. This is comparable to a physician, for whom knowledge of medicine serves as a tool. It would be a sad mistake for a medical student to turn aside from study simply to bandage fingers or swab throats, using the limited knowledge already possessed, and miss the full command of medical skills to be gained by continuing concentrated study.

The Foreign Mission Board has policies requiring certain levels of competence in use of the local language before the missionary can shift from language study into a full-time work assignment.

In a sense, the entire first term in missionary service is preparatory. Of course, the missionary does assume an assigned responsibility and accomplish something in that assignment. But the most important accomplishments of the first term are those which form the foundation for a lifetime of effective service: gaining adequate command of the language; adapting to the local culture and living conditions; building relationships, both within the mission family and with local people; finding the handle to the job assignment and learning to be productive; and gaining a broader and deeper vision of the mission to which God has led.

The furlough after the first term of missionary service is especially important. Prior to that furlough, a formal evaluation process identifies needs for further training or additional strengthening. The Foreign Mission Board conducts a special debriefing conference at the Missionary Learning Center near Richmond for missionaries on their first furlough. Arrangements are made for special courses of study, seminars, or workshops that will prepare the missionary for even more effective service after return to the field.

Continuing in-service training linked to the ongoing process of evaluation (self-evaluation, peer evaluation, and evaluation by the area director) contributes to the continuing growth of each missionary toward his or her maximum potential in missionary service.

### Life-style

Always, in the experience of the foreign missionary, two cultures interact. One is the culture the missionary takes with him. The other is that into which he moves. The distinctive elements of missionary life-style grow out of this cultural interaction as it is shaped by the missionary purpose.

### *Identification*

Successful adjustment to the new cultural setting is imperative. The process may be accompanied by culture shock in varying degrees of severity. Adaptation may be more or less complete, depending on the extent of the disparity between cultures and on the personality of the missionary. Many withdrawals from missionary service are due to failure in cultural adjustment, and many other missionaries who do not withdraw are limited in effectiveness by inadequate adjustment.[11]

The ideal in cultural adaptation is appropriate identification with local people. Absolute identification is impossible, since the missionary inevitably will retain a basic American cultural orientation. Some kinds of identification may be undesirable (as reflected in the old expression about "going native"), but a large measure of identification is inherent in the principle of incarnational missions.[12]

In spite of a desire and effort to identify, a missionary is always to some extent a bearer of another culture, whose presence tends to induce social and cultural change. This is both good and bad. It is bad in that the introducing of elements of modern Western culture may be disruptive. Some anthropologists have been quite critical of Christian missions on that score—though missionaries in the main have been much more concerned to identify with and strengthen local cultures than have representatives of government, commerce, and even science who have come in as cultural outsiders. Furthermore, many cultural changes brought by missionaries are good.[13]

In a sense, the missionary as an individual and missionaries as a group become a bridge between cultures. The Christian missionary may have begun his career with the thought that he was giving up his homeland. He discovered, however, that he did not become a "man without a country," but rather a man with two countries. This creates one of his greatest opportunities, but is at the same time one of his continuing problems. He is enriched by having two countries instead of only one. His ministry to each is magnified by his involvement in the other. But he can never feel completely adjusted in either of his countries. Thus the vital contribution of the missionary as a cultural bridge costs much painful adjustment and some probable permanent unease.

The position of the missionary in between his own culture and the culture of another land is ultimately a tale of three countries: The missionary in either of his homelands is actually a representative of the heavenly kingdom. By reference to that kingdom, the countries of earth can rightly relate to one another and rightly reform their own cultures.

### Servanthood

Appropriate identification and comfort with the bridge role are possible only from the posture of servanthood. Here missionary attitude is determinative. A servant spirit does not come naturally or easily to persons reared in American culture. Furthermore, even in our church life, we have tended to forget that *minister* means serve and have often thought of the Christian ministry in terms of authority and status. Japanese theologian Kosuke Koyama described the difference as "crucified mind, not crusading mind."[14]

American missionaries, coming from a highly developed

technological society with large and strong churches, are easily tempted to view persons of other cultures with what Stanley Soltau called "the downward slant." He commented that "as long as it is indulged in, it always checks the progress and growth of the new church and the spiritual development of its new members and also builds up a resentment and bitterness towards the missionaries."[15]

Luther Copeland expressed his own conviction that "only those who take seriously the role of servant will be able to offset the negative factors which would indicate that American missionaries cannot function effectively in the Third World."[16] Clearly, the missionary life-style must be one of servanthood.

### Community

Missionaries live in community, not in isolation. Good relationships are indispensable for fruitfulness. Missionaries become part of a mission team and mission family. In the meantime, they continue and nurture their relationship with the Southern Baptist constituency at home in America. But the most important part of their building of relationships is with people of the land where they serve. Missionaries may be tempted to remain primarily in the American or other expatriate community, but to do so blocks progress in the very purposes for which they are missionaries.

Relationships with local communities on the mission field have several aspects. Harmony and mutual congeniality with local Christian leaders are foremost. Crucial also are the cultivating of friendships and the winning of acceptance in the general population. A missionary also inevitably has a kind of "public relations" role, through contacts with official or semi-official elements of public life. The value of a good public image to the Christian cause is inestimable (Prov. 22:1).

By intention and even by specific planning, missionaries must join the various communities that make up their new world. The Foreign Mission Board seeks to structure the initial period of language study in ways that will encourage such relationships. More yet needs to be done, even if it means reducing the social interactions of the missionary family in order to stimulate greater involvement with local people. The old "compound" arrangement, in which missionary residences were all together behind a wall, is now recognized (though it has some advantages) as a hindrance to the purposes of missions.

After all, missionary life-style is intended to involve witness. But witness, except in the most superficial or formalized way, is possible only through continuing contact with persons in the non-Christian world.

An orientation module developed by the Foreign Mission Board emphasizes the evangelistic witness of all missionaries, regardless of their professional specialties or work assignments. It describes the missionary as essentially one who not only proclaims but also "demonstrates the love of Jesus Christ in a cross-cultural setting." The essential elements of missionary life-style mentioned above (a cultural identification, a spirit of servanthood, and the building of relationships in community) all point toward and contribute to what is sometimes called "life-style evangelism"—expressing spontaneously who we are in Jesus Christ.

### Special Concerns

Several special concerns related to missionary life-style need brief examination.

1. *Economic Disparity*—The common disparity in economic resources and in material standard of living between missionaries and local people poses an exceedingly complex question. It can become particularly acute in societies which really have no economic middle class, only a few very rich, and the remaining masses living in poverty. If Christian witness and Christian influence are not rendered impossible in such circumstances (a view which some consider tenable), they are at least made much more difficult for missionaries from affluent America.

The principle of identification is relevant, but it is not the only principle involved in this issue. Absolute identification in material life-style is not advisable in many or even most situations. For missionaries to have and use an antimalarial medicine may be a difference in life-style. Books and schooling for missionary children may be another. The automobile that allows mobility to fulfill the missionary's assigned task may make a great difference in material life-style.

Since the matter is so complex, the Foreign Mission Board has not felt it appropriate to take a dogmatic position, but rather to give general encouragement toward simplicity of life-style. The spirit in which a missionary uses possessions, openness, and sharing are ultimately more important than material considerations—but many persons never do get close enough to missionaries to observe their spirit, and the gospel may be judged superficially on the basis of missionary affluence. Our missionaries have probably erred more toward the side of too great an image of affluence and materialism.[17]

Elmer S. West, a Foreign Mission Board staff member, has developed a presentation and bibliography for new missionaries on the topic "Toward a Biblical Understanding of Enough." It builds on a theme expressed by John V. Taylor in the title of his book *Enough is Enough*.[18]

The concept of a Christian doctrine of enough, the principle of Christian stewardship, and concern for living patterns simple enough not to hinder the sharing of the gospel illumine one aspect of missionary life-style. They pose questions with which every missionary should wrestle personally.

2. *Missionary Support.*—The Foreign Mission Board wrestles with another side of the matter. The Board is concerned with providing missionary support that will be adequate and fair.

Persons who place high priority on material and financial rewards are not likely to become missionaries. Missionary support provisions will never make anyone rich by United States standards. But the Board does seek to assure basic continuing support and special help for unusual needs, at a level that will protect the missionary from financial anxieties. Thus missionaries can devote their full energies to the spiritual concerns of their ministry.

The Foreign Mission Board has adopted a formal statement of missionary support philosophy (see Appendix 7), and it reviews regularly the provisions needed to implement its philosophy. Benefits that are common in Christian work in the United States (medical insurance, life and accident insurance, vacations, retirement provision, and so forth) are part of the missionary support package.

Furloughs are a special consideration in missionary life-style. They are not vacations. Instead, they are brief periods when the missionary or the missionary family will be in the United States reporting in the churches, getting additional training, and meeting personal and family needs. A sliding scale relates length of furlough to the length of time spent at work on the field.

Whereas a housing allowance is provided during furloughs, actual housing (usually owned by the Foreign Mission Board) is made available for the missionary at the field location. Depending on local circumstances, that housing may compare reasonably well with current middle-class housing in American cities (perhaps an apartment), or it may be more comparable to usual American housing patterns one or two generations ago. In more developed societies, the housing and material standard of living of a local high-school teacher may offer a good model for missionaries to consider as they seek a life-style that will combine the meeting of their own needs with an appropriate image.

Missionary support includes emotional support, especially at the strategic point of family welfare. Therefore, for about 15 years the Foreign Mission Board has had on its staff a missionary family consultant to give backing and help for the personal and family needs of a rapidly growing missionary staff.

3. *Political Involvement.*—The controversial question of political involvement is another special consideration in missionary life-style. In its *Manual for Missionaries*, the Foreign Mission Board includes a statement calling for political neutrality and noninvolvement. This is a matter of long-standing policy.

Most other missions agencies have followed the same principle. Well over a century ago, one major mission board had this policy statement: "Every missionary is strictly charged to abstain from interfering in the political affairs of the country or place in which he may be situated." Mennonites, through their Council of International Ministries, have given special attention to this matter and have prepared detailed pamphlets on the issues involved.

A missionary is a guest in the country where he serves. The

kind of political involvement that is entirely proper for a citizen is not appropriate for a guest. Of course, the spiritual and moral concerns which are essential to the Christian faith do have implications for political life. Measuring the realities of the political situation and applying Christian principles to those realities is part of the Christian responsibility of local believers and their churches.

Furthermore, missionaries have sometimes been suspected or accused of being agents of the American government. The Foreign Mission Board's position of political noninvolvement gives assurance that missionaries go abroad with a spiritual purpose, not a political one.

This principle does not mean lack of concern about social conditions. Through the sharing of Christian teachings, missionaries can help introduce the influence of the gospel into the situation. Missionaries also can minister to persons on all sides of political conflicts.

In October 1974 the Foreign Mission Board adopted this formal statement: "That the Foreign Mission Board reassert its stance of political neutrality in nations where its representatives serve, its concern for persons regardless of their political convictions or involvements, its readiness to work for the spiritual and humanitarian welfare of persons on all sides during times of crisis and war, and its request to missionaries to refrain from actions or statements which might endanger other missionaries or national Christians or jeopardize the witness for Christ in any part of the world."

Of course, no statement of principle or policy can resolve all the complexities involved in this matter. Missionaries should be persons who can live comfortably with ambiguity. They need the ability to proclaim the whole gospel in good Christian conscience, while acting in harmony with the principle of political noninvolvement. They need to be "wise as serpents, and harmless as doves" (Matt. 10:16).

4. *Crises.*—A further life-style concern involves crisis situations (such as have been common, for example, much of the time in Lebanon in recent years). When such crises become acute, should missionaries remain or withdraw? Standing foreign

Mission Board policy authorizes individual missionaries and the mission organization on the field to exercise their own judgment, under the guidance of the Holy Spirit, whether to remain or to withdraw to some nearby location until the crisis passes.

Many, and perhaps most, missionaries at some time experience special danger. However, the danger element in missionary service should not be overdramatized. Most missionaries most of the time are in no more danger than is common in traffic on an American highway. Missionaries as a group are a good insurance risk, and many live to a ripe old age. However, some missionaries at some times are in places of quite serious danger.

Missionaries often judge that the importance of their ministry outweighs the risk. Actually much of the most fruitful ministry takes place in time of crisis.[19]

The cross has not been and cannot be eliminated from world missions. Sharing the gospel in a troubled world can be very costly, as evidenced in the cases of Bill Wallace, Mavis Pate, Archie Dunaway, and others killed in missionary service.

5. *Mobility.*—One further special element in missionary lifestyle is mobility. Missionaries have always moved frequently within their fields of service. Transfers between countries and even between major cultural regions of the world have now become more frequent than in earlier years. Such mobility has both advantages and disadvantages, both for missionaries and for the work.

Since the trend toward increased mobility does not seem likely to reverse, missionaries need to accept change as natural, nurturing elements of stability in their lives as a counterbalance to change, and to make unusual efforts to put roots down deep in the local culture and relate closely to local people. Meanwhile, missions administrators need to encourage good stewardship of missionary investments in language and in cultural adaptation by holding missionary transfers to a reasonable minimum.

In many respects, it is easier to be a missionary now than in earlier times. Daily life overseas is much easier, with modern conveniences often readily available. Dangers to missionary health have been greatly reduced. Transportation is simpler and more frequent. Communication has improved greatly, so there is much less sense of isolation. Changes in the world have created greater responsiveness to the gospel. Missionaries have opportunities for better training and are more perceptive and sensitive to their cultural setting.

But in some ways it is harder to be a missionary than it used to be. It is harder partly because it is easier, paradoxical as this sounds. With more exposure to a wider world, lives and roles become more complicated. If there are fewer major external problems to confront, it is easy to begin floundering in a sea of minor aggravations. Going overseas can seem so simple that we fail to recognize the deep changes needed to identify and communicate in another cultural setting. It is possible to move into missionary service without the depth of commitment required by the servant role. We may be tempted these days to listen to the many voices around us and not hear so clearly the voice of God within.

The "hardships" of the missionary life may not be as readily discernible as in earlier generations, but they are still real and still require genuineness of motivation and depth of commitment.

## Continuity

The career missionary concept assumes the importance of continuity in missionary service. Involvement in depth (not merely superficially) is a long-range matter. But withdrawals from missionary service are inevitable. The Foreign Mission Board does monitor the attrition rate in order to analyze causes for withdrawal and to find ways of increasing continuity of service.

From 1963, soon after a medical consultant was added to the Foreign Mission Board staff, there have been annual studies of attrition in our missionary forces.

Earlier, such reports were called "missionary loss" studies—but we soon recognized that the term *loss* is not entirely appropriate. Most of those who resign are not lost to the mission cause. For example, all of the Board's area directors are resigned missionaries. Many other former missionaries serve on the Foreign Mission Board staff, as missions professors in seminaries, or in other important responsibilities in Southern Baptist life.

There are a few missionaries also whose resignation is no "loss" because they were already unproductive or were sources of trouble. Other missionaries may have to spend countless hours trying to straighten out problems caused by a few. In such cases, the Board takes initiative in a resignation, since the team will be stronger without the person. This does not necessarily mean that the person cannot be a suitable servant of the Lord, but rather that he and the mission task do not fit together. Such persons are advised to project their ministry in some fitting place of service in the United States.

Those resignations that seem due essentially to missionary failure have three main causes. One is in the realm of spiritual or moral default. Another is inability to adapt to a different environment and a strange culture. The third failure area is relational—problems in working together with fellow missionaries and with local believers.

Resignations come for a wide variety of other reasons. Some missionaries are asked to join the Foreign Mission Board staff. Some have health problems that rule out continuing overseas service, though the person can serve well in this country. Some resignations are caused by serious family burdens related to children or to aged parents. Some resign to marry. Others interpret their resignations simply as "for personal reasons" or as "change of call."

Occasional comments or questions suggest a high rate of attrition in missionary forces. Numerically, of course, there are many more missionaries resigning than in earlier days. But on a percentage basis, attrition from missionary service is still not high.

For about twenty years, up to the mid-1960s, the resignation rate for career missionaries averaged about 2 percent per year. In the late 1960s the rate was above 3 percent and on up above 4 percent by the early 1970s. In the 1980s there have been signs of a downward trend to a range between 3 and 4 percent per year. By comparison with other kinds of Christian service (and recognizing the heavy stresses on missionaries), the resignation rate reflects remarkable tenacity of commitment.

There are two apparent reasons for the increase in missionary resignations that took place in the late 1960s. One was the change in American culture toward general temporariness of personal direction (described in the previous chapter). This cultural factor seems definitely to be involved in the higher resignation rate.

A second consideration is what Jesse Fletcher (a former Foreign Mission Board division director) called the "vulnerability" factor. It identifies times in missionary service and stages in the life development of individuals when conditions that may lead to resignation are more prevalent. Several of these vulnerability elements—the period in one's missionary career, the time when children are going through teenage adjustments, the need of aging parents for special attention, and the stage in personality development sometimes identified as the "middle-age syndrome"—all come into focus at about the same time, when missionaries are in their forties. This means there is extra vulnerability when missionaries reach that point in life.

Because few missionaries had been appointed in the 1930s and the early 1940s and the missionary staff was growing rapidly in the 1950s, our missionary forces for about two decades were made up of some missionaries nearing the end of their careers and a large number just beginning—but with very few in the middle years. Therefore, an unusually small portion of the missionary forces was at the main vulnerability stage. But by the late 1960s we had a cross section of missionaries at all stages of life, so the vulnerability period was affecting a larger proportion of our missionaries.

Many missionaries who resign come back after a few years, when the problem causing resignation has been resolved, and seek reappointment. Thus the net annual loss rate by resignations (minus reappointments) is only about 3 percent.

Extended experience shows that attitude is more important than circumstances in determining whether missionaries will continue in service on a long-range basis. Two missionary families may encounter identical problems, with one family becoming frustrated and withdrawing, while the other family feels challenged and puts down deeper roots. Happiness, continuity, and missionary effectiveness are essentially interrelated.

Missionary references today to the "hardships of the missionary life" are most often joking. Still, there are enough challenges to make career missionary service comparable to other roles that obviously are not for "softies" (the middle linebacker in professional football, the Marine sergeant, the teacher in a ghetto). American life with its emphasis on convenience, pleasure, prosperity, and security does not prepare persons very well for foreign missions. Missionaries for many of the more demanding places need the spiritual qualities which impelled Caleb not to ask for the fertile valley, but to accept instead the challenge of the mountains where the giants lived (Josh. 14:12). Happily for the world mission, God still gives persons those spiritual qualities.

### Notes

1. For representative examples, see unpublished thesis by Winston Crawley, *The Call to Foreign Missions Among Southern Baptists, 1845-1945* (Southern Baptist Theological Seminary, 1947).

2. That concept, for example, is central in the title of W. O. Carver's interpretation of Ephesians: *The Glory of God in the Christian Calling*, paperback ed. (1949; reprint, Nashville: Broadman Press, 1979).

3. For interpretation of the missionary call from a wide range of viewpoints, see Arthur J. Brown, *The Foreign Missionary* (New York: Fleming H. Revell Company, [1907] 1950); Ross Coggins, *Missions Today* (Nashville: Convention Press, 1963); R. Pierce Beaver, *The Missionary Between the Times* (Garden City, N.Y.: Doubleday & Company, Inc., 1968); Henlee H. Barnette, *Has God Called You?* (Nashville: Broadman Press, 1969); J. Herbert Kane, *Understanding Christian Missions*, rev. ed. (Grand Rapids: Baker Book House, 1978); and Michael Griffiths, *What On Earth Are You Doing?* (Grand Rapids: Baker Book House, 1983).

4. Kane, p. 41.

5. Ibid.

6. For analysis of process and influences in missionary calling, see the thesis cited in note 1 and also the unpublished thesis of William W. Marshall, *A Study of Selected Correlates to the Recruitment of Seminary Students as Foreign Missionaries* (Southern Baptist Theological Seminary, 1974).

7. H. Richard Niebuhr, et. al., *The Purpose of the Church and Its Ministry* (New York: Harper & Row, Publishers, 1956), pp. 63-66, especially p. 65.

8. See, for example, the section on "Qualifications for Missionary Service"

by Kane (pp. 73-84), which summarizes qualifications under the categories of physical, academic, vocational, psychological, and spiritual.

9. Baker J. Cauthen and Frank K. Means, *Advance to Bold Mission Thrust, 1845-1980* (Richmond: Foreign Mission Board, SBC, 1981), p. 80. Gradually earlier mission boards had begun sending out single women missionaries. See R. Pierce Beaver, *American Protestant Women in World Mission*, rev. ed. (Grand Rapids: William B. Eerdmans Publishing Company, 1968).

10. For another perspective on missionary orientation, see the article by James A. Scherer, "The Preparation of Missionaries in an Ecumenical Era," *Occasional Bulletin from the Missionary Research Library*, vol. 15, no. 2 (February 1964). (The bulletin is presently entitled *International Bulletin of Missionary Research.*)

11. A number of books deal at length with the entire broad theme of missionary life-style. Examples are T. Stanley Soltau, *Facing the Field* (Grand Rapids: Baker Book House, 1959) and J. Herbert Kane, *Life and Work on the Mission Field* (Grand Rapids: Baker Book House, 1980).

12. Leland Webb, *How in This World* (Nashville: Convention Press, 1974), has a chapter on identification that explores some of the questions and problems involved, pp. 49–65. See also Kane, *Understanding Christian Missions*, pp. 340–51.

13. For some ramifications of this question, see J. H. Bavinck, *An Introduction to the Science of Missions*, trans. David Hugh Freeman (Grand Rapids: Baker Book House, 1960), pp. 100–116, and Kane, *Understanding Christian Missions*, pp. 36–38.

14. Kosuke Koyama, "What Makes a Missionary?" in Gerald H. Anderson and Thomas F. Stransky, eds., *Mission Trends No. 1: Crucial Issues in Mission Today* (New York: Paulist Press and Grand Rapids: Wm. B. Eerdmans Publishing Co., 1974), pp. 117–32.

15. Soltau, p. 76.

16. E. Luther Copeland, *World Mission and World Survival* (Nashville: Broadman Press, 1985), p. 105. Note the larger context of this statement in sections on missionary attitudes and on paternalism. See also the chapter on "Leading Through Servanthood" in Ebbie C. Smith, *Balanced Church Growth* (Nashville: Broadman Press, 1984), pp. 165–76.

17. The most comprehensive exploration of this problem is that of Daniel Johnson Fleming, *Living as Comrades* (New York: Agricultural Missions Inc., 1950). More recently the Lausanne Movement and the World Evangelical Fellowship sponsored an international consultation on simple life-style, dealing with the life-style of all Christians and not just missionaries. Papers related to the consultation have been published, with Ronald J. Sider editor of *Lifestyle in the Eighties: An Evangelical Commitment to Simple Lifestyle* (Philadelphia: The Westminster Press, 1982). A brief booklet by Alan Nichols summarizing the findings of the consultation was published in 1981.

18. John V. Taylor, *Enough is Enough* (London: S.C.M. Press Limited, 1975). See also the book commissioned by the Mennonite Central Committee: Doris Janzen Longacre, *Living More with Less* (Scottdale, Penn.: Herald Press, 1980).

19. For more detailed treatment of this question see the report presented to the Foreign Mission Board in January 1981 by Don Kammerdiener, area director for Middle America and the Caribbean, and "Horizons: What is 'Safe'?" by Winston Crawley in the May 1981 issue of *The Commission*, vol. 44, no. 4:33.

# Part IV
# Objectives

For many years I have kept a clipping from that well-known "theological" work, the comic strip "Peanuts." It shows Linus during baseball season in the outfield, wearing his baseball cap, with a heavy growth of grass and weeds around him. Linus is talking to himself: "I don't mind playing right field," he says. "I don't mind standing out here in weeds over my head—really I don't. I mean if this is where I can do the team the most good, this is where I belong. . . . The only thing that bothers me is, I don't know if I'm facing the right way."

This strip speaks to the missionary situation. It reflects feelings that every missionary is likely to have at times. And it points up the importance of having the whole team facing the same direction. Common objectives make possible successful teamwork in missions.

A missions teams operates as a task force made up of persons with a wide variety of gifts and functions, but with their efforts coordinated toward a central objective. The task force concept is illustrated by the combined efforts of various military units in the South Pacific during World War II. The units involved—Army, Navy, Air Force, Marines, Seabees—were not told simply to go to the South Pacific and fight. Instead, they were given a specific task (to accomplish a landing, for example, on the island of Leyte), and each unit performed its part of that assigned task.

Similarly, if we send missionaries with instructions simply to go and do mission work, we have not been clear enough to enable them to operate as a task force. They need to have a common working objective that they all understand, toward which each individual ability, each specialty, and each unit of the work can contribute.

Southern Baptist foreign missions is not intended to be a hodgepodge of unrelated individual activities nor "parallelism" in the use of traditional missionary approaches.[1] We conceive our foreign missions efforts rather as a correlated program with a clearly defined objective and a well–focused central thrust.

Clarification of our terminology may be helpful. Specialists in planning and management use several terms, sometimes in different ways. Terms that may be used to indicate desired results include *purpose, aim, end, intention, objective,* and *goal.* The widely adopted approach of *management by objectives* has made that term especially common.

The Foreign Mission Board follows planning terminology accepted by mutual agreement in the Southern Baptist Inter-Agency Council and recorded in the planning glossary of the Southern Baptist Convention. That terminology uses *purpose* for the most general long-range and continuing direction of an organization. *Objective* is the term for intermediate or implementing statements of guiding intentions. *Goals* are specific, dated, and measurable. As further implementation, goals are made operative through *action plans.*

A chasm between theory and practice is a constant danger. A mission undertaking may be grounded in the soundest theology of mission, with well-developed and appropriate objectives, but with no real connection between the theory and what is actually done—or even with little done except the planning process.[2]

In Southern Baptist foreign missions, specific objectives appropriate to each local situation are developed on the fields, but with the expectation that all will be related to and supportive of the general objectives of the Foreign Mission Board—to keep the whole team facing in the same direction.

### Notes

1. For discussion of the concept of parallelism, see Donald McGavran, *How Churches Grow* (London: World Dominion Press, 1959), pp. 70-76.

2. T. Watson Street, *On the Growing Edge of the Church* (Richmond, Virginia: John Knox Press, 1965), pp. 39–52, has an interesting chapter on the danger of substituting theologizing and academic discussion for actual missions.

# 8
# What Are We Trying to Do?

Most Southern Baptist church members or leaders, if asked what we are trying to do in overseas missions, would probably answer along this line: We are trying to win people to Christ. Perhaps some other phrase with a similar meaning would be used, such as to share the gospel. This would be a good answer and a true answer, though usually not stated broadly enough.

### General Purpose

Our desire is not just to win some people to Christ, but rather to win the entire world to Christ. We are taught to pray for a whole world under God's rule: "Thy kingdom come. Thy will be done in earth, as it is in heaven" (Matt. 6:10).

This is what we are trying to do because we believe it is what God is doing. He is building His kingdom. Though He works in the forces of history, the heart of His purpose is bringing people into His kingdom through personal faith in Jesus Christ. Therefore, the crowning purpose of missions is the rule of God, through Christ, in the hearts and lives of all people.

This general long-range purpose can be stated in various ways. It is sometimes simply called world evangelization. The overarching purpose statement for Bold Mission Thrust refers to sharing the gospel with every person in the world. The formal stated purpose of the Southern Baptist Convention is "to bring men to God through Jesus Christ." The Foreign Mission Board program statement reflects that purpose in the Board's general objective: "To do everything possible to bring all men in other lands around the world to a saving knowledge of Jesus Christ as rapidly as possible, and to involve them in Christian growth and service as members of indigenous churches." Stated most simply and most comprehensively, the ultimate general purpose of foreign missions is the kingdom of God.[1]

## Working Objective

The most rapid and most effective realization of the long-range general purpose of missions will not be possible solely on the basis of resources moving from our own churches and denomination out to other lands. Rather, the greatest results will be achieved by developing Christian life and cultivating church resources in the mission lands themselves. Therefore, we define our specific central working objective as planting, multiplying, and strengthening churches in each land where we work. Such churches are the normal fruit of gospel witness and evangelism.

The general long-range purpose of world evangelization, or the kingdom of God, is not focused sharply enough to be a guiding objective in determining missions strategy. Our more sharply focused guiding objective is not just evangelism, but something more complete, of which evangelism is an essential and basic part but not the whole. Foreign Mission Board President Keith Parks frequently states this objective as "evangelism which results in churches." We are convinced that thorough biblical evangelism includes the developing of churches and that the church is the pivotal agency in God's plan for his world mission.[2]

Other complementary or supportive objectives are included in Southern Baptist foreign missions, but all operate in relation to the central objective with its focus on churches.[3]

According to the Foreign Mission Board philosophy statement, "New Testament churches, interdependent and autonomous under the Lordship of Christ, are to be established and multiplied as the basic units for Christian nurture and kingdom extension." That means not simply sharing the gospel, but also gathering those who respond into New Testament fellowships.

Many persons think of "church" in institutional and traditional ways. Our objective does not mean churches with a particular kind of building and organization and program, such as we are traditionally accustomed to, but rather the vital spiritual fellowships which are described in the New Testament.

A word of caution is important here. The place of human objectives and human efforts in the planting of churches is only instrumental (as is true of the church's role in relation to the kingdom). Furthermore, Southern Baptist missionaries share in the process alongside their fellow Christians of other lands. Foreign Mission Board President Keith Parks has expressed it well.

> It is important for all of us to understand that we do not speak of church planting in any possessive sense of the word. To speak of church planting in another country is not to suggest that a missionary, however gifted or committed, is alone the instrument to bring to life a new church rooted in the local soil. Yet the figure of speech communicates, for God does call missionaries to specific tasks. And in doing that task, the missionary often functions alongside another people in such servant ways that by God's grace, another *ekklesia*— another community in that strange, miraculous, marvelous institution we call church—is born.[4]

The central thrust of Southern Baptist foreign missions can perhaps be clarified by contrast with what seem to be the main objectives of some other missions organizations.

There are many mission groups, including a large number of nondenominational ones, that do not invest much effort in planting churches. They major more on widespread evangelism—an approach which is sometimes called "seed-sowing." That is, they try to bring at least some contact with the gospel to as many people as possible. They go from house to house, passing out tracts, giving a word of witness. They preach in the village marketplace, then move on to the next village to preach in the marketplace there. They may try to get Christian literature into every home in a city, or they may broadcast the gospel by radio and television. These are all forms of seed-sowing. In some cases they do only slight cultivation to follow up where the seed has been sown, and in many cases they make little or no direct effort to plant churches.

We would not disparage either those missionaries or their work. Many who serve with such mission organizations have an unusual dedication to the Lord and a genuinely sacrificial ministry. Furthermore, if seed-sowing is their special calling from the Lord, it is appropriate for them to follow that calling. But it is appropriate also for us to recognize that approach as different from what Southern Baptists for generations have considered central in our missions strategy—not that we do no seed-sowing, but that we follow the seed-sowing with diligent cultivation and with formation of churches. That is what we do in this country, and it is what we do overseas.

There are other missions agencies, many of them the main denominational mission boards, that major on various kinds of humanitarian service. They often have strong institutional ministries: schools, hospitals, agricultural projects, social centers. In many cases, there is apparently only secondary or perhaps even minimal attention to the planting of strong churches alongside those ministries.

Again, we would not disparage either those missionaries or their work. They display the love of Christ and exhibit deep personal compassion toward human need. Their ministries render valuable service and at the same time help create a climate in which Christianity is respected and the gospel gets a better hearing. Furthermore, if that is their special calling from the Lord, it is entirely appropriate for them. But again it is different from what we Southern Baptists have done through the generations, both in this country and abroad—not that we engage in no service ministries, but that in and through such ministries we give ample attention to evangelism and the planting of churches.

We have several reasons for giving churches a central place. One is our understanding of the nature and significance of the church (as seen, for example, in Eph. 3). We find this emphasis also in New Testament missions. Paul gave attention to "strengthening the churches" (Acts 15:41, RSV), and Luke felt it important to report on the welfare and strength of the churches (Acts 9:31; 16:5). Paul kept planting additional churches in new places, and he wrote repeatedly to those churches to encourage and further strengthen them. Thus we are convinced that our focus on churches is biblical.

There are sound practical reasons also for emphasizing churches. One is that the work of the missionary may be interrupted and is at most only temporary. If the main thrust of an agency is seed-sowing, when the missionaries for some reason have to leave, that seed-sowing ends. Or if the main thrust is humanitarian service, when the missionaries have to leave, those ministries are likely to end or to become government services without any continuing Christian witness. But if the main thrust has developed churches, the churches are still there after the missionary leaves. Those churches will continue sowing the gospel seed and continue a Christian ministry of helpfulness and love (though perhaps in less institutionalized form). Churches are the great hope for the future of the work.

Furthermore, missionaries coming from another land can never fully evangelize any country. At best, missionaries remain foreigners, no matter how well they may adjust to the local culture. But more significantly, there simply are not, and will not be, enough missionaries to reach everyone with the gospel. (Southern Baptist missionaries number less than one per halfmillion people in the countries where we work.) The aim is for missionary forces to be used of God to bring into existence local forces and local resources that will go far beyond what missionaries themselves might do. Evangelist Dwight L. Moody has been quoted as saying, "It is better to put 10 men to work than to do the work of 10 men."

What is needed, and is possible only through planting churches, is a chain reaction in which churches keep starting other churches so rapidly that the entire population can be reached with the gospel.

Southern Baptist foreign missions includes a wide range of relationships and activities, varying greatly from country to country. The Southern Baptist Convention program statement for the Foreign Mission Board outlines several functional programs, but on the mission fields they all cooperate to plant, multiply, and strengthen churches.[5] Witness and ministry are priority elements in Southern Baptist missions, but these are seen as having their greatest value when they are appropriately related to planting, multiplying, and strengthening churches.[6]

To be sure, work in different countries is at differing stages of development, and the various elements in the work contribute in different ways; but in each land there is the same central objective. Methods and approaches most appropriate to the accomplishing of the objective in that particular setting are brought into play. We do not think of ourselves as having an evangelistic program heading in one direction, a medical program heading in another, and an educational program with a third direction. Instead, every part of the work fits into a unified program, all focused on concern for churches.

### The Role of the Missionary

What is the missionary role in all of this? Actually, every missionary has *multiple roles*. There are some things that the missionary should be and do simply as a Christian. These include witness to the gospel and expression of Christian love in service to others. The missionary also has a role as a member of a church on the mission field.

In addition, each missionary has special gifts, training, and experience that open doors of opportunity for witness and ministry.

Each missionary has a formal assignment. Usually that assignment is an expression of the specialty for which the missionary has prepared—though sometimes the mission team will need the help of a missionary in an assignment outside his or her specialty. Fulfillment of the assigned task is an important part of the role of every missionary.

Further, each missionary functions as part of the mission, sharing in its strategy planning and adapting to that strategy. Both in personal witness and ministry and in the carrying out of an assigned task, the missionary relates what is done to the central mission objective of church planting and church development.

There are several *types of missionary assignments*, with the various types combining and complementing each other to produce a coordinated thrust. To recognize practical differences in function does not imply belittling any function. All need each other. The analogy of the parts of the body in 1 Corinthians 12 is relevant.

Many missionaries have a specific assignment for direct church development work. A person with that assignment may be called a church planter, a field evangelist, a direct evangelist, a church development counsultant, or some other descriptive term. The work is that of planting and developing churches. Obviously, that function is central for every mission field.

An essential function, if there are to be strong churches and strong denominational life, is leadership training. This involves varied programs to help prepare pastors and other leaders for the churches. In some form or other, such training must be available for every mission field.

Another vital function provides tools the churches need for development. This is the work of literature production (plus now other kinds of media resources). This function often includes development of a religious education curriculum and promotion of the spiritual life of the churches. To become strong and effective, churches need tools with which to work. They need gospel tracts, Bible study materials, doctrine study books, and many other helps.

Besides these essential functions, there are several quite valuable allies of the central mission thrust. They include programs of general education (other than church leadership training), health care ministries, and many other kinds of benevolent or social services. These may not all be present in every field, but where possible they can be sources of much help and strength. The ministries through the home and in the church rendered by many missionary wives (as described in the preceding chapter) are exceptionally valuable.

Another category of missionary assignments encompasses the many special approaches, emphases, and techniques used in missions—such as student ministries, women's work, literacy programs, music, and so forth.

Other missionaries serve in supportive roles. Common examples are mission business manager, secretary, teachers or dormitory parents for missionary children, and the field associates to area directors (who have a role combining pastoral and administrative).

Baseball offers an interesting analogy of the way a mission team functions. A baseball team is composed of players with different specialties based on their individual gifts. Each plays his own position. Together they constitute a team. However, each player comes up to bat, and each seeks to improve his batting as well as skill in his specialty. But the purpose of the team is not to have sharp pitching or good fielding or excellent individual play at any position; nor is the purpose to have a high composite batting average. The purpose of the baseball team is to win games. Both at bat and in the field, players may be asked to attempt things at which they are not so highly skilled in an effort to help the team win the game.

Similarly, missionaries are specialists, each carrying out his own function. Together they make up a team. The one thing expected of every missionary is to share in personal witness and direct evangelism. (We do not classify missionaries by referring to some as evangelistic missionaries, whereas others are not.) Every missionary participates in evangelism, just as every baseball player comes up to bat (this analogy includes no "designed hitter" rule). But the purpose of the mission is not just evangelism; nor is it any other specialized mission function. The purpose of the mission is to develop churches. There may be times when a missionary who would like to be working in some particular specialty, or would love to be involved entirely in direct personal evangelism, has to fill another assignment or fit into some other pressing need in order to strengthen the whole team and enable it to do better at developing churches.

Even if a missionary's assignment continues the same for many years, the role is still a *changing* one. The world changes, and its changes affect Christian missions. New ways are required by new days.

The world as a whole has become much more urban, more highly developed. There are better facilities both for missionary life and for mission work. Approaches used in missions can be much more varied because of increased resources. In the meantime, sharpened nationalism and both local and widespread conflicts create a challenging setting for modern mission.

Furthermore, the task of the individual missionary changes with the progress of his own work. A classic description of one expectation of the missionary is to "work himself out of a job." As local people assume responsibility for functions he has had, he assumes other functions. Readiness to accept change is a primary requirement for missionary service.[7]

The missionary role has always been a changing one. Still, in a sense, "the more it changes, the more it is the same." In other words, whether it actually changes may depend upon what we mean by "role." If we refer to the details of missionary ministries and methods, radical change is obvious. If we refer to missionary purpose and principle, we may find that the essential role is still the same—doing whatever is most needed and most effective to share the Chistian good news, minister to human need in Christian love, and plant and nurture Christian fellowships.

One way of stating the essence of the missionary function is to describe it as a *generative* role. This has a two-fold reference: to the generating of local forces and local resources on the mission field, and to continuing behind–the–scenes provision of help and strength for the work of the churches (as a generator provides power which electric motors use in their work). Some have used the term *catalytic* to express something of the same idea. In chemistry, a catalyst by its presence facilitates a chemical process. *Generative*, however, is a more active word and expresses continuing participation in what is happening.

Some old illustrations of the missionary role have compared it to a stake to which a plant is attached when it is young and weak, or to the scaffolding used when a building is being constructed. Both illustrations imply temporariness—but missionaries can continue to be helpful, even after strong churches with strong leaders have developed.

Perhaps a more apt illustration is fertilizer, or irrigation, which may be unseen but still gives added strength. This is the essential idea in the concept of the generative role of the missionary: After helping bring churches into being, the missionary continues to use his spiritual gifts in ways that bring added spiritual strength to the churches and their outreach with the gospel. In the whole process, the missionary is secondary and instrumental; Christ and His church are central.

### Notes

1. See the extended treatment of this purpose in chapter 3. Note also Johannes Verkuyl, *Contemporary Missiology* (Grand Rapids: William B. Eerdmans Publishing Company, 1978), pp. 197-98, and Lesslie Newbigin, *Sign of the Kingdom* (Grand Rapids: William B. Eerdmans Publishing Company, 1980).

2. See the earlier sections on the gospel and the church in chapter 3 in relation to our understanding of our mission purpose.

3. For broader academic considerations of various objectives that are common in world missions, see Verkyul, chapter 7, "The Goal and Purpose of Mission," pp. 176-204; and Orlando E. Costas, *The Integrity of Mission* (New York: Harper & Row, Publishers, 1979).

4. Report to the Foreign Mission Board, October 15, 1980.

5. The Foreign Mission Board program statement has been interpreted in chapter 5.

6. The holistic approach to witness and ministry will be explored more fully in chapter 13.

7. Further attention will be given to the relationship between the missionary and the maturing of mission work in chapter 9.

# 9
# What Kind of Churches?

"What if those churches get out of our hands?" The question is a natural one. I had been talking about the planting of churches in another land with a different cultural setting. The question which was raised in the discussion period reflects a very common concern.

Natural and common as it may be, it is still the wrong question. Churches do not belong in human hands; they belong in the Lord's hands.

As Baptists, we believe that every church is responsible directly to the Lord Jesus. The allegiance of Baptist churches overseas is not to the missionary nor to Southern Baptists, but to the Lord.[1] We should not think of overseas Baptist churches as extensions of our Southern Baptist denomination. They are not simply reproductions of church life here in America, including the various elements of practice and method that have grown out of American culture. They are Nigerian Baptist or Brazilian Baptist or Japanese Baptist churches, with elements of practice and method suited to their own cultures.

Baptist churches overseas unite in their own Baptist conventions (sometimes called unions), which have a friendly fraternal relationship with the Southern Baptist Convention—but without either convention having the slightest authority over the other.

In an era when nationalistic and anti-colonial feeling runs high, it is especially important for us to avoid anything that might seem to imply that Baptist churches overseas are an appendage to our own Convention here in America. (This means that they are not called Southern Baptist churches, except in a few rare cases where they have chosen that terminology themselves.)

Overseas churches and the conventions in which they cooperate gradually become stronger and more mature. As they do so, they grow their own leadership; they pay their own expenses; they assume responsibility for evangelistic outreach and for the planting of more churches; they develop forms of worship and of church life that fit the thinking and customs of their own countries. As we see these things happening, we rejoice that our missionary efforts are achieving their desired purpose.

Many persons, without knowing it, have a colonial concept of what we do in missions. They think that we are creating outposts or branches of our own churches and our own Convention— something that we brought into being, that we therefore are in charge of and operating, and that looks to us as the center of its allegiance.

The opposite principle from the colonial, and the one that fits Baptist beliefs, is the indigenous principle. Instead of thinking in terms of "Southern Baptist churches," we seek to plant New Testament churches. This phrase is commonly used among Southern Baptists to express our intention of developing churches that embody the spiritual qualities of the New Testament church.[2]

In addition to its reference to "New Testament churches, interdependent and autonomous under the lordship of Christ," the formal philosophy statement adopted by the Foreign Mission Board in 1978 speaks of "indigenous church strength as a guiding objective." This commitment was reaffirmed in the strategy statement adopted by the Foreign Mission Board staff in 1982: "Indigenous church strength continues as the central objective to give unity to planning."

### Indigeneity

Indigeneity is essential to the central Southern Baptist foreign missions objective: not simply planting, multiplying, and strengthening churches, but also a certain kind of churches—indigenous churches.

*Indigenous* is a word initially related to plant life. Its basic meaning is "native." (For example, coffee is indigenous to Arabia.) But the meaning of the word has expanded to include "being produced, growing, or living naturally in a particular region or environment."[3] Put most simply, it means "homegrown." (For example, coffee is now indigenous to Brazil.) Therefore, indigenous churches, using the broader sense of the term, are churches growing naturally and flourishing in a particular environment.

If churches are indigenous, they will be at home in their own nations, rooted firmly in their own soil—not hothouse plants imported from another land.[4]

The ideal of indigeneity has been generally recognized by missions leaders for decades. However, it did not develop early in Protestant missions history. R. Pierce Beaver has traced the process, beginning from the 17th-century Puritan missions to the American Indians and the work of chaplains of the Dutch East Indies Company in the Orient. He commented that "both missions paternalistically imposed European forms."[5]

Beaver noted the unconscious colonial mentality permeating early missions, the emphasis on "civilization," and the later concept of mother and daughter churches as hindrances to indigeneity. He summed up his impression: "It is astounding that it should have taken Protestant missionaries three hundred years to accept the indigenous church ideal."[6] By the time of the international missionary conferences at Jerusalem in 1928 and at Madras in 1938, the indigenous principle was well recognized—though perhaps still not followed very consistently.

### The Three-Self Formula

Earlier, before the term *indigenous* came into general use, concern for indigeneity was generally expressed through a well-known formula developed by Rufus Anderson and Henry Venn about 125 years ago. Anderson was secretary of the American Board of Commissioners for Foreign Missions and Venn was secretary of the Church Missionary Society—likely the strongest missionary agencies at that time in America and England.

> The two missionary statesmen in interaction defined the goal of missions as the planting and fostering of churches which would be self-governing, self-supporting, and self-propagating. This formula was speedily adopted by most boards and societies, and it eventually provided the foundation for the theory of the indigenous church.[7]

For about a century, the three-self terminology was recognized and used widely. It became the basis for the Protestant religious organization set up in China 35 years ago, when the communist government came to power. That organization, the Three-Self Movement, is still the officially recognized link between the government and the Protestant church.

### Other Analyses of Indigeneity

Though widely used in missions circles and not much debated for many years, the traditional three-self statement was never entirely satisfactory. It failed to address a major, fundamental area of concern: the relationship of church life to local culture. Discussions of indigeneity at Jerusalem and Madras gave special attention to that concern. To remedy that shortcoming, H. Cornell Goerner (then missions professor at The Southern Baptist Theological Seminary) as early as 40 years ago had added a fourth item, self-expressing, to the formula. However, that addition never became widely known outside the Southern Baptist academic setting.

In the meantime, there was growing dissatisfaction with the three-self rubric, and a number of writers on missions themes began suggesting other ways of describing the indigeneity that is appropriate for churches resulting from missions efforts.

Much of the difficulty with the traditional expression comes from its repetition of the term *self*. It seems to view churches primarily from an inward-looking perspective, when churches should be essentially upward and outward looking. Beaver pointed out the advantage of the indigenous church definition worked out at Madras as having "further eliminated any wrong ideas of introverted 'selfhood' and linked indigenization with apostolate."[8] In reaction against a colonial system, the self-sufficiency implied by repeated use of the term *self* was important, but other more outward-looking interpretations of indigenous church strength are now appropriate.

Many newer treatments of the subject have avoided all reference to *self*. But D. T. Niles, a prominent Asian theologian and missiologist, broadened the concern to examine the authentic Christian "selfhood of a church."[9] Niles interpreted the nature of a church as it is defined "by its worshipping life, by its call to mission, and by its task of secular engagement" plus "what it means for a church to be itself in relation to other churches."[10]

E. Luther Copeland, then professor of missions at Southeastern Baptist Theological Seminary, described the concept of "authentic Christian selfhood" of a church as going "beyond what is normally connoted by indigenization." He explained:

> A church has true selfhood only as it is responsibly related in faithful obedience to the Lord, who is the sovereign source of its life; in cooperation and fellowship with the universal church, whose reality it manifests in its own locality and whose universal mission it shares; and in relevant witness and service to persons in the environing culture.[11]

Apart from the apparent introversion of the traditional formula, it has had other problems, as Pierce Beaver pointed out.

> The national leadership of the young churches tended to identify the indigenous church with the self-governing church and to contend for independence, freedom from hidden control, and parity with the older churches. Missionaries and mission board executives, on the other hand, because of ever-increasing costs, were prone to equate the indigenous church with the self-supporting one, and they tried to foster that ideal. The generally imposed pattern worked against success. . . .
>
> There was far less readiness to identify the indigenous church as the self-propagating church. . . .[12]

The International Missionary Council at its meeting at Willingen, Germany, in 1948 took an entirely new approach to the matter. It described the desired indigenous results of missions in terms of: (1) relatedness to the environing culture; (2) adequately trained ministry adapted to local requirements; (3) inner spiritual life resulting in responsibility for Christian nurture and witness; and (4) membership in the church universal.[13] Though both form and terminology are entirely different, this statement still deals with the same concerns as the traditional formula, but seeks to avoid introversion and any implication of independent self-sufficiency.

Luther Copeland used a brief summary statement defining indigeneity as "the meaning and nature of the universal gospel in vital expression in relation to the environing culture."[14]

More recently, C. Peter Wagner dealt with the matter at length and proposed three signs of a mature church: (1) a church that can take care of itself; (2) a church that is a church for others; and (3) a church that is relevant to the cultural situation.[15]

Obviously, there are many possible ways to describe the meaning of indigeneity, and all of them can have value to mission leaders and church leaders as they seek indigenous church strength.

### Measurement of Progress

The traditional statement, expanded by the adding of self-expressing, still has practical value. The items should not be treated as goals in themselves, but they can be helpful measures of progress toward indigeneity. When they are so used, the larger meaning of *indigenous,* with its predominantly upward and outward reference, will need to be kept in view. Furthermore, the terms themselves will need careful interpretation.

*Self-propagation* refers to churches that will continue to propagate the gospel and to reproduce themselves by starting more churches, even apart from any concern or effort of missionaries who work alongside them. As long as churches still depend upon the enthusiasm of the missionary for their evangelistic zeal, they are still weak. The extent to which they reach out with the gospel and start new churches is a measure of their progress.

*Self-government* is a term which does not exactly fit Baptist ecclesiology (Anderson and Venn were not Baptists). We would say that a church is by nature self-governing, under Christ, from the time it comes into being. What this principle actually means is that churches are not dependent upon foreigners for leadership, but they have their own strong, capable, mature, well-trained leaders. Until churches have such leadership, they are still to that extent weak and dependent. The emerging of strong local leadership is a measure of progress.

*Self-support* means that financing for the churches and their programs comes from local sources, not from America (not even to any significant degree from the tithes of American missionaries). As long as churches need continuing dollar transfusions in order to keep going, they are in very frail condition. The extent to which the stewardship and dedication of local people provides financially for the work of the churches is a measure of progress.

*Self-expression* means forms of church life and organization and ways of doing things that suit the local culture. Many times I have suggested to new missionaries that I hope they will not immediately feel at home in the churches of the land to which they go. If they do feel at home immediately, it is probably a sign that the churches are much too American in their ways and that local people who visit them will not feel at home. If everything about church life seems foreign to the local culture, the churches are not yet really rooted in local soil. The extent to which church life expresses itself in local cultural forms is a measure of progress.

What has been said of churches needs to apply also to the developing corporate life of Baptist denominations—their associations, their conventions, their agencies and institutions. The traditional measures are relevant and helpful, and the broader and deeper concern for true indigeneity and "authentic selfhood" is vital. The pertinent question is "How much of church life is real?" If missionaries and missionary resources disappeared tomorrow, how much vitality would remain? Our objective is indigenous church strength—churches that are both real and vital.

### Contextualization

A relatively new term, *contextualization*, began to be used widely in relation to missions in 1972. The directors of the Theological Education Fund in the fund's report for that year, "Ministry and Context,"proposed the word as a replacement for *indigenization*.[16] Arthur Glasser indicated that the term itself had been coined in the late 1950s, though it did not come into common use until the 1970s.[17]

The emphasis on contextualization as a substitute for indigenization has departed entirely from the traditional three-self emphasis. Relatively little attention is given to self-propagation, self-government, or self-support, except as effective adaptation to the context impinges on those concerns. Thus the new emphasis seems to make primary the concern for self-expression— that is, the relating of gospel and church to local culture.

Furthermore, those who have promoted the use of the new term seek to focus attention especially on "contemporary social, economic and political issues."[18] In that connection, Bruce Nicholls quoted what he described as a vivid illustration of this difference in a comment by Al Krass. "Indigenizing concerns traditional culture, the kind of thing you read about in *National Geographic*. Contextualizing, on the other hand, concerns more the kind of thing you read about in *Time*. It relates to the current history of the world's culture."[19]

The central question in contextualization is the relationship of the Christian faith to culture. The dangers are foreignness or rigidity on one side and syncretism on the other. Appropriate interpretation of the gospel and adaptation of the forms of the church in terms of the local culture are essential, while maintaining at the same time the genuine essence of both gospel and church.[20]

Though Southern Baptists have not spoken much of *contextualization* (in part because it has sometimes included extreme elements), concern for an appropriate relation with local culture, which is the heart of contextualization, has been receiving growing attention and emphasis.

Some historic questions of contextualization help clarify the significance of this concern. Probably the most famous example in missions history is the "Rites Controversy" in Roman Catholic missions in China. The Pope, in Rome at a distance of thousands of miles and with only secondhand acquaintance with China, made a decision about the meaning of ancestral rites in Chinese culture, which dictated the position taken by the Roman Catholic Church in China and resulted in a major setback for Roman Catholic missions there.

Another prominent example is the question of polygamy in African society, which has been probably the major continuing problem in church life in Africa and has been a major factor in the splitting of many African denominations and the forming of what are called African indigenous churches (that is, those without connections with a Western mission organization).[21]

Current prominent examples of concern for contexualization are efforts to develop patterns of church life to fit cultures that are intimately related to other major religions. For example, there has been a movement developing messianic synagogues, which retain many elements of Jewish culture.[22] A similar approach to persons of Muslim background was proposed by Phil Parshall in *New Paths in Muslim Evangelism*.[23] As would be expected, these approaches have been controversial.[24] Furthermore, such approaches to evangelism and church life in Jewish and Muslim cultural settings have been seen as a special threat and therefore both resented and resisted by leaders of those religions.

Some approaches to contextualizing would be judged by most missionaries and missions leaders as extreme. For example, Parshall suggested the possibility of some other kind of initiation ceremony as a substitute for baptism, to avoid Muslim misunderstandings of the ceremony.[25] Later, in response to a question about the proposal, Parshall replied:

> I struggled with this and then backed off. I would be interested in seeing someone experiment with a kind of functional substitute, but it's not worth pushing because of the controversy. . . . Water baptism is biblical, universal and historical. The problem is that Muslims see this as the time when you

bail out of society, and that's exactly what we don't want them
to think. That's why I really struggled with this.[26]

Concern for contextualization in Christian missions has many
ramifications. Several can be mentioned, but without space for
detailed exploration. The entire Liberation Theology movement,
which originated among Roman Catholic leaders in Latin America, is an expression of contextualized theology.[27] The "base
ecclesial community" movement among Roman Catholics in
Brazil, beginning from 1960, has sought to relate church life to
the daily problems (the context) of poor communities.[28]

Liberation theology and the base ecclesial communities reflect
a situation in which nominal Christians are a substantial majority of the population. In much of Africa and in most of Asia,
Christians are a small minority group. In such settings, there is a
natural tendency to avoid confrontation with society as a whole.
To counteract criticism for being adherents of a "foreign religion," Christians often are especially supportive of national
viewpoints and policies. A similar tendency is seen among
Christians in communist countries. This too is a form of contextualization—though sometimes not recognized or accepted as
such by either liberal or conservative religious groups in the
United States. (Liberal groups seem to feel such conduct is
appropriate for Christians in communist countries, and probably also under Muslim governments, but not under right-wing
repressive governments. Very conservative groups question the
Christian faith of those who do not openly confront communist
governments, while making allowances for Christians who are
cooperative or keep a low profile in other authoritarian settings.)

Issues of contextualization obviously are quite complex.
Whether approached in the more aggressive way implied by
current terminology and current emphases, or under the earlier
more general models of indigeneity and self-expression, the
questions do not lend themselves to solution at a mission board
headquarters or in the churches which send out missionaries.
(Such an attempt would simply repeat the error of the pope in
the historic Rites Controversy.)

In fact, it would be arrogant to assume from outside a culture enough knowledge to decide the appropriate Christian relationship to elements of that culture. Even the missionary who has spent years adapting to a culture still cannot take the lead in developing self-expressing forms of church life. He helps self-expression best by trying to stay out of the way. Local Christians, guided by the Scriptures and the Holy Spirit, need to find the best ways of expressing the gospel in their own thought patterns and the forms of church life that will be most suitable within their own culture.[29]

## New Testament Churches

As indicated early in this chapter, the objective of indigenous church strength means developing New Testament churches. We want those churches to be deeply rooted in the local soil, to grow vigorously in their local setting. That means cultural adaptation (self-expression or contextualization). But it must also mean fidelity to the essential nature of the gospel and the church. Luther Copeland's statement summing up indigeneity as "the universal gospel in vital expression in relation to the environing culture" combines appropriately the essential (universal, unchanging) and the cultural (variable) elements in the life of New Testament churches.[30]

The problems lie in knowing how to identify which elements in church life are essential and which are variable, so as to suit the variable elements to a particular culture. When we examine the actual way in which churches are described in the New Testament and compare with the churches with which we are familiar today (whether in our homeland or on foreign mission fields), we find many dissimilarities. We have inherited traditional concepts of church that include cultural elements along with New Testament essentials, and it is not always easy to separate them.

### Cultural Overhang

When we have gone abroad as missionaries, we have naturally reproduced the pattern of church life with which we have been accustomed. That pattern has generally included a piece of land and a church building, a pastor with formal Bible school or seminary training, and details of worship, organization, and programs similar to those in Southern Baptist churches. However, when we examine the Scriptures, we do not find those elements present in New Testament churches.

Furthermore, reproduction overseas of our traditional patterns has been a hindrance in many ways—foreignness, expensiveness, and limitation on the church growth that might otherwise be possible. This problem has been named "cultural overhang."[31] It is also frequently called the Saul-David problem, on the basis of Saul's well-intended attempt to clothe David in his armor for the fight with Goliath (1 Sam. 17:38-40). The armor was unnatural for David. He used instead the sling that was natural to him, for it was part of his personal culture already.

Unfortunately, Christian tradition has clothed churches in other lands in European armor instead of letting those churches use whatever spiritual methods are appropriate to their own culture and their own experience. Churches have been weighted down with Saul's armor when circumstances have called for freedom of movement. Churches in other lands need to discover appropriate weapons for their own spiritual battles within their own cultural settings, instead of continuing to wear "Saul's armor."

Freedom to adapt New Testament principles of church life to local cultures is hard to achieve. Missionaries have preconceived notions brought from America. But local people also have preconceived notions about church, based on generations and in some cases centuries of church tradition. Even in countries where Southern Baptists are just beginning to work, there is almost always a tradition from other churches already working there.

Different cultural settings and new circumstances always call for reexamination of New Testament principles to find new and suitable applications.[32]

### Major Concerns

The objective of developing New Testament churches includes concern for the nature of the church, the forms or structures of the church, and the leadership and ministries of the church.

In nature, the New Testament church is a combination, and indeed a rhythm, of "come" and "go." Just as we breathe in and breathe out, so the church comes together to worship the Lord and goes out into the world in His name. This means the "gathered church" and the "scattered church." Our Western patterns have tended to emphasize "coming to church" and have identified the church with the building. But the church is just as much church when it is scattered doing God's work and bearing witness for God in the world as when it gathers for worship.[33]

The Bible really does not seek to prescribe specifically and clearly the forms or structures of church life. The New Testament says nothing about church buildings. Little is said about organization, and even that little seems to show patterns which vary at different times and places. Worship forms are not detailed. Ways of arriving at decisions seem to be those that were common in the cultural setting.

Leadership in the New Testament church was not based on position, status, or authority. The distinction between clergy and laity is not biblical but traditional. Ministry is service, and all the saints are called to "the work of ministry" (Eph. 4:12, RSV). The reason for having leaders is functional: They are persons to whom God has given special gifts that can be used to help equip all the saints for their work of ministry.

Apparently churches that were predominantly Jewish were organized and functioned more according to the pattern of the synagogue, whereas churches that were predominantly Gentile were organized and functioned according to prevalent customs in the Greek culture. This seems to indicate that the New Testament establishes no firm pattern of church forms or structures— that there can be officers called by various names in various settings, and that there was more flexibility in the New Testament church than our traditions may have assumed.

A stimulating suggestion in an early issue of *Missiology* provided a term that has been used frequently in more recent missiological writing. The term is based on the process of Bible translation. Literal word-for-word translations often fail to communicate meaning clearly. For effective translation, the Bible societies seek a "dynamic equivalence" translation. That is, the translator seeks first to understand the meaning of a statement in the original language, and then in the other language uses words and phrases that dynamically, livingly, effectively communicate an equivalent meaning. The words used may not be similar, but it is good translation if it communicates the essential idea clearly. The *Missiology* article suggested "dynamic equivalence churches"—churches expressing in forms suited to the cultural setting the dynamic principles that are at the heart of Christian experience and the nature of the church.[34]

### Typical Problems

There are two main problem areas in the Western cultural overhang that has tended to reproduce European or American-style churches in other parts of the world. The problems relate to properties and leadership.

The property concern may not be too serious in rural or village areas. However, it becomes acute in the major cities of our highly urbanized world.[35] Some modern counterpart of the "house churches" that were mentioned so frequently in the New Testament, or a combination of such multiple congregations with a central large meeting place for worship and celebration, seems necessary if the masses of today's urban centers are to be evangelized. The pattern of separate churches, each with its own church building and educational space, if maintained as the sole or even the primary acceptable pattern, will simply concede in advance that only a tiny portion of the population can be brought into churches.

(The problem of property can become even more serious when expensive institutions become the administrative and financial responsibility of relatively small and relatively poor churches and conventions—a question to be examined further in chapter 14.)

The expectation of a seminary-trained full-time pastor for each congregation and the traditions that give the pastor's role special status have combined to limit growth and multiplication of churches in many missions areas. Our belief in the value of full-time well-trained pastors is entirely understandable, since that ideal has been achieved only slowly and with difficulty in our own denomination. But Southern Baptists would never have become very numerous, nor would we have expanded to the entire nation, if we had demanded that ideal pattern. On the contrary, much of our growth both in earlier days and up to now has taken place through part-time or bivocational leadership.

Fortunately, in many places overseas, the vision of new work with lay leadership and of theological education by extension is beginning to break down the traditional pattern and allow the multiplying of churches more reflective of the New Testament model. (More attention will be given to church leadership in chapter 14.)

The churches sought by our objective are New Testament churches which express all the essential principles of the church as seen in the New Testament, but continue to adapt to the realities of culture.[36]

## Homogeneous Unit Principle

At the beginning of Southern Baptist mission work in the Philippines, we worked with the Chinese minority (because the work was started by displaced China missionaries). Later we were ready to expand our work to include the majority Filipino population also. At that point an argument arose as to how to proceed. Some missionaries, having worked previously in Hawaii where churches were multiethnic, felt that Filipinos and Chinese should be evangelized together and brought into churches together. Others, on the basis of language and cultural differences, urged separate approaches to the two groups. At that time (about 1950) the term *homogeneous unit principle* did not exist, but that is the issue that we were dealing with.

The term was developed by Donald McGavran as part of church growth theory (which will be considered at length in chapter 12). At first McGavran seems to have been merely making an observation, but as time passed it developed into an important principle of the church growth movement. McGavran's observation was that "men like to become Christians without crossing linguistic, racial or class barriers."[37] Through his missionary experience in India, McGavran became aware of the influence of cultural factors on evangelization. People respond to the gospel most readily if they do not have to leave their cultural setting or frame of reference in order to do so.

What McGavran began to call "homogeneous units" are now more frequently called people groups or subcultures. The principle calls for approaches in evangelism and forms of church life that are appropriate to a particular group or subculture. In a sense, it is another way of stating the concern for indigeneity or contextualization. However, emphasis is placed on the relation of the principle to effective evangelization.[38]

The homogeneous unit principle as set forth by McGavran quickly engendered controversy. It was criticized as contrary to the biblical principle of the one body of Christ and as implicitly racist. Defenders of the principle rejected any charge of racism and acknowledged commitment to the unity of the church but called attention to the biblical concept of people groups and to the appropriateness of cultural diversity within the one church.[39] Though to some extent the controversy continues, it has now moderated. In 1977, under the auspices of the theology and education group of the Lausanne Movement, a colloquium was held to examine the homogeneous unit principle and seek to harmonize the opposing views. The resulting statement reported large areas of consensus, with some remaining "points of tension and disagreement."[40]

The argument seemed to involve on one side primarily theologians and ethicists who view the matter from the perspective of a majority culture, and on the other side primarily missionaries and evangelists (often with some background in cultural anthropology) who perhaps view the matter from the perspective of a minority culture. The views of both groups are valid and need to be held in balance or in tension with each other.

The term *homogeneous unit principle* is an unfortunate one. The real concern is for persons, not for an abstract principle. Furthermore, at a time of great sensitivity about racism, the word *homogeneous* was an irritant. It is better to avoid the term entirely and simply seek the most culturally appropriate ways of evangelizing each people group or subculture.

The main point is that actual human cultures should be taken seriously (as is implied by the doctrine of the incarnation). Persons should not have to change to another culture in order to follow Christ. That was the basic question at issue in the Jerusalem conference recorded in Acts 15, and much of Paul's missionary energy was devoted to defending that principle. He maintained earnestly (in Galatians and elsewhere) that it would be a perversion of the gospel to require Gentiles to become culturally Jewish in order to become Christian. Evidently churches made up primarily of Gentiles would be Gentile in cultural forms. At the same time, Paul insisted on Christian fellowship across cultural lines (Eph. 2:13-16; Gal. 2:11-14).

Many who have opposed the homogeneous unit emphasis seem not to realize that any church actually expresses in the forms of its church life some dominant culture. For example, for centuries now the issue in Acts 15 has operated in reverse: The new question is whether Jews can receive Christ without becoming culturally Gentile. To avoid the unconscious cultural imperialism implied in that situation, in recent years such movements as messianic synagogues or Jews for Jesus have arisen.

Our temptation always is to assume heterogeneous churches made up of a wide variety of persons of different ethnic and social groups but expressing itself in the language and with the values, emphases, and forms of worship with which we personally are familiar and comfortable.

Some protest, appropriately, that all cultures are under the judgment of Christ. That truth, however, does not mean that the cultures of other persons should not be taken seriously. And missions is primarily gospel, not law or judgment. Cultural changes that are required by the Christian faith will be the work of the indwelling Spirit and the Word in the life of believers—not additional requirements for salvation.

In summary, we expect churches resulting from our mission efforts to represent many cultures and subcultures, identified with different languages and ethnic or social groups. (Incidentally, Southern Baptists have been leaders in this kind of development in the United States.[41]) We expect that all such churches will be open to persons from any racial or social background and that they will be aware of the one body of Christ and related in brotherhood with other members of that one body. The reality is not a "homogeneous unit principle," but rather the more basic biblical principle which affirms the cultural diversity of the myriads of churches which are embraced in the broader unity of the church.

## Maturity

Achieving indigenous church strength is not an event but a process. Mission work and churches are always in the process of maturing. Luther Copeland commented that, "from the biblical perspective, there is a sense in which a church is always growing toward maturity as an eschatological goal . . . while at the same time the churches are treated as though they have full responsibility for their life and mission from their beginnings."[42] Continuing development to maturity, as mentioned earlier, is part of the central church development objective in Southern Baptist missions.

Such a purpose assumes not only that individual churches will grow strong, but also that there will be appropriate denominational development through which the churches can combine their efforts in wider witness and ministry. This view assumes also a growing force of strong local leaders to exercise initiative and responsibility in the life of the churches and the emerging denomination.

Unfortunately, in many places today, independent or parachurch organizations based in America, either not understanding or not committed to the indigenous principle and its vision of mature churches with mature local leadership, employ many of the strongest leaders in their own programs. This not only deprives the local churches of the leadership they need; it also tends to separate those leaders from any local base. The results are fragmentation of Christian efforts and delay of the maturing process.

Maturing takes time. In many places overseas, because Baptist work is relatively new and because workers and other resources have been limited, everything is still relatively undeveloped. Important elements of denominational life such as seminaries and publishing centers may be comparable to such elements of Southern Baptist life several generations ago.

Even apart from limited development because of a late start, because of scarcity of workers and resources, or because of difficult situations, there is another limitation: There seem to be laws of natural growth that are hard to shortcut. Jesus stated this principle when he said, "First the blade, then the ear, after that the full corn in the ear" (Mark 4:28). Many times in mission work we find ourselves wishing we could have the full grain without taking the time required to go through the blade and ear stages, but it doesn't work that way.

Southern Baptist work in different countries is at widely differing levels of development. Generally, there is a sequence from pioneering to church planting and then to the developing of denominational and institutional programs. Increasing transfer of responsibility to local leadership follows, and finally a time when missionaries may be involved in specialized roles alongside relatively mature churches that are carrying out their own mission.[43]

The maturing process brings major changes in the relationship of the mission organization to the work and in the roles of missionaries. These changes are essential to our objective of indigenous church strength.

At the beginning of pioneer work, the missionary necessarily carries many responsibilities. He is at the center of things. Gradually, however, as work grows, well-trained local people begin to take over many responsibilities that the missionary formerly carried. In a relatively mature situation, the missionary is not likely to fill any central place of recognition and responsibility. The process by which missionaries and the mission move from center stage and transfer responsibility to the emerging churches and denomination has traditionally been called *devolution*—though the term is now archiac. Sometimes today the process is referred to as *nationalizing* of the work. More often in Southern Baptist missions it has simply been called *maturing*, or transfer of initiative and responsibility.[44]

A common way of stating the change in missionary role is that the missionary "works himself out of a job." It does not mean that the missionary has fulfilled his calling and should then return home, leaving everything cared for. It means rather that he turns over his responsibilities in a particular assignment to a local leader. But there are always other jobs waiting to be done. His own work is forever that of starting something and eventually passing it on to others.

The chief difficulty in this is the danger of paternalism. It is hard for American missionaries, trained and experienced in leadership roles, to turn over initiative to others. As Leland Webb stated it: "It's a matter of 'letting someone else drive.' Breathes there a motorist used to driving his own car who can ride calmly in the passenger seat without occasionally cautioning, 'Watch out!'?"[45] At times, missionaries doubt that the work is yet strong enough or young leaders yet experienced enough for responsibility to be transferred. Sometimes this almost amounts to advice "not to go near the water until you have learned how to swim." Experience and maturity are gained in exercising responsibility. I have commented often to missionaries that I see no reason why we Americans should have a monopoly on the privilege of making mistakes.

Sometimes the missionary paternalism expresses itself in protectiveness toward the work (or especially toward workers who have been under his or her leadership). The emotions involved are comparable to those of parents giving up their "baby girl" to be married to someone who may not take care of her in exactly the same way they have.

Sometimes paternalism seeks to link involvement in decision making with the providing of financial resources. In other words, missionaries might say that when local Christians provide the financing for a seminary (or some other object), then it will be appropriate for them to have major responsibility in decisions about it. That position is irrational and seems to be based on unrecognized condescension or even racism. After all, the money did not come from the missionaries. They are simply exercising trusteeship—and being American is not the prime qualification for trusteeship.

The answer to paternalism is the servant attitude. The spirit called for must necessarily be like that of John the Baptist when he said of the Master, "He must increase, but I must decrease" (John 3:30). In this way, local leadership will become strong and churches will take center stage, while missionaries and the mission still fulfill their generative role in the background.

In reality, the missionary moves from an administrative responsibility dealing with tedious details to a more spiritual role, lacking in authority but having the possibility of even greater influence. Many missionaries have reported a sense of release and challenging new opportunities on making such changes in assignment and role.

An outstanding indication of the maturing of churches in the Third World is rapid increase in the international missionary outreach of such churches. Mission fields have become mission bases.[46] This topic will be considered further in chapter 10.

## Conclusion

Indigenous church strength as a central objective has ramifications touching all aspects of mission strategy and methods. Keeping a clear vision of the objective, in spite of personal and cultural bias, is not easy. At best, the effort is complicated, as Luther Copeland commented:

> Nobody can give simple answers to these complex problems—or at least answers that are adequate to the varied circumstances. Eternal vigilance to discern between gospel and culture, careful study on the part of all concerned that missionary methods be true to the nature of the Christian revelation, and prayerful submission to the Holy Spirit's guidance are essential to a fair measure of success in helping churches toward authentic Christian selfhood.[47]

Ultimately our vision and our hope look to the sowing down of the world with true New Testament churches, mature in every way (Eph. 4:13-16), usable instruments for the glory of God (Eph. 3:21), making known his "manifold wisdom . . . according to the eternal purpose which he purposed in Christ Jesus our Lord" (Eph. 3:10-11).

## Notes

1. A report of Winston Crawley to the Foreign Mission Board in August 1967 treated this subject in detail. It was carried in adapted form, "It's Their Work," in *The Commission*, vol. 30, no. 11 (November 1967): 6-7, and in *The Baptist World*, vol. 15, no. 2 (February 1968): 6; then in *Baptist Men's Journal*, vol. 39 (April 1968): 12, and revised by an editor into what he called "early teenage boy dialect," in *Ambassador Life*, vol. 23 (November 1968): 8-9, under the title "Richmond is Not Our Rome."

2. For descriptions of the New Testament church, see, for example, W. O. Carver, *Christian Missions in Today's World* (Nashville: Broadman Press, 1942), pp. 65-71, and Dean S. Gilliland, *Pauline Theology and Mission Practice* (Grand Rapids: Baker Book House, 1983), pp. 181-212.

3. *Webster's New Collegiate Dictionary* (1977), s.v. "indigenous."

4. For treatment of various concerns related to indigeneity, see chapter 2, "Indigenization," in Leland Webb, *How in This World* (Nashville: Convention Press, 1974), pp. 23-48.

5. See the entire chapter, "The Missionary and the Indigenous Church," R. Pierce Beaver, *The Missionary Between the Times* (Garden City, N.Y.: Doubleday & Company, Inc., 1968), pp. 127-42. The quotation is from p. 130.

6. Ibid., p. 136.

7. Ibid., p. 133.

8. Ibid., p. 136.

9. See the chapter "The Self-Hood of a Church," D. T. Niles, *Upon the Earth* (New York: McGraw-Hill Book Company, Inc., 1962), pp. 139-69.

10. Ibid., p. 150.

11. E. Luther Copeland, "A Strategy of World Evangelization," *The Commission*, vol. 31, no. 10 (October 1968): 11. In his recent book *World Mission and World Survival* (Nashville: Broadman Press, 1985), pp. 105-106, Copeland expands that description of church selfhood.

12. Beaver, p. 137.

13. A report on "The Indigenous Church—The Universal Church in Its Local Setting," in Norman Goodall, ed., *Missions Under the Cross* (London: Edinburgh House Press, 1953), pp. 195-200.

14. Address to Conference of Furloughing Missionaries sponsored by the Foreign Mission Board in June 1966.

15. C. Peter Wagner, *Frontiers in Missionary Strategy* (Chicago: Moody Press, 1971), chapter 9, "The Emerging Church in Missions Strategy," pp. 163-64.

16. For an extended treatment of the significance and the pros and cons of contextualization, see Bruce J. Nicholls, *Contextualization: A Theology of Gospel and Culture* (Downers Grove, Ill.: InterVarsity Press, 1979). Less extensive treatment also is found in J. Herbert Kane, *The Christian World Mission* (Grand Rapids: Baker Book House, 1981), chapter 13, pp. 185-200, and in an editorial by Arthur F. Glasser in *Missiology*, vol. 7, no. 4 (October 1979): 403-10. Similar concerns had been discussed much earlier, from a European perspective and

using the term *accommodation*, in J. H. Bavinck, *An Introduction to the Science of Missions* (Grand Rapids: Baker Book House, 1960), pp. 169-79.

17. Glasser, p. 405.

18. Nicholls, p. 22.

19. Ibid.; the quote is from *The Other Side* (March 1978), p. 62.

20. This question has already been explored briefly in chapter 4. Further ramifications of the question can be investigated in the books to which reference was made there, in those listed in an earlier footnote here, and in others to which footnote references are made in the book by Bruce Nicholls.

21. For an interesting treatment of this issue, see Walter Trobisch, *My Wife Made Me a Polygamist*, new rev. ed. (Downers Grove, Ill.: Inter-Varsity Press, 1971).

22. "Christian Witness to the Jewish People," *Lausanne Occasional Papers: No. 7, Thailand Report* (Wheaton, Ill.: Lausanne Committee for World Evangelization, 1980), pp. 17-18.

23. Phil Parshall, *New Paths in Muslim Evangelism* (Grand Rapids: Baker Book House, 1980).

24. See, for example, the report of an interview with Phil Parshall, under the title "How Goes the Battle over Contextualiztion in Muslim Evangelism?" by Jim Reapsome in *Muslim World Pulse*, a publication of the Evangelical Missions Information Service, vol. 12, no. 2 (April 1983): 7-8.

25. Phil Parshall, "Contextualized Baptism for Muslim Converts," *Missiology*, vol. 7, no. 4 (October 1979): 501-515.

26. Reapsome, p. 7.

27. That movement is examined thoroughly by Gerald H. Anderson and Thomas F. Stransky, eds., *Mission Trends No. 4: Liberation Theologies in North America and Europe* (New York: Paulist Press and Grand Rapids: Wm. B. Eerdmans Publishing Co., 1979).

28. For a description of the movement, see Sergio Torres and John Eagleson, eds., *The Challenge of Basic Christian Communities*, trans. John Drury (Maryknoll, N.Y.: Orbis Press, 1981).

29. On the complications of this question, see Eugene A. Nida, noted anthropologist and linguist for many years with the Bible societies, in an article, " 'Why are Foreigners So Queer?' A Socioanthropological Approach to Cultural Pluralism," *International Bulletin of Missionary Research*, vol. 5, no. 3 (July 1981): 102-106.

30. See above, p. 200 and note 14.

31. See the chapter "The 'Cultural Overhang'" in Donald Anderson McGavran, *How Churches Grow* (London: World Dominion Press, 1959), pp. 85-92.

32. For further treatment of this theme, see an address by Winston Crawley on "New Ways for New Days," presented at an Orient missions conference in August 1957 and published in the report book of that conference. Later, an abbreviated version was presented as a report to the Foreign Mission Board in August 1962 and published in *The Commission*, vol. 26, no. 4 (April 1963): 7-9.

33. For more extended treatment of the themes of this section, with their biblical support, see Winston Crawley's Bible study messages on the biblical base for urban strategy, presented at an Asia conference on urban evangelism at Manila in November 1978 and published in the report book of that conference.

34. Charles H. Kraft, "Dynamic Equivalence Churches," *Missiology*, vol. 1, no. 1 (January 1973): 39-57.

35. See Larry L. Rose and C. Kirk Hadaway, *An Urban World: Churches Face the Future* (Nashville: Broadman Press, 1984).

36. For helpful additional insights and practical suggestions and examples, see Nicholls, p. 64; Webb, pp. 40-42; J. Herbert Kane, *Understanding Christian Missions*, rev. ed. (Grand Rapids: Baker Book House, 1978), pp. 351-59; and Paul G. Hiebert, "Sets and Structures: A Study of Church Patterns," *New Horizons in World Missions*, ed. David J. Hesselgrave (Grand Rapids: Baker Book House, 1979), pp. 217-27.

37. "Without Crossing Barriers," by missionary Medley, *Church Growth Bulletin*, vol. 8, no. 5 (May 1971): 135-37.

38. For more extensive treatments of the homogeneous unit principle, see McGavran, *How Churches Grow*, chapter 11, "Understanding Church Growth," pp. 77-84; C. Peter Wagner, *Church Growth and the Whole Gospel* (San Francisco: Harper & Row, Publishers, 1981), chapter 9, pp. 166-83; and Delos Miles, *Church Growth—A Mighty River* (Nashville: Broadman Press, 1981), pp. 96-100. See also the Summer 1983 issue of *The Enterprise*, periodical of the Canadian Baptist Overseas Mission Board.

39. For a most interesting expression of the two contrasting positions, see an extended exchange of letters between Victor Hayward and Donald McGavran published under the title "Without Crossing Barriers? One in Christ vs. Discipling Diverse Cultures," *Missiology*, vol. 2, no. 2 (April 1974): 203-24.

40. The report is published in David A. Fraser, ed., *The Church in New Frontiers for Missions* (Monrovia, California: Missions Advanced Research and Communication Center, 1983); p. 189-94.

41. Wagner, *Church Growth and the Whole Gospel*, pp. 168, 180.

42. Copeland, *World Mission and World Survival*, p. 105 (quoted from an early draft of Copeland's manuscript).

43. There have been many analyses of stages in the maturing of mission work and of churches resulting from that work. See, for example, C. Peter Wagner, *Frontiers in Missionary Strategy*, pp. 176-178, and Ralph D. Winter, in an address on "Frontier Mission Perspectives," in *Seeds of Promise*, the findings of the World Consultation on Frontier Missions '80, Allan Starling, ed. (Pasadena, Calif.: William Carey Library, 1981), pp. 83-88.

44. For an earlier discussion of the entire subject, see Bavinck, chapter 10, and especially pp. 191-99.

45. Webb, p. 42. He gives several pages of illustrations (pp. 42-46).

46. See the December 1982 issue of *Mission Frontiers*, the bulletin of the U.S. Center for World Mission.

47. Copeland, "A Strategy of World Evangelization," p. 11.

# 10
# How Do We Relate to Others?

Relationships have always been a very important concern in Christian missions.[1] Large sections of the Book of Acts (such as chapter 15) and of the Letters of Paul deal with the matter. It is quite complex, since missions involves relations in many directions and with a wide variety of persons and groups. Progress in indigeneity to a considerable degree hinges on relating well to local churches and their leaders.

All relationships in missions take place in the context of the primary relationship with God. He is the sender. The mission belongs to Him, and every relationship is to be guided by His Spirit.

Southern Baptist relationships in missions can be summed up in two categories: partnership and friendship.

## Partnership

The general concept of partnership in missions and the sending partnership which links missionaries with Southern Baptists and with one another through the Foreign Mission Board have been described already in the section on partnership in chapter 5.[2] Therefore, this section focuses on relationships on the mission field.

A basic principle of Southern Baptist foreign missions is partnership with Baptist churches and conventions in mission areas—though this principle has not always been fully understood (even by missionaries) or fully realized.

The expectation of the Foreign Mission Board and its staff is that missionaries will relate in full partnership with believers, churches, and emerging Baptist conventions in lands where they work. Partnership does not subordinate the local church or local leaders to the missionaries. They are "partners in obedience" to the Lord Jesus. Such partnership is vital, since none of us can fulfill our Lord's commission alone.

### Tensions

Partnership does not come automatically or even easily to those of different cultures and different stages in development of church and denominational life. Therefore, relationships between missionaries and churches on the fields involve many problems and frequent tensions.[3] Friction between missionaries and local leaders is fairly common, especially at sensitive stages in the development of mission work. In some cases, such friction intensifies to the point of disrupting the relationship.

Fault in such cases often lies on both sides. Missionaries may fail to understand the indigeneous objective, the desirability of partnership, and the need to adopt a servant role. They may show inconsistency or condescension in implementing policy. They often retain vestiges of paternalism. Local leaders, on the other hand, may respond with oversensitivity, or interaction between the mission and the churches may get caught in power politics of rival local leaders.

Of course, tension in itself is not bad. In many situations it is normal or even unavoidable, and it can be very valuable. If the strings of a musical instrument were not under tension, they could produce no music. If there were no tensions within the human body, it would be only a pile of meat and bones lying on the ground. Tensions need to be accepted, understood, and used constructively. This has been an intention of missionaries, missions administrators, and missiologists in recent years.[4]

### Stages

Mission-church tensions vary in nature and in acuteness with the progressive stages of development of the relationship. This is the reality behind the old joke that a missionary really has only two problems: his fellow missionaries and the nationals—who are not a problem until after they are converted. To be more exact, it is not conversion that begins to make the relationship sensitive; it is the beginning of initiative and incipient leadership on the part of the national. This may take place rather early in the life of a new congregation. With work in a new country, it usually takes 15 or 20 years before denominational development reaches the point of such special sensitivity.

In some cases, transfer of initiative and responsibility from a mission to a young convention takes place fairly smoothly. In other cases, the transition is quite traumatic. The difference seems to depend on a complicated mixture of circumstances, personalities on both sides of the tension, and the way in which transition is approached. If missionaries drag their feet, resentment and resistance build up toward an explosion. If the mission acts arbitrarily or unilaterally, relationships curdle. If cooperation with the mission becomes a political football in struggles for convention leadership and power, effective partnership is endangered.

Even well-intended interim structures, calling for proportionate representation of the mission and the convention, often do not help the transition process because they are not fully responsible to either body. They easily become a special arena for power struggles between individuals or between groups. What is needed, of course, is maturity in personality, in attitude, and in relationships on the part of all concerned.[5]

In the beginning of work, the missionary inevitably takes initiative and exercises leadership. This gives the missionary high visibility. As soon as there are local believers, the intention is to project work in partnership with those believers and with churches as they take shape. As the work develops further, the missionary becomes less prominent, while local leaders loom larger and larger in the partnership. (It is often difficult to communicate this clearly to persons here in the homeland, who are naturally interested in "what our missionaries are doing.")

As indigenous work matures, missionaries and the mission become helpers in programs of the churches and conventions, instead of having separate parallel programs of mission work. This development is sometimes called *united work* or *one work*.

*Partnership* is the more inclusive term that applies through the entire process.

Stages in the development of work can be analyzed in various ways. A helpful interpretation with special attention to partnership was given by Akiko Matsumura at Ridgecrest in June 1980 (reported in *The Commission*, October 1980). Mrs. Matsumara, described by *The Commission* as "a long-time respected leader among Japan's Baptists," commented:

> "In Japan, are Southern Baptist missionaries above, equal to, or below nationals?" That question was addressed to me in the presence of many women in Indonesia.
>
> After a moment of intensive thinking with prayer, I replied, "Baptists in Japan have gone through three stages of growth: childish dependence, adolescent self assertion, and adult appreciation and cooperation.
>
> "Baptists in Japan depended heavily on the leadership and parental care of Southern Baptist missionaries in the first stage of development. At one time we became big-headed and self assertive, glorying in the goal of independence from the Foreign Mission Board.
>
> "Now we have come to understand the heartbeat of Southern Baptists," I said. "We now appreciate more deeply than ever the dedication, love, and patience of Southern Baptist missionaries among us.
>
> "We no longer think of them either above or below us. They are our good friends and co-workers with whom we can freely share our visions and discuss problems."

Mrs. Matsumura went on to say that

> The effectiveness of Christian witness depends on two things:
>
> 1) How quickly young churches grow out of a childish dependence and adolescent rebellion and achieve adult appreciation of each other and the message of the gospel.
>
> 2) How smoothly older churches discard paternalism and domination and accept national Christians as equals in the common task of evangelizing the whole world.[6]

### Structures

Different stages in the developing relationship between missionaries and churches call for different structures. The mission structure in the pioneering stage is likely to be relatively simple. As work expands, with the probable addition of a wide range of functions, mission structure may become quite complex. With the maturing of the work, functions become increasingly the responsibility of a convention, with functions of the mission diminishing (the process of devolution). Finally, the mission functions primarily as a fellowship and support group for missionaries.

The question of mission structures was considered in great detail at a conference of evangelical Christian leaders at Greenlake, Wisconsin, in 1971. Papers presented at that conference described possible forms of mission-church relationship and examined their relative merits. Writers dealt mainly with "fusion," by which in effect the missionaries and the mission are merged into the organized denominational structure on the mission field, and "dichotomy," which retains a separate mission organization related cooperatively to the local churches and denomination. Considered also were modified forms of fusion and dichotomy. The discussion did not anticipate unanimity or finality as to structures for mission-church relationship.[7]

Some have suggested that the mission organization in older Southern Baptist mission fields should be dissolved, with missionaries relating as individuals to local churches and denominational life. The Foreign Mission Board has continued to believe in the validity and the value of a mission organization. In one country, for example, where for some years there was no mission, in more recent years the Board has arranged for the formation of a mission.

No structure is perfect. Any arrangement will involve potential problems and dangers. The main danger for the mission organization is that it will become an end in itself, concerned to maintain itself, to strengthen itself, to increase its authority and powers and functions. Constant struggle is needed to keep it a servant organization, as lean and streamlined as possible, transferring properties and functions readily to churches and denominational entities instead of holding on to them, committed to being only a means to the greater ends of mission outreach and the upbuilding of the churches. It must be essentially a partnership structure, not simply a work structure that happens to have connections with local church structures.

### Implementation

Quite naturally, forms of Southern Baptist partnership overseas vary greatly. Cultural settings differ. Work is in different stages. The history of the work affects relationships. Therefore, there is no one common recommended mission structure and no one expected partnership structure. Area directors work with mission organizations and share in consultations with local convention leadership as forms appropriate to the circumstances are developed.

Individual missionaries are expected to be members of local churches on the field and to be involved in the life and work of those churches. At times they may be chosen by the churches as representatives in various aspects of denominational life. In principle they relate within those churches as individual Christians, without any special status based on their being missionaries. Of course, in many cases their work responsibilities mean that they are away from their own churches much of the time (like persons in denominational work in the United States).

Normally, the mission and the convention as separate entities cooperate without either exercising control over the other. Areas of cooperation are based on agreement. The convention may be involved in some projects in which the mission has no cooperative involvement. The mission also will have concerns (particularly those related specifically to the care of missionaries) in which the convention probably is not involved. The partnership can be strengthened by mutual openness, sympathetic understanding, and support in prayer even in relation to endeavors that are not cooperative.

True partnership must rest on clear understandings between mission leaders and church leaders. Faulty communication is a frequent source of problems. This is true especially when any changes are being considered. Action without consultation proves disruptive. In some cases, understandings about ways of working together are put in writing. We have felt that formal contracts generally are not desirable—since they tend too easily toward legalism, with extended quibbling over details, whereas the relationship is intended to be a spiritual partnership.[8]

Many international meetings (usually regional) have been sponsored by the Foreign Mission Board to involve church leaders and mission leaders in discussing various Christian ministries, and sometimes also in discussing mission-church relations. From such conferences have come numerous practical suggestions that have strengthened Southern Baptist partnership with Baptists in other lands.

The Foreign Mission Board's commitment to partnership is clearly spelled out in the formal strategy statement adopted by the Board's Executive Management Group in 1982. The "focus" section of the statement refers twice to partnership with local Baptist churches and conventions. A list of implementing guidelines includes the following relevant items:

> Insofar as possible, entry to new countries is at the invitation of and in relation with existing Baptist churches.
> Partnership with existing churches and conventions is of highest importance. The nationalizing of leadership and planning roles as rapidly as possible gives expression to this developing partnership.
> With the growth of local Baptist strength, transition in the form of missionary ministries is to be expected.
> Some form of mission organization is retained as the most practical approach to cooperative endeavor.

### Special Arrangements

In the broader context of our ongoing partnership with Baptist churches and conventions overseas, the Foreign Mission Board now promotes several specialized partnership arrangements. They probably by now have become generally known to Southern Baptists.

One of the arrangements is partnership evangelism. It is a plan that involves a Southern Baptist church with a specific church overseas for a special evangelistic effort. Although pastor led, it is basically a program for the laity. Preparation may require about six months, with the team from the American church going overseas for about two weeks and conducting an actual evangelistic campaign of one week, Sunday to Sunday.

Partnership missions is a plan for cooperation between a Southern Baptist state convention and a Baptist convention overseas. The two conventions agree on projects which they will undertake together over a period of three or four years. An example was a special three-year evangelistic effort in Brazil with the partnership of the Texas convention, leading up to the 100th anniversary of Baptist work in Brazil in 1982.

Partnership projects involve various special ministries. Some are construction projects. Others are evangelistic. Choir tours are a common example. An exchange program of a Southern Baptist university with a university overseas is another example. Also, there are partnerships between Southern Baptist hospitals and Baptist hospitals overseas. Possibilities for partnership projects are numerous and varied.

### Prayer

The most important element of partnership in world missions is prayer partnership. All other partnerships, both the broad ongoing ones and the specific programmatic ones, are empowered only through faithful partnership with the Lord and with one another in prayer.

### Friendships

Missionaries, mission organizations, and the Foreign Mission Board are involved in many relationships that are not as close as the sending partnership with Southern Baptists and the partnership on the fields with Baptist churches and conventions there. Those other relationships can be reckoned as Christian friendships.

### With Other Christians

Southern Baptists and the Baptist conventions with which we are partners are by no means the only Christians in lands where we work. In fact, in most cases, Baptists are definitely a minority of the Christians present, and in some cases a very tiny minority.

In the United States, and especially in the South, Southern

Baptists can be so surrounded by other Baptists and so involved in Baptist church activities that relating to other Christians becomes a rather low item on the agenda. Overseas, Christians of various denominations are drawn together by their overall minority status in the total population. Friendly relationships with other Christian individuals and groups becomes a valuable part of missionary life and work. The thoroughly biblical concern for Christian unity (John 17:21; Eph. 4:3-6,13; 1 Pet. 2:17b) is much less likely to be neglected.

The missionary overseas is likely to come into contact with the ecumenical movement and to face questions regarding ways of cooperating with other Christians. The word *ecumenical* comes from a Greek word that means "the inhabited world." Therefore, the general meaning of ecumenical is simply worldwide. The modern Christian ecumenical movement grew out of concern for the worldwide spread of the gospel and worldwide fellowship of believers. It has now come to refer mainly to organizations that relate Christians across denominational lines. Luther Copeland commented that "the ecumenical movement includes the various attempts to bring Christians together in an expression of their unity in mission. Unfortunately, sometimes mission tends to be lost from sight in the commendable eagerness to get together."[9]

The Foreign Mission Board encourages cordial friendship and many kinds of cooperation with other Christian groups. One of the implementing guidelines in the staff strategy statement adopted in 1982 is, "Southern Baptist mission work is carried on in the context of the larger Christian family and in cordial relationship and increasing correlation with the work of other denominations." The central principle of such relationships is fellowship and cooperation without entanglement or diversion from the mission task. As is evident from the terms used, this guideline and this principle are not laws. They are not applied rigidly. Instead, specific opportunities for cooperation are evaluated on their own merits.

The Southern Baptist *Curriculum Scope Document* on the teaching of missions stated the situation well.

Christians differ on ways to express unity and to cooperate.

> Southern Baptists are generally cooperative in spirit while avoiding structural relationships. For example, the Southern Baptist Convention is a member of the Baptist World Alliance but has never accepted membership in the World and National Councils of Churches. Nevertheless, the "Statement of Baptist Faith and Message," approved by the Southern Baptist Convention in 1963, contains an article on 'Cooperation' which manifests a positive spirit toward cooperation with other Christians. . . .
>
> In missionary efforts, Southern Baptists enjoy cordial relationships with various other Christians and cooperate in a number of ways, though generally informally. The Foreign Mission Board for several years was affiliated with the Foreign Missions Conference of North America, until the latter elected to merge with other interdenominational councils to form the National Council of Churches in 1950. Southern Baptist missionaries generally find it easy to express Christian unity in situations abroad where Christians are far less numerous than in the United States.[10]

Aside from the warm friendships that individual missionaries may have with persons of other denominations, mission organizations face the relationship question in three main ways. One has to do with membership in councils of churches. In most cases such councils are open only to "churches"—that is, to denominational bodies. Therefore, a mission organization would not be eligible for membership. In some places, membership has been opened to mission organizations also. However, the position of the Foreign Mission Board has been that it is more appropriate for indigeneous Baptist conventions or unions to become members of such bodies if they feel it is the right thing to do. Mission organizations are discouraged from affiliating.

Missions do become sponsoring bodies for various united institutions. The most common of these are language schools (after all, there is no special Baptist doctrine of the Chinese language) and schools for missionary children (to provide them an American type of education). At times there is participation in other institutions. (For example, the beginning of Southern Baptist work in India involved assignment of a medical missionary couple to the interdenominational Christian hospital at Vellore.)

Involvement in joint projects is even more common. These are temporary, and they frequently include a much wider range of Christian groups. (For example, many mission and church bodies may work together in disaster relief after an earthquake or may share together in the sponsoring of a Billy Graham evangelistic campaign.) Southern Baptist missionaries often have leadership roles in such joint projects.

In general, our Southern Baptist approach values and urges spiritual unity, while exercising a good bit of caution about organizational alliance, which in many cases has turned out to involve attempted control by some central group or office.

Several special aspects of relations with other Christians need to be mentioned.

One is joint mission efforts with other Baptist groups. An early example was the University of Shanghai, founded jointly by Southern Baptists and American Baptists (then known as Northern Baptists) in 1905. More recently, these same Baptist mission organizations have worked cooperatively in Okinawa. Southern Baptists have had a cooperative work with Australian and New Zealand Baptists in Bangladesh. These are a few examples of a relation that involves partnership as well as friendship.

Comity is another special issue. Though less common today, comity agreements were a prominent part of overseas missions for many years. They were agreements which assigned specific geographic areas for the mission ministries of the different denominations, with the understanding that each denomination would work only in its assigned area. Perhaps a major city would be considered an open area in which all denominations would feel free to work. By policy, at least for many decades, the Southern Baptist Foreign Mission Board has not participated in formal comity agreements. At some times and places, there have been informal understandings. Always there has been the intent of Christian courtesy—seeking friendship and harmony with workers of other denominations, avoiding locations too close to other churches, resisting any temptation toward "sheep stealing," or especially toward the luring away of any "shepherd" (that is, any pastor or worker) from another denomination.

Parachurch organizations pose an entire range of questions.

The Foreign Mission Board and its missionaries seek to maintain friendship with the many Christian organizations at work in the overseas setting. Sometimes, however, involvement at the program level would cause confusion. This may be even more likely if the parachurch organization arises within Southern Baptist life and seeks its personnel and support exclusively or almost entirely from Southern Baptists. Both within the home constituency and on the field, such organizations may seem to be a branch of the Foreign Mission Board, or else a substitute channel for Southern Baptist foreign missions—but without having the well-defined ongoing partnership represented in the sending process by Southern Baptist structures and on the field by long-standing cooperative arrangements. The Foreign Mission Board and its missionaries seek to stay on friendly terms with parachurch organizations, while making as much use as possible of the contributions they might offer to the work, provided there can be enough clarity of relationship to avoid misunderstanding and problems.

Another important consideration is the freedom of Baptist conventions to make their own decisions about interdenominational relations. In many cases, conventions with which we work are members of national councils of churches in their own countries and of the World Council of Churches. Through such participation, they help inject into those councils more of the Baptist understanding of the Scriptures and the church and help to stimulate within those councils growing concern for evangelism and mission outreach.

A further special complication is the cleavage that has developed across the years between the organizations and leaders of the ecumenical movement on the one hand and the main evangelical missions groups (primarily smaller denominations and independent missions societies) on the other hand. Southern Baptists have not adhered to either of these movements but have maintained informal contact and ad hoc involvement with both.[11]

It has been my privilege and pleasure for a good many years to share in many organizations, meetings, or seminars that have involved mission leaders, either separately or together, from these two wings of current Protestant missions. I have participated as an individual, not a formal representative of the Foreign Mission Board; but my presence was often due to my role on the Foreign Mission Board staff. This is typical of the way Southern Baptist missionaries across the world relate to other Christians as friends and co-laborers in the cause of Christ.

### With the General Public

It is important for missionaries to remain on good terms with the general public, remembering that they are guests in the country. (The idea of the "ugly American," though missing the point of the book title, is now generally understood as an important caution for Americans overseas.) Being a good neighbor in the overseas community involves learning to relate well to persons in government and in business, to community leadership, to the American or other foreign community, and to visitors from the United States.

Since "a good name is rather to be chosen than great riches" (Prov. 22:1), missionaries must not ignore local customs, evade laws, criticize and condemn, compete for special favors, bribe, argue, show off, or "throw their weight around." Personality traits, careless habits, or thoughtless actions that might be overlooked or understood in their own cultural setting can be interpreted overseas as typical of all missionaries or even of the Christian faith.

Christian courtesy and kindness are essential. In places where concern for "face" is part of the culture, missionaries need to be exemplary in protecting the face of local people and indifferent, if possible, to slights that might make them lose face. There are times when a mission might appropriately use modern publicity techniques, but with great caution. Keeping in the background, maintaining a low profile, and sticking to the servant role are generally more appropriate.

Paradoxically, the best in missionary public relations is not advertising or promotion of the missionary and the mission but self-forgetfulness and self-giving in order to display Christ. The principle is that of spiritual victory through the cross.

### With Persons of Other Religions

Relating to adherents of other religions is part of the broader relationship with the general public, and the same principles of

Christian attitude and behavior apply. But this specific subject is important enough to deserve separate notice.

Essentially the missionary approach is to persons (as was pointed out in chapter 4), but the missionary needs unusual sensitivity to the religious situation.

In addition to the helpful treatment by D. T. Niles, which was cited in chapter 4, a perceptive summary of the missionary approach to other religions is given in the *Curriculum Scope Document* on missions of the Southern Baptist Missions Education Council. There the following suggestions are offered as a framework: witness, respect, fairness, understanding, dialogue, and a theological perspective.[12]

Witness, of course, is fundamental. "The first responsibility, then, is for the Christian to know his own faith and be prepared to give a personal testimony concerning it. . . . The intent of the Christian witness is that those who hear be brought to a faith commitment to Christ."[13]

Respect and fairness should be the normal Christian attitude toward others, reflective of the Golden Rule (see Luke 6:31 and also 1 Pet. 3:15). Understanding is very important. Hendrik Kraemer, in his definitive *The Christian Message in a Non-Christian World*, suggested a congenial understanding.[14] The missionary needs to understand the terminology, the history and beliefs, the values, and insofar as possible the psychology of the religion that is prominent where he serves. It is important to realize that much religion is "popular" religion—that is, attitudes and customs that may not be understood fully by most of the people and may not represent the formal beliefs of the religion as explained by its scholars. The missionary needs to understand both the popular expression of the local religion and its more formal and normative beliefs.

Dialogue in the strict sense of the word refers to "planned conversations and discussions involving adherents of different religions."[15] These take place occasionally in overseas missions and can be helpful "to build bridges of understanding."[16] However, most conversations and witness are much less formal.

The question of theological perspective has already been explored in chapter 4. The *Curriculum Scope Document* suggests that "what is to be hoped for is that Christians will hold the conviction of the uniqueness and finality of Jesus Christ in hearts that love and respect and sympathize with all persons in their religion or lack of it."[17]

## Internationalization

Possible *internationalizing* of Christian world missions has received growing attention in recent years. The concept is not new. It was implied in the term "Mission in Six Continents," which was the theme of the 1963 Mexico City meeting of the Commission on World Missions and Evangelism of the World Council of Churches. The closing message from that conference included this statement: "We believe that the time has now come when we must move onwards to common planning and joint action. The fact that Christ is not divided must be made unmistakably plain in the very structure of missionary work."[18] A decade later, Emilio Castro indicated that "a multiple traffic system, under the name of ecumenical sharing of personnel, is being constructed which will separate funding from personnel and channel the support of Christians in all parts of the world for the exchange of missionary forces in all possible directions."[19] These statements actually spoke more to a concept than to an established structural reality. Nevertheless, internationalizing of missions has been an increasingly prominent theme.

Increase in the number of missionaries being sent out from Third World nations augments the interest in internationalization. In many cases, missionaries from the Third World and missionaries from the Western world are joined in international mission teams—though of course there are also many cases in which Third World missions agencies project their efforts separately, as the Western agencies have done for generations.

The growth of foreign mission efforts by Third World churches has been remarkably rapid. Special attention is being given to "transforming mission fields into mission bases."[20] Lawrence E. Keyes has been a leader in analyzing and interpreting missions from the Third World base.[21]

A 1972 study showed 203 Third World missionary-sending agencies, with almost 3,000 reported missionaries. The 1980 research indicated 368 agencies with nearly 11,000 reported missionaries and an estimated total of 13,000 missionaries. By now Keyes and others estimate that there are more than 15,000 missionaries from Africa, Asia, Oceania, and Latin America.[22]

Not all of these Third World missionaries are "foreign" missionaries, in the sense of working beyond their own national boundaries. Many work in cross-cultural situations within their own nations, as is evident from examining agency by agency the detailed information compiled by Keyes.[23] Even in foreign missions, many of the Third World missionaries minister among people of their own language, nationality, and/or culture. Therefore, comparisons with the work of Western missions agencies (to which the same consideration applies, but only to a limited extent) is not easy. What is obvious, however, is that Christians in the Third World are engaging in cross-cultural or international missions on an amazing scale.

In this process, problems and questions that have concerned Western missionaries and agencies in the past are now being faced also by the new Third World missionaries and agencies. Furthermore, the presence of this growing host of Third World missionaries tends to create an entirely new context for Christian world missions.[24]

Structures designed for international cooperation in missions have begun to develop. An example formed along racial and cultural lines is the Chinese Coordination Centre of World Evangelism, based in Hong Kong.

Interest of the Baptist World Alliance in world missions strategy development is an example of a fairly common denominational or confessional direction. The alliance is basically a fellowship rather than a program organization. Discussion of international cooperation in missions has centered in a related organization, the Baptist International Mission Secretaries, which meets annually in connection with the meeting of the BWA General Council or the Baptist World Congress and is itself a consultative body, not a program organization. The Southern Baptist Foreign Mission Board is fully involved in these discussions and in other alliance activities.

The real advance in internationalized missions programs has taken place through joint efforts involving two or more missions agencies at specific places and for specific projects. Several examples of such joint efforts relating Southern Baptists to the missions agencies of other Baptist conventions have been mentioned already on page 229. Now, however, such cooperative arrangements are being developed more and more frequently with Third World Baptist missions agencies. The Brazilian Baptist Convention, which now has 84 missionaries in 16 countries, relates with Southern Baptists in international partnership in several countries. A recent case representing even more clearly the concept of an international mission team is the beginning of Baptist missions in the Netherlands Antilles jointly by Venezuelan Baptists and Southern Baptists. Foreign Mission Board encouragement for this kind of development is reflected in one of the guideline statements in the strategy document: "Internationalization of missions is being strengthened through exchanges or cooperative arrangements with other Baptist conventions."

One unresolved question about internationalized mission efforts is the extent to which Southern Baptists should provide financing for the world mission outreach of other Baptist groups. In the past, the Foreign Mission Board has provided large sums of money to assist in local evangelistic and in home missions endeavors of Baptist unions and conventions across the world. Our general practice up to now has not provided funds for their foreign missions endeavors, on the principle that supporting their own foreign missions efforts will do more to stimulate enthusiasm and spiritual strength. However, this practice is now beginning to be reexamined and may change.

A possible promising new step in international partnership is an anticipated linkage in global planning of the Foreign Mission Board and many of the Baptist conventions with which the Board works in ongoing partnership. At the recommendation of Board President R. Keith Parks, the Board adopted in April 1983 this proposal: "That the Southern Baptist Foreign Mission Board consult all interested Baptist bodies with whom we are linked in a working relationship to discover better strategies for jointly sharing Jesus Christ with everyone in the world before the end of this century."[25] Exploration of the proposal, looking toward a possible implementation, is continuing.

In a missions setting that demands increasingly close partnership, and with increasing international complexity, our missionaries (and our denomination) are challenged to seek the deepest possible level of Christian mutuality in relation with brother and sister believers around the world.

### Notes

1. W. O. Carver made that concern the theme of one of his lectures in his overview series on missions published as *Christian Missions in Today's World* (Nashville: Broadman Press, 1942).

2. For further treatment of the sending partnership by others than Southern Baptists, see: from the perspective of other major denominations, R. Pierce Beaver's chapter on "The Missionary and His Home Church," in *The Missionary Between the Times* (Garden City, N.Y.: Doubleday & Company, Inc., 1968), pp. 143-58; and from the perspective of independent missions, Virgil Gerber, ed., *Missions in Creative Tension* (South Pasadena, Calif.: William Carey Library, 1971), pp. 52-56, 124-43; and C. Peter Wagner, ed., *Church/Mission Tensions Today* (Chicago: Moody Press, 1972), pp. 53-72.

3. For an academic and comprehensive treatment of such relationships, see chapter 12 in Johannes Verkuyl, *Contemporary Missiology*, trans. and ed. Dale Cooper (Grand Rapids: William B. Eerdmans Publishing Company, 1978), pp. 309-40.

4. See for example the books cited above edited by Virgil Gerber and C. Peter Wagner. They reflect preparatory papers, reaction comments, and follow-up interpretation of a conference on "Missions in Creative Tension," held at Greenlake, Wisconsin, in 1971, with about 400 mission and church leaders called together under the sponsorship of the Evangelical Foreign Missions Association and the Interdenominational Foreign Mission Association. A more recent book dealing with the same subject is W. Harold Fuller, *Mission–Church Dynamics* (Pasadena, Calif.: William Carey Library, 1980).

5. Appendix 9 includes a chart produced by the Foreign Mission Board in connection with the 1974 study series on "Strategy on Foreign Missions," which illustrates partnership arrangements in foreign missions, both with the sending churches and with the churches and convention on the field.

6. Akiko Matsumura, "Working as Partners," *The Commission*, vol. 43, no. 10 (October 1980): 7-9.

7. See the chapters by Louis L. King and George W. Peters in *Missions in Creative Tension*, Virgil Gerber, ed., pp. 154–230. For a statement on this subject from a leader of the ecumenical movement, see Emilio Castro, "Structures for Mission," in Gerald H. Anderson and Thomas F. Stransky, eds., *Mission Trends No. 1: Crucial Issues in Missions Today* (New York: Paulist Press and Grand Rapids: Wm. B. Eerdmans Publishing Co., 1974), pp. 157-63.

8. E. Luther Copeland has a helpful summary of principles of partnership in *World Mission and World Survival* (Nashville: Broadman Press, 1985), pp. 107-109.

9. Ibid., p. 124. The larger section from which this quotation is taken is a helpful overview of concerns related to "Christian unity and cooperation."

10. *MEC Curriculum Scope Document, Task: Teach Missions* (Nashville: Missions Education Council, SBC, 1984), p. 96.

11. For contrasting perspectives on interdenominational relations, see, for the "ecumenical" or "conciliar" viewpoint, "Joint Action for Mission and Missions," T. Watson Street, *On the Growing Edge of the Church* (Richmond: John Knox Press, 1965), pp. 68-82; and for the "evangelical" viewpoint, Warren W. Webster, "The Nature of the Church and Unity in Mission," in David J. Hesselgrave, ed., *New Horizons in World Mission* (Grand Rapids: Baker Book House, 1979), pp. 243-63.

12. *MEC Curriculum Scope Document, Task: Teach Missions*, pp. 96-99. See also Copeland, pp. 127-32.

13. Ibid., pp. 97.

14. Hendrick Kraemer, *The Christian Message in a Non-Christian World* (Grand Rapids: Kregel Publications, 1963), as for example, p. 140.

15. *MEC Curriculum Scope Document, Task: Teach Missions*, p. 98.

16. Ibid.

17. Ibid., pp. 98-99.

18. R. K. Orchard, ed., *Witness in Six Continents* (New York: Friendship Press, 1964), p. 174.

19. Emilio Castro, "Editorial: Structures for Mission," *International Review of Mission*, vol. 62, no. 248 (October 1973): 393-98.

20. That phrase is the theme of the December 1982 issue of *Mission Frontiers*, the bulletin of the U.S. Center for World Missions. See further the January 1983 issue.

21. See especially his definitive study based on 1980 research, with projections for 1981, published as *The Last Age of Missions* (Pasadena, Calif.: William Carey Library, 1983), and his article "Third World Missionaries: More and Better," *Evangelical Missions Quarterly*, vol. 18, no. 4 (October 1982), pp. 216-24.

22. See Keyes, *The Last Age of Missions*, p. 75.

23. Ibid., Appendix 2, pp. 129-203.

24. For examination of some of these issues, see J. Herbert Kane, *Understanding Christian Missions*, rev. ed. (Grand Rapids: Baker Book House, 1978), pp. 359-70; Chun Chae Ok, "Third World Missions: A Personal Perspective," in Waldron Scott, ed., *Serving our Generation* (Colorado Springs: World Evangelical Fellowship, 1980), pp. 137-48; and Mok Chan Wing-wan, "Issues Facing Asian Cross-Cultural Missionaries," a January 1983 special report from *Bridging Peoples*, vol. 2, no. 1, published by O. C. Ministries.

25. For further details, see the column by R. Keith Parks, "Partners in Strategy," *The Commission*, vol. 46, no. 5 (June-July 1983): 2.

# 11
# How Far, How Fast, for How Long?

The central working objective in Southern Baptist foreign missions is to plant and to multiply strong indigenous churches through partnership with Baptist churches and conventions in other lands. But in how many lands? And in which lands? The objective needs specific practical definition as to where and when. Such definition is implied by asking how far and how fast Southern Baptist missions should expand and how long formal involvement should continue.

Ideally, the mission of the church should be carried out everywhere immediately. God intends that everyone should hear the gospel (1 Tim. 2:4; 2 Pet. 3:9). The mission extends to the ends of the earth (Acts 1:8). We must take full advantage of present opportunities (John 4:35; 9:4; Eph. 5:16).

However, it is not possible for Southern Baptists to do the entire work of Christian missions in all lands. We would spread our efforts so thin as to have little effectiveness. Furthermore, there are many places where other Christian groups are already doing wonderful work. We need the Holy Spirit's leadership in determining what new fields to enter, how to relate most appropriately to mature work in our older mission fields, and also what to do about countries that seem to be "closed."

## Entering New Fields

Southern Baptist foreign missions expansion has been quite rapid (as pointed out already in chapter 1). The number of countries served by Southern Baptist missionaries has grown from 19 at the end of 1947 to 105 at the end of 1984. That is a net average increase of more than 2 countries per year. But Southern Baptist missionaries still serve in less than half the countries of the world. (The *World Christian Encyclopedia* lists 223 countries.[1]) The Lord's comment to Joshua about the entry of the Hebrew people to the Promised Land can be applied symbolically to Southern Baptist foreign missions: "There remaineth yet very much land to be possessed" (Josh. 13:1).

How are decisions made as to when to move into new fields? And why is one field chosen rather than another? What guiding principles determine how far and how fast Southern Baptist missions expands?

There are several important and strong reasons for moving as far and as fast as possible. One is the argument of human need. Most of the world's people have not yet heard the gospel of salvation. Perhaps every land today has a few Christians, and most have churches and also missionaries of some Christian denomination, but there is still far more to be done than all Christians together can do. Thus the appeal of spiritual need pulls Southern Baptists on toward more mission fields.

An even stronger and more important cause for going as far and as fast as we can is our deep conviction of the command and the personal leading of our Lord. It has been nearly 2,000 years since He commissioned His followers to take the gospel to every person on earth. Surely no one would claim that we have gone or are going too fast.

Still another reason for rapid advance into new areas is the urgency of the world situation today. We must enter doors while they are open. Thus we seek to go as far as we can and as fast as we can "while it is day" before "night cometh, when no man can work" (John 9:4).

If we could follow completely the logic of overwhelming human need, the clear command of our Lord, and the challenge of our day, we would indeed go everywhere immediately. But there are sound reasons why that is not possible. Christians live and work always in a tension between the divine ideal and practical realities.

Limitation of resources for world missions—both in committed lives and in money—is a major hindrance. Available resources have to be used in a way that will not be so scattered as to be wasteful.

There are external obstacles also: nationalism, visa limitations, inflation, war or civil strife, and resistance from other religions or cultures. A main determining factor in entering a country is an open door.

Missionaries on the field and Foreign Mission Board staff members give much time, thought, and prayer to the best placement of both missionaries and funds. Progress of the work is evaluated carefully. Possible fields are studied to see which are unusually needy and which show responsiveness that will likely yield more fruit. Urgent need, sizable opportunity, and strategic timing are major elements in the decisions.

The Board's long-range plans propose continuing outreach to additional countries at a rate approaching that in the recent past. A stated Bold Mission Thrust intention for AD 2000 calls for "missionaries at work in at least 125 countries as God may lead."

Entering a nation is so obvious a news item that it may overshadow significant expansion into other regions of lands we already serve. For example, some countries already entered have provinces of more than a million persons in which we have no missionaries. The fuller Bold Mission Thrust statement anticipates expansion into "broad areas within countries already entered" as well as the entering of new countries.

## Concentration/Diffusion

The question of how far and how fast to expand to new fields is one expression of a continuing tension that pervades all mission work—tension between concentration and diffusion (or extension).

Should mission resources and efforts be concentrated heavily in a few places to develop very strong work? Or should they be spread broadly to have at least some influence on as many persons and as many places as possible? No easy answer can be given.

As a matter of fact, in mission planning neither extreme is appropriate as the sole rule—neither complete concentration nor complete diffusion of mission efforts—but instead a balance of the two in a way appropriate to the resources available and to the circumstances.

Missionaries occasionally say to the Foreign Mission Board, "We believe you should not enter any more countries until you first reinforce our efforts here and give us more tools to work with." This is a clear-cut expression of the tension between concentration and diffusion.

The same tension applies to details of mission planning. Should additional missionaries be assigned to strengthen existing work in a great central city, or should they be sent out to smaller cities and to towns and villages that are still untouched? In health-care ministries, should we provide a few fine hospitals that can give the highest quality of medical care, or should we plan for many bush clinics to give at least some healing touch to as many people as possible? Similar questions arise in broadcasting work, in theological education, in relief ministries, and other aspects of missions. (These questions will be examined further in chapter 14.)

A central example of this tension is seen in the long–range plans related to Bold Mission Thrust. Those plans declare an overarching purpose of trying to share the gospel with every person in the world by the end of the century. That statement obviously emphasizes diffusion. If foreign missions strategy were determined solely by that purpose, we would extend our efforts far and wide—but extremely thin—around the world. Actually, the remainder of the Bold Mission Thrust document identifies principles and intentions that imply more concentrated effort along a number of lines. Thus there is a built-in tension between concentration and diffusion. The Foreign Mission Board's plan for the remainder of the century projects a balance of diffusion with concentration.

Some Foreign Mission Board emphases in recent years have tended toward greater concentration. The program of foreign missions advance that began in 1948 defined the anticipated advance in terms of more missionaries, more fields, and more financial backing. But the next forward thrust that was proposed in 1964 and especially the Bold Mission Thrust adopted in 1976, while containing those elements, have included also strengthening and deepening missionary efforts in many additional ways. Furthermore, the adding of many new categories of missionary specialization has the effect of leaning toward concentration.

The historic stance of Foreign Mission Board administration has encouraged diffusion (as, for example, in continuing emphasis on entering new fields). The reason is very simple: The concentration side generally takes care of itself without anybody having to push it. When persons go overseas, their human nature is still human nature. Missionaries naturally feel deeply a need to concentrate in order to strengthen work in which they are engaged. Thus the Foreign Mission Board through its staff keeps urging continuing outreach toward whole nations and the whole world.

### Responsive/Neglected

Two strong emphases in current missiology have been interpreted and promoted in many books and articles. Both emphases have become by now concerns of many Southern Baptists (including many Southern Baptist missionaries). One lays stress on reaching populations that are most responsive to the gospel. The other urges increased work among populations that have been neglected in gospel outreach. Both had their roots in the church growth movement (which will be examined specifically in the next chapter). But the two emphases give rise to a dilemma in missions planning, since they move in opposite directions.

Tension between these emphases is a typical expression of the concentration/diffusion tension. Emphasis on responsive peoples is essentially a call for concentration of mission efforts. Emphasis on neglected peoples is a call for more diffusion.

The importance of responsiveness is sometimes stated so strongly as to imply that missionaries should be sent almost exclusively to ripe harvest fields, with at most only token forces in more difficult and unresponsive settings. The reasoning is that God has made certain fields ready for harvest in our day and that the mission opportunity in such fields is so urgent as to demand absolute priority. That reasoning is valid up to a point, and in a less extreme form it must certainly be a major element in planning for missions—but not the sole determining principle.

If immediate responsiveness had always been a major principle, not much foreign mission work would ever have been done. Fields that are now most responsive were once difficult. Part of the change results from God's use of the forces of history, apart from missionary effort; but much of it is due to long years of difficult and often unrewarding work by pioneer missionaries. We must not take a "hard–shell" position about the hope for responsiveness in fields that are still slow and difficult, leaving it to God to make them responsive when He pleases, without effort on our part. Planting and watering and cultivating precede harvest. In some cases, there must be first a period of removing stones before plowing and planting can take place.

The factor of responsiveness, important as it is, must be balanced with the factor of divine command which impels us to keep reaching out, not neglecting or ignoring any field, no matter how difficult, until the gospel is preached to "every creature" (Mark 16:15).

As with the broader tension between concentration and diffusion, balance is the key concern. The Foreign Mission Board does make responsiveness a very important element in its planning, but it also keeps entering new fields where large response may be many years in the future. We retain and live within the tension of outreach as well as ingathering, plowing and planting as well as reaping.

Ralph Winter has had major impact on current missiological thought by pointing out the large population blocs that dominate the remaining task of world evangelization—the Chinese, the Muslims, and the Hindus. Whereas those groups constitute by far the largest part of the non-Christian world, the number of missionaries serving among them is relatively small. If neglected peoples are to be given priority attention, which will be necessary if everyone in the world is to hear the gospel, then special effort must be made to multiply missionaries and mission outreach in those population areas.[2]

From another perspective, which reflects our Southern Baptist concern for personal relationship with Christ, the people of

Europe (both West and East) are an additional large bloc needing to hear, understand, and respond to the gospel. Though Europe is in large measure nominally Christian, its people are largely secularist and materialist in actual belief and life.

Alongside attention to these neglected regions of the world, Southern Baptist foreign missions invests large resources in some of the outstanding responsive areas of the world today— Africa, Brazil and other parts of Latin America, Korea, and the Philippines, for example. The principle is both/and, not either/ or.

## People Groups

Increasingly, mission efforts focus on people groups rather than nations. This focus relates closely to the identifying of neglected or responsive populations (as described in the previous section) and also to the homogeneous unit principle (discussed in chapter 9). The question of how far our mission work is projected must consider people groups, not just nations. Much of the most significant new outreach in the coming years will be among additional people groups in nations where we are already at work.

### The Concept

In earlier planning for missions and reporting on missions, it has been common to make nations the basic unit. Without realizing it, we may have thought that people in a particular nation were all very much alike. An apt analogy might be a cloud, which is homogeneous: Wherever you may touch it, it is all water vapor. By contrast, the true nature of any nation is richly varied, more like a mosaic (the traditional analogy used by the church growth movement) or like a patchwork quilt.[3] Mission efforts need to be targeted specifically on each of the varied population elements that make up a nation.

*People groups* seems to be the least ambiguous term to designate the different parts of the population mosaic. They can also be referred to simply as *peoples* (and a single group then called *a people*).

For some years, the generally accepted definition for people group has been "a significantly large grouping of individuals who perceive themselves to have a common affinity for one another."[4] As an interpretation of that formal definition, a fuller statement has been used. "A people group is a part of society that has some basic characteristics in common that cause it to feel a sense of oneness, and set it apart from other groups. It may be unified by language, religion, economic status, occupation, ethnic origin, geographic location, or social position."[5]

In other words, a people group is any social group with enough distinctiveness, unity, and self-awareness to be an identifiable special group. Probably the simplest example is a tribe. A people group is not just a gathering of persons (though it is not necessarily permanent). It is usually not an organization. It may be large or small—though the concept generally indicates more than just an extended family. To some extent there is overlapping of people groups within society; that is, a person may belong to more than one identifiable people group. Major people groups, though, are the separate units that combine to make up the population of a nation.[6]

Using the term *people* in this way is actually a reflection back to the New Testament. People is the equivalent of the Greek word *ethnos*, from which we get the modern English word *ethnic*. The New Testament speaks of *ta ethne*—the peoples. And so this emphasis picks up a biblical concept and places it in a current sociological frame of reference. In New Testament times, modern "nations" (composed of many people groups) did not exist. Therefore, biblical references to nations actually refer to ethnic or people groups. *The Gentiles* is a term roughly synonymous with *the nations* and refers collectively to all the non-Jewish people groups.

Indeed, the Great Commission is a specific command that every people group in the world be brought into discipleship to Jesus. It is only indirectly relevant to "making disciples" of individuals. The basic command is to disciple *panta ta ethne*, all the peoples of the world.[7] To be fully biblical and to fulfill the Great Commission, we need to plan to evangelize ethnic groups.

Current missiological usage identifies two categories of people groups: ethnolinguistic and sociocultural. The former corresponds closely to biblical usage, but many strategy principles in missions apply similarly to both groups.

### Its Development

As indicated earlier, emphasis on people groups arose from the church growth movement. Donald McGavran's influential book *The Bridges of God* (1955) centered in the concept of "people movements," in contrast with the "mission station approach" which had been traditional in McGavran's missionary experience in India. At the beginning of the book, McGavran asked "How do peoples become Christians?" and noted that "every nation is made up of various layers or strata of society."[8] He chose the term *people* intentionally as "a more universal word than 'tribe', 'caste' or 'clan' " and as "more exact than 'group.' "[9]

By 1959, in *How Churches Grow,* McGavran was stating the case in a broader context than India and in more general terms.

> The church in its multitudinous forms is likely to think of people amongst whom it works as Chinese, Indonesians, Africans, or Indians. To the extent that it does this, it labours under an illusion—that those with whom it works are fundamentally a homogeneous population; that one person is very much like another; and that all have the same background, culture, psychology and racial characteristics.
>
> The reality is otherwise. A nation is usually a conglomerate of peoples, sometimes bound together by language, religion and culture and sometimes divided by just these factors.[10]

The Mission Advanced Research and Communication Center (MARC), founded by World Vision in 1966, has centered its work on people groups. Ed Dayton, its director, has been strongly influenced by McGavran.[11]

The *peoples* terminology was used in a 1972 consultation on "The Gospel and Frontier Peoples" to give attention to "frontier missons among tribal peoples."[12]

The International Congress on World Evangelization held at Lausanne, Switzerland, in 1974 further advanced general interest in people groups. By that time the additional term, *unreached people* (meaning an unreached people group), had come into focus and was a central theme at the congress. For the congress MARC had prepared a directory listing about 450 "unreached peoples." From 1979, such directories have been published annually.[13]

The term *unreached people* points out that there are some people groups which do not yet have the gospel effectively planted within their own cultural settings. The concept has been defined, interpreted, and restated in the past ten years through a process led primarily by the strategy working group of the Lausanne Committee for World Evangelization (LCWE), with Peter Wagner as chairman. Results have been shared in the unreached peoples volumes already mentioned and in a practical strategy workbook developed by Edward R. Dayton, founder and director of MARC, under the title *That Everyone May Hear: Reaching the Unreached*.[14]

For a time, the working definition of an unreached people was "a group that is less than 20 percent *practicing* Christian." This interpretation was explained:

> It is estimated that when 20 percent of the people are Christians, the church within the group no longer needs outside evangelists. For all intents and purposes this group is no longer "unreached." To put it another way, the reached group of people is one that is *more* than 20 percent Christian. It is assumed the church(es) within it can complete the evangelization of the group. (Notice that the major task of world evangelization will be done by Christians with their neighbors. The *cross-cultural* task is only to reach each group.)[15]

In the late 1970s, Ralph Winter coined the phrase "hidden people" to refer to people groups with virtually no Christians or churches. Since *unreached people* was being given such a broad definition, some narrower term was needed to represent peoples having little or no contact with the gospel. The idea in the word *hidden* was that the people groups had been neglected or overlooked, even though in some cases they might be living among Christians of some other social group. Winter began also to use the term *frontier missions* for outreach to hidden peoples.

Efforts to refine and implement the people group approach continued. The strategy working group of the Lausanne Committee sought to refine the unreached peoples concept further, breaking it down on a percentage basis into hidden people, initially reached, minimally reached, and possibly reached. Ways of analyzing potential receptivity to the gospel were suggested—for example, the Engel scale of movement toward Christ, originally proposed by James Engel of the Wheaton Graduate School; and a resistance/receptivity scale.[16]

The Lausanne Committee sponsored another world consultation at Pattaya, Thailand, in 1980. It studied strategies for evangelizing major population groups of the world, a topic with relevance to the peoples concept, though not specifically focused on it.

Another international conference in 1980 was the World Consultation on Frontier Missions at Edingburgh, Scotland. It was promoted and developed by Ralph Winter and focused sharply on hidden peoples and thus by inference also on those major world population blocs that include most of the hidden peoples. Winter used an estimate of 16,750 hidden peoples in the world, assumed to constitute half the world's population. The conference theme was "A Church for Every People by the Year 2000."

### Recent Questions and Problems

Since 1980 there have been continuing efforts to clarify concepts and terminology related to unreached peoples and to develop plans for correlation in reaching them. Ralph Winter's U.S. Center for World Mission is devoted entirely to this purpose. Its news bulletin, *Mission Frontiers,* continues to spotlight frontier missions, having for a time encouraged churches and mission agencies to "adopt a people" (though later Winter came to feel that the phrase sounded paternalistic).

More recently the term *hidden people* has been downplayed because it has been subject to considerable misunderstanding. *Unreached people group* is the currently recommended term. The criterion of "20 percent practicing Christian" as the outer boundary for unreached peoples has been dropped (and by implication also the smaller percentages that were identified as initially, minimally, or possibly reached). There has been agreement to identify unreached peoples by the definition that was used for hidden peoples at the Edinburgh consultation: "Those cultural and linguistic subgroups, urban or rural, for whom there is as yet no indigenous community of believing Christians able to evangelize their own people."[17]

A more recent revision is: "Among which there is no indigenous community of believing Christians with adequate numbers and resources to evangelize this people group without outside (cross-cultural) assistance."[18]

There is still much ambiguity in the people group emphasis. Winter's figure of 16,750 has no clear statistical base and is apparently much too large if it is taken to mean ethnolinguistic groups. A count of sociocultural groups could be almost unlimited in number. David Barrett in the *World Christian Encyclopedia* identifies about 9,000 people groups (ethno-linguistic) in the world, with only about 1,000 "unreached."[19] This figure is based on groups "less than 20 percent evangelized"—which is far different from less than 20 percent practicing Christians.

The *Unreached Peoples* volumes lump together in their listing both ethnolinguistic groups and those identified by social or vocational criteria. Even so, the 1983 volume lists only 3,690 groups. It would be much less confusing and the lists would be much more helpful if there were separate lists for ethnolinguistic groups and sociocultural groups.

Even with all the ambiguities, however, the concept of unreached people groups and the emphasis on planning to reach them with the gospel through cross-cultural missions is of great value.[20]

### The Southern Baptist Approach

Both in general worldwide planning done by Foreign Mission Board staff and in detailed local planning on the mission fields, evaluation of needs and opportunities in terms of people groups helps answer three main questions: (1) What groups may have been overlooked or neglected in the sharing of the gospel? (2) Which groups are currently especially open or responsive? (3) Are there any groups of unusual strategic importance for the reaching of the entire nation with the gospel?

In Southern Baptist foreign missions, even before the modern emphasis on people groups developed, spontaneous attention was given in most places to specific people groups. Such attention has now increased. Thus Southern Baptist missionaries are more involved with tribal groups that are to a large extent unreached with the gospel. In response to an informal inquiry in 1980, Foreign Mission Board area directors reported work among 20 such groups. A significant example is the intensive and highly successful effort among the Giryama people in coastal Kenya, which was projected about a decade ago.

Although tribal peoples are the most obvious focus of concern for unreached peoples, the concept applies to many other aspects of Southern Baptist missions. For example, the extensive worldwide ministry through English-language churches, which the Board began to promote in the mid-1950s, is a focus on a special people group: Americans residing overseas and/or the general international community in major cities.

Another illustration is the Bangkok Urban Strategy, developed jointly by the Baptists of Thailand and Southern Baptist missionaries.[21] The plan involved a survey by a sociologist to identify within the city of Bangkok a large number of "neighborhoods" which might be considered as separate places to begin Christian ministries. In effect, this was an identifying of different people groups in Bangkok. The entire phenonomen of urbanization, which defines increasingly the context of missions, calls for growing use of the people group approach.

Some advocates of the people group approach insist that it should displace the earlier approach to nations. The Foreign Mission Board accepts the new emphasis as an addition, not a replacement, as indicated in the Board's strategy statement: "Although . . . increasing attention is being given to the peoples concept, we continue using the nation as the main planning unit. The major reason is partnership with Baptist bodies that are organized on a national basis." Thus in planning, both in the

Foreign Mission Board offices and on the fields, concern for people groups is expressed within the context of concern for partnership.

### Moratorium

The suggestion of moratorium in missions is a more sophisticated way of saying, "Missionary, go home!"[22] The idea is not new. For many years some groups of Christians have felt that the number of overseas missionaries should be reduced. Mission boards of several denominations have made this a matter of standing policy. They base it on the principle that when the church has been planted in a particular area it becomes the responsibility of that church to evangelize the area.

However, the term *moratorium* came into prominence and became a common discussion topic in the 1970s. A proposal for temporary withdrawal of missionaries was first made in East Africa in February 1971. The emotion that fueled the moratorium movement built to a peak by 1974, when a call for moratorium was officially adopted at a meeting of the All-Africa Conference of Churches (though even that organization soon moderated its position). By late in the decade, attention was being given to the underlying causes for the proposal, but without much continuing backing for the proposal itself. It had never been widely supported outside Africa. (Hugh Smith, staff member with the Overseas Ministries of American Baptist Churches, told of a Chinese layman in Thailand who commented that moratorium "sounds like a place where they keep dead bodies—and I think that's where that idea belongs!")[23]

Previously in this chapter we have examined mainly outreach to new fields—how far to go and how fast. The moratorium question relates to old fields of mission work—how long should work continue? After a certain length of time, or at a certain stage of development, does further missionary presence become counterproductive?

The moratorium proposal embraces the entirely valid point that indigenous freedom, indigenous initiative, and indigenous responsibility are essential for church strength and for continued rapid spread of the gospel. However, if moratorium is taken as an absolute principle, it hinders the increasing of Christian forces devoted to world evangelization. At the Lausanne Congress on World Evangelization in 1974, the idea of moratorium was discussed at considerable length by participants from all continents. It was rejected as an absolute, though the values of indigenous freedom, initiative, and responsibility were fully recognized and strongly supported.

In Southern Baptist missions, we have not declared a moratorium. On the contrary, both the Foreign Mission Board and the Southern Baptist Convention adopted a plan to double our missionary forces across the world between AD 1975 and AD 2000. This has led to questions. Sometimes persons from other Christian groups ask, "Why are Southern Baptists seeking to increase the number of missonaries, when many other Christian leaders feel that a moratorium is in order today?" Sometimes from within Southern Baptist life comes the question, "Does the Foreign Mission Board have plans for reduction or withdrawal of missionary forces in older fields of work?"

Occasionally someone will cite the phasing out of Foreign Mission Board involvement in Hawaii as a model—not realizing that missionaries have not been phased out, but home missionaries are serving there instead of foreign missionaries, since Hawaii is now a state.

One guideline in the Foreign Mission Board's formal strategy paper is: "With the growth of local Baptist strength, transition in the form of missionary ministries is to be expected, but not automatic withdrawal or moratorium." This guideline points out that the Foreign Mission Board has no arbitrary plan for withdrawal. Neither is there an arbitrary policy to prohibit withdrawal. Each situation is examined on its own merits. The presumption favors continuing to send missionaries in response to continuing needs and opportunities.

An outstanding case in point is Brazil, where Baptist work is now more than a century old and is well established, mature, and vigorous. With more than 300 Southern Baptist missionaries already serving in Brazil, some question why we continue sending more missionaries instead of beginning to phase out our missionary forces.

There are several obvious reasons. Perhaps no one of them by itself would be compelling, but together they make a strong case (typical also of principles applicable to other countries).

Many from our churches who offer themselves for missionary service have a clear impression of a call to serve in Brazil. In some cases, this impression of the Lord's leading is based on earlier experience with Brazil or Brazilians, or on the influence of missionaries to Brazil.

We continue to receive from Brazil requests for large numbers of additional missionaries. Many of these requests for persons for specific assignments are originated by Baptist churches or state conventions there, or by agencies of the Brazilian Baptist Convention. This means that our Brazilian Baptist brethren still want us to send more missionaries.

The need for additional Christian workers in Brazil is great. Evangelical believers constitute only a very small percentage of the population. Spiritism is a strong factor in Brazilian life. Though Baptists number about 600,000 there are still some states with populations in the millions with relatively few Baptist churches.

This is a day of special spiritual opportunity in Brazil. There is a harvest to be reaped because of the openness and responsiveness of the people.

In any land where Baptist work is well established and strong, the roles of missionaries are different from what they are in lands where Baptist work is new, small, and still weak. But missionaries to help in outreach to new areas or additional people groups and who have a servant spirit to stand alongside and help the efforts of local Baptist churches and conventions are still needed and still valuable.

### "Closed" Areas

Missionaries cannot go at all into some countries. There are also several former Southern Baptist mission fields which missionaries have had to leave (the current missions maps produced by the Foreign Mission Board show 11 such countries). The existence of such "closed" countries places limits on how far and how fast we can move into world missions outreach.

## Meaning

The idea of *closed countries* must be used with considerable caution. Often the term may be more confusing than helpful.

It is hard even to draw up a list of countries that do not allow foreign missionaries. Some countries definitely can be listed. But there are others that may admit missionaries for special purposes or for limited time periods—or provided no publicity describes the arrangement as mission work. Degrees of openness and closedness merge from one into another without any sharp dividing line.

Timing is also a factor. Countries which allowed missionaries a few years ago may not allow them today. Other countries which were closed to missionaries have now opened their doors.

A list prepared in the Foreign Mission Board offices in 1982, with a broader scope, identified 96 countries "where missionary residence is not possible or advisable" (at the time of the survey). Many were very small countries which might be open, but would have low priority in Foreign Mission Board planning because of other more urgent needs. The *World Christian Encyclopedia,* published that same year, listed 25 countries as closed to foreign missions, plus 24 "partially-closed."[24]

Trying to maintain a current reliable list is not the only problem about closed countries. A more important concern is a proper understanding of what the concept really means. It can easily be misunderstood.

Of course, no country is closed to the presence of God. He does not need a visa and residence permit from any human government. For generations prior to 1873, Japan had public notice boards proclaiming that if the Christian God Himself came to Japan, He would pay for it with His life—but God was at work there anyway.

Countries that do not allow foreign missionaries are not closed to the often vibrant witness of local believers. Rumania and Burma are examples of closed countries where Baptist churches are unusually vigorous.

Countries that may be labeled closed are usually not closed to opportunities for Christian fellowship across national borders—

and for the continuing mutual interest, concern, and prayer that result from such fellowship.

In actuality, very few countries are entirely closed to all possibilities for Southern Baptist involvement and help. We believe our very best help in other lands is given by missionaries living and working there—but when that is impossible, there are other valuable ways we can help Christians of such lands to strengthen their church life and to share their witness.

### Causes

The reality of so many closed countries (and of serious limitations and difficulties for Christian missions in other countries) has been interpreted as a kind of fallout. "Fallout is something you cannot escape, whether or not you had anything to do with its cause." Widespread nationalism and the multiplying of totalitarian governments are suggested as main causes.[25]

In some cases, to avoid endangering local Christians, "strategic withdrawal" of missionaries is recommended.[26] This is what Southern Baptist missionaries have done in some cases, such as Nicaragua, where temporary withdrawal was suggested by leaders of the local Baptist convention.

Some interpreters have seemed to blame the Christian mission movement for political changes that have brought the closing of doors, though generally Christians have not been that large a factor in the situation. David M. Paton, in his well-known book *Christian Missions and the Judgment of God*, appeared to lean in that direction in interpreting modern China. However, his actual conclusion was: "The practical reasons for the ending of the missionary era in China are of course external to the Church and the Mission; and they are political."[27] It is difficult to agree with his further conclusion that "the end of the missionary era was the will of God."[28] To be sure, it can be understood as within his permissive will. It did bring a forced "moratorium" on the presence of missionaries, and in retrospect much indigenous growth of Christian faith in China is evident—but the end of the missionary era accompanied political developments which meant suffering and death for millions of people. I believe it is sounder to understand closed doors as circumstances which

God allows and which he can overrule and even use for his own glory (Gen. 50:20; Ps. 76:10).

## Ministries

Developing the most acceptable and most effective ways to help the Christian cause in closed countries is very important. In presentations to the Foreign Mission Board in September 1980, Ted Ward (professor at Michigan State University and knowledgeable evangelical missions consultant) stressed the urgency of finding ways to cross inhospitable borders for Christian witness. He emphasized bivocational missionary ministries and the value of the witness of potential "lay missionaries," persons who travel or live overseas in the normal course of their own employment.

In principle, the Foreign Mission Board's arena is global—all nations outside the United States. Therefore, the Board gives continuing attention to nations which are in some sense or to some degree closed to traditional missionary ministries. In 1983 formal guidelines were developed under the title "Ministry Development Plan for Countries Where We Do Not Have Missionaries." The plan includes a variety of possible approaches to meet differing circumstances.[29]

The Laity Abroad program of the Foreign Mission Board, which in 1984 was in contact with and provided materials and other help for 1,749 persons, is an important part of the ministry plan. Approximately half of the countries represented by contacts of the Laity Abroad office are countries where Southern Baptists currently have no missionaries.

Much of what is done in relation to countries that restrict normal missionary activity maintains a very low profile. In some cases, publicity would make the ministry impossible. Governments may permit and even welcome programs that could become an embarrassment to them politically if promoted too aggressively. Therefore, the Foreign Mission Board does not publicize all its involvement in such ministries.

Even for the most difficult situations, it may be possible to do at least something. For example, beginning in July 1984 the Foreign Mission Board began to share in a weekly gospel broadcast for Albania, which is perhaps the world's most strongly anti-religious nation.

An approach in which the Foreign Mission Board relates cooperatively with the Home Mission Board and with National Student Ministries seeks to evangelize students and other temporary residents from other lands, so they may then return to their own lands for Christian witness and ministry.[30] Many Southern Baptists have an opportunity for indirect ministry in some closed country through kindness and through witness to persons who come to America from other countries.

### Conclusion

The question explored in this chapter involves great variety and much complexity. Many factors affect the rapidity and the extent of Southern Baptist movement into new fields and decisions about continuing ministries in older fields.[31] In response to such complications, flexibility combined with a clear sense of direction is essential. The philosophy statement of the Foreign Mission Board affirms:

> The board is committed to a strategy of entering new countries, as well as ministering to neglected areas in countries already entered, as God may lead. It believes attempts should be made to communicate the gospel via mass media to countries where missionaries either cannot go or are prevented from preaching.
>
> Both responsive and unresponsive fields must be served. The Great Commission gives no warrant for neglecting so-called "unresponsive" fields.
>
> The board's philosophy should be kept comprehensive enough and flexible enough to accomplish, in future circumstances and altered times, the will of our sovereign Lord and the expressed wishes of the supporting constituency.

The strategy document has a section explaining major strategy concerns, including several dealt with in this chapter (major population blocs that are relatively unevangelized, closed areas, the peoples concept, responsive areas, urbanization, and strategic timing). The section then summarizes:

The Foreign Mission Board does not take any one of these concerns as its sole or even its major strategy determinant. Its strategy seeks to be an appropriate combination of all of these emphases, giving to each due attention. This approach is much more complex and more difficult than a strategy approach based on only one principle. . . . The exact place of these various elements in Foreign Mission Board strategy is dynamic rather than static.

As these chapters on objectives have affirmed, churches are the key to the entire process.[32] The central concern of the Foreign Mission Board is to do everything possible, in as many lands and among as many peoples as possible, in full partnership with local Baptist churches and conventions, to plant, to multiply, and to strengthen indigenous churches—that the gospel may be shared with all, and that God's kingdom may come and His will be done on earth, as it is in heaven (Matt. 6:10).

### Notes

1. For a brief discussion of the problem of determining how many countries there are, see Winston Crawley's column, "Horizons: How Many 'Countries' Should be on the List," in the October-November 1983 issue of *The Commission*, vol. 46, no. 8: 73.

2. For the main thrust of Winter's emphasis, including charts and diagrams, see the reports of his presentations at the Lausanne Congress on World Evangelization in J. D. Douglas, ed., *Let the Earth Hear His Voice* (Minneapolis: Worldwide Publications, 1975), pp. 213-41; at the World Consultation on Frontier Missions which he sponsored at Edinburgh in 1980, in Allan Starling, ed., *Seeds of Promise* (Pasadena, Calif.: William Carey Library, 1981), pp. 45-99, especially pp. 92-95; and at an Evangelical Consultation on Frontier Missions at Wheaton in 1983, in David A. Fraser, ed., *The Church in New Frontiers for Missions* (Monrovia, Calif.: Missions Advanced Research and Communication Center, 1983), pp. 83-100. Large charts and diagrams presenting this theme visually and updated periodically are available from the U.S. Center for World Mission.

3. This analogy has been suggested by Charles Harvey, of the Canadian Baptist Overseas Mission Board, in an article in the periodical published by that board, *The Enterprise* (Summer 1983): 1-2.

4. Edward R. Dayton, ed., *That Everyone May Hear: Reaching the Unreached,*

3rd ed. (Monrovia, Calif.: Missions Advanced Research and Communication Center, 1983), p. 18.

5. "Appendix A: Unreached Peoples Questionnaire," Edward R. Dayton and Samuel Wilson, eds. *Unreached Peoples '83* (Monrovia, Calif.: MARC [Missions Advanced Research and Communication Center], 1983), p. 494.

6. For detailed treatment of the concept of people groups and the related concept of unreached peoples, see Dayton, *That Everyone May Hear;* Edward R. Dayton and David A. Fraser, *Planning Strategies for World Evangelization* (Grand Rapids: William B. Eerdmans Publishing Company, 1980); and the annual *Unreached Peoples* volumes published since 1979 by MARC, with C. Peter Wagner, Edward R. Dayton, and Samuel Wilson as editors. Interesting overviews of the people group concept are available in the Summer 1983 issue of *The Enterprise,* the periodical of the Canadian Baptist Overseas Mission Board, and in the March/April 1983 (vol. 2, no. 2) issue of *World Christian,* a publication of the U.S. Center for World Mission.

7. On this point see further the column of Winston Crawley, "Horizons: Clarifying the Command of the Great Commission," in *The Commission,* vol. 46, no. 5 (June-July 1983): 73.

8. Donald Anderson McGavran, *The Bridges of God* (London: World Dominion Press, 1955), p. 1.

9. Ibid., p. 13.

10. Donald Anderson McGavran, *How Churches Grow* (London: World Dominion Press, 1959), pp. 40-41.

11. See a detailed explanation in "The New World of Missions: Are They Hidden or Unreached" in the March 1980 issue of the *MARC Newsletter,* pp. 4-5.

12. R. Pierce Beaver, ed., *The Gospel and Frontier Peoples* (South Pasadena, Calif.: William Carey Library, 1973), p. 1.

13. See Peter Wagner and Edward R. Dayton, eds., *Unreached Peoples '79* (Elgin, Ill.: David C. Cook Publishing Co., 1978) and its annual successors.

14. Dayton, cited in note 4.

15. Ibid., pp. 31, 32.

16. Ibid., pp. 42-47.

17. Starling, p. 61. These decisions were reached at a meeting in 1982 of representative persons involved in missions planning and analysts with interest in people groups, including this author.

18. Dayton and Wilson, *Unreached Peoples '83,* pp. 494-98, 499.

19. *World Christian Encyclopedia,* p. 19; see also pp. 105-115.

20. Incidentally, E. Luther Copeland indicates a preference for "unevangelized" rather than "unreached" in *World Mission and World Survival* (Nashville: Broadman, 1985), p. 36, though actually the two terms are not equivalent in meaning.

21. Ronald C. Hill, *Bangkok: An Urban Arena* (Nashville: Convention Press, 1982).

22. See the earlier book with that title by James A. Scherer, *Missionary Go Home!* (Englewood Cliffs, N.J.: Prentice-Hall, Inc., 1964).

23. For thorough reviews of the moratorium discussion, including its basis in real problems that need continuing attention, see Copeland, pp. 93-101; J. Herbert Kane, *The Christian World Mission: Today and Tomorrow* (Grand Rapids: Baker Book House, 1981), chapter 12, pp. 173-84; and W. Harold Fuller, *Mission-Church Dynamics* (Pasadena, Calif.: William Carey Library, 1980), pp. 99-109.

24. *World Christian Encyclopedia*, pp. 129-30, 799-801.

25. Ted Ward, "The Future of Missions: Hangovers, Fallout, and Hope," in David J. Hesselgrave, ed., *New Horizons in World Mission* (Grand Rapids: Baker Book House, 1979), p. 25.

26. Ibid., p. 26 and note 4 on p. 32.

27. David M. Paton, *Christian Missions and the Judgment of God* (London: SCM Press Ltd., 1953), pp. 50-51.

28. Ibid., p. 51.

29. For brief amplification and some examples, see "Horizons: Which Ones Are 'Closed'?" by Winston Crawley, *The Commission*, vol. 47, no. 6 (August 1984): 7.

30. See further Winston Crawley's column, "Horizons: Gates to Closed Places Could Swing Open," *The Commission*, vol. 46, no. 7 (September 1983): 65.

31. For a variety of examples taken from Eastern and Southern Africa, see the 1983 mission study book by John Cheyne, *The Imperative Impulse* (Nashville: Convention Press, 1983).

32. Compare the statements by Paton (p. 58): "The work of missions is the planting of the visible Church in all its completeness in areas where it has never existed or has now ceased to exist. This may also be expressed by saying that missions have as their aim the growth of the Church to its divinely appointed limits which are identical with the geographical distribution of the human race. . . . The aim of missions is not primarily to save souls, but to provide the permanent means by which souls may be saved."

# Part V
# Strategy

The word *strategy* is applied to mission work today both wide-ly and frequently; but in most cases the term is used very loosely, almost as a more impressive synonym for *methods*. I feel it is much more meaningful to reserve the term for a special kind of careful and thorough general planning.

The word originated as a Roman military term. In military affairs it refers to an overall plan for employment of resources for maximum military effectiveness. It is used in contrast with an-other term, *tactics*, which refers to specific detailed actions that support and implement the general strategy. According to that pattern, details of mission methods and approaches would be understood as part of mission tactics. Strategy then would refer to the overall long-range plan for coordinating actions and al-locating resources for greatest effectiveness.

As indicated in the Introduction, the Foreign Mission Board did not make formal reference to mission strategy until 1965, but both the process and many principles of strategic planning were followed by staff and missionaries in earlier generations. The concept of an overall plan for missions was not new.[1]

Some perhaps would question the legitimacy of the strategy concept in missions. Persons of an independent temperament might prefer freedom to follow at all times the impression of the moment, instead of being limited by a plan adopted earlier. Some might even interpret strategy as seeking to limit the Holy Spirit. Jesus, however, spoke favorably of efforts to understand and evaluate circumstances (Luke 12:56) and to estimate re-sources available to accomplish one's purposes (Luke 14:28-31). And the missionary efforts of Paul, both as recorded in Acts and as reflected in Paul's epistles, are full of references to planning. We are convinced that God is ready to provide guidance in the planning process and that the Holy Spirit leads groups as well as individuals. These beliefs find spiritual confirmation at many points. Therefore, we believe that strategic planning is a valid and appropriate part of biblical missions.

According to the Foreign Mission Board's philosophy state-ment, "Long-range strategy planning, in the view of the board, is consistent with its stewardship obligations (1) toward our great God and his eternal purpose, and (2) toward the supporting churches."

Much has been written in recent years about mission strategy. Sometimes the term itself has not been used, even though content relates to strategy. Johannes Verkuyl, for instance, in his book on contemporary missiology, follows a section on "The Goal and Purpose of Mission" with a section on "Ways and Means."[2] More specifically, however, strategy is addressed by Harold R. Cook in *Strategy of Missions: An Evangelical View;* [3] by Edward R. Dayton in a small practical strategy planning workbook, *That Everyone May Hear: Reaching the Unreached;*[4] and by Edward R. Dayton and David A. Fraser in their comprehensive volume focused on the people group approach, *Planning Strategies for World Evangelization.*[5]

The Foreign Misision Board moved to formal concentrated attention to strategy in preparation for the decade of the 1970s, when the Overseas Division which had been created in 1968 led in preparation of a "Strategy for the Seventies."[6] To implement that plan, each area director (then called area secretary) was to instruct each mission in his area to consider setting up a committee for planning and review of strategy or to assign that function to some appropriate existing committee, unless the mission already had a formal strategy planning process. Also, a proposed general approach to strategy planning was shared with missionaries at the annual conference of furloughing missionaries in 1971.[7]

In January 1976 the Foreign Mission Board adopted the comprehensive and detailed long-range plan outlined in "Foreign Missions Looks Toward AD 2000." That plan was accepted by the Southern Baptist Convention in June of that year, becoming part of the new Bold Mission Thrust. The document included a summary of principles of Southern Baptist foreign missions. The first of those principles stressed indigenous churches and partnership (two themes already emphasized in earlier chapters of this book). The interpretation of that principle also included this statement about strategy.

The Foreign Mission Board maintains an overview of

missions strategy throughout the world in line with instructions given to it by the Southern Baptist Convention. It draws up overall strategy guidelines, takes initiatives, and helps to coordinate efforts and plans in other parts of the world. It seeks to cultivate the work of Japanese Baptists, Nigerian Baptists, Brazilian Baptists, etc., in their proper spheres.

National and local strategy formulation overseas usually takes final focus on the basis of initiatives taken by national leaders and missionaries. Overseas plans and strategies are not formulated at the Foreign Mission Board and passed down a chain of command to missionaries, churches, and denominational entities in foreign countries.

The Holy Spirit must be given free rein. The spirit may lead Baptists in foreign groups to follow methods and procedures different from our own, but we all serve the Lord Christ.[8]

Obviously the Foreign Mission Board has been placing increasing emphasis on strategy. This has been expressed most clearly through the adoption of a formal strategy position paper by the Board's Executive Management Group in April 1982. That document interpreted the strategy concept in this way:

Strategy deals with the "how" question. In foreign missions, it refers to an overall plan for managing resources most effectively to carry out the missionary purpose.

The developing of strategy inevitably rests in the broader context of a philosophy of missions and theology of mission, which identify the "what" and "why" of missions. . . .

The document described the essential design of our mission strategy by quoting the still-valid statement from the earlier "Strategy for the Seventies."

The essence of strategy is the managing of resources for greatest effectiveness. The need for strategic planning rests in the assumption that resources available are limited, that not all the fine things that might be done and should be done actually can be done, and that therefore hard choices are necessary if available resources are to be used in ways most vital to total effectiveness.

Maximum results require coordination of resources and efforts in a unified program directed toward a central objective. Our strategy is not, and in the nature of the case cannot be, a matter of simply doing more of everything we do. Neither should it be a range of separate programs and projects carried out independently of each other. Increased mission thrust is possible only through comprehensive planning for the best stewardship of mission resources.

Strategic planning calls for the relating of every part of the work to the objectives of the whole. The central objective to give focus to planning in each field is the developing of indigenous church strength. This includes evangelism and is related to varied ministries. The objective is not to be understood narrowly or shortsightedly, and the exact combination of approaches and proportionate allocation of resources must be adapted to local conditions.

Similar considerations apply to the Foreign Mission Board in its decisions regarding the world and our mission efforts as a whole. Resources must be allocated in such proportions as to bring greatest overall accomplishment.

Many of the concerns mentioned in these overview statements about Southern Baptist foreign missions strategy have been explored in earlier sections of this book. Strategy rests in theology of mission (our understanding of God and His purpose both for the world and for His church) and in a philosophy of missions (a general understanding as to what we are trying to accomplish). These were dealt with at length in chapter 4. They constitute the why and what of Southern Baptist missions. Strategy involves the determining of specific objectives (such as indigenous churches and partnership, dealt with in Part IV) and the translating of those objectives into approaches and methods, which will be the substance of Part V. (A major element in our approach, the emphasis on career missionaries, has been considered already in Part III.)[9]

This question of strategy can be illustrated by a football player anticipating a game. He knows what he wants to do; he wants to help win the game. But the strategy question is How? His planning could be approached so narrowly as for him simply to ask himself, *What shall I do on this play? What move shall I make?* That is only part of the question. Since football is a team sport, he considers his own actions in the context of another question, What shall *we* do on this play? The move that a specific player makes depends on what the team is doing, not just on one player's personal idea.

For strategy to work, there must be a team plan. The plan for each play is determined in the even larger context of a game plan—which, of course, makes allowance for interim decisions along the way, depending upon circumstances, and for possible major alteration of the game plan itself if necessary.

Mission strategy involves this correlation of individual plans and actions with group plans and actions, within the larger picture of a long-range plan which is the overall strategy. It is obvious from the illustration that strategy is not so much a specific decision or position as it is a process, with general long-range planning being implemented by many decisions and adaptations along the way. Strategy in essence is dynamic.

Part V deals with global strategy as understood and implemented by the Foreign Mission Board. A parenthetical but critical question concerns the world mission strategy of Southern Baptist individuals and churches—which in the main seems to be lacking. That is to say, most individual and local church decisions, such as church budget decisions, are not made as implementation of a conscious world strategy—with a clear purpose and comprehensive plan that determine the allocating of resources and move steadily toward the objective of world evangelization. Such a world missions strategy would require using minimal resources to maintain our churches and denominational structure, so as to devote maximum resources to missions outreach through our cooperative channels. This concept which distinguishes between base and outreach is not part of the thinking and planning of most Southern Baptists.

Part V considers first two major concerns in foreign missions strategy, followed by a general examination of methodology and then analysis of a special question that is focal in many strategy discussions.

Before we review the various elements in mission strategy, I suggest two cautions, both related to continuing openness to the Holy Spirit's leadership. Lesslie Newbigin wrote:

> My own experience as a missionary has been that the significant advances of the church have not been the result of our own decisions about the mobilizing and allocating of "resources." . . . By obediently following where the Spirit leads, often in ways neither planned, known, nor understood, the church acts out the hope which it is given by the presence of the Spirit who is the living foretaste of the kingdom.[10]

And Harold R. Cook commented:

> The Spirit has never revealed the whole of His strategy. Like every good general, He reveals to each of his men the part that concerns him, and often only a step at a time. To those who have the larger responsibilities He gives a larger vision of His plans. But no one can claim to know them all. . . .
>
> The Lord expects us to use the wisdom He has given us. He expects us to deliberate, to work diligently, to lay sound plans. But most of all He wants us to be men under His control, doing all these things in the Spirit.[11]

This is why the Foreign Mission Board philosophy statement, in the paragraph that emphasizes strategy planning, ends by saying, "Throughout the process, the Holy Spirit must have free rein for guidance and for power."

### Notes

1. Note for example that Edmund Davidson Soper in his widely used book on *The Philosophy of the Christian World Mission* (Nashville: Abingdon Press,

1943) devoted an entire major part to "The Strategy of the World Mission." He noted the relationship between strategy and tactics on p. 235.

2. Johannes Verkuyl, *Contemporary Missiology* (Grand Rapids: William B. Eerdmans Publishing Company, 1978), Sections VII and VIII, pp. 176-225.

3. Harold R. Cook, *Strategy of Missions: An Evangelical View* (Chicago: Moody Press, 1963).

4. Edward R. Dayton, *That Everyone May Hear: Reaching the Unreached*, 3rd. ed. (Monrovia, Calif.: Missions Advanced Research and Communication Center, 1983).

5. Edward R. Dayton and David A. Fraser, *Planning Strategies for World Evangelization* (Grand Rapids: William B. Eerdmans Publishing Company, 1980).

6. The document is a part of the Foreign Mission Board minutes as a report of Winston Crawley, then director of the Overseas Division, to the Foreign Mission Board, SBC, in May 1970.

7. These implementation steps were reported to the Foreign Mission Board, SBC, at its March 1972 meeting by Winston Crawley. Further steps in the strategy emphasis were reported in April 1974.

8. Implications of this statement of principles were interpreted by Winston Crawley in a report to the Foreign Mission Board, SBC, in March 1979.

9. *Perspectives on the World Christian Movement: A Reader,* ed. Ralph D. Winter, Steven C. Hawthorne, et. al. (Pasadena, Calif: William Carey Library, 1981) brings together articles on the entire range of the why and how of missions.

10. Lesslie Newbigin, *The Open Secret* (Grand Rapids: William B. Eerdmans Publishing Company, 1978), pp. 71-72.

11. Cook, pp. 122-23.

# 12
# What About Church Growth?

This is not the place for an exhaustive analysis of the church growth movement—its history, principles, contribution, and possible problems (which would require an entire book). Notes at the end of this chapter and the Bibliography give references for those who want to explore the matter further. The intention here is to provide enough background information for adequate understanding of how the church growth emphasis is involved in Southern Baptist foreign missions.

### History

The church growth movement is now 30 years old. Peter Wagner, a leader and frequent spokesman of the movement, says that "the historical event now regarded as the beginning of the movement was Donald McGavran's publication of *The Bridges of God* in 1955."[1] In *The Bridges of God* (with the subtitle "A Study in the Strategy of Missions"), McGavran presented his conclusions about emphases needed in world missions, based on 31 years of missionary experience in India.[2]

Incidentally, McGavran himself has sought to downplay that interpretation of the movement's origin. He has written:

> It is in no sense a new movement. It is simply a continuation of the essential emphases of the Early Church and every great forward movement in the Church from that time to this. Do not, I beg of you, think of it as an American invention of 25

years ago. Classical biblical missions believed in church growth.[3]

Most of the distinctive tenets of the church growth movement can indeed be traced in earlier Christian missions. Some of them had been strongly urged by earlier writers, such as Roland Allen in *Missionary Methods: St. Paul's or Ours?* (1912) and *The Spontaneous Expansion of the Church* (1927).[4] It remains true, however, that only the perceptiveness of McGavran combined a number of insights into a well-defined strategy, and only the promotion of that strategy by McGavran gained the following that made it a movement.

The rapid spread of interest in church growth came initially from the continuing teaching and writing of McGavran. As time passed, others joined him in teaching church growth principles and in writing to explain and apply them.[5] McGavran's teaching gained momentum through the Institute of Church Growth, which he founded in 1961 in Eugene, Oregon. In 1965 it was moved to Pasadena, California, to become the School of World Mission of Fuller Theological Seminary. There it attracted other teachers and a large number of students from many lands (both missionaries on furlough and national church leaders).

Further books by McGavran expounding church growth doctrine include *How Churches Grow* (1959);[6] *Church Growth and Christian Mission* (1965),[7] a symposium including R. Cal Guy of Southwestern Baptist Theological Seminary, Melvin L. Hodges, and Eugene Nida; and his definitive work, *Understanding Church Growth* (1970).[8]

Other important instruments of the church growth movement have been the *Church Growth Bulletin*, founded in 1964, which now has the title *Global Church Growth Bulletin;* the Church Growth Book Club, founded in 1970; and the William Carey Library, which was founded in 1969 by Ralph D. Winter to publish books on missions, especially including church growth themes.[9]

McGavran's focus of attention from the beginning had been the spread of the gospel among unreached and responsive people groups around the world. In 1972, however, he and Peter

Wagner began applying church growth principles to the United States. That application has been expanded, with Win Arn as the leader. By now there is a special organization, the Institute for American Church Growth, with its own periodical, *Church Growth: America.*

The church growth movement has met a good bit of resistance and has sparked considerable controversy.[10] Early critics of the church growth movement tended to question the legitimacy of so much emphasis on numerical growth. It was partly in response to those critics that Allen R. Tippett wrote *Church Growth and the Word of God.*[11] More recently, questioning of church growth has reflected growing concern among evangelicals for the social dimensions of the Christian faith—what is sometimes called "the cultural mandate." Peter Wagner has dealt with that concern in *Church Growth and the Whole Gospel.*[12]

## Central Themes

McGavran has been a fertile thinker and a prolific writer. Many others with similar gifts have joined him in the church growth movement. Therefore, a mountain of material emphasizing church growth has been published, making it difficult for anyone to state briefly the main views of the movement. Almost any brief statement will omit some point which might be considered highly significant. However, I will attempt a statement of some central church growth themes as I see them.[13]

### Discipling All the People Groups

Basic to the entire approach of McGavran and other church growth leaders is an understanding of and emphasis on the central thrust of Christ's commission to his church as the discipling of all the people groups of the world. This is the imperative in the Great Commission (Matt. 28:18-20), whereas the other verbs in the commission are participles. Much attention is given to the Greek phrase *panta ta ethne,* all the peoples. Therefore, the concept of people groups as separate ethnolinguistic and cultural entities is prominent in church growth thought.

### Research and Measurement

If people groups are to be discipled, they need to be identified. The insights of sociology and anthropology are employed as research tools. The world is perceived not in mass nor as billions of individuals, but in terms of social and cultural units.

Research further seeks to measure progress toward the discipling of specific people groups and to discover factors that affect progress in discipling, either positively or negatively.

### Cross-Cultural Evangelism

Special attention is given to the process of sharing the gospel with people groups that have not yet been discipled. This process involves messengers taking the gospel into new cultural settings. Identifying unreached people groups is a means to this end.

To clarify the meaning of cultural distance and the need for cross-cultural evangelism, McGavran developed a scheme by which evangelism within one's own cultural setting is designated as E-0, with numbers reflecting degrees of cultural difference up to E-3 for evangelism within a culture radically different from one's own. (Church growth leaders have developed similar schemes for other aspects of church life, such as discipling, missions, and Christian leadership.)

### The Primacy of Evangelism

Christian nurture (or *perfecting*, in the term early favored by McGavran) follows discipling. The commitment of faith by which persons become disciples comes about through communication of the gospel—that is, through evangelism (Rom. 10:17). In the Great Commission, discipling precedes baptizing and "teaching them to obey." Therefore, the first obligation of the church toward any people group is evangelism.

### Identification of Hindrances

McGavran and his associates have given much attention to elements in Christian life and work which hinder outreach to additional people groups and their rapid discipling. A comprehensive list of such hindrances would be a very long one. For example, in *How Churches Grow* McGavran has successive chapters on the "cultural overhang," the "tremendous pressure" to "perfect," "gradualism," and the "prison of previous patterns." These are typical concerns.

### Concentration on the Responsive

Research by those concerned for church growth not only seeks to identify unreached peoples, but also to locate those people groups or those population elements which are most open and responsive to the gospel ("ripe harvest fields"). Church growth theory then urges major investment of efforts where the current response is greatest.

### Cultural Adaptation

Effective discipling of people groups requires approaches that are appropriate to each particular culture. The gospel should be presented in ways that minimize foreignness and harmonize insofar as possible with indigenous patterns. Persons should be able to come to Christ without having to cross cultural barriers. From this general principle of cultural adaptation arises what is usually called the "homogeneous unit principle." Another important consideration related to culture patterns in many societies is the validity of "people movements," a central emphasis in *The Bridges of God*.

### Reproducible Models

Forms of church life and of evangelistic outreach need to be readily reproducible in the local cultural setting and with local resources, rather than being an artificial imported pattern. This is especially true of leadership models. Great emphasis is placed on types of leadership that are normal within the culture—which often means primarily lay or bivocational leadership. The rapid spread of theological education by extension (TEE) has been linked to this emphasis of the church growth movement.

## Multiplication Through New Units

Much of the most rapid growth of membership in Christian bodies takes place in new work. Therefore, the beginning of new congregations is a potent element in church growth.

## Evaluation

Any movement as prominent and as aggressive as the church growth movement inevitably generates considerable response. Much of it has been controversial; some of it has been sympathetic. Most missiologists who are not themselves adherents of the church growth school note valuable contributions it has made, but note also some faults and limitations.[14] For example, writers generally supportive of the movement have commented that "the church growth model is not applicable to every situation,"[15] that "church growth that does not go on beyond numbers counted on membership lists is defective,"[16] that "a strategy which calls for church growth, but which at the same time does not call for adequate teaching, will eventually fail,"[17] and that "the proponents of church growth, with few exceptions, have emphasized the human factors and all but overlooked the divine factor."[18]

It is unfortunate that the church growth approach has sometimes been promoted with such aggressive lobbying as to make detached evaluation difficult. The result has been unneeded controversy and polarizing of attitudes, both among missiologists and among missionaries. A cooler and more balanced approach could take advantage of helpful insights for Christian missions contributed by the movement without losing sight of other complementary principles in Christian missions.

## Relation to Southern Baptist Foreign Missions

Many concerns of the church growth movement were already an important part of Southern Baptist missions before that movement developed. Southern Baptists have been strongly evangelical and evangelistic. Church planting and church growth have been major emphases in our missions efforts at home and abroad. Therefore, we have been committed to the primacy of evangelism and to the importance of multiplying congregations. We have stressed cross-cultural missions and cultural adaptation. Some characteristics of the mission efforts which McGavran observed and reacted against in India were never prominent characteristics in most Southern Baptist missions. All in all, we were predisposed to agree with most of the church growth emphasis.

In the past 30 years, our work has been definitely influenced by the church growth movement. Some of its terminology has been adopted. We have now, for example, four regional consultants for evangelism and church growth as part of our mission staff. Some church growth precepts have become more prominent in our strategy planning. Noticeable examples are the people group concept and the homogeneous unit principle (which have been interpreted in earlier chapters).

Yet the church growth approach, as typically promoted by its leaders, is not the only or even the dominant element in Southern Baptist foreign missions strategy. Perhaps one reason is that we were already committed to many things the movement promotes, and we continue doing them without thinking of them as part of a "church growth" package.

Furthermore, our foreign missions philosophy and strategy have always been eclectic. That is, we have adopted insights, concepts, or approaches derived from many different sources, if we feel they can be useful and are harmonious with our basic understanding of our mission and with the main thrust of our work. Thus we have never felt ourselves to be adherents of some particular school of missions thought.

There is nothing in the Foreign Mission Board's philosophy statement that comes specifically from the church growth movement (with the possible exception of the clarification that the Board is committed to both responsive and unresponsive fields). The strategy statement includes three typical church growth items (major unreached population blocs, the peoples concept, and responsive areas) in a series of thirteen major strategy concerns—and then indicates that "the Foreign Mission Board does not take any one of these concerns as its sole or even its major strategy determinant."

## Foreign Mission Board Stance

In response to the question posed by the title of this chapter (What About Church Growth?), the Foreign Mission Board would answer with a resounding yes. Concern for church growth is an integral part of our foreign missions strategy. Our answer to the question is yes—and more! Our commitment to church growth is understood and applied in harmony with other important considerations.

Because the church growth approach has been aggressively promoted and almost as aggressively resisted, we approach it with some caution. We do not want to be classified either with the promoters or with the resisters. We want our missions philosophy to rest on its own base and to be measured by fidelity to the Scriptures and to the realities of who we are and what our world is like—not by the extent to which our philosophy and practice in missions correspond to a particular package of missions theories.

On the one hand, we recognize a need for caution that we do not fall into the trap of rationalizing any failure or ineffectiveness in our mission work by criticizing features of church growth theory.

On the other hand, we want to be quite careful not to be misled by thoughtless commitment to church growth ideas into some hidden pitfalls. There might be a danger of making an arbitrary a priori judgment on an approach or method (such as opposing institutions automatically, regardless of their nature or ministry). There may be a danger of narrow or shortsighted emphasis on growth (such as doing things quickly ourselves, instead of following the slower route of helping local churches and local leaders learn to do them). There may be a danger of polarization of groups of missionaries backing different methodologies (instead of the "both-and" approach that is ultimately more fruitful).

Fully aware of these cautions, we intend still to seize the potential of the church growth emphasis. We expect both staff and missionaries to be informed about and to exploit insights for effective missions that come from that source. For example, a major contribution of McGavran's early book *The Bridges of God* is recognition that new believers should not be separated from their natural social context—since their relationships with family and acquaintances are bridges over which God intends the gospel to spread.[19] Any missionary can profit from that insight, without having to subscribe to every detail of church growth theory or trying to force an application of every detail to his own situation. Missionaries are encouraged to read widely, receiving light on their task from the whole range of missiological writing. They will find in the works of church growth leaders much that will be helpful.

Essentially, however, Southern Baptist foreign missions seeks to achieve an objective that is broader and deeper than church growth. That is why I have preferred a different term, *indigenous church strength*. This is the term used to express the guiding objective in Southern Baptist foreign missions, both in the Board's philosophy statement and in its strategy position paper.

A major reason for selecting a different term is that *church growth* apparently is often understood rather narrowly. Although I believe the main spokesmen of the movement have not intended such a narrow understanding, many people hear the term as a reference entirely to numerical growth. Adding persons to the Christian fellowship is a vital part of missions, but missions should also result in other kinds of church growth.[20] I believe the broader scope will be more readily evident if we use another term.

Churches need to become strong numerically. They need to become strong also in worship and spiritual life; in understanding of the Scriptures and in prayer; in moral uprightness and ethical sensitivity; in compassionate ministries to those around them; in warmth of Christian fellowship; in stewardship of their gifts and resources; in leadership; in influence on society, for justice and reconciliation; and in evangelistic and missionary vision and outreach.

Southern Baptist foreign missions have in view both the concern and the central objective of trying to help churches in lands around the world to become strong in these and other appropriate ways as instruments for world evangelization and as demonstrations of the glory of God.[21]

## Notes

1. C. Peter Wagner, *Church Growth and the Whole Gospel* (San Francisco: Harper & Row, Publishers, 1981), p. x.

2. Donald Anderson McGavran, *The Bridges of God* (London: World Dominion Press, 1955).

3. In a manuscript prepared for an address to Southern Baptist Foreign Mission Board staff in early 1981.

4. Roland Allen, *Missionary Methods: St. Paul's or Ours?* (London: World Dominion Press, 1912; reprinted, Grand Rapids: Wm. B. Eerdmans Publishing Co., 1962) and *The Spontaneous Expansion of the Church* (London: World Dominion Press, 1927; reprinted, Grand Rapids: Wm. B. Eerdmans Company, 1962).

5. For a detailed summary of the development of the church growth movement, see Delos Miles, *Church Growth: A Mighty River* (Nashville: Broadman Press, 1981), chapters 1-5, pp. 9-49.

6. Donald Anderson McGavran, *How Churches Grow* (London: World Dominion Press, 1959).

7. Donald Anderson McGavran, ed., et al., *Church Growth and Christian Mission* (New York: Harper & Row, Publishers, 1965).

8. Donald A. McGavran, *Understanding Church Growth* (Grand Rapids: William B. Eerdmans Publishing Company, 1970).

9. For more detail on these and other advocates of the church growth movement, see Miles, pp. 11-13.

10. Difference between ecumenical and conservative evangelical philosophies of world mission, which form the background for much of the controversy, were explored in a book edited by Norman A. Horner, *Protestant Crosscurrents in Mission* (Nashville: Abingdon Press, 1968). McGavran himself compiled and edited a book dealing directly with the controversy: Donald McGavran, ed., *Eye of the Storm: The Great Debate in Mission* (Waco, Texas: Word Books, 1972).

11. A. R. Tippett, *Church Growth and the Word of God* (Grand Rapids: William B. Eerdmans Publishing Company, 1970).

12. Wagner, cited in note 1.

13. For a more extensive analysis, weighted toward American church growth, see Miles, chapters 6-9, pp. 50-106. Johannes Verkuyl in *Contemporary Missiology* (Grand Rapids: William B. Eerdmans Publishing Company, 1978), pp. 189-90, gives a summary which greatly overstates McGavran's positions, as a prelude to opposing them.

14. For a fairly representative selection of evaluations, see Miles, chapters 11-12, pp. 124-46; Verkuyl, pp. 190-92; Orlando E. Costas, *Christ Outside the Gate* (Maryknoll, N.Y.: Orbis Books, 1982), chapter 3, pp. 43-57; J. Herbert Kane, *The Christian World Mission: Today and Tomorrow* (Grand Rapids: Baker Book House, 1981), chapter 14, pp. 201-12; and James A. Scherer, "The Life and Growth of Churches in Mission" in *Mission Trends No. 1: Crucial Issues in Missions Today*, ed.

Gerald H. Anderson and Thomas F. Stransky (New York: Paulist Press and Grand Rapids: Wm. B. Eerdmans Publishing Co., 1974), pp. 165-77.

15. James F. Engel and H. Wilbert Norton, *What's Gone Wrong with the Harvest?* (Grand Rapids: Zondervan, 1975), p. 57.

16. Edward R. Dayton and David A. Fraser, *Planning Strategies for World Evangelization* (Grand Rapids: William B. Eerdmans Publishing Co., 1980), p. 131.

17. Ibid., p. 319.

18. Kane, p. 212.

19. McGavran, *The Bridges of God*, p. 23.

20. See the emphasis on "growing better" and "growing broader" in Ebbie C. Smith, *Balanced Church Growth* (Nashville: Broadman Press, 1984), pp. 35-37.

21. This chapter's content is expressed in brief summary in Winston Crawley's column, "Horizons: What 'Church Growth' Means," in the May 1983 issue of *The Commission*, vol. 46, no. 4:75.

# 13
# What About Human Need?

In principle, *human need* encompasses all kinds of need—physical, material, emotional, educational, social, and spiritual. Human nature is complex and mysterious. We are "fearfully and wonderfully made" (Ps. 139:14). Spiritual need, however, has generally been taken for granted as a concern of Christian missions, whereas involvement of missions with other aspects of human need has sometimes been questioned.

Differences of opinion about Christian approaches to physical, material, and social needs have spawned enough controversy to make this an especially important concern in missions strategy, and one that deserves specific examination.

Southern Baptists generally have thought of their mission work at home or abroad primarily in spiritual terms. The expected and stated purpose has been to share the gospel so as to lead persons to faith in Christ. In earlier days, there was little question as to the legitimacy and centrality of this purpose.

More recently, missionaries on furlough have observed that it seems easier to arouse Christian people's interest and concern with accounts or pictures of physical and material needs than by presentation of spiritual needs. Similarly, Christian young people have seemed to lean more easily toward callings that minister to obvious physical or material needs. Certainly the general population is much more sympathetic toward such ministries than toward the spiritual ministries of Christian missions. We may well wonder how much relativism and materialism have crept into our own thinking without our awareness.

## Historical Setting

Material and social concern has been part of Christianity from the beginning. New Testament evidence is far too voluminous to cover fully here. It began, of course, with Jesus, who linked love of neighbor with love of God in his response to an inquiry about the greatest of all commandments (Mark 12:28-31). He illustrated social concern in many of His parables—for example, the good Samaritan (Luke 10:29-37), the rich man and Lazarus (Luke 16:19-31), and the judgment of the nations (Matt. 25:31-46). He expressed His compassion through many miracles of physical healing. In the ministry and teachings of Jesus, there was no separation or polarizing of spiritual and physical ministries.

Concern for people's physical and material needs carried over into the early church. The Book of Acts records healings and distribution of material help "as any had need" (Acts 2:45, RSV). Paul urged doing good to all (Gal. 6:10), and James gave pointed admonition along that line (Jas. 1:22; 2:15-16; 4:17).

Through the centuries of Christian history, believers have been prominent in initiating or leading many efforts for human welfare (such as hospitals, orphanages, prison reform, abolition of slavery, and opposition to many forces that would blight human life).

The same has been true in the outreach of Christian missions across the world. William Carey, the pioneer of the modern Protestant mission movement, led the way through a lifelong crusade against some social evils of that day in India. What was true of Carey has been typical also of countless missionaries in succeeding generations and in all parts of the world.[1] The social impact of Christian missions was so extensive that James S. Dennis, between 1879 and 1906, took three volumes, entitled *Christian Missions and Social Progress*, to review the subject.[2]

Though there were natural differences in emphasis by various persons and at diverse times and places, and though the main thrust of Christian missions was spiritual, looking toward salvation of individuals and planting churches, there was no serious polarization of spiritual and social concerns in missions until this century. The cleavage arose from several background developments. Biblical criticism led some to doubt the origin and the principles of the Christian faith. Increasing comparative knowledge of other religions led some toward religious relativism. About the same time, a philosophy of social progress was growing out of the theory of evolution. The social emphasis of Walter Rauschenbusch and others who followed resulted in what came to be called the Social Gospel.

Attention to the social concerns that are appropriate to the Christian faith was really very much needed, and it could well have been added to the spiritual concerns of the Christian faith in a thoroughly biblical and fruitful harmony. But many persons, influenced by the uncertainty and relativism that were developing at the same time, backed away from the traditional gospel core of faith and salvation. They began to stress social concerns as if they were the only Christian gospel. In reaction, many of those who were still committed to the fundamentals of biblical faith resisted that Social Gospel, but with it resisted also the social concerns that biblical faith should have included. Thus in the early decades of this century polarization developed between Christians emphasizing human spiritual need and other Christians emphasizing physical, material, and social needs.[3]

The polarized emphases have carried over into the modern setting as a major distinction between what are sometimes called "conciliar" and what are called "evangelical" groups in modern Protestant church life. Conciliar groups are related to national and/or world councils of churches and are primarily the traditional mainline denominations. Evangelical groups are smaller denominations or others which choose not to affiliate with church councils and which emphasize the gospel (the "evangel"). There is much blurring of lines between the two groups, and use of the labels is in many cases misleading; but for most of the middle decades of this century there was a readily discernible difference between those stressing complete commitment to meeting spiritual need and those urging much more commitment to meeting social needs.

This polarization has been evident in relation to the world mission of the church. For example, in 1973 representatives of the evangelical position and the conciliar position were asked to respond to the question: "What is 'mission' today?" The evangelical response (by Arthur F. Glasser) stressed the spiritual mission of the church. The conciliar response (by Tracey K. Jones, Jr.) stressed the social, economic, and political responsibility of the church.[4]

The conciliar theme of meeting social needs has continued to develop over a period of several decades. The process can be traced through reports of periodic meetings of the World Council of Churches and of its Commission on World Mission and Evangelism. The new slogan of "humanization as the goal of mission" came into focus through the fourth assembly of the World Council of Churches in 1968.[5] Following the rise of liberation theology, liberation became another common motif.[6] These emphases have led also to new definitions of the mission of the church in terms of changing the structures of society.[7]

As conciliar views seemed to move further and further from the spiritual concerns that are essential to the gospel, evangelicals entered into sharp debate with the new positions that were being proclaimed.[8]

In the past few years, there has been some evidence that the conciliar camp is beginning to add again a stronger emphasis on evangelism, alongside the continuing emphasis on social concerns. At the same time, and much more markedly, evangelical leadership has begun to stress social concerns, alongside the continuing major stress on evangelism.

This evangelical view that gives serious attention to the meeting of human material and social needs as an element of faithfulness to the gospel and to the Scriptures is sometimes called a "new evangelicalism." It has actually been in the making for several decades, ever since some prominent and strongly evangelical Christian agencies devoted to relief and other social welfare ministries came out of World War II and the years that immediately followed. However, the Congress on World Evangelization at Lausanne, Switzerland, in 1974 was pivotal in bringing spiritual ministries and social ministries together in the thought of evangelical leaders. The congress focused on the spread of the gospel, but many of the papers presented and the final statement from the conference included also the importance of ministries to all kinds of human need.[9]

Since the Lausanne meeting, there have been many expressions of growing evangelical commitment to social ministries. The "option for the poor" so clearly stated as a current direction by the Roman Catholic Church has been reflected in evangelical writing. Topics related to development and social justice have been discussed in a number of conferences of evangelicals.[10] In 1980 a commission of the World Evangelical Fellowship sponsored a "Consultation on the Theology of Development."[11] In that same year Waldron Scott, who was then general secretary of the Fellowship, published a book on the social responsibilities of the church.[12] Other recent books by evangelicals express similar commitment to "the whole gospel," including social concerns along with spiritual concerns.[13]

Southern Baptists have not been very much involved in these developments, though influenced to some extent by them. We are not affiliated with the National Council of Churches or the World Council of Churches. We have been evangelical in beliefs and emphases, but have not been affiliated with evangelical organizations or active to any great extent in independent non-denominational circles which have supplied much of the evangelical leadership.

Occasional Southern Baptist tension over social issues may reflect what we have heard and read about the Social Gospel—but probably mainly reflects a strongly pietistic stance and differences of opinion as to the appropriate Christian response to specific social issues. Except in our universities and seminaries, we have been largely unaware of discussions taking place on themes such as "What is mission today?" We experience some of the same tensions, and similar developments can be traced in recent decades of Southern Baptist life, but polarization and controversy have been less severe among us than in the broader Christian scene. Even so, the validity and importance of Christian ministry to human physical, material, and social needs are becoming more and more widely recognized among Southern Baptists.

## Holistic Missions

From the beginning, Southern Baptist foreign missions ministries have been holistic; that is, they have addressed the whole person in an actual life situation, not just the soul.

Even though there has sometimes been a tendency in the United States to polarize evangelism and ministries to physical or social needs, as if they were opposed to each other, that has seldom been the case in overseas missions. Compassionate attention to all kinds of human need has been more typical. Note, for example, the school for girls started by Henrietta Hall Shuck in Hong Kong, the appointment of a Southern Baptist missionary physician in 1846, and the sharing of food with famine-stricken people by Lottie Moon (and many other missionaries). Missionaries quite naturally reached out in Christian love to relieve the intense physical and material suffering of those around them.

Despite very limited personnel and funds, medical work (now preferably called health-care ministries) became common in Southern Baptist foreign missions from about the beginning of this century. Other kinds of benevolent and human needs ministries gradually expanded also. Orphanages and goodwill centers were added fairly early. Relief programs were common in times of emergency. Informal agricultural projects were initiated several generations ago; formal agricultural work is newer. By now many vocational categories for which missionaries are appointed relate to some phase of what is broadly called "human need ministries."

Though the idea and the reality of holistic ministry have characterized Southern Baptist foreign missions from the beginning, the term is fairly new and formal statements interpreting the concept are also new (as is true of most strategy concepts).

When foreign missions strategy was made a special study theme for Southern Baptist churches for 1974, one of five strategy principles identified in chapter titles by Leland Webb was "Involvement: Responding to Human Needs."[14] Baker James Cauthen (former Foreign Mission Board executive director) frequently explained the complementary relationship of witness and ministry in missions by commenting how appropriate it is for a missionary to go to the field with a Bible in one hand and a loaf of bread in the other. The Board's long-range plans, adopted in January 1976, stated this fundamental principle: "Evangelism and church development will be maintained as the imperatively central thrust. Compassionate ministries are no less insistent as expressions of obedience and examples of Christian compassion in action." Linking witness and ministry in one principle reflects what is sometimes called the "Great Command" of Jesus, which linked love of God and love of neighbor.

The formal Foreign Mission Board philosophy statement adopted in 1978 expresses the same truth in different words: "The task of missions supremely and imperatively is to make disciples, to baptize them, and to teach them to observe all that Christ commanded. It includes all the world—every creature— every generation. The task of missions is also to minister compassionately to those who are hungry, thirsty, strangers, lack clothing, sick, imprisoned, and so forth."

These statements of foreign missions principle are rooted in the purpose of the Southern Baptist Convention itself. The Convention constitution describes that purpose as "the promotion of Christian missions at home and abroad and any other objects such as Christian education, benevolent enterprises, and social services which it may deem proper and advisable for the furtherance of the kingdom of God." The Board's philosophy statement indicates that "human need worldwide requires accentuated attention to health care and disease prevention, benevolent and social ministries on an expanding scale, hunger relief and compassionate responses to crisis situations." The strategy document adopted by the Board's Executive Management Group in 1982 states the same principle, again in different words: "Our concern is for the whole person, with no polarization of witness and ministry."

John R. Cheyne, the Board's senior consultant for human need ministries, set forth this theme in a paper on "An Approach Toward a Theological Understanding of a Holistic Response to Human Need," presented at a conference of Baptist International Mission Secretaries in 1983 in Buenos Aires. A key statement affirms that the missionary, "whatever the primary assignment, will deal with the whole person in terms of the whole need in the context of the particular situation. He will see himself as ministering in the name of Christ and addressing those human hurts (whether defined as spiritual or physical) which keep men from comprehending, receiving and manifesting the life of Christ through faith."

Holistic ministry harmonizes with a holistic view of human nature, like that expressed in the biblical concept of *shalom*—usually translated as peace, but having the much broader connotation of wholeness or general welfare.

An apt example of such missionary ministry was the preacher with an evangelism assignment who regularly met the mobile medical team as it came for a leprosy clinic. He brought a basin of water and a towel and washed the dust from the ulcerated feet of the patients as preparation for their examination by the doctor. That expression of loving service, he explained to them, represents the love that God has expressed toward us all in Jesus.

### Ministry Programs

In the 1960s the Southern Baptist Convention developed formal program statements for all Southern Baptist boards, institutions, and other agencies. As mentioned earlier, the objective of the Foreign Mission Board was defined as: "To do everything possible to bring all men in other lands around the world to a saving knowledge of Jesus Christ as rapidly as possible, and to involve them in Christian growth and service as members of indigenous churches." That general statement is supplemented by a list of nine more specific objectives, one of which is: "To minister to human need in Christian love through service agencies, such as schools, hospitals, clinics, good will centers, and publishing houses."

Assigned responsibilities of the Foreign Mission Board are arranged under six programs, beginning with a program of support for foreign missionaries and a program of evangelism and church development in foreign lands. The next two programs, providing for schools and student work and for publication work, relate both to evangelism and to needs of the churches for leadership and tools—but they also minister to the general public. The other two programs, providing for hospitals and medical care and for benevolent ministries, are essentially human need ministry programs. Thus the Southern Baptist Convention recognizes that human need ministries do play and will continue to play a very large part in Southern Baptist foreign missions.

The Scriptures tell us that Jesus came preaching, teaching, and healing (Matt. 4:23). His example is taken as a guide by Christians and churches today. The preaching aspect of missions is expressed mainly through programs of evangelism and church development, the teaching aspect through schools and through literature, and the healing aspect through medical and benevolent ministries. The healing ministry, in some form, cannot be omitted or neglected if we are to minister to the whole person in the name of Jesus. Preaching relates to the needs of the soul, teaching nurtures the mind, and healing ministers to both body and emotions. The healing ministry involves concern for all aspects of personal health and wholeness of life.

In addition to revealing, expressing, and sharing the love of Christ, medical and benevolent ministries also often open people's hearts to hear and respond to the message of salvation. Many lands at first could be entered by missionaries only through medical and other benevolent ministries. A general atmosphere hostile to the gospel may be made favorable by Christian ministries of love and mercy.[15]

### Relief and Development

The Foreign Mission Board's benevolent ministries in foreign lands have been carried out across the years primarily through ongoing programs of work, with missionaries specifically assigned to them. An example would be a Christian social work program through a community center. Another would be an agricultural program led by an agricultural missionary. But the Board's program statement also recognizes the need for emergency relief projects. It speaks of "administering relief in foreign countries in crises created by wars, storms, earthquakes, famines, and other calamities."[16]

Long before the program statements were developed, the Foreign Mission Board was recognized by the Convention as the normal Southern Baptist channel for meeting emergency relief needs overseas.

Immediately after World War II, Southern Baptists engaged through the Foreign Mission Board in a major relief and rehabilitation effort overseas, which had a special offering goal of three million dollars. Afterward, the Board continued to receive small sums year by year designated for relief overseas, but the sums increased only when there was a major disaster; and even then the increase usually was not large.

In the 1970s the pattern of Southern Baptist giving for relief changed. The realities of natural disasters and of dire famine began to be brought into Southern Baptist homes through television news reports. As a result, throughout Southern Baptist life, there was a remarkable surge of interest in and concern for response to disasters. Previously, though our missionaries were surrounded by pathetic needs—poverty, malnutrition, disease, illiteracy, and sometimes war or insurrection and seas of refugees—and though the Foreign Mission Board sought to inform Southern Baptists about continuing needs and special crises, limitations of the communication process meant that most Southern Baptists had only very limited awareness of the severity of human need in other lands and of the ways in which our missionaries were ministering.

Relief contributions flowing from the churches through the Foreign Mission Board increased rapidly in the late 1970s. Such funds had generally been well under $100,000 per year until 1974. In response to a severe earthquake in Nicaragua in 1972, the Board allocated over $100,000 from general funds for emergency aid.

Growth in relief contributions actually began in 1974. The hurricane in Honduras that year and the earthquake in Guatemala elicited a flood of response. Both nations were near enough to the United States for the disasters to have strong impact. In addition, public news media were playing up severe famine conditions in the Sahel region of Africa. Southern Baptist overseas relief contributions neared $300,000 in 1974 and amounted to more than $1,600,000 in each of the next two years, before dropping back to approximately $890,000 when there was no major disaster near at hand and when the Sahel famine had eased.

General concern for world hunger was continuing to grow, and contributions stimulated by that concern would build to even higher levels in years that followed.

As this response to overseas disasters began to build, the

Foreign Mission Board moved to take advantage of it, in hope that it meant more than a passing interest of Southern Baptists. In late 1974 Board staff began developing a formal disaster response plan. A staff member was named in 1975 as disaster response cordinator. Each mission organization on the field was asked to designate a person as disaster response coordinator and to name a committee to evaluate relief needs and implement relief programs.

Many Southern Baptists were beginning to speak or write about the urgency of world need in general, about specific crisis situations, about the importance of Christian influence on government decisions related to hunger and development, about appropriate Christian life-style in a needy world, and about channels for Christian contributions to meet human need. The Southern Baptist Convention Executive Committee in 1975 reaffirmed the mission boards as the recognized Southern Baptist channels for relief ministries in the United States and overseas. Concerned individuals began to request a special day of emphasis on world hunger in the Southern Baptist calendar—a suggestion which was implemented beginning in 1978.

With the instituting of World Hunger Day, Southern Baptist giving toward overseas hunger and relief ministries escalated rapidly, nearly doubling each year for three successive years (1978-1980). Growth in the annual amount given has slowed down, but by 1984 the total amount was $7,210,376. By now also the Foreign Mission Board staff to handle world hunger and relief concerns has expanded, with two consultants for human need ministries.

It is not surprising, with such rapid increase of funds for relief, that several problems developed. One that has not been solved yet is lack of enough missionaries on a long-range basis with special training for and commitment to relief and development ministries. Most of those who have been deeply concerned for world hunger and have done extensive speaking and writing on the subject have said comparatively little about this aspect.[17]

The Foreign Mission Board has had to give special training in relief and disaster response to missionaries already in service, who assume this responsibility as a sideline. For example, a quite detailed disaster response manual was developed by 1981, and conferences for coordinators were held in many parts of the world.

At the same time, the Foreign Mission Board was seeking to clarify for Southern Baptists the approaches that are being followed in hunger and relief ministries. Some donors thought that their gifts would be used only for distributing food, whereas the Board sought mainly to help people become able to grow their own food. Many donors wondered about the buildup in relief funds over a period of months and felt that all funds should be spent immediately—not realizing that reliable and effective relief ministries need time for preparation and care in implementation. Very few were aware of the costs added to the ongoing foreign missions program for the administering of relief or the added workload for missionaries and staff. Board President R. Keith Parks spoke to those concerns in a report to the Board in March 1982, which was disseminated to Southern Baptists through Baptist Press and other communication channels.

The Foreign Mission Board is firmly committee to the development approach in its response to hunger and other urgent needs. As Parks stated in his report:

> The Foreign Mission Board is committed to enabling people to learn to plant or to fish or to work in order that they can be self-supporting. It takes longer to plant and harvest rice than to cook and eat it, but it's worth more. It takes longer to assist someone to become self-supporting than to give him a gift, but it's worth more. While in the crisis event food distribution is carried out, the long range approach can save lives for generations. This ministry also provides contact and time that allows a spiritual ministry.[18]

The Board and its missionaries are involved in many development projects overseas, seeking insofar as possible to use what is called "appropriate technology"—that is, methods that can be followed by local people without reliance upon expensive imported machinery or supplies. An example is the sloping agricultural land technology (SALT) developed at the Baptist Rural

Life Center on Mindanao, in the Philippines, which was given an achievement award by the Crop Science Society of the Philippines.[19]

By now the commitment of Southern Baptists to world hunger and emergency relief ministries seems to have stabilized. Contributions continue to grow gradually, and the relief and development portion of our overseas effort is well related to other parts in our holistic missions approach.

### Structural Change

As mentioned earlier, much emphasis has been given in recent years, especially by Roman Catholics and by Protestants of the conciliar group, to humanization and liberation. The responsibility of the church toward implementing those concerns has been described as working to "change the structures of society." At times this purpose has been proposed as the primary or perhaps almost the only purpose of mission.[20]

This trend in missions thought is well summarized in the title of a videotaped lecture given by Bishop Lesslie Newbigin at the Overseas Ministries Study Center in 1982. The lecture title is "Service, Development, Revolution." For generations all Christian mission work included service ministries. Since World War II, development projects have become increasingly prominent. During the past two decades, emphasis has shifted to political movements aiming at social change.[21]

To the extent that this approach calls for political action in overseas mission areas, the Southern Baptist Foreign Mission Board and its missionaries would not join in (see the earlier section on political involvement).

Christians in other countries can make their own decisions, under the leadership of the Holy Spirit, as to how best to work within their own political settings for justice and human rights. The problems are complex, but it is certainly a valid principle that seeking to prevent human suffering is better than simply ministering to those who suffer.[22]

### Cohesion

Many Christian denominations and other groups separate the function of evangelism and church planting, done by a mission board, from the function of benevolent ministries, done by relief agencies or special parachurch organizations. We are convinced that it is better for the two to be combined. Our cohesive approach ties all kinds of human need ministries together, whether they minister primarily to spiritual need or primarily to physical and social need.

Combining evangelism and church development with compassionate ministries gives the clearest testimony to the full meaning of the gospel and has the greatest long-range effectiveness, both in meeting material needs and in accomplishing spiritual purposes. Our missions philosophy and strategy intend to keep witness and ministry together in a holistic Christian mission.

Board President R. Keith Parks, in speaking of hunger and relief ministries, said: "The 'cup of cold water' must be in Jesus' name to distinguish it from the humanitarian or political gesture. The local church is the best context for this witness. . . . This ministry will be done in the name of Jesus. It will augment evangelism and church growth. It will be an appropriate part of the total Southern Baptist foreign mission effort."[23] What was said regarding relief ministries is equally true of all ongoing health care and benevolent ministries. Those compassionate activities are a natural expression of the Christian heart, impelled by the Holy Spirit. Missionaries seek to do such work in ways which will also do most to strengthen gospel outreach and facilitate the developing of churches.

By intent and by policy, Southern Baptist missionaries and/or Baptist church and convention representatives on the mission fields are involved in the actual administration of relief projects and relief funds. We do not channel these funds through governments or other secular agencies. The servant role of the church in ministry to others is a vital expression of its calling.

Comments of John E. Mills, area director for West Africa, in his March 1984 report to the Foreign Mission Board, are representative of the significance of human need ministry in the cohesive thrust of Southern Baptist missions worldwide.

Drought, famine, disease, coupled with a population explosion, have added to the burden of poverty that reduces life to a struggle for survival for multiplied millions in West Africa—and many die.

How can Southern Baptist missionaries do effective work under these conditions? We cannot ignore them. "If anyone has material possessions and sees his brother in need but has no pity on him, how can the love of God be in him?" (1 John 3:17) Unapologetically, we are trying to meet human needs in the name of Jesus and demonstrate Christian love. We cannot do all that needs to be done, but we are doing a significant amount to minister in meeting crisis needs as well as working in developmental projects to help avert future crises. . . .

But we cannot forget that the greatest needs in West Africa are spiritual. Spiritual death is worse than physical death. We dare not degenerate into becoming relief workers and developers only. Careful attention is being given to assure that all that is done is really done in Jesus' name. All meeting of human needs is shot through and through with an evangelistic witness. I believe that in so doing we are opening doors to entire communities, and that more rather than fewer people are coming to know Christ and finding in Him life abundant and eternal. . . .[24]

Missionary reponse to all kinds of human need involves many continuing problems. Human failings and limited resources lead to some inconsistencies. Differing individual gifts place missionaries more in direct evangelism ministries or more in human need ministries—but all within the one body, in which there is no polarizing of witness and ministry, but rather one cohesive holistic mission thrust.

## Notes

1. For a brief review, see the chapter dealing with "Humanitarian Service" in J. Herbert Kane, *Understanding Christian Missions* (Grand Rapids: Baker Book House, 1978), pp. 328-38.

2. James S. Dennis, *Christian Missions and Social Progress*, 3 vols. (New York: Fleming H. Revell Company, 1897-1906).

3. Johannes Verkuyl in *Contemporary Missiology* (Grand Rapids: William B.

Eerdmans Publishing Company, 1978) has sections on "The Goal of Forming a Christian Society," which was primarily a European emphasis, and "The Goal of the 'Social Gospel,' " pp. 192-96.

4. These brief statements are included in Gerald H. Anderson and Thomas F. Stransky, eds., *Mission Trends No. 1: Crucial Issues in Mission Today* (New York: Paulist Press and Grand Rapids: Wm. B. Eerdmans Publishing Co., 1974), pp. 5-11.

5. *International Review of Mission: Humanization and Mission* vol. 60, no. 237 (January 1971). For an evangelical evaluation of this theme, see the chapter on "Humanization or Salvation?" in J. Herbert Kane, *The Christian World Mission: Today and Tomorrow* (Grand Rapids: Baker Book House, 1981), pp. 155-71.

6. Gerald H. Anderson and Thomas F. Stransky, eds., *Mission Trends No. 4: Liberation Theologies in North America and Europe* (New York: Paulist Press and Grand Rapids: Wm. B. Eerdmans Publishing Co., 1979) is devoted entirely to liberation theologies. See also Johannes Verkuyl and H. G. Schulte Nordholt, *Responsible Revolution*, trans. and ed. Lewis Smedes (Grand Rapids: William B. Eerdmans Publishing Company, 1974).

7. See Verkuyl on "The Goal of Improving the Macrostructures," in *Contemporary Missiology*, pp. 196-97.

8. An excellent summary of the debate, from an evangelical perspective, is given by Arthur F. Glasser and Donald A. McGavran in *Contemporary Theologies of Mission* (Grand Rapids: Baker Book House, 1983).

9. The Lausanne Covenant, produced at the Congress, included a statement on social concern: "Here too we express penitence both for our neglect and for having sometimes regarded evangelism and social concern as mutually exclusive," in *Let the Earth Hear His Voice*, ed. J. D. Douglas (Minneapolis: World Wide Publications, 1975), p. 4.

10. See the papers and report from a recent conference at Wheaton, Illinois, in Tom Sine, ed., *The Church in Response to Human Need* (Monrovia, Calif.: Missions Advanced Research and Communication Center, 1983).

11. Papers presented and the statement issued are found in *Evangelicals and Development: Towards a Theology of Social Change*, ed. Ronald J. Sider (Exeter, England: The Paternoster Press, 1981).

12. Waldron Scott, *Bring Forth Justice: A Contemporary Perspective on Mission* (Grand Rapids: William B. Eerdmans Publishing Company, 1980).

13. For example, C. Peter Wagner, *Church Growth and the Whole Gospel: A Biblical Mandate* (San Francisco: Harper & Row, Publishers, 1981) and Orlando E. Costas, in a chapter entitled "The Whole World for the Whole Gospel: Recovering a Holistic Legacy for the 1980s," in *Christ Outside the Gate* (Maryknoll, N.Y.: Orbis Books, 1982), pp. 162-73. See also the interesting suggestions of John J. Jonsson in "An Elliptical Understanding of Mission and Its Roles," *Missionalia*, vol. 11, no. 1 (April 1983): 3-10.

14. Leland Webb, *How in This World* (Nashville: Convention Press, 1974), chapter 5, pp. 91-113.

15. Ibid. Various examples of human need ministries are given by Webb.

Also a constant stream of current examples is reported in *The Commission* and in Foreign Mission Board press releases through Baptist Press.

16. SBC, *Annual*, 1967, p. 91.

17. See Winston Crawley, "Horizons: The (Almost) Missing Ingredient," in the September 1981 issue of *The Commission*, vol. 44, no. 7:54.

18. R. Keith Parks, "Hunger and Relief Ministries in the Context of Foreign Missions," Foreign Mission Board *Minutes*, March 1982, p. 4.

19. For an overview of development concerns related to the Third World, see the brief conference report volume (ed. by Ronald J. Sider) cited in note 11.

20. Compare Verkuyl on "The Goal of Improving the Macrostructures," pp. 196-97. See also the summary of this development in Glasser and McGavran, pp. 150-56.

21. For an exposition of that viewpoint, see the chapter on "Mission as Action for God's Justice" in Lesslie Newbigin, *The Open Secret* (Grand Rapids: William B. Eerdmans Publishing Company, 1978), pp. 102-34.

22. For further treatment of this subject, see "Horizons: Christians and Government," Winston Crawley's column in the February-March 1983 issue of *The Commission*, vol. 46, no. 2:61.

23. Parks, cited in note 18.

24. Foreign Mission Board *Minutes*, March 1984.

# 14
# What About Methods?

In most discussions of mission strategy, methods are the main focus of interest. We are coming to the topic late—intentionally, since methods need to be understood in a much larger context. Discussing methods without defining that larger context is speaking in a vacuum.

Two missionaries on furlough may begin talking about mission methods. One says, "I believe Method A is the best method to use in foreign missions." The other says, "No, that's not right. Method B is the best method." Actually they may both be exactly right: Method A may be best today for the country where missionary A is serving, and Method B best where missionary B is serving. But their discussion has taken place in a vacuum because they have not identified the larger context to which each missionary method relates.

Much of what is written or said about mission methodology falls short by failing to set methodology in the appropriate context.

## Context

There are several essential elements in the context within which missionary methods are determined and evaluated (though persons involved in decisions about methods may not be aware of these elements). They function as background which should condition or even determine decisions that are being made, but it is possible for them to be overlooked—and then wrong methods are likely to be chosen for wrong reasons (habit, bias, or imitation of others).

### The Planning Sequence

In discussing mission strategy with new missionaries, I generally introduce the topic of methods and then move to the place of methods in a normal planning sequence. I begin by asking a simple question, "Is using an ax a good method?" Then I wait for a response from the new missionaries, one of whom before long will probably say, "Well, that depends—it depends on what you are trying to do." Using an ax can be a very fine method for splitting kindling wood, but it would not be a good method for getting rid of a fly on a dinner plate. Suitability of a method depends on the objective.

Mission objectives, in turn, as implied in Part IV, grow out of a philosophy of missions. And our philosophy (the way we understand our mission, as expounded in chapter 4) rests in an understanding of God and his purpose—that is, in a theology of mission.

The normal planning sequence which is the implicit framework for determining and evaluating mission methods can be diagrammed in this way.

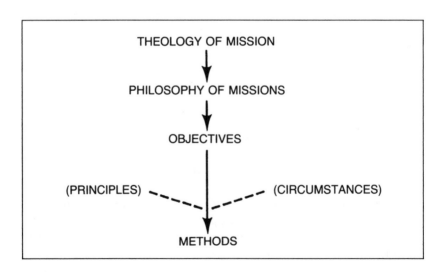

The diagram places methodology appropriately at the end of the process. Objectives are translated into methods in terms of the general principles of human nature and of the Christian faith, and also in terms of the widely varied circumstances encountered throughout the world.[1]

### General Principles

Perhaps it should go without saying that any method which defies or ignores the realities of human nature is destined to fail. In Christian ministries, methods certainly also should harmonize with the nature of the gospel and the character of the Christian life. Unfortunately, it is possible to cite in missions history many instances of unwise or inappropriate methods.

In the 140 years of Southern Baptist history, the Foreign Mission Board has developed a generally accepted missions philosophy, including main principles to guide its mission strategy.[2] By now, many of those principles have been formalized in the Board's philosophy and strategy statements. They have been explained in earlier sections of this book.

Therefore, mission methods should be developed and evaluated in the context of all that has been said earlier about how we understand our mission, about incarnational missions and holistic missions, and especially about the fundamental objective of indigenous church strength.

### Current Plans

Mission organizations on the field are guided by the philosophy and objectives established in the Foreign Mission Board's planning process and current plans. Long-range plans of the Board, covering the final quarter of this century, have been determined already, as reported in the Bold Mission Thrust document "Foreign Missions Looks to AD 2000."

The Board's Office of Overseas Operations develops "priority concerns" as the central step in its planning. Priority concerns are specific working objectives for specific time periods. Guidance is given to the missions through a strategy planning workbook and through the leadership of area directors and their associates. Appendix 10 includes a diagram of the formation of priority concerns and a list of concepts identified by Charles W. Bryan, senior vice president for Overseas Operations, as guides that set their directions.

### Specific Situations

The importance of circumstances in the determining of appropriate methods cannot be overemphasized. Most arguments about methods on the mission field arise from failure to analyze either objectives or circumstances or both. Even if the basic long-range objective is exactly the same, methods used must be adapted to circumstances. (Preaching in the city plaza may be an excellent missionary method in Brazil, but preaching in the city plaza in Yemen would result only in expulsion from the country.)

Even in the same place, circumstances change and methods need to change with the passing of time. The use of a method becomes part of the circumstances, and continued use brings into play the law of diminishing returns. (Holding a week of special evangelistic meetings this year may be a very fine method, but holding a week of special evangelistic meetings every month will not do.)

## Central Axiom

As I interpret mission methods to new missionaries, using a diagram (see p. 298) to show methods in context, I have sought to bring our central axiom of mission methodology into sharp focus by saying, "Even if you forget everything else that I have said about this diagram, there is one thing that I hope you will remember: I hope you will remember the *s* on the end of the word *method*."

We are committed to plurality in mission methods—not a single prescribed way, but a wide variety of approaches and methods. Missions principles and missions objectives have continuing validity and force, but forms of missions activity are almost infinitely variable.

This central axiom related to methodology was included as a basic principle in the introduction to the Bold Mission Thrust document adopted in January 1976. The principle was stated:

The methodology is comprehensive and flexible. Our commitment is not to one method to the exclusion of others. Every method which God will honor should be employed where feasible and possible. Comprehensive methodology is inclusive of all such methods.

Some mission organizations exist to promote one method exclusively. Our commitment to a comprehensive methodology may expose our work to certain problems which such organizations do not face. The polarization which can result from the magnification of one method over another can have unfortunate consequences.

Methods, procedures, and organizational forms are being called into question by changing times. New ways will be found to do old and new things. Care will be taken to preserve necessary functions—even though forms may have to change radically.

The heart of this statement was incorporated briefly in the formal philosophy statement of the Foreign Mission Board, adopted in June 1978. "Methodology should be kept comprehensive and flexible. Every method which God will honor should be employed where feasible and possible."

The two words *comprehensive* (sometimes *inclusive* has been used as a synonym) and *flexible* sum up the meaning of this central axiom of Southern Baptist foreign mission methodology.

## Implications

No exact prescription to accomplish world evangelization is available—not even a brief list of recommended methods that taken together will meet the need. Every missionary or missions administrator has yearned at times for one simple clear universal method as the answer to all our problems. Some new missionaries have expected their orientation program to include operating instructions for the missionary method they would use on the field. Sometimes missionaries wrestling with a difficult situation seemed to hope that the area director on his next visit would bring in his briefcase the very method that they needed.

But there is no escaping the struggle involved in clarifying objectives and analyzing circumstances and finally, through study, discussion, and prayer, reaching a decision on the method or methods to be used.

For that reason, missionaries and missions administrators need to observe developments around them thoughtfully, read widely and discriminatingly, and cultivate the arts of analysis, synthesis, and adaptation.

There is always a temptation to focus on a single approach, holding to it even when circumstances may not be suitable and perhaps insisting that it be followed by others in quite different situations.[3] Some in fairly recent years have popularized the phrase *the indigenous church method*. The phrase is misleading and unfortunate in two respects. It speaks of "the" method, when there are actually many methods that can help toward indigenous churches. Furthermore, "indigenous church" is not a method but an objective. Thus the phrase confuses method and objective and assumes only one method of reaching the objective. In reality there are many methods to be used in many different times and at many different places, according to the specific need of the situation.

When I was a young man, I was urged to pray that someone would discover the cure for cancer. Now we know that there are many different kinds of malignancies and that there are also many different approaches that can be helpful in treating them. Methods are plural because circumstances are plural.

Furthermore, methods change because circumstances change. There is no fixedness or finality in mission methodology. We should not be misled by the title of Roland Allen's book *Missionary Methods: St. Paul's or Ours?*[4] The title implies that we should be following Paul's missionary methods. A better title would have been, Missionary Principles: St. Paul's or Ours? The New Testament describes but does not prescribe methods in missions. Methods used by Paul reflect principles that are permanently valid. The details of methods were appropriate to the cities of the Roman Empire in the first century, but times have changed. We need to discover in our day and for our specific settings the methods that will best express New Testament principles. Thus in a constantly changing world mission methodology must be dynamic.[5]

Another temptation in mission methodology is polarizing. New methods are often promoted by contrast with old methods, as if any old method were now automatically passé and only new methods were worthwhile. There is frequent dichotomy also between institutional and noninstitutional methods in missions. Occasionally, some would set evangelism on the one hand over against ministries to human need on the other, or seed-sowing and church planting over against Christian nurture and church strengthening (*perfecting* in McGavran's terminology). Polarization seems to be a spontaneous tendency in human nature.

Southern Baptist missionaries are urged to avoid any such inclination. Our foreign mission methodology is inclusive (there is an *s* on the end of *method*). This means that we follow a "both-and" approach, not an "either-or" approach.

To illustrate, in medicine there are the old standard treatments by drugs and surgery, and new treatments such as radiation therapy. The discovery of the new methods has not made the old ones worthless. Nor should a physician decide in advance never to use surgery because it is too expensive, or never to use drugs because they are too slow and uncertain. Approaching a decision about treatment in such an arbitrary way would be malpractice. Instead, the physician will analyze the circumstances and recommend a method of treatment appropriate to the circumstances.

A further danger in mission methodology is fragmentation. A mission is made up of many persons with varied gifts and opinions. To avoid controversy, the mission may be tempted to let each missionary determine his own method and be a kind of "lone ranger." It takes hard work and skill in group process for a mission to arrive at a cohesive strategy, in which all parts of the mission work cooperate in a united program. Every approach or method needs to be both planned and evaluated in terms of contribution to the total strategy of the mission.

As the principle stated by the Foreign Mission Board in January 1976 suggests, it may be much easier and may sound more dramatic to identify one rather narrowly defined method and then to promote and emphasize that method. This is an advantage that some independent mission agencies have. But we are committed to a comprehensive mission program. We believe that this has been historically the strength of Baptist development—that it has used a wide variety of methods. Therefore, for our overseas mission work we project *comprehensive* methodology, *unified* in a focused program, *balanced* as to the different parts of the program, *flexible* to change methods as circumstances change. Mission strategy, after all, is not arbitrary and static. It is a dynamic process.

### Functions

Mission methods can be analyzed and classified under a variety of functions. Traditionally there have been three main functions—evangelism, education, and medicine (or preaching, teaching, and healing). In more recent decades, many other mission functions have been added.[6]

The most clear-cut functional outline for Southern Baptist foreign missions is the official program statement of the Foreign Mission Board, adopted by the Southern Baptist Convention in 1966.[7] That statement summarizes foreign mission work under several functions (which have been mentioned in chapter 13). When the program statements were being developed, there was understanding between Foreign Mission Board leadership and SBC Executive Committee leadership that the basic planning approach in foreign missions is not functional but geographic. However, the functional program statement was preferred for description and reporting of foreign missions. In actual work on the fields, both in planning and in implementation, the various functions combine into a united program, with the relative prominence of the different functions depending on circumstances and needs in a particular field.

From time to time, the Board has been urged to adopt a functional administrative approach for some specific aspect of its work. Generally these urgings have come from persons who view the matter from an American perspective rather than from the field perspective. An example would be a proposal that all health-care ministries around the world be managed by a director of health-care ministries on the Foreign Mission Board staff.

However, that course would lead to fragmentation of mission efforts. Therefore, the Board has remained committed to the basic geographic approach (see earlier treatment of this principle in chapter 4).

An interesting side effect of this distinctive system is seen in relationships of Foreign Mission Board staff with staff of other Southern Baptist agencies. In the case of most agencies, "program leaders" are persons with functional assignments. For the Foreign Mission Board, however, area directors are the "program leaders." For a few functions, the Foreign Mission Board does have staff specialists, who serve as consultants (see chapter 4).

The program statement of the Foreign Mission Board is intended to be all-embracing. That is, it intends to place within the assignment of the Foreign Mission Board any and all methods that may be appropriate and helpful in foreign missions. It is a valuable document for reference, especially for the defining of relationships between the Foreign Mission Board and other SBC agencies. Its statement of functions is inevitably somewhat arbitrary, since mission methods can have multiple purposes and are interrelated in ways that make neat categorizing difficult.

Another way of stating functions in missions has been introduced already in the section on missionary roles (see chapter 9). Missionary assignments were there grouped in terms of the way different functions contribute to the central objective of indigenous church strength. For understanding mission strategy, that is a more helpful analysis than the sections of the board's program statement. (Those sections might seem to imply parallelism in mission strategy instead of a unified program with a central thrust.)

Obviously, it is not possible to examine every mission function in detail here, since entire books are devoted to only one function (such as literature work or broadcasting). Attention can be given to only a few special aspects of mission methodology in order to provide a reasonably clear overview.

### Human Need Ministries

Already, in the preceding chapter, considerable attention has been given to human need ministries. These are "valuable allies" that complement the central thrust of evangelism that results in churches. Prominently treated in the preceding chapter were health-care ministries (formerly commonly called medical missions)[8] and relief and development ministries. However, the scope of human need ministries is much broader. For example, persons with a high level of training in professional social work are useful in a number of ways in modern missions.[9] A specialty that has expanded rapidly in recent years in Southern Baptist missions is agricultural ministry, which is especially critical now because of the threat of world hunger.

### Educational Work

Another valuable ally of evangelism and church planting is educational work. The Foreign Mission Board's program statement for schools and student work recognizes several purposes and values of educational missions: meeting pressing educational needs, winning students to Christ and ministering to their spiritual needs, and preparing Christian leaders. From the earliest days of modern missions, schools have played a prominent part. They have ranged all the way from kindergarten through university. Outstanding examples at the higher academic level are Seinan Gakuin in Japan and Hong Kong Baptist College.

Formerly, it was more or less assumed, when we began work in a country, that we would start schools at various educational levels. With Southern Baptist advance into so many new fields in the past 40 years, opening schools has not been an automatic expectation. In many places, the local educational system is adequate. Furthermore, schools can be quite expensive and are subject to special government controls and cultural pressures. Thus the Foreign Mission Board has been taking initiative in developing schools only in a few very special situations, with less developed local educational systems and with general resistance to Christianity. In some other places, Baptist churches and conventions have become strong enough to begin their own schools (with encouragement and perhaps assistance from Southern Baptists).

Baptist schools are intended for educational evangelism. They offer some of the very finest evangelistic opportunities, and many are outstanding as evangelistic agencies. At the same time, even schools for general education have a role in preparing Christian leaders. Many of the strongest Baptist leaders around the world, both preachers and laypersons, have come through Baptist school systems.

There are other peripheral but still important contributions of educational institutions. Christians who have received a higher education are able to earn better incomes, so schools help the churches to become self-supporting. Schools minister also to the community in general, as an expression of Christian interest in human welfare. This in turn gives Christianity and the Baptist denomination a good reputation in the community. Schools help to permeate pagan cultures with Christian ideas and ideals. From Baptist schools come possible future leaders of society, and even those who may not become Christian during their course of study generally develop favorable attitudes toward Christianity and missions. In a great many ways, schools for general educational purposes are valuable allies of the Christian mission cause.

Though there are many lands in which it has not seemed possible or appropriate to begin Baptist schools, the student population is strategic in every land. Many of the things that were formerly accomplished in mission work through Baptist schools are accomplished now through Baptist student ministries in government schools or other schools. Often a student center is used as a base for the student ministry. In other cases, plans are developed for helping churches to project their own student ministries. The student population is often the social group most responsive to the gospel. Special ministries for students frequently include and in some cases even specialize on those at the high school level.

The Foreign Mission Board recognized the critical urgency of student ministry by listing special attention to evangelizing of students and youth among the formal intentions of Bold Mission Thrust.[10]

### Evangelism and Church Development

The central functional thrust in Southern Baptist missions is evangelism and church development (to which the human

needs ministries and educational ministries are complementary). The Foreign Mission Board program statement identifies
the program of evangelism and church development as dealing
with activities for "directly presenting the gospel to people" and
for "the establishment and nurture of churches."[11]

Of all the Foreign Mission Board's assigned programs of work,
this has by far the broadest scope. Even a brief review of several
elements involved shows how very complex the program is. For
example, it includes a wide variety of direct evangelistic approaches—such as pioneer evangelism in new fields, outreach
efforts from established centers of work, rural and village work,
urban evangelism, special campaigns or crusades, and development of plans for and training for personal witness.

Included also are ministries directed toward special groups. A
prominent part of the program is English-language church
work, to evangelize either overseas Americans or the cos-
mopolitan English-speaking community in major cities around
the world. However, there are also important evangelistic approaches to many other special groups (such as youth evangelism, efforts among tribal populations, work with refugees,
ministries to the deaf, and so forth).

(Approaches in missions that make use of modern media have
been included up to now in the program of evangelism and
church development, but will be reserved for discussion a little
later.)

Activities and methods described to this point may be compre-
hended very broadly under the term *seed-sowing*. That is, they
have to do with scattering the gospel seed, sharing the message
in a wide variety of settings, through various media, and directed toward different persons or groups. However, the Foreign
Mission Board approach moves on from evangelism to church
development. Seed that is sown needs cultivation and then
harvesting, with the gathering of believers into congregations
and with a wide range of activities to strengthen those congregations.

This program of work envisions further the developing of
associations and conventions, with the mission organization
assisting and strengthening the evangelism and church development programs of those local Baptist bodies.[12]

In addition to the central and indispensible function of the missionary assigned to general evangelism (whose role has been described in chapter 7), there are a large number of missionary specialties that relate directly to church development. They include religious education, music, stewardship, men's work, women's work, camp programs, and the like. A major concern in church development is the kind of evangelistic follow-up and Christian nurture that will avoid or minimize two major problems in Christian work overseas. One is the large number of persons in relatively responsive fields who make a profession of Christian faith but never follow through to baptism. The other is the large number of persons in some settings who drop out as "back door" losses from the churches.

### Media Support

Training of leaders and provision of tools are functions that are vital for the growing of strong churches. A current comprehensive term for the providing of tools is *media support*. This includes both print media (publication work, literature and literacy, Bible distribution) and other types of media, such as audiovisual or electronic (radio, television, or cassettes). These are primarily tools for communication, either within the church or toward the general public.

Communication is not the whole task of missions, but it is essential to that task. Much of the communication involved in missions is directed to individuals or small groups, but a large and growing part is communication through mass media—that is, through forms of communication that transmit a message to large numbers of people at the same time.

In essence such communication is not new, but modern tools have vastly expanded the extent and the size of the audience. For four centuries the printing press has served as a remarkable medium of mass communication, with still many advantages over some of the more recently developed tools, in that printed materials can be read and reread again and again.

Electronic media are well recognized as offering tremendous potential for Christian missions. Especially the use of radio in missions has developed phenomenally in the past 60 years.

Involvement of Southern Baptist missionaries in radio ministries, which began in the very early days of radio, has expanded remarkably since World War II. At the same time there has been increasing use of the newer medium of television. Recording and/or broadcasting studios have been established in many lands, and Baptist conventions are increasingly responsible for planning and developing broadcast ministries.[13]

There is great current interest among Southern Baptists in wider use of mass communications media. All who are concerned for the spread of the gospel naturally want to take full advantage of these valuable tools. Furthermore, mushrooming world population and a sense of urgency regarding gospel outreach in this century heighten the importance of mass media.

Publication and literature ministries have been a part of modern missions from the beginning (an early associate of William Carey in India was a printer). Much of the work of Baptist publishing centers provides tools for the nurture of believers and the strengthening of churches (Bible study and training materials, doctrinal books and booklets, devotional materials, and so forth). In addition, some aspects of literature ministry are directed toward the general public. These include publication and distribution of Bibles and Scripture portions (often in connection with the Bible societies),[14] evangelistic tracts, periodicals for general readers, newspaper publicity and advertisements, and Bible correspondence courses. Both Scripture distribution and the use of Bible correspondence courses have greatly increased in very recent years.[15]

For a number of years, audiovisual media have been widely used in missions. These media have included motion picture films (some of them produced by Southern Baptist missionaries) and especially a growing cassette ministry.

### Leadership Training

In a concentrated thrust for strong indigenous churches, with missionaries in a generative role, no function seems more vital than that of developing leadership. Traditionally this function has centered in institutions to train pastors and other church workers. Often those institutions overseas have been called seminaries, even though in many cases (by comparison with

American institutions) they might be at the Bible school or Bible institute academic level. Some, of course, are fully comparable to American seminaries.

In recent decades it has become apparent that those institutions have prepared only a portion of the leadership needed for rapid multiplication of churches and for indigenous church strength. The rapidly growing movement for theological education by extension (initiated by Presbyterians in Guatemala in 1963) has supplemented what was being done in more formal theological institutions. By now theological education by extension (commonly called TEE) is a well-recognized part of Christian leadership training in many lands.[16] Unfortunately, some interpreters and missionaries in some fields have fallen into the trap of polarizing institutional leadership training and theological education by extension. This is sometimes followed by a pendulum swing between the two emphases. A "both-and" approach would be more constructive.

The need for church leadership is really quite broad and calls for a whole spectrum of training programs. I generally illustrate this with a pyramid. (Others have used similar schemes, with or without the diagram, but with the number of classifications and the descriptions varying.) Church leadership can be classified in this way:

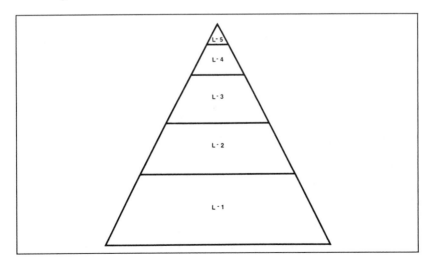

The broad area at the base represents layworkers within the local church, with training programs usually being part of a church religious education curriculum. The next segment represents workers in outreach ministry. They are still essentially laypersons with responsibility in evangelism and in the beginning of Bible study or fellowship groups. The third segment represents pastors of smaller churches. Many of them will often be bivocational. It is for them and the outreach workers that theological education by extension is primarily intended. The fourth segment represents fully trained pastors of town and city churches. They are generally trained in a Bible institute or seminary program. The small segment at the top of the pyramid represents persons who are prepared to become seminary teachers or to fill other specialized roles in denominational life. These positions often require advanced academic training, either in their own country or in some other country. A well-rounded leadership training program for work in any field will make some kind of provision for all segments of church leadership.

Many other specialized functions fall within the several classifications outlined by the Foreign Mission Board's program statement. In addition, of course, there are supportive roles, such as administration, which also affect mission methodology.

### Situations

A fundamental principle in methodology is that approaches and methods must be adapted to circumstances. Since situations in which mission work is carried on are almost infinitely varied, methods also must be similarly varied. There is no way to give even a simple classification of all the different types of mission situations. At best, only a few situational factors of unusual importance can be mentioned.

Much of what has been written about mission methods has presupposed pioneer missions in tribal settings. In our day, despite the emphasis on unreached peoples, that situation represents only a small part of the world mission. Some interpreters of missions have assumed that methods found successful in such settings can be applied universally—but that is not the case.

Donald McGavran's book *The Bridges of God*[17] had immediate relevance to missions in India. Many insights shared in that book can be adapted to other mission situations, but the methods described cannot be treated as a package applicable everywhere. The same is true of the popular book by Melvin Hodges, *On the Mission Field: The Indigenous Church*.[18] It applies primarily to a rural and small-town setting within the dominant Roman Catholic culture of El Salvador. Its suggestions will fit fairly well in other situations that are comparable—but not without radical adaptation, for example, in the cities of Japan.

Religious climate is a major situational factor affecting mission methods.[19] One nation may be practically a spiritual vacuum; another may be undergoing religious change; a third may be nominally Christian, with special readiness for the gospel; while a fourth may be experiencing Islamic resurgence and thus may be especially resistant to the gospel. Analysis of the religious setting is an important part of missions strategy planning.

Observers have sometimes disregarded the public relations value of medical and educational ministries, even referring lightly to an "airwick" philosophy of missions. If such observers worked for five years as missionaries in an extremely responsive situation, and then for another five years in an extremely resistant situation, I believe they would be less likely to disparage methods that help to produce an open and receptive attitude toward the gospel.[20]

Attention to special social groups has already been mentioned in connection with the people group concept. Demographic analysis is very valuable. In many places today there is need for special attention to older persons. On the other hand, there have been situations where adults were substantially impervious to the gospel, but young people could be reached; and they would eventually grow up and become a mature church.

Money for mission work generally has been rather limited. However, for about twenty years, from the late 1940s to the late 1960s, with inflation relatively low and with Southern Baptists committed to missions advance, Southern Baptist mission work was relatively prosperous. That was true both by comparison with many other mission agencies and by comparison with earlier and with more recent Southern Baptist funding for missions. The peak percentage allocation of Cooperative Program funds for foreign missions came in 1964, and current Bold Mission Thrust allocations have not reached that level. With higher inflation in more recent years, actual purchasing power available per Southern Baptist missionary has declined significantly in the past 15 years. This has tended to return Southern Baptist missions to the financial situation that prevailed before 1948 (though without the debt that was such a severe hindrance in the 1920s and 1930s).

Limited funding means especially a shortage of money for capital purposes (such as church land and buildings). Therefore, methods that do not depend on church properties bought with mission funds become essential.[21] Bivocational mission ministries also become increasingly important in a situation of limited mission funding.

Recent rapid urbanization throughout the world makes financial problems more acute. Mission work in rural or semirural areas can be relatively inexpensive. To try to undertake the same things in crowded cities is usually quite expensive or extremely complex or both. If typical American patterns of church life are followed, the number of churches and the number of people who can be reached with the gospel will be few. House groups in some form may be part of the solution.[22]

This need for special methodology, based on limited resources and current urban realities, encounters the serious barrier of traditional concepts of church and ministry. In many difficult mission situations, a major hindrance to rapid multiplication of churches is a traditional view of pastoral leadership. This has often been compounded by programs of leadership training that copy European or American models and by patterns of financial assistance that may give the impression that a church is impossible without a full-time, highly trained and paid leader.

For many years, the number of Baptist churches in Brazil has been almost double the number of pastors. Some have lamented this situation, feeling it to be a serious flaw. On the contrary, I see it as a sign of vigor—an indication that the spread of the gospel and the planting of churches have not been prevented by arbitrary traditional views. This does not mean that there is anything wrong with having a well-trained, full-time pastor. That is ideal. However, most New Testament churches seem to have managed without that ideal (and without buildings). Our approach should be "both-and" rather than "either-or"—the ideal where possible, and other patterns where the ideal is not possible.

Another present-day development greatly affects especially institutions like schools and hospitals. Increasingly the needs which these mission ministries have met are being filled by government schools and government hospitals. This poses a challenge to modern missions to adapt in the best way possible to this new situation, while continuing to express Christian compassion through helping ministries.

In some cases mission schools and hospitals become government institutions. The mission board can then use the same resources of personnel and funds in other less institutionalized ministries. In many cases the schools and hospitals become agencies of a maturing local Baptist convention.

The trend in new mission fields and in new outreach with helping ministries is toward less formal approaches (such as community health or primary health care in the medical arena). Again, this does not mean that existing schools and hospitals have no further usefulness. Some adaptation is often needed, but there are often fine contributions yet to be made by such mission agencies. The approach again is "both-and"—that is, capitalizing on the best current possibilities for already existing work, while moving into additional opportunities with new work.

Severe restrictions imposed by government or by cultural pressures create the most difficult situations for missions and therefore often call for the most unusual mission methods. For example, Southern Baptist missionaries have served in some countries by affiliation with earlier work sponsored by other mission groups (as, for example, in Sudan and in Nepal). Unusual approaches have been projected for India because permission for missionary residence there is very limited in comparison with the large population and the great mission need and opportunity.

All this is to say that we face a world of boundless variety and change. Its kaleidoscopic conditions challenge us to move beyond business as usual, both in the projection and support of our mission efforts and in the approaches and methods used.

## Special Concerns

The central emphasis in Southern Baptist missions is on churches—on attitudes that will let them be indigenous, and on methods that will help them become strong. These major concerns have been examined already. However, there are also some perennial tensions and problems in methodology that require missionary awareness and understanding. A few of those special concerns can be dealt with briefly.

### Concentration and Diffusion

One such concern is the tension between concentration and diffusion, which has already been explored in chapter 11.[23]

### Priority and Proportion

Another special concern is the distinction between priority and proportion. *Priority* (or perhaps more frequently in the plural form, *priorities*) is a very common word in current writing and speaking about missions. It can be a helpful word as a stimulant to thoughtful reexamination of what we are doing. It is entirely possible to go on unthinkingly in a routine of mission effort by habit and tradition, whereas a question about our priority or priorities can initiate wholesome new strategy studies. In many of its uses, however, the word *priority* is vague or even misleading. It is perhaps more useful in preaching than in planning, more helpful as a stimulant to analysis than as a guideline in the planning process.

Priority means "firstness." Occasionally the word is used to describe only a time sequence, but it usually states an order of importance and urgency. If strictly interpreted, it will mean that whatever has priority must be done, regardless of whether it is possible also to do the things that might rank second, third, and fourth in importance and urgency. For example, we can speak of giving priority to evangelism. However, the task of evangelism could use more than all of our resources and still not be completely done. Thus on a strict interpretation there would be no personnel or funds committed to any other kind of mission endeavor.

Of course, we do not carry any priority to that strictly logical conclusion. The result then is that the word becomes vague in meaning, a more impressive synonym for importance. In that sense it is common to use the plural *priorities* instead of the singular. But the tendency then may be to add more and more priorities, as everything that seems important joins the list. Neither the singular nor the plural form of the word really tells us how important or how urgent a particular part of the work may be. They are good words for raising the question of need and urgency, but something else is needed as a guideline in the planning process.

A helpful distinction can be made between *projects,* which are one-time endeavors with a definite completion point, and *programs,* which are continuing long-range operations. Priority is the appropriate word in planning for projects: Project A is to be done, then Project B, and afterward Project C if enough resources remain. For ongoing programs (sometimes called systems), *proportion* is a much more appropriate and useful word. It represents the way program planning is actually done. (*Emphasis* is a word with secondary value, to help in adapting proportions to current and changing needs.)

This can be illustrated in our individual families. We may have various projects in mind: replacement of the family car, a vacation trip, a new tree or new fence for the yard, and so forth. We decide which one has priority and save up money toward that purpose, with the others waiting until some future time. In the meantime, the ongoing needs of the family for shelter and clothing and food and health care and so forth are programs, each with its proportion in the family budget. The needs of a child who becomes ill will call for special emphasis on the health-care portion of the budget for a while. Except for the projects (which are in a sense "extras"), the word priority is really not applicable. Proportion and emphases are the operative planning concepts.

Similarly the main continuing concerns of mission strategy are handled primarily in terms of proportion and emphases, while the concept of priority applies primarily to capital or other special projects. All of these (whether priority, proportion, or emphases), in order to have validity, need to be grounded in a clear sense of purpose. The fundamental question to be asked again and again in the planning process is, With this as our purpose, what proportion of our resources should we invest in each of the various programs that contribute to the purpose?[24] The Foreign Mission Board in its philosophy statement makes explicit its belief "that proportion and balance are both desirable and necessary" in mission methodology.

### Function and Form

The distinction between function and form is an important consideration in mission methods. All of us, because of past experiences, have certain forms associated in our minds with the functions they express. For instance, when we think of preaching, we may automatically think of a man standing behind a pulpit at 11 o'clock on Sunday morning in our own home church. Preaching is a function; but all the rest of that picture is form (the man, the pulpit, the building, the time).

A critical adjustment for missionaries is learning how to carry out important spiritual functions without dependence on the particular American forms to which they have been accustomed.

A missionary may be tempted to feel that since Jesus came healing, a new wing for the mission hospital is a necessity. Healing indeed is a vital Christian function—but a hospital wing is a form.

It is rare indeed for missionaries to be able to exercise their functions overseas in exactly the same forms they used in America. Most missionaries with general evangelism (or church planting) assignments have been pastors in the United States; very few are pastors overseas. They have to learn to fulfill their ministries in new forms. Those new forms are usually much simpler and less expensive than would be expected or normal in America, since mission funds are so limited. Furthermore, and more important, the forms need to be appropriate to the local culture—and preferably reproducible by local persons using local resources. The missionary needs to pray that he will be delivered from dependence on accustomed forms, in order to be usable in the function to which he is called.

These questions then are the gist of many strategy decisions: In this particular context, which functions are appropriate to our purpose? How much of each function is needed? In what forms? Or how structured? (Note here the "Saul-David problem," to which reference was made earlier in chapter 9.)

One special aspect of this matter is the place of institutions on the mission field. (*Institution* usually means a more or less permanent organized entity of mission work, perhaps involving property and a regular staff.) However, the very use of the term tends to be misleading. Some missiologists, particularly followers of the church growth movement, have taken a fairly strongly anti-institutional stance. As a result, for many persons the term has a built-in negative connotation. Although it is not likely that the term will disappear, for good mission planning it would probably be better if the term *institution* were never used at all.

After all, in a less restricted sense, a church is an institution. An association is an institution. Even a family is an institution. No sound evaluation can be made by labeling something as an institution and thereby feeling opposed to it. The appropriate question is, What is the best form for implementing this important function in this setting? In nearly every case, with the passing of a bit of time, the form will become to some extent "institutionalized." This can happen even to a method of planting churches. Then comes indeed a danger that the form itself, the tradition related to it, and its own momentum will overshadow the function it is intended to express and make it too rigid to change as needed in new circumstances.

### Personnel and Program

There is a wholesome tension always between mission programs and the "real live missionaries" who administer them. Each missionary has personal gifts, interests, opinions, emphases. The way a program is implemented is shaped in part by the individuality of the missionary.

This is both good and bad. It is good to have enough flexibility in a program to take advantage of the gifts and strengths of personnel related to the program. But it can become harmful if the direction of the program itself is altered to fit someone's personal agenda.

A major problem in missions arises from this reality: The entire operation is carried out by persons with flaws. Thus the result at best is less than ideal. Policy and procedure need to protect the purposes of the work from too much distortion by the peculiarities of the workers.

It is important, therefore, for each mission to be aware of the danger of distortion and to learn how to help personnel to fly in formation, instead of each simply doing his own thing. (In a vivid phrase, some missionaries have trouble learning to "color inside the lines.")

### Mobility

Missiologists today emphasize the importance of remaining flexible enough to respond readily to new opportunities. Bogging down in the ruts of established work is unfortunate. Mobility in missions is recognized as highly valuable.

At times mobility in missions has been promoted in extreme form (perhaps in connection with the church growth movement's emphasis on responsiveness). Advocates of mobility have seemed to propose radical shifting of large numbers of missionaries from one country to another to respond to an unusual opportunity.

For practical reasons, such radical shifting is not advisable. Missionaries are not pawns on a chessboard. They are persons, often with families. They have learned languages and adapted to cultural settings. They have developed relationships. It would be very poor stewardship and would be traumatic for missionaries if they were shifted arbitrarily to a new cultural setting, to learn another language and to build relationships with another group of people, uprooting their families in the process.

Furthermore, radical shifting would be devastating to the

work in which such missionaries were already engaged. It would make no sense to pull missionaries out of work in Thailand, where good cultivation has been done and a harvest is beginning to appear, to send them into the ripe Korea harvest. After all, seminaries and churches in the United States can much more readily spare some of their personnel and can find replacements for them much more readily than Thailand (or some other mission field).

What is really needed, of course, is large numbers of persons already on the field, already knowing the language, already adapted to the culture, already involved in the work when the great harvesttime arrives.

So the Foreign Mission Board does not promote the idea of mobility as a shifting of missionaries between countries (approving such transfers only when there are special justifying circumstances). Our approach does emphasize mobility within a particular cultural setting. No missionary should consider himself wedded to a particular location and job assignment. Flexibility is the key word. The missionary should be ready to move into new opportunities as they develop.

Narrowing of the sense of calling is an unfortunate observable tendency in missionary experience. Many a missionary goes to the field committed (as should be the case) to whatever is needed for the best contribution to the evangelization of the chosen field. But after a time, the missionary has become accustomed to a particular city, a particular specialization, a particular role, a particular assignment. Often with new developments that change the situation, or even with normal maturing of the work, that missionary should make a change—perhaps even back to a more general role. But too often the concept of calling has narrowed down from a general missionary calling to the one assignment which is no longer appropriate—and the missionary withdraws from the field and resigns. In a spiritual and emotional sense, the missionary needs to be a sojourner, "living in tents" like Abraham, Isaac, and Jacob (Heb. 11:9, RSV). This is not easy, as anyone who has been through a time of transition can testify, but it is an important element in good mission strategy.

## Process

Probably little attention needs to be given here to details of the planning process (by which strategy is developed and methods determined), either in the Foreign Mission Board offices or on the fields. After all, the content of planning, which has been under consideration through many chapters, is much more important than the procedures used. Those procedures are comparable to planning procedures in many Southern Baptist agencies and institutions. Details vary from country to country and area to area and from time to time, but the general outlines of the process are fairly well fixed. The Foreign Mission Board has a formal plan for planning, and the Office of Overseas Operations administers similar plans for the fields.

The system is basically one of management by objectives. It has been formalized only in very recent years. Some aspects of the plan are still in process of completion.

The Office of Overseas Operations has used the term *priority concerns* as a somewhat broader and more flexible equivalent of *objectives*. The term applies to directions within a particular planning period—perhaps three to five years, as the case may be. Some of the priority concerns are more like projects in nature, while many are more comparable to emphases. Some are specific expressions, within a designated time frame, of ongoing directions which are part of the Foreign Mission Board's general strategy (such as "evangelism that results in churches") or of Bold Mission Thrust.

Whether in the home offices or on the fields, objectives (or priority concerns) are implemented through goals and action plans.

Research is an increasingly important part of the entire process, with the wonders of modern data processing to help. An example of a specific Foreign Mission Board research project is the developing of a data base on approximately 2,200 cities of the world, which are expected to have populations of 100,000 or more by the end of the century—a project being conducted jointly with David B. Barrett, editor of the *World Christian Encyclopedia*, and with the Southern Baptist Center for Urban Church Studies.

A key element in the entire process is the counsel of area

directors and their associates as missions wrestle with questions of strategy and methodology. The area directors bring to the discussion their own experience and observations in many countries, collective input from discussions within the staff of the Foreign Mission Board, and missiological insights from reading and from seminars. They are persons with a broad general understanding, not only of their own regions of the world but also of missions principles and methods.

## Creativity

Missionaries are encouraged to experiment. In most cases, they have wide areas of freedom in performing their assigned tasks. A high level of creativity is greatly to be desired.

It is probably relatively easy to be creative in ways that fit our own traditional patterns and depend on increasing mission resources—but creativity in methods that will not be limited by traditional patterns or American resources is most urgently needed. It is impossible to estimate the potential value of one creative idea for a reproducible approach in evangelism and church planting—an idea that can multiply the effectiveness of field resources and expand the outreach of the churches.

We long to see a mushrooming of churches, in which their vigor reaches such a level that they multiply themselves over and over again, and more and more rapidly, until an entire nation receives the gospel.

Obviously these questions of strategy and methodology are complex and demanding. This chapter has only barely touched the high points of relevant principles and concerns and offered some very general observations on them. It has all been rather abstract. The concrete reality of dealing with mission methodology takes place in the struggle of a mission to discover its direction—in the cooperative and creative experience of research and study and discussion and prayer until God's will is discerned.

## Notes

1. See, for example, chapters entitled "Theology Produces Methodology" and "Know Your Objectives" in Charles Brock, *The Principles and Practice of*

*Indigenous Church Planting* (Nashville: Broadman Press, 1981), pp. 15-20,29-37. Brock's book is an excellent treatment of church planting methodology in the specific setting of the Philippines.

2. The process of development of strategy principles is traced by Jesse C. Fletcher in "Foreign Mission Board Strategy," *Baptist History and Heritage,* vol. 9, no. 4 (1974): 210-22.

3. An interesting example is the controversy of Missionary T. P. Crawford with the Foreign Mission Board a century ago. Crawford insisted that the Board should adopt as worldwide policy those methods which he felt were advisable in his mission field. See Baker James Cauthen, et al., *Advance: A History of Southern Baptist Foreign Missions* (Nashville: Broadman Press, 1970), pp. 85-86.

4. Roland Allen, *Missionary Methods: St. Paul's or Ours?* (London: World Dominion Press, 1912; reprinted, Grand Rapids: Wm. B. Eerdmans Publishing Co., 1962).

5. As illustrative expansion on this theme, see "Thinking About Strategy," Edward R. Dayton, in the *Lausanne Communique,* a publication of the Strategy Working Group of the Lausanne Committee for World Evangelism, reporting the conclusion from studies and discussion by the group that "there is *no* one grand strategy for world evangelization."

6. For general summaries of mission functions from differing perspectives, see Johannes Verkuyl's chapter on "Ways and Means" in *Contemporary Missiology* (Grand Rapids: William B. Eerdmans Publishing Company, 1978), pp. 205-25; and J. Herbert Kane on "Methodological Imperatives" in *Understanding Christian Missions,* rev. ed. (Grand Rapids: Baker Book House, 1978), pp. 297-338. Functional summaries of Southern Baptist missions are found in Baker J. Cauthen and others, *By All Means* (Nashville: Convention Press, 1959); and in Baker J. Cauthen and Frank K. Means, *Advance to Bold Mission Thrust* (Richmond: Foreign Mission Board, SBC, 1981).

7. See SBC, *Annual,* 1966, pp. 60-67.

8. For further treatment of the Southern Baptist approach in health-care ministries, see the "Report to the Board: Overseas Division," Winston Crawley, director, attached to the Foreign Mission Board *Minutes* for March 1975 and February 1978, and the mission study book by Franklin T. Fowler, Senior Medical Consultant for the Foreign Mission Board, *Sick and Ye Visited Me* (Nashville: Convention Press, 1975).

9. For examination of this potential, see "Report to the Board: Overseas Division," by Winston Crawley, director, attached to Foreign Mission Board *Minutes,* September 1977.

10. Frank K. Means, "Foreign Missions Looks To AD 2000," *The Commission,* vol. 39, no. 6 (June 1976).

11. SBC, *Annual,* 1966, p. 62.

12. This functional aspect of Southern Baptist missions was the annual mission study theme for 1978. In fact, from 1975-1979, annual foreign missions study focused on programs of work of the Foreign Mission Board. Therefore,

those study books provide a comprehensive survey of functional approaches in Southern Baptist missions.

13. In connection with a special study of overseas broadcasting work requested by the Southern Baptist Convention, the director of the Overseas Division, Winston Crawley, made special reports to the Foreign Mission Board on various aspects of broadcast ministries at that time. See Foreign Mission Board *Minutes*, October 1968, February 1969, and September 1970.

14. For a general treatment of Bible distribution in missions, see Eugene A. Nida, *God's Word in Man's Language* (New York: Harper & Row, Publishers, 1952).

15. See the report of Winston Crawley, director of Overseas Division, to the Foreign Mission Board on publication work in the Foreign Mission Board *Minutes*, February 1977.

16. For a summary of the movement see F. Ross Kinsler, *The Extension Movement in Theological Education*, rev. ed. (Pasadena, Calif.: William Carey Library, 1981).

17. Donald Anderson McGavran, *The Bridges of God* (London: World Dominion Press, 1955).

18. Melvin L. Hodges, *On the Mission Field: The Indigenous Church* (Chicago: Moody Press, 1953).

19. Various religious situations are reviewed in Gerald H. Anderson and Thomas F. Stransky, eds., *Mission Trends No. 5: Faith Meets Faith* (New York: Paulist Press and Grand Rapids: Wm. B. Eerdmans Publishing Co., 1981).

20. For relevant practical treatment of this and related subjects, see James F. Engel and H. Wilbert Norton, *What's Gone Wrong With the Harvest?* (Grand Rapids: Zondervan Publishing House, 1975).

21. See Winston Crawley's column, "Horizons: Money Pinch Felt in Church Properties," in the January 1984 issue of *The Commission*, vol. 47, no. 1:74.

22. See the October 1982 report of Winston Crawley, vice-president, Office of Planning, to the Foreign Mission Board.

23. The matter is considered in more detail in the report of the director of Overseas Division, Winston Crawley, to the Foreign Mission Board in December 1969 and March 1977; see Foreign Mission Board *Minutes*.

24. For elaboration of this topic, see the report of the director of Overseas Division, Winston Crawley, to the Foreign Mission Board in December 1974 and July 1979, attached to Foreign Mission Board *Minutes*.

# 15
# What About Self-Support?

Treating self-support in a separate chapter may seem strange, as may also the location of the chapter.

Self-support was explained in chapter 9 as one of the traditional measures of progress toward indigenous maturity. In reality, self-support is likely the least important of those measures. Vigorous evangelistic outreach, strong leadership, and adaptation to the cultural context are probably all more significant for essential indigeneity and for effective ministry.

Furthermore, if additional attention needs to be given to self-support for practical reasons, this could well be included as one of the "special concerns" introduced in the chapter on methods. (As a matter of fact, that is where I have treated it for some years in strategy discussions with new missionaries.)

A separate chapter is being devoted to self-support because of the prominence it has had in the writing, teaching, thinking, and planning of many persons involved with missions (whether academically, administratively, or in actual missionary service). Concern for self-support has sometimes seemed to override other important strategy concerns. Some persons, indeed, if asked the meaning of *indigeneity,* would reply that the term means self-supporting churches. Thus the broader and deeper meaning of indigeneity can be distorted, and progress toward church maturity and strength can be hindered. To avoid the possibility of such distortion and such hindrance, adequate attention needs to be given to proper understanding of self-support.

Within the broad context of mission strategy, two chief topics were lifted out for priority treatment. Those were the church growth concept and holistic mission ministries. Consideration of those themes was placed ahead of the general chapter on methods because of their importance. In the total strategy picture, self-support is much less significant. It is being treated here as a kind of extended footnote to methodology, needing more specific scrutiny and more space than would be expected as a minor subpoint in the chapter on methods.

## Money and Missions

Those who place considerable stress on self-support may be tempted to view the matter rather narrowly. For example, it is possible to take a doctrinaire position of giving no financial assistance to churches, but at the same time to employ local workers as evangelists or place large sums of money in the hands of missionaries to do things that churches might help do if there were a partnership plan. Self-support needs to be considered in the wider context of the total place of money in mission ministries.

In Christian missions, as we are well aware, there are other values much greater than money. Investment of life and the spiritual qualities of the Kingdom are much more significant. In a time of crisis, this becomes evident. (For example, a missionary who was part of a group that walked from Burma to India during World War II told of persons in the group throwing money away because carrying a given weight of food to sustain life was more important than carrying the same weight in coins.)[1]

However, money is important. In modern society almost every aspect of life (for the Christian as well as the non-Christian, and including every kind of church activity) involves the use of money. In fact, that was already true to a large degree in New Testament times. Paul was part of a money economy: He did not grow his own food and make his own clothing. Because money is such a vital part of the life of organized society, mission work is largely dependent on money for its continuation.

Money has little or no intrinsic value. Its value depends on the possibility of exchanging it for goods and services, as reflected in dictionary definitions ("medium of exchange, measure of value, and means of payment"). However, there is a sense in which money does represent human life—for it serves as a channel through which a person's time, talent, and energy can be transferred to places and purposes to which the person may not have immediate access. This is one element in Christian stewardship. The money of a Christian can become a spiritual force in the world. Indeed, the combined concepts of Christian mission and Christian stewardship seem to require that money be used in missions to the greatest possible effect.

This then reaches the basic question, not whether to use money in missions, but how money can best be used. Some underlying principles can be suggested.

1. The kingdom of God obviously will not be built, nor the mission of the church accomplished, primarily by money. When we deal with money, we are involved with something that is only instrumental and not essential (in the basic meaning of that word) to the Christian calling.

2. At the same time, it is important to note that any attempt to separate money from life tends to be artificial and perhaps even arbitrary. Money has become an almost inseparable part of human experience. (Attempts to eliminate the use of money in missions often actually turn out only to hide its use.)

3. The well-known biblical statement does not condemm money itself as the "root of all evil," but rather the love of money. Thus we are granted freedom to use money, but we are also given a caution about wrong attitudes that may arise in its use.

4. Money is of neutral moral value. In itself, it is neither good nor bad. It can be used in ways that are harmful to the user and to others. On the other hand, it can have constructive uses as a tool to accomplish good.

5. Any human arrangement can be expected to have both advantages and disadvantages. This is therefore true of any plan for use of money. A particular plan will need evaluation in the light of objectives and circumstances, for measurement of relative advantages and disadvantages. (There may then be the further problem of human error and failure in the carrying out of any plan.)

6. The same concerns that apply to decisions about use of money on mission fields need also to be applied to arrangements for mission organization, staffing, and other general overhead expenditures. Decisions about all such expenditures need to reflect the central mission objective and need to express the sense of stewardship implied in the strategic concept of maintaining a lean base in order to commit resources mainly to outreach.

The whole question of the relationship between money and missions is exceedingly complex. Ability to finance even the sending out of missionaries can depend on developments in local economies and the international economy and on government financial policies and regulations. The possibility of developing church strength along traditional lines depends on local economic systems and economic strength. All these complexities cannot be explored here in detail.[2]

### Dangers

"How many times I have wished that we could do missionary work without money!" That comment by Luther Copeland reflects what many of us have felt at one time or another.[3] Copeland goes on to describe the serious difficulties that can arise from the contrast between the affluence of our missionary home base and the poverty typical of many mission fields.

> Relatively affluent churches of the United States (and other western nations) are doing missionary work in cooperation with churches in the developing nations, churches often severely limited in economic and perhaps in personnel resources. How can we use our greater wealth of finance and personnel without breeding in our partner churches a spirit of servility and dependence which violates and hampers selfhood? How can money be used in missionary work without its being coercive? How are missionaries to avoid the spurious authority which inheres in purse strings?[4]

Many negative consequences of financial aid are obvious (and are by no means limited to foreign situations). Even help to individuals runs the risk of producing "rice Christians"—persons who claim to be Christians in the hope of financial benefit. Some of the terms commonly used in missions, such as *subsidy* and *sending and receiving*, imply a condescending relationship. The desire some have expressed in recent years for a possible "moratorium" in missions has arisen in large part from that kind of uncomfortable relationship.

The basic problem addressed by the self-support emphasis is the danger that money may be used in ways that actually hinder the objective of indigenous church strength. That danger is real and serious.

There are many potential traps in the use of money. Mission funds have been used widely to establish and perpetuate models of church life and of institutional ministries based on Western culture and tradition. Thus young churches around the world have been outfitted precisely like David in Saul's armour. The same has been true of denominational organization, which has often been top-heavy. No matter how willingly missionaries transfer responsibility to local leaders, the pattern has already been set, and any shift to something simpler and more culturally appropriate is exceedingly painful.

In many cases missionaries are reluctant to transfer responsibility, and so continue to administer various kinds of assistance. A missionary may be surrounded by mission employees to whom he is paymaster. He may be tempted to use funds to build a personal following or to control decisions being made by local churches and their leaders.

Too much help too soon and too long quite naturally breeds a spirit of dependency. The expectation of continuing aid is very hard to break. The recipient is not likely to break it, and the donor breaks it only at the cost of ill feelings and controversy.

Resentment (rather than appreciation) is the emotion that is most natural and frequent in dependency situations. The resentment is compounded if there is any trace of condescension or manipulation by persons who control the money. For missionaries or the mission to be making decisions about local leaders is an almost foolproof recipe for anti-missionary feeling.

Ready availability of foreign funds tends to stunt the growth of biblical stewardship and generosity on the part of new believers and their churches. Teaching and training for stewardship are simply felt to be unnecessary or even irrelevant, as long as someone else will pay the bills.

A system in which local leaders are supported largely by funds from the United States sets up a wrong relationship for those leaders. Instead of being related directly and primarily to churches, they relate primarily to the mission. In extreme cases, they may think themselves to be employees of the mission. Once the pattern is established, persons may enter seminary with the expectation of a good job as a church leader after graduation, and even with the hope of lifelong "social security" through that employment. Sometimes church leaders as a group then operate about like a labor union to protect their position.

Even when a partnership arrangement has been worked out, and local leaders share or assume decision-making responsibility, the possibility of problems is not removed. To be sure, the missionary is no longer guilty of (or suspected of) using control of funds to manipulate. The guilt or suspicion is simply transferred from the foreigner to those local leaders who now have decision-making responsibility. Also, this power often becomes a bone of contention between aspiring leaders—and some young Baptist conventions have been split by the power struggle.

A principal fault in many plans for financial aid is simply that money continues to be poured year after year into the same old work, instead of being released by growing self-support so that it can be devoted to new outreach.

## Complexity

From the preceding summary of dangers, it should be clear that a very strong case can be made for providing no financing in any form to churches that develop from mission work. There is no need to attempt here a full statement of that case. The books of Roland Allen, Melvin Hodges, Donald McGavran, and many others who emphasize church growth and what is sometimes called "the indigenous method" are well known to modern missiologists. A number of mission agencies have adopted a firm policy of providing no financial assistance.

That position also brings problems. An outstanding one is that there are many parachurch or independent mission organizations that will offer good salaries to well-qualified workers. Developing self-supporting churches that are strong in stewardship and can support their pastors well is difficult and often slow—especially if there has been a history of dependency. Sometimes also a relationship with a foreign organization will give status and perhaps the possibility of occasional international travel. Many of the organizations that provide these employment opportunities have no commitment to the indigenous principle. They believe in local preachers employed by an American organization with American funds as the best way to do mission work. The effect, however, is to rob churches striving to be self-supporting of the leadership they need in order to become strong.

Another complication is that individual missionaries (where policy rules out the use of mission funds) are tempted to use special gifts they may receive, or their own personal funds, to help churches, workers, or special projects. In one Southern Baptist mission field where the mission was seeking to implement a nonassistance policy, such individual end runs around the policy came to be called "Baptist Underground Missions."

Even where missionaries resist that temptation, in many settings the tithes of missionaries still are a problem. Suppose, for example, that a missionary family working in a destitute area believes in giving a tithe of income through the church in the community where the family lives. Most churches in newer places of work are relatively small. The tithe of the misionary family might amount to more than all the giving of the other members put together. Technically that church could be called self-supporting, though heavily dependent on foreign funds. Having one family contributing that large a portion of the church's resources cannot help distorting any attempt at democratic decision making by the church. Furthermore, if that missionary family moves away, programs that have been undertaken on the basis of available resources will undergo sudden crisis. The question of missionary tithes is itself a complex one, with no easy answer.

Mission strategy must be dynamic. It involves many interrelated concerns. No one principle should be applied dogmatically. Even a thoroughly sound aim like self-support has many ramifications.

Actually self-support (except in very special circumstances or in a carefully limited sense) should not be taken as a goal in missions. If taken as a goal, it is one of the easiest in the world to attain. All that is necessary is that there be no church building, no pastor, no literature, no program of training or outreach—and self-support is achieved. Surely vitality, strength, and effectiveness are more worthy goals. The desire for self-support can be a helpful stimulus and tool, and progress toward self-support is a valuable indicator of growing church strength—since any church that needs constant "money transfusions" to keep it going is obviously not in vigorous health.

### Foreign Mission Board Viewpoint

The approach of the Southern Baptist Foreign Mission Board to the use of money is rooted in two basic principles: trusteeship and outreach. Money channeled through the Foreign Mission Board is a sacred trust from Southern Baptist individuals and churches. It is intended as a spiritual resource for outreach with the gospel. Therefore, the Board seeks to use funds (following sound administrative practice) for maximum effectiveness in pursuit of its overall purpose of world evangelization, through the planting, multiplying, and strengthening of churches.

### *Basic Position*

The principles of trusteeship and outreach do not rule out use of money to help overseas churches. The arguments of others in support of a nonassistance policy are seen as cautions or danger signals, not as a prohibition. In other words, the fact that money can be used in missions in harmful ways does not necessarily mean that there is no such thing as constructive use of money.

We are sure that there are many circumstances in which Christian concern calls for using money to help individuals—as in responding to emergency relief needs, for example.

Our practice (as in other strategy matters) has been flexible. We look to the judgment of persons at work on the fields to identify constructive ways of using money. If a mission organization decides that its policy, in light of local circumstances, should be a nonassistance policy, the Board supports that mission decision. If another mission, in light of its local circumstances, plans a strategy that allows assistance, with appropriate safeguards, the Board is ready to support that decision too.

A century ago, a strong Southern Baptist missionary leader in China, T. P. Crawford, insisted that the Foreign Mission Board should rule out any use of funds for aid to churches anywhere in the world, but the Board refused to adopt that arbitrary position.[5]

For the first century of Southern Baptist mission work, there was little money to give. In the twenty-five years immediately following World War II, the Board had larger resources, but they diminished sharply in purchasing power in the 1970s. Unless that trend is reversed, missionaries may face again stringent conditions similar to those in earlier generations. In the meantime, some other mission agencies have "made a virtue of necessity," espousing strongly the principle of nonassistance, when in fact they have had no money to provide.

Whether funds have been relatively scarce or relatively plentiful, the Foreign Mission Board has maintained consistently through the years its flexible approach, allowing this question to be decided on the fields in relation to circumstances and in the context of total strategy. The formal strategy statement adopted by the Board's Executive Management Group in 1982 includes this guideline. "Policies should stimulate self-support but without any arbitrary requirement that might hinder growth and strength."

The term *subsidy* should be avoided. Its connotation almost unavoidably suggests condescension and dependency, plus the probable expectation that the subsidy will continue indefinitely. Even *assistance* may not escape those dangers entirely, but it can more easily be interpreted as assistance to a specific project or for a specific purpose, and within a designated time span.

The primary concern for self-support relates to churches. Serious problems arise when a church becomes dependent on outside financing to carry on its own life and work. The concern does not apply to nearly the same degree in other parts of mission work. For example, in evangelistic outreach to new areas of a country, no grave problem is created by a partnership arrangement in which outreach is supported jointly by funds from the churches and funds from the mission.

Continuing mission participation over a period of many years in funding for other aspects of a comprehensive mission effort, such as broadcasting, publications, theological education, or health-care ministries, seldom causes very much problem. Such ministries presumably will move gradually either toward self-support or toward full support by the local church constituency. Even so, mission funds might still be used for special projects— all within a framework and an atmosphere of partnership.

Other than churches, the main area where self-support is of great importance is convention structures and expenses. As in the case of churches, the Foreign Mission Board has not taken an arbitrary position ruling out any help toward such convention expenses—but it does urge strongly that convention structures be kept lean rather than top-heavy, and that churches and their leaders give high priority to full support of their own convention.

In essence this approach envisions three tiers. The established churches and their convention operations are to rest as fully as possible on the local financial base of their own stewardship. Agencies and programs of the convention may involve continuing mission partnership in providing funds, but with local sources becoming increasingly responsible. New outreach and special projects (including some capital provisions) may be an area of long-range financial partnership. Concern for self-support is to be understood and applied in ways that will contribute best to indigenous church strength and to effective outreach.

### Guidelines

Istead of self-support as a focus of interest and effort, we urge concentration on seeking the wisest and best ways to use financial resources in missions. The search is not easy, and the answers we find are seldom simple and final. From years of experience, however, some guidelines for wise use of missions money have been identified.

1. All money for missions is received as a sacred trust, having been contributed in many cases sacrificially, by persons desiring to send the gospel to everyone in the world. Plans for use of money should reflect that trust and that intent. Responsible stewardship calls also for good business practice.

2. General principles of strategy planning apply. Basic commitment to the maturing and vitality of the churches and to effectiveness in gospel outreach must be kept clearly in view. Plans for moving toward that central objective must be carefully adapted to the local situation. (For example, in rural and small-town areas, probably little financial aid to churches should be expected, but more help may be appropriate in urban settings.)

3. It is not necessary or desirable to reproduce in other lands the pattern of church life that is found in the United States.

4. The concept of partnership in Christian ministry and outreach between local Christians and missionaries should permeate all financial planning. Any distinction between "giving and receiving churches" is inappropriate. The mission is not giving to the churches. The mission and the churches together are giving for Christian ministries and gospel outreach.

5. Basic responsibility for finanacial support of churches rests with their own members. They are responsible for selecting their leaders and for providing suitably to meet the needs of such leaders (whether they are lay leaders, bivocational, or full-time professional leaders). That responsibility extends to whatever provisions are appropriate for medical emergencies and for retirement. Serious problems easily develop, and growth of the work is hindered, if workers look to the mission rather than to their churches as the expected source for any of these provisions.

6. Mission money for any program or the meeting of any need should be a supplement to, and not a substitute for, funds provided by the congregations. Therefore, the financing of any project should not begin with an offer of money from the mission. It should begin with discussion of the need for the

project and enough prayerful consideration to arrive at common concern for the project. Next in order should come an evaluation of the probable local resources available. Only then is it timely to examine the possibility of financial participation by the mission.

Unless there is enough local interest to generate significant local funding, the project is likely to be merely something artificially stimulated by the mission, but without any enthusiastic participation of church members. Missionaries easily tend to be activists and approach things promotionally, instead of allowing time for local initiative and the growth of local support.

Loan funds are a common solution to church property needs. Such funds leave responsibility ultimately with the local congregation, but they provide help which the congregation might not be able to get elsewhere.

7. One-time help on a project basis (especially for local church and convention needs) runs much less risk of creating dependency than does continuing month-by-month assistance. Therefore, it is wise to spend considerable time discussing and developing a system that will provide financing for special needs, but not for current expenses. If a mission is already involved in a plan that provides regular funds for convention overhead, it should begin discussions pointed toward allocating the funds for particular projects.

In many situations, mission financial grants will be given mainly to help with church buildings. This should be clearly interpreted and understood as a one-time grant—not implying any mission responsibility for upkeep or repair of the building. (I wear a watch which was a gift to me, but I would not go to the donor and ask him to pay when the watch needs repair.)

8. There may be special circumstances that justify operating budget assistance to a young congregation (or a fledgling convention). In such cases, the provision should be for a clearly understood limited time only.

The most likely reason for aid to a church would be to enable it to have full-time trained leadership, even when the church is relatively young and small. The intention is to help the church to become large and strong rather rapidly. If several years have passed, and the church has not grown large and strong enough to support its pastor, obviously the aid is not accomplishing its purpose. Presumably, then, that particular place of work at that particular time can reasonably sustain only a bivocational pastor or a layleader—in which case the assistance should be phased out and should be used for beginning other new work. It is not the intention of the Foreign Mission Board for its funds to be used on a continuing basis to maintain established churches.

Perhaps five years, on a gradually diminishing basis, should be the maximum length of help to a church. Even that length can easily create a spirit of dependency, with resentment as the amount of help decreases. A less risky arrangement is a two- or three-year "grubstake," with the definite understanding that it is intended to get a new work going and that the new congregation afterward will arrange for the kind of leadership that fits its financial strength. That approach, well explained and fully understood from the beginning, gives strong support to the principle that foreign mission funding should concentrate on planting and multiplying churches.

9. All decisions about the amount or kind of material provision for church leaders and workers should be made by local churches, or by appropriate representative committees of local leaders (perhaps a convention committee, where one exists). Missionaries and the mission organization should not be involved in such decisions. Salary levels and housing provisions for pastors, for workers in church ministries or outreach, and for convention leaders should all be determined by local people. The mission can appropriately indicate the extent of its possible participation, but it should not do so in a way that seems to determine the total amount that the worker will receive.

Ideally, it is better for the administering of aid funds and of budgets of ministry agencies to be transferred as soon as possible from missionaries to local leaders and local committees. This will express symbolically the partnership in ministry and outreach toward which local churches and Southern Baptists are contributing as they are able.

## Conclusion

Our financial resources are limited, but we do not have to say, "Silver and gold have I none" (Acts 3:6). Since we do have some money, we cannot avoid the complications that go with use of money. More important, we have the privilege of the stewardship that accompanies availability of money. God gives us the money in order that it may be used wisely and well toward the accomplishing of his world purpose. We must keep learning how to avoid using money in ways that hinder, and discover, by the leading of God's spirit, ways that will make mission money a great blessing, not merely a necessary evil.

### Notes

1. Paul Geren, *Burma Diary* (New York: Harper & Brothers Publishers, 1943), p. 34.

2. For earlier extended treatments of the subject, see vol. 5, "The Economic Basis of the Church," in the Reports of the International Missionary Conference at Madras, India, *The World Mission of the Church* (New York: International Missionary Council, 1939), pp. 98-104 and J. Merle Davis, *New Buildings on Old Foundations* (reprint, New York: International Missionary Council, 1947). More recent treatments from two quite different perspectives are found in Johannes Verkuyl, *Contemporary Missiology* (Grand Rapids: William B. Eerdemans Publishing Company, 1978), pp. 320-26 and J. Herbert Kane, *The Christian World Mission: Today and Tomorrow* (Grand Rapids: Baker Book House, 1981), pp. 109-19. Much has been written about the subject in books related to the church growth movement.

3. E. Luther Copeland, *World Mission and World Survival* (Nashville: Broadman Press, 1985), p. 106.

4. Ibid (quoted from an early draft of Copeland's manuscript).

5. The controversy between Crawford and the Foreign Mission Board included other concerns. The self-support aspect of it is reviewed by Jesse C. Fletcher in "Foreign Mission Board Strategy," *Baptist History and Heritage*, vol. 9, no. 4 (1974): 214-15.

# Part VI
# Future

# 16
# What Next?

Walter de la Mare, an English poet, wrote of "poor Jim Jay" who "got stuck fast in yesterday." Woe be to us if we get stuck there with him! We Southern Baptists must turn our faces toward tomorrow and accept anew and willingly from our Lord's hands the committal of a world task that is far from finished. No matter how true that it is not our task alone but one we share with Baptist co-workers in other lands and with Christian brethren of other denominations, we still must discharge our own stewardship. In God's sight, we must do the part He expects of us.

Earlier chapters have reviewed highlights of Southern Baptist foreign missions up to the present and have sought to describe clearly the combination of objectives and principles that guides us. In this chapter we examine the unfinished business that still awaits us.

## Bold Mission Thrust

This year marks the ninth birthday of Bold Mission Thrust, the Southern Baptist world missions projection for the last twenty-five years of the century. The background, beginnings, and general outlines of Bold Mission Thrust, plus progress up to the present, were described in chapter 3 and the concept was further interpreted in chapter 4. As we look to the future, we inevitably raise again the questions that were asked at the beginning: Can it be done? Is world evangelization really possible?[1]

From the first, many thought it was presumptuous for Southern Baptists to talk of preaching the gospel to all the people in the world by the year 2000. But we have never meant that we expect to evangelize the whole world by ourselves, while other Christians simply stand by and watch us do it. A number of other Christian groups have stated world evangelization as their intention also, and many Christians throughout the world are deeply involved. The task will demand that the full resources and best efforts of all Christians be wholly committed to gospel outreach. Bold Mission Thrust expresses our desire to do our full part alongside all our fellow believers.

Even so, the remaining task of world evangelization is so awesome that from the human perspective it seems clearly impossible.

In recent years, some enthusiastic persons have claimed that modern technology makes the sharing of the gospel with everyone possible at last. That assertion can be credible only if "in principle" or "in theory" is attached to it. In reality, hundreds of millions of the world's people have no chance to hear any Christian broadcast. Multitudes have no radios. There is no broadcasting at all in many of the world's languages, and no Christian broadcasting in an even larger number. Government regulations prevent such broadcasting in many places, or prohibit ownership of shortwave radios that might receive an international broadcast.

At best, there are immense barriers of language and culture; of law, ideology, and customs; of remoteness, poverty, and prejudice that prevent not just a few people but countless millions from hearing the gospel. All this is in addition to the severely limited resources, both in persons and in financing, for sharing the gospel in those places where it is least known.

Multiplied miracles will be required for everyone in the world to hear the gospel in this century.

Is Bold Mission Thrust then merely a promotional gimmick to encourage us to do a little more in our regular church programs? Or is it simply a high-sounding theme that helps us to feel good because we are talking about doing something great—even though we may not do much about it? This can indeed be the case, and it is the great danger we face in Bold Mission Thrust—

the danger that we will not be genuinely dedicated to world missions.

It is easy to talk glibly about Bold Mission Thrust and world evangelization without taking any action that is really bold or making any actual costly commitment. We are simply kidding ourselves if we think that Bold Mission Thrust can be possible without our giving up some things that we would like to have for ourselves, our families, and our churches.

At least up to this point, there is every indication that Southern Baptists do intend to stick with the idea of Bold Mission Thrust as a constant challenge to ourselves. Many wondered initially whether the entire emphasis would be only a fad. In the past, most Southern Baptist emphases have lasted only a short time. Continuing with a major denominational theme seemed rather unlikely. However, awareness of the theme and interest in it seem to have grown fairly steadily during the past nine years. In 1985, the concept of Bold Mission Thrust is alive and well among Southern Baptists.

### Mid-Course

The preceding section has dealt mainly with the depth of commitment of Southern Baptists to Bold Mission Thrust. What about the progress of the mission thrust?

At first, following adoption of the Bold Mission plans in 1976, there was little evidence of change in the normal progress of Southern Baptist missions. For three or four years, any effects of Bold Mission Thrust were difficult to identify. That would normally be expected, since it would require time for enthusiasm to build up in the churches. By now the thrust does seem to have lifted bold mission off the launching pad, and momentum is increasing.

Mission statistics each year are reviewed and a summary is prepared to show progress toward Bold Mission Thrust challenges. A copy of the most recent summary, reflecting statistics at the end of 1984, is in Appendix 11.

Mid-range projections have been developed to serve as a connective between the Board's long-range Bold Mission Thrust projections and ongoing current planning. The mid-range projections point toward the end of calendar year 1990. In addition, desirable growth rates for a four-year period (1983-1986) have been identified. Copies of these are in Appendixes 12-13. They express the outlook of Foreign Mission Board staff as of early 1982, based on Bold Mission Thrust progress to that date.

Another revealing way of analyzing where we stand in Southern Baptist foreign missions mid-course in Bold Mission Thrust is to consider an average Southern Baptist foreign mission field. Totals for the number of missionaries and the annual budget are so large that they may be confusing or misleading. They can seem to imply that no more missionaries and no more mission money are needed. Or they may simply be so large that it is hard to comprehend them. Breaking down the entire mission effort to an average field can help make it comprehensible. Therefore, such an analysis, using the latest statistics available in early 1985, is included in Appendix 14.

A few comments on the data may help still further: The population of an average field is more than 16 million (with India not included in the computation, since its population is so large and the region served by Southern Baptists has been relatively limited). The number of Southern Baptist missionaries in the average field has not changed very much for a good many years. Our increasing number of missionaries is matched by an increasing number of fields, so the ratio of missionaries per field remains about the same. Missionaries in the average field are engaged in a wide range of ministries, such as are carried on both by state conventions and by Southern Baptist Convention agencies in this country. There are a number of Southern Baptist churches that have an annual budget larger than the foreign missions budget for an average field with more than 16 million people.

These realities emphasize the immensity of the unfinished world mission task and the strategic importance of the Board's philosophy of church multiplication, with missionaries in a generative role.

## Moment of Truth

The *moment of truth* is a phrase that is used to refer to any decisive time. The moment of truth determines and reveals clearly how things will come out.

We may have reached by now the moment of truth for Bold Mission Thrust. Both on the fields and in our Convention, radical changes will be needed soon if the intentions of Bold Mission Thrust are to be realized. (I am not referring here to the great overarching purpose, but to the more specific intentions spelled out in the Bold Mission Thrust documents.)

On the fields, the main problem area (as indicated earlier) is the challenge of tenfold multiplication of churches in the final quarter of the century, along with similar increases in baptisms and church membership. This is not only the most difficult of the Bold Mission Thrust proposals but also the most important, since multiplication of churches is central in Southern Baptist foreign missions strategy and is the true hope for world evangelization.

Tenfold multiplication of churches in 25 years would have required an average annual net gain of almost 9.7 percent. The rate of net gain thus far, while higher than it had been prior to 1979, is still only roughly 7.7 percent. Now for the remaining years of the century, if the challenge is to be met, the annual rate of increase will need to be almost half again higher than it has been thus far. That kind of increase in the planting of new churches seems entirely feasible, but it will not come easily. Area directors and missionaries must keep this concern in the forefront of their thinking and planning, and must encourage the churches and conventions with which they work to develop specific programs for accelerated church planting. The Board's Office of Overseas Operations is already giving concentrated attention to this concern.

At the home base, what is urgently needed now is a new thrust in giving for missions to support the already evident acceleration in missionary personnel and in mission work overseas. In the initial years of Bold Mission Thrust, Southern Baptist giving for foreign missions did not increase enough to counteract inflation at home and abroad and match the growth in missionary personnel. Therefore, funding for missions programs has been pinched more and more.

In 1984 the Lottie Moon Christmas Offering fell almost 2 million dollars below its goal, and the amount for foreign missions from the Cooperative Program was almost 3 million dollars below the projection in the Convention operating budget. In both cases, increases did roughly match United States inflation plus net growth in Southern Baptist membership—which left per-member giving for foreign missions (adjusted for inflation) just about where it had been. *That level of giving can hardly be called bold.* The average per-member Southern Baptist gift for foreign missions, through the Cooperative Program, the Lottie Moon Christmas Offering, and special designated gifts, still amounts to less than the cost of mailing one first-class letter per week. If we take world evangelization seriously, we surely must do better in financing it.[2]

For several years there has been a distraction in Southern Baptist life—a controversy that has threatened Southern Baptist unity and concentration on our world mission calling. Southern Baptists, with all our diversities of viewpoint, need to unite again around the Great Commission and our stewardship of the gospel for the nations.

Halfway commitment will not meet the challenge of such a tremendous era in world affairs. We will need to break out of our routines, both in our overseas ministries and in the backing given to those ministries by our churches. The world population explosion, modern improvements in transportation and communication, the unusual resources in the hands of Southern Baptists, and the uncertainties of the future combine to make it imperative that our churches reach out to the whole world now.

Although there is still danger that Bold Mission Thrust may simply fizzle out, there are encouraging signs that timing may be right for a second surge of missions emphasis. In 1985 the Convention will be launching the formal promotional theme for the final five years of this decade. That theme is "Total Missions." During the same period the Cooperative Program should receive new impetus through the Planned Growth in Giving program, which seeks to encourage individual church members, churches, and state conventions to give increasing percentages of their resources for missions outreach. The interest of state conventions in partnership missions arrangements with overseas conventions is spreading. Many vocational groups among Southern Baptists have organized for involvement in missions (medical and paramedical personnel, farmers, lawyers, and so forth). The Foreign Mission Board is moving toward a probable global consultation, involving missionary-sending Baptist conventions with which we have partnership relations. Perhaps most encouraging of all is the continuing increase of candidates seeking appointment as missionaries.

Still, in this moment of truth when Bold Mission Thrust may hang in the balance, there are solemn questions we all need to ask ourselves about that half of our world's people who have not yet heard the gospel: Should they hear only if getting the message to them is easy or convenient? Only if it costs us little or nothing? Only if we need to take no risks? Only when our own needs have all been met? Only if others pay the price in lives or in money? Only if we individually can live where we would choose and do the work we would prefer in the way we would want to do it?

Of course we want everyone in the world to hear the gospel, but how are they to hear if we bypass the cross?

### Looking to the Future

John Schaar of the University of California at Santa Cruz has described the future as "not a result of choices among alternative paths, offered by the present, but a place that is created—first in mind and will, next in activity."[3] Southern Baptists through their foreign missionaries are involved in creating the future.

Futurism, or futurology, is a rapidly growing field of general public interest. The World Future Society, founded in 1966, lists nearly 200 books and audiovisual cassettes dealing with the future. *The Futurist* magazine even had an article on "The Future of Futurism" in April 1983.[4] Prominent news periodicals have put out special issues dealing with the future in considerable detail. Religious organizations and religious periodicals have also made projections for the future based on current trends.[5] Of course, persons making such projections recognize the large part that entirely unanticipated changes will play in the actual future as it develops.

Southern Baptist foreign missions leaders have made projections also, with special focus on world missions. At the consultation on foreign missions sponsored by the Foreign Mission Board at Miami Beach, Florida, in 1975, I presented a paper on "The Missions Task Ahead," looking forward to this final quarter of the twentieth century.[6] Bill O'Brien, executive vice-president of the Foreign Mission Board, sketched a global Baptist fellowship scenario to introduce the 1980 adult foreign missions study book, *Mission for Tomorrow*.[7] Clark Scanlon, executive assistant in the Foreign Mission Board's Office of Overseas Operations, has written on trends in foreign missions for *The Baptist Program*.[8]

A stimulating view of the future was presented by the new Foreign Mission Board president, R. Keith Parks, in the October 1980 issue of *The Commission*. Parks wrote:

I expect there will be:

| MORE | LESS |
|------|------|
| Change | Rigidity |
| Mobility | Structure |
| Partnerships | Unilateralism |
| Financial Needs | Buying power |
| Missionary personnel | Dependence on missionaries |
| Accountability | Defensiveness |
| Strategy planning | Confusion and ambiguity |
| Administrative guidance | Frustration and waste |
| Local leadership | Missionary control |
| Poverty | Equality |
| Hunger | Food |
| Danger | Stability |
| Urgency | Complacency |
| Witnessing | Tolerance |
| Responsiveness | Neutrality |

Each pair of words or phrases represents two sides of one concept. Each expression bulges with meaning and implication. The inevitability of many of these changes is certain. Our options are simple:
1) We can ignore the onrushing tide and be engulfed.
2) We can resist it and be shattered.

> 3) We can initiate some change and adapt to others and be
> blessed and a blessing.
> May we have courage and clarity of vision as we keep the
> world in view.[9]

Although we cannot know the future in any sure detail, we do know the general direction of God's purpose. Therefore, we are deeply determined to keep moving forward in foreign missions, as God may enable and guide us. It is reasonable to expect that any missions advance in the decades immediately ahead will be aptly described by the familiar phrase *advance through storm*.[10]

If we focus our examination on the next 15 years, the remainder of the twentieth century, we will probably find still relevant the suggestion at the Miami consultation in 1975.

> Within the span of only 25 years, even statements, forms
> and structures may not change radically on a broad scale.
> They are subject to more rapid change than in earlier decades,
> and in limited or local experience "future shock" can be
> severe, but history still suggests that "great changes come
> about gradually."[11]

Furthermore, nearly all that was said in that report about the world ahead and about the challenges looming ahead of us is still relevant. (Those themes have been addressed already in this book more fully than was possible in the 1975 address.) The possible directions mentioned at that time are in most cases being implemented.

Now, nine years into Bold Mission Thrust, we look to the future from a different vantage point. Much has been done in these nine years to strengthen the planning processes of the Foreign Mission Board and the missions on the fields and to strengthen the strategic thrust of our objectives. These processes which have been set in motion have their own growing momentum. Any increasing number of missionary appointments strengthens the incarnational contribution of Southern Baptists to world evangelization. Greatly enlarged relief and development funds make possible more effective holistic ministries.

Accentuated attention to evangelism that results in churches is the spearhead of continuing mission thrust.

From this vantage point, I suggest four areas of special additional emphasis for the years just ahead.

*One area is research.* The Foreign Mission Board has engaged in a variety of research projects for years. Most of those have been relatively small projects related to pending management decisions. Now, with staffing that has developed in the past few years and with vastly improved computer possibilities, much more extensive and far-reaching research should be possible. Currently a broad data base of world survey information and report data from Southern Baptist missions over a period of years are being computerized. Furthermore, there are exciting opportunities for linking Foreign Mission Board research with other significant centers of research on Christian missions.

*A second area for increasing emphasis will be the interaction between mission fields and the home base.* Communication back and forth across the world has become increasingly simple and reliable. Immediate reports from the fields are being incorporated into communications to Southern Baptist churches through the Baptist Telecommunication Network (BTN). The Foreign Mission Board is involving itself more directly with the Southern Baptist constituency in several arenas (missionary recruitment, volunteer enlistment, partnership missions and partnership evangelism projects, development, Cooperative Program promotion, and intercessory prayer). More is being done already, but much more needs to be done to personalize the partnership of Southern Baptists in the churches with their missionaries overseas.

*Another growing emphasis is internationalizing of world missions.* This must increase in ways that will preserve both the authenticity of partnership between Baptists from different nations and different conventions and the integrity of the trusteeship relation with sponsoring conventions. The proposed consultation on global partnership between Southern Baptists and related Third World Baptist missionary-sending conventions is a vital move in that direction.

*As a further emphasis, for the actual mission work on the fields, I suggest the love of God as a possible unifying theme,* encompassing three elements: proclaiming the love of God in every way possible (evangelism), embodying the love of God (incarnational and holistic ministry), and the community characterized by and expressive of God's love (the fellowship of the church). In the words of the popular song of a few years ago, "What the world needs now is love"—and "Herein is love," that God "loved us, and sent his Son" (1 John 4:10).

### Potential—*If!*

Southern Baptists in the years ahead can be a great potential instrument for world evangelization. But that potential cannot be realized just by commitment and action of the Foreign Mission Board and its missionaries. It can be realized *if* Southern Baptists as a whole respond to the challenge.

Surely "now is the time" (see 2 Cor. 6:2) to share the gospel with the whole world.[12] If Southern Baptists turn their attention to other concerns or spend their energies and resources on larger church buildings and more staff to serve where we are and reach our own people, God will raise up other groups to be His instruments for discipling the nations. But if we fulfill our stewardship of all the blessings God has given us and carry out the purpose for which He has created us, we will be captured by an overwhelming vision of the unreached peoples of all lands and will devote ourselves—all we are and all we have—for their salvation.

This can happen only through a recovery of the biblical principle of mission support. Recently we have become so caught up in the idea of personal participation that many in our churches have little enthusiasm for studying the outreach of the gospel and supporting that outreach with gifts and with fervent persevering prayer. When Paul and Barnabas went out as missionaries, the believers in Antioch were involved with them through mission support. Later, as Paul ministered in Athens and Corinth and elsewhere, believers at Philippi were his faithful supporters. In the Third Letter of John, believers were commended for their love and backing for missionaries, and were encouraged "to send them on their journey as befits God's service" (v. 6, RSV). We are then clearly instructed that "we ought to support such men, that we may be fellow workers in the truth" (v. 8, RSV). I can participate personally in only a tiny corner of God's world mission, but I can be a supporter all across the world through my gifts and my prayers.

An ancient Greek philosopher observed that if he had a lever long enough and a place on which to rest the fulcrum, he could move the world. We understand the physical principle involved: Through the use of a lever, even a small force can be applied in such a way as to move an enormous object. The same is profoundly true in a spiritual sense. We have in the gospel of Jesus Christ the lever by which the world can be lifted toward God. That lever rests on the sure and unshakable base of God's redemptive purpose. What is still needed to lift our world toward God is lives applied to that lever, lives fully committed to the loving worldwide missionary purpose of our Lord.

Many observers have pointed out that pastors are the key to enlarged world missionary vision in our churches. Other members exert an influence, especially through the missionary organizations, but many church members do not participate in those organizations. The pastor is the one who has broader access to the entire membership and who can give effective leadership for missions if that has high priority in his own life and ministry.

Unfortunately, the proximity of local needs, pressures from persons with other priorities, and the emphases promoted by other churches and other pastors often displace high-priority commitment to missions outreach. This is true even with many pastors who had a high degree of world mission vision when they were seminary students. Imperceptibly that vision fades. Over the coming 10 to 20 years, recovery of the missionary vision and enthusiastic pastoral leadership for missions outreach will be essential if Southern Baptists are to be and do what God expects in the fulfilling of his world purpose.

In 1904, at a time of high enthusiasm for world evangelization, the Student Volunteer Movement for Foreign Missions published a book by John R. Mott on *The Pastor and Modern Missions* with the subtitle "A Plea for Leadership in World Evangelization."[13] The fact that the book has been so long out of print and that there has been no recent substitute for it reveals the widespread turning to other and more localized interests on the part of most American churches.

The *if* involved in the fulfilling of the Southern Baptist potential for world missions may well depend on the extent to which pastors take seriously their responsibility and privilege of leadership toward the discipling of the nations.

Two analogies may be helpful in clarifying our stewardship of the gospel. One is a business analogy. Though some persons are uncomfortable about comparing business with spiritual affairs, Jesus felt free to make such comparisons and commented that "the children of this world are in their generation wiser than the children of light" (Luke 16:8).

In a sense, Southern Baptist churches and our leaders have responsibility for managing a business. (*Steward* is merely another term for manager.) The business in which we have management responsibility is not a production business. The product, which is the gospel, has already been made available. Ours is a distribution and service business.

We have received instructions from the owner of the business. His instructions are that we "disciple the nations"—that is, that we distribute the product worldwide.

Fulfilling our management responsibility should call for careful planning to analyze needs and opportunities. Then sales personnel should be located in terms of those needs and opportunities, keeping in mind the basic operating objective of worldwide distribution. (Actually as Southern Baptists we have not done very well at allocating personnel on the basis of discipling the nations, but have tended to concentrate most of the entire force in one relatively small area.)

Another concern in effective management is keeping down overhead expenses so as to put the most resources possible into sales outreach. This requires constant concern to distinguish between overhead and outreach, to maintain the essential base for the operation as economically as possible, and to release increasing resources for outreach. (As Southern Baptists we have not done too well at this, often making decisions in our church life without any thought of keeping down overhead expenses so as to invest more in the business objective.)

When we report to the owner, we are tempted to describe the

"fine things we are doing"—the attendance, the contributions, the correctness of beliefs and practices, the smoothly functioning organization, the building and equipment, the activities, the fellowship, and so forth. These signify a good and strong base. But how well are we doing at discipling unreached social groups such as those in our inner cities, in the youth subculture, the migrant workers, the state university intelligentsia, the internationals in our midst, or the far more numerous racial, cultural, and social groups far out across the world, most of whom have never yet heard the gospel at all?

An observer might well be tempted to ask, "Is this any way to run a business?"

Another analogy—a kind of modern parable for our churches and our Convention—is the exploration of space. Many of us saw by television the successful completion of the moon missions. We saw also the great supporting organizations that made such a mission possible: the production of the rockets, the launch site at Cape Kennedy, and the mission control center at Houston. It was all very impressive.

That entire system existed as a gigantic base for outreach to a new space frontier. No part of the operation existed to maintain itself or to serve itself. All were dedicated to the moon mission.

Similarly, the church of Jesus Christ has an earth mission. Churches do not exist to maintain themselves or to serve themselves, but as a great base for outreach to the world. What gives Baptist churches and conventions their highest significance is their global mission thrust. We have "a story to tell to the nations." This is our very reason for being.

## A Prayer

O loving Father, "this is life eternal, that they might know thee the only true God, and Jesus Christ, whom thou hast sent" (John 17:3).

Use us, we pray, to make Thee known, to tell the gospel story by life and word, each one of us in just that place where needed most.

And help us send the good news on beyond us with all our

energies, until the very last person on earth has a chance to hear—even now in our own day.

Let this be our passion, we pray in Jesus' name!

### Notes

1. See articles by Winston Crawley under these titles: "Can It Be Done?" *Contempo*, vol. 11 (November 1980): 2, and "Is World Evangelization Really Possible?" *The Quarterly Review*, vol. 40, no. 3 (April, May, June 1980): 4.

2. See articles by Winston Crawley, "The Cooperative Program Is Vulnerable" in *The Baptist Program* (November 1978): 14, and "Horizons: 'Moment of Truth' for Bold Mission Thrust?" in the December 1983 issue of *The Commission*, vol. 46, no. 9:65.

3. John H. Schaar, "Decadence and Revitalization," *Legitimacy in the Modern State* (New Brunswick, N.J.: Transaction Press, 1981), cited in the April 1979 issue of the newsletter *Footnotes to the Future*.

4. The article, though written from a secular perspective, verges on spiritual implications. See Barbara Marx Hubbard, "The Future of Futurism," *The Futurist*, vol. 17, no. 2 (April 1983): 56-58.

5. An interesting example is an entire issue of *Ambassador Life*, the Southern Baptist "boys' magazine with a world outlook," vol. 20 (February 1966).

6. Published in adapted form as "The Task Ahead" by Winston Crawley in *The Commission*, vol. 39, no. 3 (March 1976): 22-25.

7. That book deals also broadly with the theme of looking to the future. See Bill O'Brien, *Mission for Tomorrow* (Nashville: Convention Press, 1980).

8. A. Clark Scanlon, "Additions Are Not Enough, We Must Multiply," *The Baptist Program*, August 1981, pp. 14-15.

9. R. Keith Parks, "The Future of Missions: Change," *The Commission*, vol. 43, no. 10 (October 1980): 2 (inside front cover).

10. This is the title which Kenneth Scott Latourette gave to the final volume of *The History of the Expansion of Christianity: Advance Through Storm*, vol. 7 (New York: Harper & Row, Publishers, 1945), covering missions advance in the period from 1914 to 1944.

11. Winston Crawley, "The Task Ahead," p. 23.

12. Elements of challenge presented as characteristic of the Orient in 1968 are characteristic also of the entire world today. See Winston Crawley, "Now is the Time," *The Commission*, vol. 31, no. 10 (October 1968): 18-19.

13. John R. Mott, *The Pastor and Modern Missions: A Plea for Leadership in World Evangelization* (New York: Student Volunteer Movement for Foreign Missions, 1904).

# APPENDIXES

## Appendix 1

## Foreign Mission Board Philosophy Statement

### (Adopted June 29, 1978)

What is the Foreign Mission Board's philosophy of world missions? One dictionary definition of "philosophy" is "the *most general beliefs, concepts, and attitudes* of an individual or group." In that sense, the board does have a philosophy, but only rarely have attempts been made to reduce it to concise, written form.

Our philosophy of world missions is derived from the Bible, Christian history, the historical context of the nineteenth and twentieth centuries, our denominational history and polity, more than a century of missions experiences, and spiritual insights of divine origin.

It finds expression in the Great Commission; the purpose of the Southern Baptist Convention; the original mandate and subsequent instructions given to the Foreign Mission Board by the convention; the board's policies and mode of operation; and the board's actions, programs, and positions taken since 1845. While needed changes have occurred, and more undoubtedly will be necessary, there are certain enduring basics in our mission philosophy which time, experience, our people, and our great God, have tested and strongly approved.

God has an eternal purpose, expressive of His love for mankind, and missions is an integral part of God's plan for the achievement of that purpose. Mission ministries are motivated by Christian love, concern for human need, the impelling of the Holy Spirit and the revealed will of God.

The Great Commission makes the overseas task the responsibility of each Christian and each church. Churches exist and cooperate for the purpose of world outreach and kingdom extension.

The task of missions supremely and imperatively is to make disciples, to baptize them, and to teach them to observe all that

Christ commanded. It includes all the world—every creature—
every generation. The task of missions is also to minister compassionately to those who are hungry, thirsty, strangers, lack
clothing, sick, imprisoned, etc.

The enlisting, appointment, sending, and support of an ever-
increasing number of God-called, and otherwise qualified,
missionaries is the priority responsibility of the Foreign Mission
Board. If nothing else could be done in foreign missions, the one
indispensable thing would be the sending and supporting of
missionaries.

The board regards as basic the concept of the career missionary. The board is committed to the use of short-term and volunteer personnel, but the overwhelming, long-term need is for
career missionaries who are committed to the truth of the incarnational principle—"the Word became flesh and dwelt among
us"—dwelling among the people of some other land on a long-
term basis.

The board is committed to a strategy of entering new countries, as well as ministering to neglected areas in countries already entered, as God may lead. It believes attempts should be
made to communicate the gospel via mass media to countries
where missionaries either cannot go or are prevented from
preaching.

Both responsive and unresponsive fields must be served. The
Great Commission gives no warrant for neglecting so-called
"unresponsive" fields.

The great over-arching objective is to provide every person on
earth with the opportunity to hear the gospel.

New Testament churches, interdependent and autonomous
under the lordship of Christ, are to be established and multiplied as the basic units for Christian nurture and kingdom extension.

Evangelism and church development are the central objectives of missionary labors.

Adequate ministerial and lay leadership training is to be provided by theological schools, theological education by extension, and religious education programs in the churches.

Ministries to students and Christian education through
schools are encouraged.

The magnitude of the missionary task demands vastly increased, and much improved, use of the mass media: the printed page, radio, television, and other audiovisual techniques.

Human need world-wide requires accentuated attention to health care and disease prevention, benevolent and social ministries on an expanding scale, hunger relief, and compassionate responses to crisis situations.

Under modern conditions, there are multiplied opportunities for reinforcing mission efforts through a variety of volunteer short-term projects and through involvement of non-missionary personnel living in the overseas setting.

The board has considered its responsibility in geographic and functional terms, and has decided that the geographic element is basic and fundamental from the standpoint of administrative outlook and organizational arrangements. This is justified because of the nature of our world and the character of our Baptist polity.

Long-range strategy planning, in the view of the board, is consistent with its stewardship obligations (1) toward our great God and his eternal purpose, and (2) toward the supporting churches. Strategy planning involves several fundamental principles: indigenous church strength as a guiding objective; missionaries and the mission organization in a generative (or helping) role; decentralized planning to give greatest play to local initiative and responsibility; increasing significance of national leadership and national Baptist conventions and agencies. Throughout the process, the Holy Spirit must have free rein for guidance and for power.

The board has responsibility to elect the executive director and other appropriate staff. The director, with the assistance of this staff, is responsible to the board in: administration, policy recommendations, overall mission strategy, financial planning, supervision of other staff and missionaries, oversight of stateside activities and field work and cultivation of wholesome relationships with overseas Baptist constituencies. The board evaluates staff recommendations in its decision-making role of: appointing missionaries, choosing fields of service, establishing policies, allocating financial resources, and determining other appropriate matters.

The board conducts a unified program, not a collection of separate programs. It believes that proportion and balance are both desirable and necessary. Methodology should be kept comprehensive and flexible. Every method which God will honor should be employed where feasible and possible.

The board recognizes that it has responsibilities in homeland cultivation. This is one of the paradoxes in Southern Baptist life. The board was created to be a channel for the missionary efforts and resources of the churches, which the convention elicits, combines, and directs. Yet the people in the churches look to the board for information, inspiration, motivation, and leadership.

The board's philosophy should be kept comprehensive enough and flexible enough to accomplish, in future circumstances and altered times, the will of our sovereign Lord and the expressed wishes of the supporting constituency.

## Appendix 2

### Foreign Mission Board Strategy Statement

(Adopted by EMG, 4/8/82, and revised 1/85)

I. PURPOSE AND USE OF THE PAPER

The position paper on Foreign Mission Board strategy serves alongside other basic planning documents, and especially in relation to the Foreign Mission Board's statement of philosophy, as a guide in planning on the fields and in the Richmond office. It is essentially a staff working document and not a formal delineation of board policy or a public relations release. However, its content is useful as background for understanding and interpretating Southern Baptist foreign missions, as well as for planning.

II. DEFINITION AND RELATIONSHIPS

Strategy deals with the "how" question. In foreign missions, it refers to an overall plan for managing resources most effectively to carry out the missionary purpose.

The developing of strategy inevitably rests in the broader context of a philosophy of missions and theology of mission, which identify the "what" and "why" of missions. Therefore, the concerns of this paper relate closely to the content of background documents interpreting the biblical foundations for foreign missions and the Foreign Mission Board's philosophy.

It is difficult to make an absolute distinction between philosophy and strategy statements (though strategy should be more sharply defined and practical). The statement of Foreign Mission Board philosophy includes many concepts which may more properly come under the heading of strategy.

III. INTRODUCTION

The essence of strategy is the managing of resources for greatest effectiveness. The need for strategic planning rests in the assumption that resources available are limited, that not all the fine things that might be done and should be done actually can be done, and that therefore hard choices are necessary if available resources are to be used in ways most vital to total effectiveness.

Maximum results require coordination of resources and efforts in a unified program directed toward a central objective. Our strategy is not, and in the nature of the case cannot be, a matter of simply doing more of everything we do. Neither should it be a range of separate programs and projects carried out independently of each other. Increased mission thrust is possible only through comprehensive planning for the best stewardship of mission resources.

Strategic planning calls for the relating of every part of the work to the objectives of the whole. The central objective to give focus to planning in each field is the developing of indigenous church strength. This includes evangelism and is related to varied ministries. The objective is not to be understood narrowly or shortsightedly, and the exact combination of approaches and proportionate allocation of resources must be adapted to local conditions.

Similar considerations apply to the Foreign Mission Board in its decisions regarding the world and our mission efforts as a whole. Resources must be allocated in such proportions as to bring greatest overall accomplishment.

IV. STRATEGY CONCERNS

There are a number of urgent concerns emphasized by segments of current missions leadership, any one of which might well serve as a major strategy directive for missions today. Each such concern deserves careful consideration in the development of strategy and the deployment of personnel and other resources.

(1) The overarching objective stated in the Foreign Mission Board's plan for the remainder of this century calls for *everyone to hear the gospel*. That intention would point toward rapid entry into as many fields as possible, spreading of missionary forces as widely as possible and greatly acceler-

ated use of mass media. If taken apart from any moderating influence of other concerns or principles, it would lead to a totally "seed sowing" approach worldwide.

(2) *Major population blocs* that are relatively unevangelized are another current focus of missions emphasis. Frequently mentioned are those populations identifiable as Muslim, Chinese and Hindu. Under the same principle, both the Communist bloc and the secularist Western European bloc should also be included.

(3) *"Closed" areas*, in which traditional missionary approaches are impossible or quite difficult, offer another special challenge.

(4) The *"peoples" concept* suggests a focus of effort on unreached people groups and perhaps especially on those with the least contact with the gospel (sometimes called "hidden" peoples).

(5) In recent decades there has been great emphasis on the importance of concentrating on *responsive areas*.

(6) *"Open doors"*—represented by ready availability of visas, a cordial welcome from local Baptist churches and conventions, freedom of operation and large available populations needing to hear the gospel—constitute another forceful incentive.

(7) *Strategic timing* can be an important determinant in strategy decisions. Some doors open briefly and then close. Good foundations may have little value unless strong building is done on them. Crisis situations call for timely response.

(8) *Urbanization*, as one of the most obvious and most significant trends of today's world, presents a special challenge to mission planners. Persons migrating rapidly to cities become uprooted, alienated and winnable for a short time. Once they are settled, there are new barriers that require new approaches. Mass media can be especially effective among concentrated urban populations.

(9) *Neglected groups and special problems* are frequently recommended as an appropriate concern of missions agencies. (Groups such as blind persons or the illiterate, and problems like alcoholism, malnourishment or family planning

are examples.) The concept is that mission agencies should not continue to do things that local governments and national Christian bodies are able to do, but should be pioneering in calling attention to additional needs and offering models for the meeting of such needs.

(10) *Transfer of responsibility* to local entities under local leadership is frequently suggested as a major direction for modern missions. This direction would point to concentrating resources on the training of local leadership and the establishing and strengthening of local Christian structures. Some interpret this principle in terms of the phasing out of mission organizations and perhaps even of missionary involvement entirely (the call for "moratorium" is an example). Our approach is based on a changing but continuing missionary role in a partnership relation.

(11) A special emphasis for many years in some missions circles has been the *benevolent ministries* side of the Christian mission. Especially in relation to world hunger, relief and development needs, this has become a growing concern of Southern Baptists. In foreign missions, ministry and witness have been carried on together from the early years of the FMB.

(12) *Volunteerism and short-term assignments* have become a growing trend in modern missions. Some other denominations have turned largely to short-term missionary involvement as their main personnel pattern. In Southern Baptist life, volunteers in large numbers have offered themselves to help in special (usually brief) overseas mission opportunities.

(13) *Accelerated church multiplication* is a central element in Bold Mission Thrust, and an element that is especially relevant to the board's philosophy.

The Foreign Mission Board does not take any one of these concerns as its sole or even its major strategy determinant. Its strategy seeks to be an appropriate combination of all of these emphases, giving to each due attention. This approach is much more complex and more difficult than a strategy approach based on only one principle. Periodic review is necessary by strategy planners in all parts of our missions operation, to make sure that some vital aspect is not being overlooked or neglected. The exact place of these various elements in Foreign Mission Board strategy is dynamic rather than static.

## V. FOCUS

Mission strategy is grounded in biblical principles, guided by the Holy Spirit, and undergirded with prayer.

Although a number of concerns need to be kept in perspective, and increasing attention is being given to the "peoples" concept, we continue using the nation as the main planning unit. The major reason is partnership with Baptist bodies that are organized on a national basis.

Planning on the fields, in the immediate context of the work, is emphasized (but in some natural tension with overall planning).

Career missionaries, functioning in a generative role and in partnership with local churches and conventions, are primary wherever possible.

Indigenous church strength continues as the central objective to give unity to planning.

Other strategy principles are understood and applied within the context of these that constitute the focus for our strategy planning.

## VI. IMPLEMENTING GUIDELINES

Guidelines are used in dynamic ongoing strategic planning. "Strategy is not so much position as process."

These statements are additions to or expansions of the strategy references in the board's philosophy statement and in the "principles" set out as an introduction to the board's long-range plans. Continuing attention in strategy planning needs to be given, of course, to each of the major strategy concerns already listed in section IV.

(1) No arbitrary numerical limits are placed on the appointing and sending out of missionary personnel.

(2) In the allocating of available mission funds, continued priority is given to the maintaining of missionaries.

(3) Improved and innovative arrangements are being devel-

oped for bivocational missionary service, especially where traditional approaches are difficult.

(4) Southern Baptist mission work is carried on in the context of the larger Christian family and in cordial relationship and increasing correlation with the work of other denominations.

(5) Internationalization of missions is being strengthened through exchanges or cooperative arrangements with other Baptist conventions.

(6) Insofar as possible, entry to new countries is at the invitation of and in relation with existing Baptist churches.

(7) Partnership with existing churches and conventions is of highest importance. The nationalizing of leadership and planning roles as rapidly as possible gives expression to this developing partnership.

(8) With the growth of local Baptist strength, transition in the form of missionary ministries is to be expected, but not automatic withdrawal or moratorium.

(9) In principle, a work extends to the entire country in which we serve, with no formal comity limitations.

(10) Contextualization or acculturation of the developing Baptist work, but without dilution or syncretism, is to be facilitated.

(11) Missionaries are expected to acquire an effective command of local languages and to devote themselves to cross-cultural witness and ministry.

(12) Our concern is for the whole person, with no polarization of witness and ministry.

(13) Relief ministries are carried on as an integral part of the mission program, rather than through a separate organization.

(14) Use of mass media is coordinated with the remainder of the mission program, to undergird program priorities for greatest effectiveness.

(15) Administrative procedures seek to keep as much planning as possible within the field context.

(16) Some form of mission organization is retained as the most practical approach to cooperative endeavor.

(17) Existing institutions and others that may be needed in the

future are to be used as effectively as possible, while guard-
ing against undue "institutionalization."
(18) Policies should stimulate self-support but without any arbitrary requirement that might hinder growth and strength.

Other strategy considerations may need to be added to this list
from time to time in the future, especially as points come under
discussion on which the board's position needs to be clearly
stated.

## Appendix 3

### Foreign Missions Looks Toward AD 2000

BASIC PRINCIPLES

God's eternal purpose in Christ Jesus our Lord was determined centuries before Paul wrote about it. Man's disobedience and sin made atonement necessary. God attempted to speak to errant mankind in various ways. Finally, He sent His Son who "died for our sins," "was buried," and "was raised on the third day."

Before Christ ascended to return to the Father, He instructed His disciples and sent them forth on the same mission the Father had given Him. He gave them the Holy Spirit to empower and enable them in their world-encompassing task. All believers were expected to be witnesses, learners, priests, and ministers. Some were called to be apostles (missionaries); many received a diversity of spiritual gifts, for the good of all and for building up the body of Christ.

What God has done creatively and redemptively in times past—and continues to do—points the way. The redeemed are expected to bring God's eternal purpose to fulfillment. It is God who redeems, but men are the instruments of a redeeming God.

People who know the gospel ("good news") have inescapable obligations toward other people and areas where the gospel is not known. God intends to make known His redemption through the church to the farthest extremities of the universe. Missions is an integral part of God's eternal purpose.

God has the whole world in His hands. Every person is somebody of worth. Life, for every person, is a sacred trust to be cherished, shared, and judged by peers, by history, and by God Himself. God is concerned about the people—all the people—of the world, regardless of status or condition. His concern reaches out in love, across all manmade barriers designed to create separation and discrimination, to all who need forgiveness and newness of life.

God sees men as whole persons, rather than as compartmentalized beings. Although the Bible refers to a man's body, soul, mind, and spirit, these aspects of his being cannot be separated without destroying him. Man does not live by bread alone, but he cannot live without it. His soul resides in a finite being, but it is destined for immortality. Man's mind, untrained at birth, has all the potential that God and heredity have given it. It is not the will of God for man's mind to remain in darkness, or for man's spirit to exist in willful disobedience and rebellion against God.

Man has many needs. Ministry in the name of Christ requires attention to all of them, beginning with his basic need for God. Neighborliness, according to the two great commandments, is next to godliness. The world's hungry, thirsty, sick, ignorant, superstitious, lonely, disadvantaged, enslaved, deprived, disaster-ravaged, imprisoned people are not to be "passed by on the other side." As the second commandment says, "you shall love your neighbor as yourself."

Basic to the work of Southern Baptist world missions are certain principles whose validity has long since been established.

1. New Testament churches are independent and autonomous under the lordship of Christ. The Foreign Mission Board is committed to the principle of indigenous churches, conventions, and institutions on foreign fields, consistent with New Testament norms, including Christian partnership. Strong encouragement will continue to be given to national leadership, administration, and self-support.

The Foreign Mission Board maintains an overview of mission strategy throughout the world in line with instructions given to it by the Southern Baptist Convention. It draws up overall strategy guidelines, takes initiatives, and helps to coordinate efforts and plans in other parts of the world. It seeks to cultivate the work of Japanese Baptists, Nigerian Baptists, Brazilian Baptists, etc., in their proper spheres.

National and local strategy formulation overseas usually takes final focus on the basis of initiatives taken by national leaders and missionaries. Overseas plans and strategies are not formulated at the Foreign Mission Board and passed down a chain of command to missionaries, churches, and denominational entities in foreign countries.

The Holy Spirit must be given free rein. The Spirit may lead Baptists in foreign groups to follow methods and procedures different from our own, but we all serve the Lord Christ.

2. A unified program—not a collection of separate programs—is essential. The overseas task includes evangelism, church development, theological and leadership training programs, mass media ministries, publications ministries, health care ministries, benevolent and social ministries, and disaster relief and world hunger programs.

Such a unified program calls for a unified, as opposed to a fragmented, administration. Southern Baptists have one unified program of overseas missions which has many facets.

3. Proportion and balance are both desirable and necessary. This applies to countries, as well as programs of work. With so many needs, in so many places, Southern Baptists can ill-afford to direct all their effort to either a single country or a single program of work. Coordinated planning is the Board's role as it weighs available resources over against compelling needs.

4. The methodology is comprehensive and flexible. Our commitment is not to one method to the exclusion of others. Every method which God will honor should be employed where feasible and possible. Comprehensive methodology is inclusive of all such methods.

Some mission organizations exist to promote one method exclusively. Our commitment to a comprehensive methodology may expose our work to certain problems which such organiztions do not face. The polarization which can result from the magnification of one method over another can have unfortunate consequences.

Methods, procedures, and organizational forms are being called into question by changing times. New ways will be found to do old and new things. Care will be taken to preserve necessary functions, even though forms may have to change—radically.

5. The Foreign Mission Board regards as basic the concept of the career missionary. Short-term and volunteer personnel make significant contributions, and the Foreign Mission Board is committed to the use of these categories. But the overwhelming,

long-term need is for career missionaries, who are committed to the truth of the incarnational principle—"the Word became flesh and dwelt among us"—dwelling among the people of some other land on a long-term basis.

6. Missionaries go to their fields to share the gospel of Christ and minister to human need. They do not involve themselves in political or commercial affairs. They are recognized as people who are dedicated to the purpose of Christian witness and service. Anything that will make unclear that image will greatly handicap their efforts, and, in some places, make impossible their residence in the country.

7. Evangelism and church development will be maintained as the imperatively central thrusts. Compassionate ministries are no less insistent as expressions of obedience and examples of Christian compassion in action.

8. The "Great Commission" makes the overseas task the responsibility of each Christian and each church. Churches exist and cooperate for the purpose of world outreach and kingdom extension. Our world and our perverse generation demand greater efforts—much greater—between now and AD 2000.

## Appendix 4—FMB Organization Chart

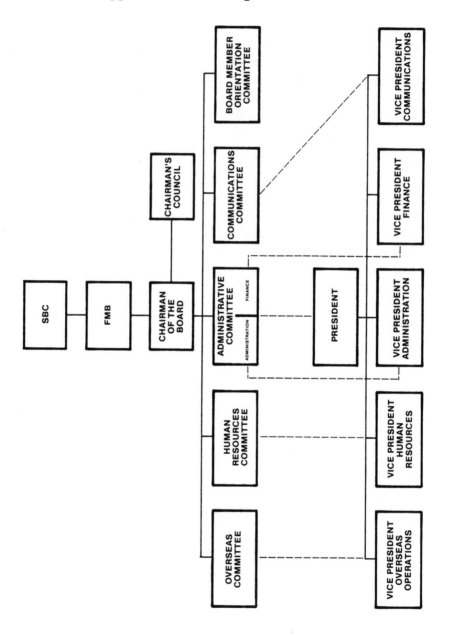

## Appendix 5—FMB Staff Organization Chart

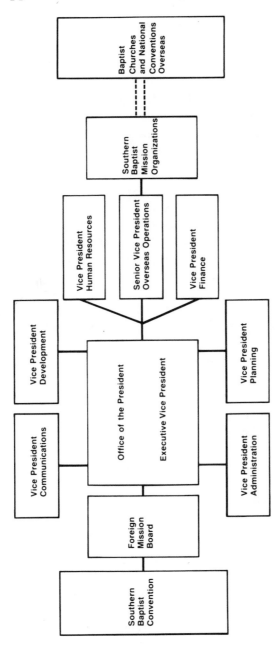

## Appendix 6

## Chart of Personnel Categories

A. MISSIONARY

1. *Career Missionary:* Persons ages 24-45, appointed for long-range service.
2. *Missionary Associate:* Persons ages 35-60, commissioned for four-year term (repeatable).

B. AUXILIARY

1. *Journeymen:* College graduates, through age 26, commissioned for two-year term (non-repeatable).
2. *Special Assignment:* Persons employed for 9-24 months of special overseas service.
3. *Mission Service Corps:* Persons serving 4-24 months and receiving no stipend. (Under exceptional circumstances they are provided transportation to and from the field.)

C. STUDENT/RESIDENT

1. *BSU Summer and Semester Workers:* Selected and supported by Baptist Student Union.
2. *Medical Receptors/Residents:* Receptors are medical school students who serve a minimum of eight weeks. Residents are MDs who serve a minimum of 12 weeks.

D. VOLUNTEER

These persons serve up to four months and receive no financial provision from the FMB.

(Note: Missionaries, journeymen and special assignment personnel with two-year assignments are reported in the "missionary count." Other special assignment personnel and the remaining categories are reported in the annual "volunteer" count.)

## Appendix 7

## Mission Support Philosophy

### (Adopted June 29, 1978)


I. The Call of God
   A. The missionary goes to the field and serves in response to the call of God. The Foreign Mission Board serves as a channel to enable and support the missionary.
      In the case of marriage, husband and wife are considered full-time missionaries (whether on the field or on furlough).
   B. The Foreign Mission Board and its staff have a stewardship responsibility to Southern Baptists and the missionaries. The board is responsible to establish and maintain support arrangements that are appropriate, fair, and of greatest benefit to the total mission task.
   C. Missionaries have a stewardship responsibility to carry out their missionary ministries in line with the principles and policies of the Foreign Mission Board and the Southern Baptist Convention.
II. The Concept of Support
   A. A support system seeks to make equitable and adequate provision for the financial needs of all missionaries. It is more appropriate than a salary system. Salary systems base compensation on specialization, qualification, assignment and responsibility.
   B. The Foreign Mission Board support system focuses on providing financial undergirding at the points of normal basic need and major financial pressures.
   C. Periodic reexamination of the missionary support structure will be undertaken by the Foreign Mission Board.
      Review and adjustments will be made to maintain the fairness of the overall support level.

# Appendix 8

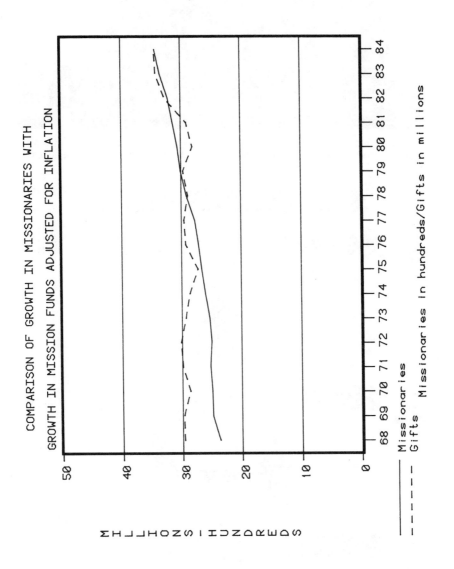

## Appendix 9

# FIELD--HOME RELATIONSHIPS

This chart shows the complex interaction that emerges as the participants in mission work increase. These expanding relationships are discussed in the adult study book, *How In This World,* chapter I.

## GOD'S DIRECTION--OVER ALL

### 1. MISSIONARY

The individual missionary has first of all a relationship with God, who guides him through the Holy Spirit.

**MISSIONARY**

### 2. CHURCH

If the missionary is sent by a church, there is an added relationship as the Spirit leads the church to accept this sending responsibility.

**CHURCH**

### 3. CHURCHES

As several churches share in the sending, the relationship expands, with each of the sending churches guided by the Holy Spirit.

**CHURCHES**

# 4. BOARD

The churches need a channel through which to work together in supporting the missionary. For Southern Baptists, this channel is the Foreign Mission Board, which also seeks God's leadership.

# 5. MISSION

As missionary personnel increases in number on a field, the missionaries organize into a Mission. Again, they move with the Holy Spirit's leading.

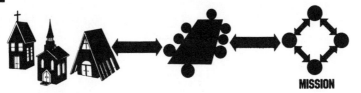

# 6. CHURCH

The formation of a church on a mission field brings still another relationship, involving Mission and church, both related to God through the Holy Spirit.

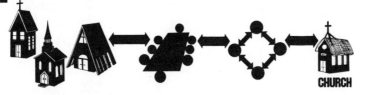

# 7. CHURCHES (CONVENTION)

When additional churches are formed, the churches may decide to cooperate with each other in an organizational way. The convention or group of churches does its work through the Holy Spirit's guidance.

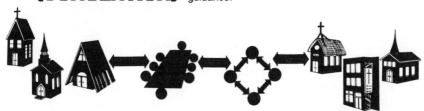

# GOD'S DIRECTION-UNDERLYING ALL

### THE FORMATION OF PRIORITY CONCERNS
### IN OVERSEAS OPERATIONS
### FOREIGN MISSION BOARD, SBC

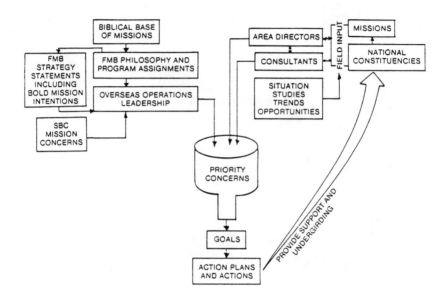

## Appendix 10

## Guiding Concepts
## for
## Formation of Priority Concerns

Charles W. Bryan, Senior Vice-President
Office of Overseas Operations

1. *Recognizing:* We recognize that God wants his good news in Christ announced to all the world's people and that, as a part of the Kingdom family, Southern Baptists must share its human work.
2. *Evangelizing:* We will do ministry and witness in many ways, but always with the central thrust of evangelism that results in churches.
3. *Multiplying:* We will spare no effort to encourage and facilitate the multiplication of disciples, the development of leaders and churches.
4. *Mobilizing:* We will seek to enlist every Southern Baptist and all colleagues in Baptist churches, here and overseas, and other Christians in a dedicated world evangelization effort.
5. *Optimizing:* We will use to the maximum all possible ministries and appropriate program assignments to share the good news of Jesus Christ.
6. *Personalizing:* We will do our work as team members who affirm each other's spiritual gifts and remain sensitive each to the other in the fellowship of mutual caring and appreciation.

# Appendix 11

## BOLD MISSION THRUST STATISTICAL UPDATE
### December 31, 1984

| Item/Numerical Challenge 2000 | Beginning Figure (1975) | Previous Report (1983) | Latest Report (1984) | Increase 1983 to 1984 | Yearly % Increase 1975-84 | Current Status |
|---|---|---|---|---|---|---|
| Missionaries 5,000 | 2,667 | 3,346 | 3,432 | 2.57% | 2.84% | Ahead |
| Countries 125 | 82 | 102 | 105 | 2.94% | 2.79% | Well Ahead |
| Volunteers 10,000 | 1,200 | 4,735 | 6,213 | 31.21% | 20.05% | Well Ahead |
| Churches 75,840 | 7,584 | 13,586 | 14,791 | 8.87% | 7.70% | Behind |
| Churches/Chapel Combination 184,890 | 18,489 | 30,581 | 32,570 | 6.50% | 6.49% | Behind |
| Membership 8,960,630 | 896,063 | 1,708,568 | 1,910,483 | 11.82% | 8.78% | Behind |
| Baptisms 807,470 | 80,747 | 146,149 | 156,326 | 6.96% | 7.62% | Behind |
| Seminary Enrollment # | 3,797 | 7,284 | 8,913 | 22.36% | 9.95% | Ahead |
| Theol. Education by Extension* # | 3,433 | 7,171 | 7,833 | 9.23% | 14.74% | Ahead |

*Enrollment first reported in 1978; columns 5/6 refer to a six-year period.
#No numerical challenge established.

## Appendix 12

### Mid-Range Projections to 1990
(Adopted by EMG, 4/8/82)
(Minor revisions, 10/82)

Mid-range projections serve as an intermediate stage between the board's long-range plans (up to AD 2000) and the more thorough short-range planning in a sliding five-year sequence.

Projections in brief outline are for the end of calendar year 1990. That will be 15 years into Bold Mission Thrust. It will be nine years from the latest statistical reports in hand at the time of adoption of these projections.

Work will be conducted according to the missions philosophy stated in the board's official philosophy statement (adopted in 1978) and in the principles for Bold Mission Thrust (adopted in 1976).

Plans for the decade are as follows:

1. To give continuing emphasis to evangelism that results in churches, with the developing of indigenous church strength as the central aim to give focus to planning in each field.
2. To reaffirm and reinforce the ongoing overarching purpose and the nine stated intentions of Bold Mission Thrust.
3. To add or strengthen programs related to major strategy concerns, as set forth in the position paper on strategy.
4. To project numerical challenges for 1990 at levels that will be on course toward the target figures for AD 2000.
   (1) 4,000 missionaries. (This will require an average increase of 2.7 percent per year through the decade.)
   (2) 110 countries.
   (3) 10,000 volunteers.
   (4) 30,000 churches with 3,400,000 members and 300,000 baptisms. (These figures incorporate an annual increase of 10 percent per years in churches and membership and 10.5 percent per year in baptisms.)

(5) Seminary enrollment of 12,500 and TEE enrollment of 17,500. (These figures continue the percentage gain in seminary enrollment in the period from 1975 to 1980 and roughly match the projected gain in churches.)

(6) Income increased by 5 percent per year after adjustment for inflation (2.24 percent annual increase in purchasing power per missionary).

## Appendix 13

Desirable Growth Rates for 1983-86
(Approved by EMG, 4/8/82)

1. Net gain of three percent per year in career missionaries.
2. Net gain of two new countries per year.
3. Increase of 10 percent per year in volunteer involvement.
4. Net gain of 10 percent per year in churches and in combined total of churches and chapels.
5. Increase of 12 percent per year in baptism and church membership.
6. Increase of 10 percent per year in students in theological schools and 12 percent in TEE.

## Appendix 14

### An Average Southern Baptist Mission Field (1984)

I. Population—16,831,024
   Note: For comparison purposes, roughly equal to Georgia
         and Florida combined. (India not included in this
         computation as its large population would distort the
         picture.)
   Percentage Evangelical Christian—3.5% (589,086 persons).
   Unevangelized age 15 and above—approximately
   10,359,200 persons. (Most of these have never really heard
   the gospel at all.)

II. Years of Southern Baptist Work—24
    Number of Missionaries—33 (about one Southern Baptist
    missionary per half million people)
    Approximately 13 career couples (7 in "field evangelism")
              1 associate couple
              3 singles (career, associate, and/or special project)
              2 journeymen

    *Types of Work:*
    Evangelism and church development ("field evangelism")
    Leadership training (including a small seminary)
    Publishing
    Broadcasting
    Student Work
    Religious education and music promotion
    Perhaps also schools, medical work, social work, agri-
       culture, other specializations and relief ministries.

III. Current Field Data (approximate):
     Churches                    140
     Mission Points              170
     Membership               18,324

| | | | |
|---|---|---|---|
| Baptisms | 1,500 | | |
| (1 for each 11 members) | | | |
| National Pastors | 123 | | |
| Local Contributions | $737,547 | ($40.25 per member) | |

| | $ | $ | $ |
|---|---|---|---|
| IV. Mission Expenditures 1984 | | | 1,201,918 |
| Field Expenditures | | 1,054,314 | |
| Personnel | 714,541 | | |
| (Sending and supporting missionaries $21,653 ea.) | | | |
| Work Funds | 195,025 | | |
| Capital | 144,748 | | |
| Stateside expenditures | | 147,604 | |

(Administration and Communication—12.3%)

*NOTE:* Probably over half of the Protestant and evangelical preachers in the whole world serve in the United States.

*Sources of data used for calculations:*
"Countries Where Southern Baptist Missionaries Serve" (listed in order of entrance)
Foreign Mission Board Annual Statistical Report for 1984
"Foreign Mission Board, SBC, 1984 Expenditures" from Office of Finance
"Political and Geographical Entities to Which Southern Baptist Missionaries are Under Appointment." (India is omitted as the large population would distort the average; therefore, the average mission is based on 104 countries.)
*World Christian Encyclopedia,* David B. Barrett, editor
1984 World Population Data Sheet

# BIBLIOGRAPHY

## General Missiological References

Anderson, Gerald H., and Thomas F. Stransky, eds. *Mission Trends No. 1: Crucial Issues in Missions Today.* New York: Paulist Press and Grand Rapids: Wm. B. Eerdmans Publishing Company, 1974.

_____. *Mission Trends No. 2: Evangelization.* New York: Paulist Press and Grand Rapids: Wm. B. Eerdmans Publishing Company, 1975.

_____. *Mission Trends No. 3: Third World Theologies.* New York: Paulist Press and Grand Rapids: Wm. B. Eerdmans Publishing Company, 1976.

_____. *Mission Trends No. 4: Liberation Theologies in North America and Europe.* New York: Paulist Press and Grand Rapids: Wm. B. Eerdmans Publishing Company, 1979.

_____. *Mission Trends No. 5: Faith Meets Faith.* New York: Paulist Press and Grand Rapids: Wm. B. Eerdmans Publishing Company, 1981.

Barrett, David B., ed. *World Christian Encyclopedia.* London: Oxford University Press, 1982.

Kane, J. Herbert. *Understanding Christian Missions.* Rev. ed. Grand Rapids: Baker Book House, 1978.

Verkuyl, Johannes. *Contemporary Missiology.* Trans. and ed. by Dale Cooper. Grand Rapids: Wm. B. Eerdmans Publishing Company, 1978.

Wilson, Samuel, ed. *Mission Handbook: North American Protestant Minis-*

*tries Overseas*. 12th ed. Monrovia, Calif.: Missions Advanced Research and Communication Center, 1979.

Winter, Ralph D. *Twenty-Five Unbelievable Years, 1945-1969*. South Pasadena, Calif.: William Carey Library, 1970.

Winter, Ralph D., Steven C. Hawthorne, et al., eds. *Perspectives on the World Christian Movement: A Reader*. Pasadena, Calif: William Carey Library, 1981.

### Theology and/or Philosophy of Missions

Anderson, Gerald H., ed. *The Theology of the Christian Mission*. New York: McGraw-Hill Book Company, Inc., 1961.

_____. *Witnessing to the Kingdom: Melbourne and Beyond*. Maryknoll, N.Y.: Orbis Books, 1982.

Blauw, Johannes. *The Missionary Nature of the Church*. New York: McGraw-Hill Book Company, Inc., 1962.

Boer, Harry R. *Pentecost and Missions*. Grand Rapids: Wm. B. Eerdmans Publishing Co., 1961.

Costas, Orlando E. *The Integrity of Mission*. New York: Harper & Row, Publishers, 1979.

Glasser, Arthur F., and Donald A. McGavran. *Contemporary Theologies of Missions*. Grand Rapids: Baker Book House, 1983.

Kraemer, Hendrik. *The Christian Message in a Non-Christian World*. Grand Rapids: Kregel Publications, 1963.

Newbigin, Lesslie. *The Open Secret*. Grand Rapids: Wm. B. Eerdmans Publishing Company, 1978.

_____. *Sign of the Kingdom*. Grand Rapids: Wm. B. Eerdmans Publishing Company, 1980.

Niles, D. T. *Upon the Earth*. New York: McGraw-Hill Book Company, Inc., 1962.

Stewart, James S. *Thine Is the Kingdom*. New York: Charles Scribner's Sons, 1956.

Vicedom, Georg F. *Mission of God: An Introduction to a Theology of Mission*. Trans. by Gilbert A. Thiele and Dennis Hilgendorf. St. Louis: Concordia Publishing House, 1965.

## Missions Strategy

Allen, Roland. *Missionary Methods: St. Paul's or Ours?* London: World Dominion Press, 1912. Reprint. Grand Rapids: Wm. B. Eerdmans Publishing Co., 1962.

_____. *The Spontaneous Expansion of the Church.* London: World Dominion Press, 1927. Reprint. Grand Rapids: Wm. B. Eerdmans Publishing Company, 1962.

Beaver, R. Pierce. *American Protestant Women in World Mission.* Rev. ed. Grand Rapids: Wm. B. Eerdmans Publishing Company, 1968.

_____. *From Missions to Mission: Protestant World Mission Today and Tomorrow.* New York: Association Press, 1964.

_____. *The Missionary Between the Times.* Garden City, N.Y.: Doubleday and Company, Inc., 1968.

_____, ed. *The Gospel and Frontier Peoples.* South Pasadena, Calif.: William Carey Library, 1973.

Buhlmann, Walbert. *The Coming of the Third Church: An Analysis of the Present and Future of the Church.* Maryknoll, N.Y.: Orbis Books, 1977.

Cook, Harold R. *Strategy of Missions: An Evangelical View.* Chicago: Moody Press, 1963.

Coote, Robert J., and John Stott, eds. *Down to Earth: Studies in Christianity and Culture.* Grand Rapids: Wm. B. Eerdmans Publishing Company, 1980.

Costas, Orlando E. *Christ Outside the Gate.* Maryknoll, N.Y.: Orbis Books, 1982.

Dayton, Edward R., and David A. Fraser. *Planning Strategies for World Evangelization.* Grand Rapids: Wm. B. Eerdmans Publishing Company, 1980.

_____, eds. *That Everyone May Hear: Reaching the Unreached.* 3rd. ed. Monrovia, Calif.: Missions Advanced Research and Communication Center, 1983.

Douglas, J. D., ed. *Let the Earth Hear His Voice.* Minneapolis: World Wide Publications, 1975.

Eagleson, John, and Sergio Torres, eds. *The Challenge of Basic Christian*

*Communities.* Trans. by John Drury. Maryknoll, N.Y.: Orbis Press, 1981.

Engel, James F., and H. Wilbert Norton. *What's Gone Wrong with the Harvest?* Grand Rapids: Zondervan, 1975.

Fleming, Daniel Johnson. *Living as Comrades.* New York: Agricultural Missions Inc., 1950.

Fraser, David A., ed. *The Church in New Frontiers for Missions.* Monrovia, Calif.: Missions Advanced Research and Communication Center, 1983.

Fuller, W. Harold. *Mission-Church Dynamics.* Pasadena, Calif.: William Carey Library, 1980.

Gerber, Virgil, ed. *Missions in Creative Tension.* South Pasadena, Calif.: William Carey Library, 1971.

Gilliland, Dean S. *Pauline Theology and Mission Practice.* Grand Rapids: Baker Book House, 1983.

Hesselgrave, David J. *Communicating Christ Cross-Culturally.* Grand Rapids: Zondervan Publishing House, 1978.

_____, ed. *New Horizons in World Missions.* Grand Rapids: Baker Book House, 1979.

Hodges, Melvin L. *On the Mission Field: The Indigenous Church.* Chicago: Moody Press, 1953.

Horner, Norman A., ed. *Protestant Crosscurrents in Mission.* Nashville: Abingdon Press, 1968.

Johnstone, P. J. *Operation World: A Handbook for World Intercession.* Kent, England: STL Publications, reprinted 1979.

Kane, J. Herbert, *The Christian World Mission: Today and Tomorrow.* Grand Rapids: Baker Book House, 1981.

_____. *Life and Work on the Mission Field.* Grand Rapids: Baker Book House, 1980.

Keyes, Lawrence E. *The Last Age of Missions.* Pasadena, Calif.: William Carey Library, 1983.

Kinsler, F. Ross. *The Extension Movement in Theological Education.* Rev. ed. Pasadena, Calif.: William Carey Library, 1981.

Longacre, Doris Janzen. *Living More with Less*. Scottdale, Penn.: Herald Press, 1980.

McGavran, Donald Anderson. *The Bridges of God*. London: World Dominion Press, 1955.

_____. *How Churches Grow*. London: World Dominion Press, 1959.

_____. *Understanding Church Growth*. Grand Rapids: Wm. B. Eerdmans Publishing Company, 1970.

_____, ed. *Eye of the Storm: The Great Debate in Mission*. Waco, Texas: Word Books, 1972.

_____, et al., eds. *Church Growth and Christian Mission*. New York: Harper & Row, Publishers, 1965.

Miles, Delos. *Church Growth—A Mighty River*. Nashville: Broadman Press, 1981.

Mott, John R. *The Pastor and Modern Missions: A Plea for Leadership in World Evangelization*. New York: Student Volunteer Movement for Foreign Missions, 1904.

Nicholls, Bruce J. *Contextualization: A Theology of Gospel and Culture*. Downers Grove, Ill.: InterVarsity Press, 1979.

Nida, Eugene A. *God's Word in Man's Language*. New York: Harper & Row, Publishers, 1952.

Orchard, R. K. *Missions in a Time of Testing*. Philadelphia: The Westminster Press, 1964.

Parshall, Phil. *New Paths in Muslim Evangelism*. Grand Rapids: Baker Book House, 1980.

Scott, Waldron. *Bring Forth Justice: A Contemporary Perspective on Mission*. Grand Rapids: Wm. B. Eerdmans Publishing Company, 1980.

Sider, Ronald J., ed. *Evangelicals and Development: Towards a Theology of Social Change*. Exeter, England: The Paternoster Press, 1981.

_____. *Lifestyle in the Eighties: An Evangelical Commitment to Simple Lifestyle*. Philadelphia: The Westminster Press, 1982.

Sine, Tom, ed. *The Church in Response to Human Need*. Monrovia, Calif.: Missions Advanced Research and Communication Center, 1983.

Smith, Ebbie C. *Balanced Church Growth.* Nashville: Broadman Press, 1984.

Starling, Allan, ed. *Seeds of Promise.* Pasadena, Calif.: William Carey Library, 1981.

Street, T. Watson. *On the Growing Edge of the Church.* Richmond: John Knox Press, 1965.

Taylor, John V. *Enough is Enough.* London: S.C.M. Press Limited, 1975.

Tippett, A. R. *Church Growth and the Word of God.* Grand Rapids: Wm. B. Eerdmans Publishing Company, 1970.

Verkuyl, Johannes, and H. G. Schulte Nordholt. *Responsible Revolution.* Trans. and ed. by Lewis Smedes. Grand Rapids: Wm. B. Eerdmans Publishing Company, 1974.

Wagner, C. Peter. *Church Growth and the Whole Gospel.* San Francisco: Harper & Row, Publishers, 1981.

_____. *Frontiers in Missionary Strategy.* Chicago: Moody Press, 1971.

_____. *On the Crest of the Wave: Becoming a World Christian.* Ventura, Calif.: Regal Books, 1933.

_____, ed. *Church/Mission Tensions Today.* Chicago: Moody Press, 1972.

_____, Edward R. Dayton and/or Samuel Wilson, eds. *Unreached Peoples.* Annual edition. Elgin, Ill.: David C. Cook Publishing Company and/or Monrovia, Calif.: MARC [Missions Advanced Research and Communication Center].

Warren, Max. *Partnership: The Study of An Idea.* London: SCM Press, 1956.

## Southern Baptist Missions Approaches

Brock, Charles. *The Principles and Practice of Indigenous Church Planting.* Nashville: Broadman Press, 1981.

Carver, W. O. *Christian Missions in Today's World.* Nashville: Broadman Press, 1942.

_____. *Missions in the Plan of the Ages.* New York: Fleming H. Revell Company, 1909. Reprint. Nashville: Broadman Press, 1951.

Cauthen, Baker J., and Frank K. Means. *Advance to Bold Mission Thrust.* Richmond: Foreign Mission Board, SBC, 1981.

_____, and others. *By All Means*. Nashville: Convention Press, 1959.

Cheyne, John. *The Imperative Impulse*. Nashville: Convention Press, 1983.

Coggins, Ross. *Missions Today*. Nashville: Convention Press, 1963.

Copeland, E. Luther. *World Mission and World Survival*. Nashville: Broadman Press, 1985.

Crawley, Sadie T. *World Awareness*. Nashville: Convention Press, 1963.

DuBose, Francis M. *God Who Sends: A Fresh Quest for Biblical Mission*. Nashville: Broadman Press, 1983.

Fowler, Franklin T. *Sick and Ye Visited Me*. Nashville: Convention Press, 1975.

Hill, Ronald C. *Bangkok: An Urban Arena*. Nashville: Convention Press, 1982.

Igleheart, Glenn. *Interfaith Witnessing: A Guide for Southern Baptists*. Richmond: Foreign Mission Board, SBC, 1984.

Inter-Agency Council. *A Basic Understanding of Southern Baptist Missions Coordination*. Nashville: Inter-Agency Council, SBC, 1972.

McClellan, Albert. *Meet Southern Baptists*. Nashville: Broadman Press, 1978.

Means, Frank K. "Foreign Missions Looks Toward AD 2000." *The Commission* 39, no. 6 (June 1976).

Missions Education Council. *MEC Curriculum Scope Document, Task: Teach Missions*. Nashville: Missions Education Council, SBC, 1984.

O'Brien, Bill. *Mission for Tomorrow*. Nashville: Convention Press, 1980.

Rose, Larry L., and C. Kirk Hadaway. *An Urban World: Churches Face the Future*. Nashville: Broadman Press, 1984.

Webb, Leland. *How in This World*. Nashville: Convention Press, 1974.

### Journals

*Evangelical Missions Quarterly*. Published each January, April, July, and October by Evangelical Missions information Service, Inc., Wheaton, Ill.

*International Bulletin of Missionary Research*. Published quarterly in January, April, July, and October by the Overseas Ministries Study Center, Ventnor, N.J.

*International Review of Mission*. Published quarterly by the Commission on World Mission and Evangelism of the World Council of Churches, Geneva, Switzerland.

*Missiology: An International Review*. Published quarterly January, April, July, and October by the American Society of Missiology, Pasadena, Calif.

*The Commission*. Published monthly except for three double-month issues (February-March, June-July, October-November) by the Foreign Mission Board, SBC, Richmond, Va.

# INDEX